Slaves and Slaveholders
in Bermuda

1 6 1 6 – 1 7 8 2

Slaves and Slaveholders

in Bermuda

1 6 1 6 – 1 7 8 2

Virginia Bernhard

University of Missouri Press

COLUMBIA AND LONDON

5   4   3   2   1   03   02   01   00   99

Library of Congress Cataloging-in-Publication Data

Bernhard, Virginia, 1937–
    Slaves and slaveholders in Bermuda / Virginia Bernhard.
        p.   cm.
    Includes bibliographical references and index.
    ISBN 0-8262-1227-1 (alk. paper)
    1. Slavery—Bermuda Islands. I. Title.
    HT1105.B47B47   1999
    306.3'62'097299—dc21   99-34249
                                                             CIP

⊗™ This paper meets the requirements of the
American National Standard for Permanence of Paper
for Printed Library Materials, Z39.48, 1984.

Text design: Elizabeth K. Young
Jacket design: Susan Ferber
Typesetter: Bookcomp, Inc.
Printer and binder: Thomson-Shore, Inc.
Typeface: Galliard

*The University of Missouri Press gratefully acknowledges the generous
assistance of the University of St. Thomas in the publication of this book.*

For Jim

History doesn't happen to cultures.
It doesn't happen to races.
It happens to people.

George C. Wolfe

Contents

List of Tables and Maps xi

Preface xiii

Acknowledgments xvii

1 The First Colonists, White and Black 1

2 From Servitude to Slavery 49

3 Too Little Land, Too Many Slaves 94

4 A Living from the Sea 148

5 Freedom and Control 191

6 Families, White and Black 234

Conclusion 273

Appendix A Bermuda-Registered Vessels Bringing Blacks into
    the Port of New York, 1716–1742 279

Appendix B Bermuda-Registered Vessels Bringing Blacks to Virginia,
    1710–1766 283

A Note on Bermuda Sources 287

Works Cited 291

Index 307

Tables

1. Census of the Eight Tribes, 1622 27

2. Indian Indentures, ca. 1636–1661 57

3. Size of Landholdings, 1663 104

4. Heads of Households by Gender, 1663 105

5. Tenants and Resident Owners, 1663 106

6. Whites and Blacks in Bermuda, 1774 238

7. Maritime Bermuda, 1774 247

8. White and Black Populations of Pembroke Parish, 1723–1773 250

9. Census of St. George's and the Tribes, 1764 270

Maps

Bermuda Islands xx

Norwood Survey Map, 1663 95

Preface

In the summer of 1977, while doing research at the Huntington Library on seventeenth-century promotional tracts about the New World, I came across a 1622 document entitled "Bermudas, Orders and Constitutions for the Plantation of the Summer Ilands." Until that moment Bermuda had existed in my mind only as an occasional travel advertisement promising pink beaches and blue waters. Like most colonial historians I had bypassed the smallest of England's colonies, a place about the size of Manhattan Island, six hundred miles off the coast of North Carolina. It suddenly occurred to me that Bermuda was the second oldest English colony in the New World, founded in 1612, only five years after the settlement at Jamestown, Virginia, and yet I knew next to nothing about its history. A bibliographical search turned up a slender volume, *An Introduction to the History of Bermuda,* by W. F. Craven, who noted, "In the study of American colonization the Bermudas have been largely overlooked, the significance of their history for the most part lost to sight."[1]

In 1980, when my husband asked me where we ought to go for a vacation cruise, I answered without hesitation, "Bermuda." There were indeed pink beaches and blue waters, but there was also a fascinating mix of people, a population two-thirds black and one-third white, whose apparent good will and good manners toward each other struck me as a remarkable twentieth-century achievement. Moreover, most of them—black and white—were the descendants of people who had come to Bermuda in the seventeenth century. I visited the Bermuda Archives and discovered a treasure trove: a collection of colonial history sources dating from the 1612 commission of Richard Moore, Bermuda's first governor. My fascination with Bermuda history and my determination to learn more of it date from that August afternoon in 1980. As I saw more of the islands and their people, one central question kept coming to mind: What was the history of race relations in a country where blacks and whites had lived together for more than three hundred years on a group of islands totaling only twenty-one square miles?

1. W. F. Craven, *An Introduction to the History of Bermuda* (Williamsburg, Va., 1938), 11.

In the course of teaching undergraduates at the University of St. Thomas, other questions presented themselves. During a U.S. survey course, I wondered how Bermuda's early years compared with Virginia's: Was there a "starving time" in Bermuda? Did the Englishmen there refuse to work, as they did at Jamestown? Did Bermuda colonists scramble to grow tobacco and little else as Virginia's first settlers did? Of course, the all-important questions also presented themselves: When did the first blacks arrive in Bermuda? When and why were they enslaved? In class I recounted to my students the arrival of the "20 and odd Negroes" brought to and sold in Virginia in 1619 by the captain of a Dutch ship, and pointed out how little we know about their history. That was 1980. We still know little about those blacks, but now we know that they were not the first blacks in Virginia. In 1995 a scholar discovered a document in the Ferrar Papers at Magdalen College, Cambridge University, showing that there were thirty-two blacks—fifteen men and seventeen women—in Virginia *before* that Dutch ship arrived.[2] That is one of the delights of history: You never know when something unexpected may turn up.

That one piece of new information about blacks in early Virginia alters our understanding not only of that colony's history but also of the history of blacks in the burgeoning transatlantic community that took shape in the 1500s. The Spanish and Portuguese began taking Africans out of Africa to use as laborers in the New World, but the English also transported the occasional African to England, more as a curiosity than anything else, and by the early 1600s a small number of blacks lived and worked in English homes or aboard English ships.[3] At least one or two of them found their way to Virginia. By the time the first English colonies were founded, blacks were scattered all over the transatlantic world, some of them multilingual, able to converse in Spanish, Portuguese, Dutch, or English, and skilled in sailing, navigation, trading, and other occupations. These are the blacks Ira Berlin has dubbed "Atlantic creoles," about whom little except their presence is known.[4] Some of them may have been among the first blacks who came to Bermuda.

As I began to delve into Bermuda records on two subsequent vacation trips in the early 1980s I discovered that, unlike the murky origins of the first

2. The scholar was William Thorndale, who reported his findings in "The Virginia Census of 1619," *Magazine of Virginia Genealogy* 33 (1995): 155–70. See also Engel Sluiter, "New Light on the '20 and Odd Negroes' Arriving in Virginia, August 1619," *William and Mary Quarterly* (hereafter, *WMQ*), 3d ser., 54, no. 2 (April 1997): 395–98.

3. Robert McColley, "Slavery in Virginia, 1619–1660: A Reexamination," in *New Perspectives on Race and Slavery in America: Essays in Honor of Kenneth M. Stampp,* ed. Robert H. Abzug and Stephen Maizlich (Lexington, Ky.: University of Kentucky Press, 1986), 11–24, discusses the little-known presence of Africans in England from the 1550s to the early 1600s.

4. Ira Berlin, "From Creole to African: Atlantic Creoles and the Origins of African-American Society in Mainland North America," *WMQ*, 3d ser., 33, no. 2 (April 1996): 251–88.

blacks in Virginia, the arrival of the first black in Bermuda can be precisely documented. In 1616, according to an early Bermuda governor, the ship *Edwin* had arrived from the West Indies, bringing with her "one Indian and a Negroe (the first thes Ilands ever had)."[5] From that time on, Bermuda's racial history would be that of a multiracial society quite different from that of other English colonies in the New World. While thousands of Africans were brought to labor on the sugar plantations of the Caribbean and later in the tobacco and rice fields in the southern colonies on the mainland, Bermuda's first blacks were brought, not for their labor, but for their expertise as pearl divers and cultivators of West Indies plants and tobacco. They were valued as workers, of course, but in the beginning they were important because they possessed skills and knowledge that the English colonists did not have. But in the end, like the rest of the Africans who were brought to the New World, Bermuda's blacks— and Indians too—became slaves. The origins of that slavery, its nature, and its effects on blacks and whites in Bermuda from the 1600s to the end of the eighteenth century are the subjects of this book.

The study of slavery has always been one of the richest veins in colonial history, and in recent years the literature has been enlarged by scholarly debates over the origins of slavery, the racial attitudes of the English, the chronology of the conversion from white to black labor, and the complex relationship between slavery and racial prejudice. Historians of slavery have pursued one question, perhaps above all the others: Which came first, racism or slavery? Despite decades of scholarly diligence, the solution to this chicken-or-egg problem remains elusive. Part of the answer may lie in Bermuda.

5. Nathaniel Butler, *Historye of the Bermudaes or Summer Ilands,* ed. J. Henry Lefroy (London: Hakluyt Society, 1882), 84. The original is an unsigned manuscript (Sloan MSS, no. 750) in the British Museum, attributed to Nathaniel Butler, governor of Bermuda from 1620 to 1622.

Acknowledgments

This book has been long in the making. I am grateful for the patience of colleagues, too numerous to name, who have been obliged to listen to my accounts of my research adventures in Bermuda since the 1980s. My husband, Jim Bernhard, has done yeoman service as a travel companion and archival assistant, as well as reading drafts, too numerous to count, and offering criticisms and encouragements. Two of my children, Paul and Anne, took time from their respective college and graduate school vacations to tabulate inventories and make databases. Catherine, their elder sister, taught me how to go downhill on a moped in Bermuda one summer.

Parts of this research were published in earlier articles. The first, "Bermuda and Virginia in the Seventeenth Century: A Comparative View," appeared in 1985 in the *Journal of Social History* and is now part of chapters 1 and 2. "Beyond the Chesapeake: The Contrasting Status of Blacks in Bermuda, 1616–1663," was published in the *Journal of Southern History* in 1988. I am indebted to that journal's editor, John Boles, and its associate editor, Evelyn Thomas Nolen, for their valuable suggestions. I owe a similar debt to the Houston Area Southern Historians, an informal association of area scholars who meet at Rice University six times a year to discuss works in progress. My presentation of a paper on Bermuda slave rebellions before that group resulted in an article, "Bids for Freedom: Slave Resistance and Rebellion Plots in Bermuda, 1656–1761," in *Slavery and Abolition* in 1996. Edward Cox was especially helpful with advice about publishing that piece and was also kind enough later to read parts of the book manuscript.

Elaine F. Crane, Elaine Breslaw, and Susan Westbury also read early versions of parts of this work and gave me sound advice. My study of Bermuda is the better for conversations with Jessica Kross, Les Rudnyanszky, Elizabeth Kessel, Joe Hawes, Karen Kupperman, Cary Wintz, Bob McColley, Dan Littlefield, Paul Finkelman, Alden Vaughan, and my faculty colleagues at the University of St. Thomas.

The initial phase of the research was made possible by a grant-in-aid from the American Council of Learned Societies in 1985. Further study and travel expenses were defrayed by a National Endowment for the Humanities travel grant in 1987 and a University of St. Thomas Faculty Development Research Grant in 1990.

My debts to the staffs of the University of St. Thomas Doherty Library, especially Mark Landingham, and Rice University's Fondren Library, are many. In Bermuda, Grace Rawlins, Patrick Burgess, and Shernette Peniston made me feel at home in the Bermuda National Library, and in the Bermuda Archives, Sandra Rouja, John Adams, Karla Hayward, Sylvie Gervais, Nan Godet, and Lorna Doyles deserve special mention. Margaret Lloyd of the Bermuda National Trust introduced me to the Historic Buildings Project. Michael Jarvis shared his work on St. George's with me, as well as his dissertation on colonial Bermuda. I owe a debt to the late Bermuda scholars Vernon Ives and Cyril O. Packwood for their own contributions to Bermuda history and their encouragement of mine. I should also like to thank James E. Smith, whose work on slavery laid some groundwork for my own.

Had it not been for the research and the friendship of two other Bermudians, A. C. Hollis Hallett and his wife, C. F .E. Hollis Hallett, whose respective works are cited in the "Note on the Bermuda Sources" at the end of this volume, my work would have taken much longer. Archie Hallett supplied me with copies of documents I might have missed, and Keggie advised me on the intricacies of Bermuda genealogy. Besides their hospitality to my husband and me on several visits to Bermuda, both Halletts generously read and criticized my entire manuscript. Cecil and Lee Dismont, the owners of Mazarine-by-the-Sea, the guest house that became my home away from home in Bermuda, were kindness itself. This book is the richer for the conversations my husband and I had with the Dismonts on Bermuda, past and present.

In the final stages, the enthusiasm of Beverly Jarrett, director of the University of Missouri Press, and the expertise of Julie Schorfheide were most welcome. The diligence and good humor of Doug Willis, my undergraduate research assistant at the University of St. Thomas, proved invaluable, as did the help of two other students, Kristina Hebert and Charles Sommer.

Slaves and Slaveholders
in Bermuda
1 6 1 6 – 1 7 8 2

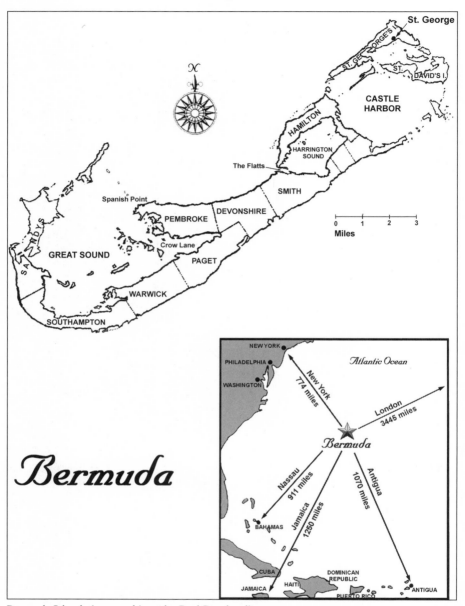

Bermuda Islands (map and inset by Paul Bernhard).

1 The First Colonists, White and Black

In 1610 the English writer William Strachey, shipwrecked off the Bermuda coast, described the islands as "so terrible to all that ever touched on them . . . that they be called commonly, *The Devils Ilands,* and are feared and avoyded of all sea travellers alive, above any other place in the world." A year later Shakespeare wrote *The Tempest,* set on a remote tropical island and believed to have been inspired by the shipwreck that stranded Strachey and his fellow passengers on the uninhabited islands of Bermuda. Mariners had long avoided Bermuda, calling it the "isle of devils" because of the danger of shipwreck on its treacherous underwater reefs.[1] In more recent times historians of European colonization have also bypassed Bermuda, preferring the larger, richer terrain of the Americas and the Caribbean islands. Yet here on this small island group 600 miles off the coast of North America, a multiracial society composed of Europeans, Africans, and American Indians developed earlier than in any other English colony, giving Bermuda a history unique in the annals of colonization. The first black and the first Indian residents arrived within four years of the colony's founding in 1612, and by 1699 "Negroes, Molattoes, and Indians"—most of them slaves—made up 38 percent of the population. Like Shakespeare's Prospero in *The Tempest,* who was the master of Ariel, the sprite, and Caliban, the savage, English colonists in Bermuda were masters of individuals toward whom they had ambiguous feelings. The history of slaveholders and slaves in Bermuda may help to illumine a set of problems that continue to engage scholars of the Atlantic community: the origins of

---

1. William Strachey, "A True Reportory of the Wracke, and Redemption of Sir Thomas Gates Knight; upon, and from the Ilands of the Bermudas . . . ," in *Hakluytus Posthumus or Purchas His Pilgrimes,* ed. Samuel Purchas (Glasgow: J. MacLehose and Sons, 1905–1907) 19:5–72. For a description of the discovery of Bermuda and excerpts from early Spanish and English narratives of the islands, see J. Henry Lefroy, ed., *Memorials of the Discovery and Early Settlement of the Bermudas or Somers Islands, 1515–1685* (1877; reprint, Toronto: University of Toronto Press for the Bermuda National Trust, 1981), 1:1–55. See also Butler, *Historye of the Bermudaes or Summer Ilands;* John Smith, "Generall Historie of Virginia, the Somer Isles, and New England . . . ," in *The Complete Works of Captain John Smith,* ed. Philip L. Barbour (Chapel Hill: University of North Carolina Press, 1986), 2:169–391; Richard Norwood, *The Journal of Richard Norwood,* ed. and intro. by W. F. Craven and Walter B. Hayward (New York: Bermuda Historical Monuments Trust, 1945); and Richard Norwood, "Relations of Summer Islands . . . ," in *Pilgrimes,* ed. Purchas, 19:179–92.

1

racism, the evolution of slavery, and the complex relationships between masters and slaves.[2]

Bermuda's recorded history begins with the name "la bermuda" on a Spanish map of 1511.[3] But Spain, bent on finding riches in the New World, had little interest in colonizing so small a place, and the islands lay uninhabited for nearly a hundred years. Named for Juan de Bermudez, a ship captain who probably discovered them sometime before 1511, these remote, volcanic islands became a landmark, but rarely a landing, for vessels plying the Atlantic. The colonial history of Bermuda begins in 1609, when the Virginia Company sent nine ships laden with provisions, 500 colonists (including William Strachey), and a deputy governor for its fledgling settlement at Jamestown. In command of the flagship *Sea Venture* was Admiral Sir George Somers, for whom the Somers Islands were to be named.[4] On July 25, 1609, a violent storm in the mid-Atlantic scattered the fleet. One vessel was lost, seven of the others eventually made their way to Virginia, and the foundering *Sea Venture* was wedged between two rocks off the east coast of Bermuda. The ship's company of 140 men and 10 women went ashore on what is now called St. George's Island, where they spent a not unpleasant 10 months. Some of them, in fact, were reluctant to leave for the struggling colony of Virginia, where they believed that "nothing but wretchednesse and labour must be expected."[5]

These marooned English colonists seem to have found Bermuda, with its tropical vegetation, its clear blue waters, and its balmy climate, the nearest they had come to the paradise promised in early descriptions of the New World. There was an incredible abundance of food: game birds, wild hogs, huge tortoises, "great craw-fishes," and "rocke fish . . . so great two will load

2. See, for example, the entire issue of *WMQ*, 3d ser., 54, no. 1 (January 1997), entitled "Constructing Race: Differentiating Peoples in the Early Modern World." James Walvin, *Questioning Slavery* (New York: Routledge, 1996), surveys the topic in its transatlantic context from slavery's origins to abolition. See also Stephan Palmié, ed., *Slave Cultures and the Cultures of Slavery* (Knoxville: University of Tennessee Press, 1995); Kim F. Hall, *Things of Darkness: Economies of Race and Gender in Early Modern England* (Ithaca, N.Y.: Cornell University Press, 1995); and Bernard Bailyn and Philip Morgan, eds., *Strangers within the Realm: Cultural Margins of the First British Empire* (Chapel Hill: University of North Carolina Press, 1991). For a historiographical review of the literature, see Alden T. Vaughan, "The Origins Debate: Slavery and Racism in Seventeenth-Century Virginia," in his *Roots of American Racism: Essays on the Colonial Experience* (New York: Oxford University Press, 1995), 136–74. See also McColley, "Slavery in Virginia."
3. Peter Martyr, *Legatio Babylonica* (1511). The map is reproduced in Lefroy, *Memorials,* 1:3.
4. According to seventeenth-century writer John Chamberlain, the Virginia Company considered the name *Virginiola* but chose *Somers Islands* as a pun on Sir George Somers's name and the "temperate ayre" of the islands. See *The Letters of John Chamberlain,* ed. N. E. McClure (Philadelphia: American Philosophical Society, 1939), 1:334.
5. Lefroy, *Memorials,* 1:40.

a man."[6] Bermuda's birds and fish, unaccustomed to the behavior of humans, were tame enough to be caught by hand. Even the weather pleased the English visitors: "noe cold ther is beyonde English Aprill, nor heate much greater than a hott July in France."[7] In the winter of 1609–1610, while their countrymen in Virginia were reduced to eating "doggs Catts Ratts and myce . . . to feede upon Serpents and snakes and to digge the earthe for wylde and unknowne Rootes,"[8] the survivors of the *Sea Venture* feasted on turtle stew, roast pig, and other island delicacies. They explored the islands, salvaged what they could from the wreck of the *Sea Venture,* and built two small ships, the 70-ton *Deliverance* and the 30-ton *Patience,* aboard which they sailed to Virginia in May 1610. Finding the settlers there near starvation, they consulted with the Virginians and dispatched Sir George Somers to Bermuda for food. The 63-year-old admiral died before he could complete this expedition. His body (except for his heart, which he requested be buried in Bermuda) went back to England, along with reports of Bermuda.[9] In 1611, as a new supply of provisions and colonists revived the Virginia colony, a number of Virginia Company stockholders hopeful of establishing another foothold in the Western Hemisphere invested the sum of £2,000 to plant a colony in Bermuda. The newly founded Somers Islands Company shared a common membership with the Virginia Company, their stockholders "consisting in great part of the selfe same persons."[10] For example, Sir Thomas Smith, the first governor of the Virginia Company, was also the governor of the Somers Islands Company, and his successor and rival in the Virginia Company, Sir Edwin Sandys, was one of the eight major proprietors of Bermuda.

In 1612 the Somers Islands Company's appointed governor, Richard Moore, sailed to the islands with 60 colonists to establish the first permanent settlement in Bermuda, which was to become the second successful English colony in the New World. When the *Plough* arrived on July 11, 1612, three of Somers's men who had stayed in the islands presented the newcomers with "an acre of good corne ripe and ready for the gatherour: numbers of pompions [pumpkins], Indian beanes, many tortoises ready taken; and good store of

6. Barbour, ed., *Complete Works,* 2:348.

7. Butler, *Bermudaes,* 1, 9.

8. George Percy, "A Trewe Relacyon of the Procedeinges . . . in Virginia," in *Tyler's Quarterly Historical and Genealogical Magazine* 3 (April 1922): 259–82 (quotation, p. 267).

9. The place where Somers's heart was buried is now Somers Park on Princess Street in St. George's, Bermuda. On Somers's life, see F. J. Pope, "Sir George Somers and His Family," *Bermuda Historical Quarterly* (hereafter, *BHQ*) 4, no. 2 (1947): 57–61.

10. *The Records of the Virginia Company,* ed. Susan M. Kingsbury (Washington, D.C.: Government Printing Office, 1906–1935), 2:408. The Bermuda charter and the names of the first 117 "adventurers" are in Lefroy, *Memorials,* 1:83–100.

hogge-flesh salted and made into flitches of bacon."[11] Moore and his colonists came ashore at St. David's Island, but on July 13 they moved to nearby Smith's Island, where the three men, Robert Waters, Edward Chard, and Christopher Carter, had been living since 1610. While waiting for the new arrivals, the three men had also made a "fortunate find": Floating in the offshore waters was a quantity of ambergris (produced in whales' stomachs and used in perfume making) worth £9,000. At a time when a laborer in England might make £12 to £25 a year, the ambergris represented a handsome fortune indeed.[12]

From its founding the Bermuda colony grew steadily, without the misfortunes that befell its sister colony on the mainland, where brackish water, meager rations, and fear of Indians gave a nightmarish quality to Virginia's first few years. By autumn of 1612 Bermuda's first permanent settlement and seat of government was the town of St. George's on the island of the same name. Unlike the Virginia colonists, Bermuda's first settlers had good water (St. George's had a "fresh water well"), plenty of food, and no natives to placate.[13] The worst that happened in Bermuda in the first few years was an infestation of rats that escaped from a visiting ship and multiplied by the hundreds in 1614. The number of settlers grew rapidly from the original 60 to about 600 in the first two years.[14] Because of Governor Moore's zeal in setting the colonists to building houses and forts in the first two years, they neglected to plant enough corn, and the result was a serious shortage of grain. For a few months, at least, Bermuda colonists experienced something of the hunger that plagued their counterparts in Virginia. Some of the new Bermuda settlers, weakened, perhaps, from the long Atlantic voyage and suffering the hardships of establishing themselves in a new land, lacked the will to fish or gather food and reportedly starved in their houses.

Colonist Richard Norwood's description of the Bermudians' plight in 1614 might have been written about Virginia in 1609–1610: "Being destitute of food, many dyed, and wee all became very feeble and weake, whereof some being so, would not; others could not stir abroad to seeke reliefe, but dyed in their houses: such as went abroad were subject, through weaknesse, to bee suddenly surprized with a disease we called the Feages, which was neither paine nor sicknesse, but as it were the highest degree of weaknesse, depriving

11. Butler, *Bermudaes,* 20. On the founding of the colony, see Craven, *Introduction,* and Terry Tucker, *The Islands of Bermuda* (Hamilton, Bermuda: Island Press, 1970), 111–12.
12. On the ambergris, see Butler, *Bermudaes,* 18–19, 21–23, 28–29. On wages in England, see Edmund S. Morgan, *American Slavery/American Freedom: The Ordeal of Colonial Virginia* (New York: W. W. Norton and Company, 1975), 94, 106–7, and John J. McCusker and Russell R. Menard, *The Economy of British America, 1607–1789* (Chapel Hill: University of North Carolina Press, 1988), 245–49.
13. Butler, *Bermudaes,* 13, 87.
14. On the rapid population growth, see Lefroy, *Memorials,* 1:721.

us of power and abilitie for the execution of any bodily exercise, whether it were working, walking, or what else."[15]

Governor Moore then called a temporary halt to his various construction projects and dispersed about 150 of the sickliest settlers to one of the yet uninhabited islands. There, unlike the Virginia colonists sent by John Smith to catch fish, who "in 6 weekes . . . would not agree once to cast out their net," the Bermuda colonists caught birds and fish in such quantities that some died of overeating.[16] Although Norwood noted that "there were many in those times that died daily for want of victuals," the majority survived, including the original 60 settlers. Eventually the food shortage was alleviated by supplies from England. Except for this brief episode of famine and illness, there is nothing in Bermuda's early history to compare with the hardships in Virginia or with the awesome death tolls in the mainland colony in the next few years.

While more than half the settlers who arrived in Jamestown in 1607 were dead within a year, those who went to Bermuda fared much better. Five years after the first settlement, Lewis Hughes, a Bermuda clergyman, exulted that "not one of all those threescore that first beganne this Plantation was dead."[17] By 1615 Bermuda had more than 600 inhabitants, while Virginia, founded five years before Bermuda, had only 350 survivors from nearly 1,200 who had sailed to the mainland colony since 1607.[18] Much of the mortality among settlers in Virginia was due to disease: dysentery and typhoid from contaminated river water and malaria from mosquito-infested swamps. The first Bermuda settlers, on the other hand, were lucky enough to find good water at the start. The "wisest and most provident among them bestowed a curious search for fresh water, the which also, haveing digged but a small depth into the bowells of the earth, at the very first essaye, flowed out upon them, to good satisfaction." They exulted that "diseases (unless meerely accidentall),

15. Norwood, "Relations of Summer Islands," 182. The sickness called the "Feages" is unidentified, and the origin of the name itself is unknown, according to the *Oxford English Dictionary,* which cites John Smith's use of it in his "Generall Historie . . . ," in *Complete Works,* ed. Barbour, 2:357.

16. Barbour, ed., *Complete Works,* 1:263. On Moore's governorship, see Butler, *Bermudaes,* 28–44, and William Frith Williams, *Historical & Statistical Account of Bermuda* (London, 1848), 25.

17. Lefroy, *Memorials,* 1:77.

18. On the troubles in Virginia, see Carville V. Earle, "Environment, Disease, and Mortality in Early Virginia," in *The Chesapeake in the Seventeenth Century: Essays on Anglo-American Society,* ed. Thad Tate and David Ammerman (Chapel Hill: University of North Carolina Press, 1979), 95–125; Karen Ordahl Kupperman, "Apathy and Death in Early Jamestown," *Journal of American History* 66 (June 1979): 24–40; Virginia Bernhard, " 'Men, Women and Children' at Jamestown: Population and Gender in Early Virginia, 1607–1610," *Journal of Southern History* 58, no. 4 (November 1992): 599–618.

are strangely and, indeed, wonderfully rare and uncommon here."[19] The state of public health in Bermuda could help explain why, in the initial period of settlement, the Bermudians worked and the Virginians did not.

Trees were as difficult to fell and fields as hard to till in Bermuda as they were in Virginia, but the Bermuda colonists did not suffer from the curious lassitude that made work a problem the first year in Virginia. In Bermuda, where the climate was mild all year, the colonists worked from dawn to 9 A.M. and from 3 P.M. to sunset—roughly the same hours as the Virginians—but Bermuda's governor was more successful than Virginia's early leaders in governing the labor force. Except for John Smith, who left Virginia in 1609, Virginia's leaders seemed unable to keep order in the first few years. But Richard Moore, the man chosen by the Somers Islands Company to govern Bermuda, was in his way as remarkable and capable a leader as Smith. Moore, who brought his wife and family to Bermuda, left no written history of his adventures in the New World, but he kept order, delegated responsibility, and saw to it that his colonists had enough food to eat and enough work to do. As Smith himself wrote of Moore, "Although he was but a Carpenter, he was an excellent Artist, a good Gunner, very witty and industrious: he built and laid the foundation of eight or nine Forts . . . mounting in them all the Ordnance he had, preparing the ground to build Houses, plant Corne, and such Fruits as they had." As ship after ship arrived with new settlers, the governor "distributed and fitted everyone to his employment and labour."[20] Compared to the labor troubles in Virginia, Moore's efficient deployment of workers must have seemed a remarkable feat, indeed. In the first decade of settlement, from 1612 to 1622, the colonists constructed eight forts, a "faire house of lime and stone" for the seat of government in the town of St. George's (this Italianate statehouse, built in 1620, still stands), and a large cedar-beamed house on the west end of the main island for one of their early governors, Daniel Tucker.

In this island colony, as in Virginia, tobacco, the plant first introduced to Europeans by the Indians in Columbus's time, would soon become a moneymaking crop. But Bermuda had far less land than Virginia, and by 1617 every inch of land in the Bermuda islands had been surveyed and parceled out to planters. The survey was the work of Richard Norwood, a remarkably talented young man brought to the islands in 1613 by the Somers Islands Company. Then 23 years old, Norwood had already made a name for himself in London by inventing a diving bell, and the Company hired him to use it to look for pearls in Bermuda's waters. When that project proved unsuccessful, the Company employed his engineering skills in a survey of the

19. Butler, *Bermudaes,* 13, 205.
20. Barbour, ed., *Complete Works,* 2:354; Butler, *Bermudaes,* 25–26, 35.

islands. By 1617 his detailed survey of the entire island group was completed. As instructed, Norwood divided Bermuda's lands outside the Company's property in St. George's into eight areas called "tribes," each containing approximately 1,250 acres.[21] These divisions were named for eight of the colony's principal investors. Land ownership in Bermuda was restricted by law to 250 acres, or 10 shares, as the 25-acre allotments were called, for each individual in a given tribe. Nevertheless, by shrewd trading, some of the first proprietors quickly amassed holdings in more than one tribe. For example, Robert Rich, who became the second Earl of Warwick in 1619, and his cousin Nathaniel Rich became Bermuda's largest landholders, with a total of 650 acres between them in four different tribes: Southampton, Warwick, Devonshire, and Hamilton.[22]

Bermuda's small size dictated the development of its resources and shaped much of its history. As early as 1620 the Somers Islands Company had complained that "the Barmudas was sould unto them for a farr greater quantitie of Land then they now find it to be."[23] Life, as well as land, in this 21-square-mile island colony was marked by severe limits: Everything from profits to wages to the killing of young tortoises was closely regulated, either by the Somers Islands Company or the colonial legislature. The Bermuda Assembly, composed of two elected representatives and a bailiff from each of the eight tribes, held its first session in 1620, with Governor Nathaniel Butler presiding. Voters had to own one share of land. The Assembly was later increased from 24 to 40 members, with five members from each of the tribes.[24] The Governor's

---

21. For a biographical sketch of Richard Norwood, see Vernon A. Ives, ed., *The Rich Papers: Letters from Bermuda, 1615–1646* (Toronto: University of Toronto Press, 1984), 401. See also Colin Benbow, "Norwood's First Survey," *BHQ* 32, no. 3 (1975): 48–52. The *Oxford English Dictionary* lists an archaic meaning of *tribe* as "a division of territory or land allotted to a family or company." Robert Rich used it in 1617 to designate the sections in Norwood's survey. By the end of the seventeenth century Bermuda's tribes were called parishes, but *tribe* would continue to appear on maps until the 1770s. For the naming of the tribes, see Butler, *Bermudaes*, 105–6; Lefroy, *Memorials*, 1:99–100; Barbour, ed., *Complete Works*, 2:370–71.

Norwood divided the tribes into 1,250 acres each, but he sometimes used 24 acres as one share, and sometimes 25, in his accounts of individual holdings. The 25-acre-per-share figure has been used in this study.

22. A list of shareholders in 1620 compared with the list of 1622 illustrates changes in landholdings. Ives, *Rich Papers*, 349–52, 241–44; on the Rich family, see 387–91. Richard Norwood's "A Mapp of the Sommer Ilands" (1626), in the Bermuda Archives, indicates the division of land into tribes and shares in the first survey and lists the shareholders. See Lefroy, *Memorials*, 1:viii, 5 n, and Margaret Palmer, *The Mapping of Bermuda: A Bibliography of Printed Maps and Charts, 1548–1970* (London, 1983). There is a copy of the 1622 map in Ives, *Rich Papers*, end pocket.

23. *Records of the Virginia Company*, 1:425.

24. Henry Wilkinson, *Adventurers of Bermuda: A History of the Island from Its Discovery until the Dissolution of the Somers Island Company in 1684* (London: Oxford University Press, 1933),

Council, originally chosen by the governor from nominees from each tribe, by the 1650s was appointed by the Somers Islands Company; and after Bermuda became a crown colony in 1684 the council members, reduced from 14 to 12, were appointed by the Lords of Trade. Justices of the peace, at first called bailiffs, who had served as members of the council in the 1620s, were appointed by the council after the 1680s. They served as the principal officers in the parishes, calling parish meetings, conducting elections for Assembly and jury service, and officiating over courts to decide parish disputes and petty crimes. The Assembly was enlarged by 1622 from four to six representatives (two bailiffs, four burgesses) from each tribe, plus eight burgesses from the "general lands" at St. George's. Under the Orders and Constitutions of 1622 the Assembly was ordered to meet every second year, but the existing records suggest that it met when called. Election of representatives from the tribes was by voice vote, as an early record from Pembroke indicates, stating that at a meeting of most of the residents, four representatives to the Assembly were elected by a "plurality of voices." Twice each year, in May and November, six jurors from each tribe were chosen in the same manner.

In 1620 the Governor's Council was made up of a representative from each of the eight tribes, plus the colony's four clergymen and the sheriff. A batch of 15 laws regulating the growing of tobacco and corn and the hiring of servants occupied the first legislative session, reflecting the primary concerns of the landlords and their tenants. Like Virginia's first lawmakers, the Bermuda Assembly found it necessary to require tobacco-mad colonists to grow a certain amount of corn. Poultry was to be penned up when the corn was planted, so that the corn could grow, and a public store of corn was to be kept in every tribe, to guard against "the improvidence generally crept in amongst the inhabitants."[25] The colony's craftsmen—carpenters, bricklayers, blacksmiths, coopers—were each allotted two acres for a house and garden and were forbidden to grow any tobacco. Their wages (paid in tobacco, the colony's currency) were also limited. A 1623 law set two pounds of tobacco per day for the wages of "artificers" such as carpenters and stonemasons, and one pound of tobacco per day for unskilled laborers. Tobacco was so precious a commodity that in 1623 the Assembly made stealing it a felony, and the punishment for stealing, death.[26] Bermudians also regulated the use of the islands' natural resources. In 1622 the Assembly passed what might be called

---

175. For an overview of Bermuda's governmental structure, see A. C. Hollis Hallett, *Chronicle of a Colonial Church: Bermuda, 1612–1826* (Pembroke, Bermuda: Juniperhill Press, 1993), 350–73. For a compilation of the acts of the first Assembly, see Lefroy, *Memorials*, 1:165–79.

25. Butler, *Bermudaes*, 200–202; Lefroy, *Memorials*, 1:174–75.

26. Lefroy, *Memorials*, 1:307–8.

the first conservation laws in North America, restricting the killing of young tortoises and the indiscriminate cutting of the islands' cedar forests.[27]

In Bermuda's early years it was not tortoises or cedar but tobacco that most colonists looked to for their livelihood. The first crop, planted on the island of St. George's in 1613, was spoiled "by want of knowledge and skill, pruninge, curinge, and makeinge of it up." In 1616 the Somers Islands Company tried to remedy this situation by sending over "Mr. Tickner, a skilfull planter & curer of tobacco," but the results are unrecorded.[28] Landlords were mostly absentee in the first generation of settlement, leasing their land to individual tenants or acquiring indentured servants to work it. In the early years most tenants worked "on halves," sending half their crop yield to the landlord and keeping the other half for themselves. Whatever the arrangement, the lease-holder or independent planter put as much of his meager acreage as he could into tobacco, hoping to turn a profit in the English market. Most of the individual holdings were quite small: Of 156 separate properties listed in 1622, 89, or 57 percent, were two shares (about 50 acres) or less. Not all the land in a share was suitable for cultivation. In 1620 John Dutton lamented this deficiency in a letter to Nathaniel Rich: "You must understand, Sir, that none of the best shaires in the Ilands will admitt past 8 or 9 ackrs to be faulen of any use. In some of them, 5 or 6, others not singly to be lived on." The amount of acreage actually devoted to tobacco is not clear. A 1623 report to the Privy Council observed: "It is but very little of the ground that is imployed for that purpose [growing tobacco]; for . . . every man . . . doth not imploy above one acre or an acre & halfe usually to make a Tobacco garden. All the rest he keepes to nourish his familie with Corne, Victualls & Provisions."[29] In 1622 the Virginia Company, "in consideration of the great defect of the quantity of Land in the *Summer Ilands*" assigned the plantation known as Bermuda Hundred in Virginia to provide additional land and income for Bermuda.[30]

Moreover, for these transplanted English colonists, the growing of tobacco itself was difficult. The following complaint of some Bermuda planters could stand equally for planters in Virginia in the early years of tobacco growing:

> . . . there is as much difference betweene a husbandman's sowing of wheate . . . in England, and planting Tobacco . . . in Somer Islands, as is betwixt black and white The husbandman hath his land ready for the plough, and his houses built; wee noe such thing He hath his beast of labor to plough his land, wee none but our hands, his wheate beeing sowen his labor and charge is little or none till harvest ours is

27. Butler, *Bermudaes,* 200.
28. Ibid., 29.
29. John Dutton to Nathaniel Rich, October 17, 1620, in Ives, *Rich Papers,* 207; "Draft of a Petition to the Commissioners," May 1623, ibid., 267.
30. Lefroy, *Memorials,* 1:228.

daylie and hourely, his crop being housed his care and charge is ended, then is our care greatest and our danger most, yea of so tickle and dangerous a nature is this Tobacco . . . that one houres neglect or the least want of helpe may spoyle a whole years cropp.[31]

In early Bermuda, as in Virginia, labor was a precious commodity: "That man commonly that hath the most helpe doth make the best tobacco." Tobacco, unlike wheat or corn, was a labor-intensive crop: Seedlings had to be planted, then transplanted to fields; the seedlings weeded and hoed; the "suckers," or new growth, kept picked off each plant to make it produce large leaves; the mature plants cut, dried, and packed for shipment. And Bermuda's tobacco fields were at the mercy of the winds from the Atlantic: A sudden wind from "north west-north, north east, or at east wch is comon" could ruin a crop in a few hours.[32] Southampton and Warwick Tribes, with fields on the south shore, were the best for producing tobacco.

In Bermuda as in Virginia in the first decade of settlement, not all of the colonists were willing workers. In 1620 colonist John Dutton wrote to Nathaniel Rich, "For my owne parte, Sir, I was never bread to the Labor of the bodye, neither came I heather to that end." Others who came to Bermuda, like those who came to Virginia, registered their dismay at the amount of work required. In 1619, seven years after Bermuda's founding, the Reverend Lewis Hughes observed that "some of the new commers are almost at a stand and do sigh to see how many trees they have to fell and how theire hands are blistered." Even the tenants complained. John Dutton wrote to the Earl of Warwick: "Your Lordships people are much discontented because they have not, as others, searvants sent them; 3 or 2 apprentizes at the least to every Master of a Famely would give them greate incouraidgement."[33] The apprentices, waifs or orphaned boys sent from England by the Somers Islands Company, usually to serve for 10 years, were a welcome addition to the labor force. The Virginia Company sent boys to Jamestown, but usually for terms of seven years.[34] As Dutton observed, "One boye with a man is able to raise twise as much as of him selfe." Laboring for a single man was difficult: "How harsh it is to some of them, I am Sencibell, who, wearied with the labors of the daye, comeinge home, must beate corne, fetch water, gett and dress his owne victuales."[35] To alleviate this problem the Somers Islands Company in 1621 sent "certaine

31. Ibid., 433.
32. Ibid., 434.
33. John Dutton to Nathaniel Rich, October 17, 1620, in Ives, *Rich Papers,* 207; Lewis Hughes to Nathaniel Rich, August 12, 1619, ibid., 137; Dutton to the Earl of Warwick, January 20, 1619/1620, ibid., 143. On the aversion to hard labor, see also Butler, *Bermudaes,* 75–76.
34. One hundred children from London were sent to Bermuda in 1619. Ives, *Rich Papers,* 240, 382; see also Morgan, *American Slavery,* 116.
35. Dutton to the Earl of Warwick, January 20, 1619/1620, in Ives, *Rich Papers,* 143–44.

young maydes (or, at the least, single women) . . . to make wives for such single men as would paye one hundred poundes of tobacco apeece for every one of them." The Company also sent "two Virginian virgins," young Powhatan women who had been members of the retinue of the Princess Pocahontas on her visit to England in 1616. She was then called Rebecca and was the wife of Virginia colonist John Rolfe. After her untimely death in England in 1617, the young women who had attended her were sent to Bermuda. One died at sea, but the other was married in Bermuda in 1621 "to as fitt and agreeable an husband as the place would afford" with a nuptial feast for a hundred persons. This may have been Bermuda's first interracial marriage. The "Virginian mayde" and her spouse sailed on to Virginia in 1622.[36]

Even for a married man, life as a tobacco planter was far from easy. The history of one such planter, a colonist named Marmaduke Dando, affords a view of an ordinary English colonist's life in Bermuda's early years. In 1617 Dando and another colonist, William Smith, took out a seven-year lease on one share of Nathaniel Rich's land in Southampton Tribe. The yearly rent would be £12.10. Nathaniel and his cousin, Robert Rich, the future Earl of Warwick, were absentee landlords in Bermuda. Nathaniel's younger brother, Robert, however, served as the family's agent in Bermuda. In 1617 the young Robert wrote to Nathaniel that the rent would be in "good English mony, which payment you need not to doubt of." The share of land would be "clered, planted with vines and other fruitts and 2 sufficient howses builded upon it, gardens payled [fenced] in, Tobaco planted." Dando and Smith, said Rich, were men of good character with "bouth wives and Children."[37]

Young Robert Rich was confident that Dando, Smith, and the other tenants would prosper, since he predicted that tobacco would bring "half a crowne [2 shillings, sixpence] a pound." If all went well, one 25-acre share, allowing for some acreage for corn and other food crops, might produce 400 pounds of tobacco in a year, a harvest worth £50 in the early years of the tobacco boom. But all of Bermuda's shares of land were not equal, and landlords' financial arrangements with tenants varied. Robert noted that Dando and Smith "could rent better land att 2 shillings an accer" (£2.10 per year), but their agreement with Nathaniel Rich included a bonus: It provided for one of the pair to return

---

36. Butler, *Bermudaes,* 271–72, 284.

37. Robert Rich to Nathaniel Rich, May 25, 1617, and February 22, 1617/1618, in Ives, *Rich Papers,* 21. Young Robert Rich's obvious satisfaction in recording his plans for these Bermuda colonists to plant crops, build houses, and make fenced gardens reinforces Patricia Seed's argument that English settlers established their cultural claim to the land by making gardens and building houses, while the French did so by planting a flag and the Spanish by reading a proclamation. See Seed, *Ceremonies of Possession in Europe's Conquest of the New World, 1492–1640* (Cambridge, Eng.: Cambridge University Press, 1995).

to England every two years. This provision would allow them to trade or buy goods, "to make the best of ther commodities as they cane." They would need to do that, given the inferior quality of their land. The Dando/Smith lease was a narrow strip of wooded, hilly land approximately half a mile long and 600 feet wide, running from James Bay and the Great Sound on the north to Port Royal and the Atlantic Ocean on the south. Although the property contained patches of level ground, these amounted to no more than five or six acres. Robert Rich observed that the land at Port Royal, which was partially covered with palmettos, cedars, and mangroves, "wilbee a long time a clereing." The terrain, he thought, would be "good for goatts and Cowes," but as yet he did not have any livestock.[38]

Dando and Smith took up their lease in December 1617, and two months later, Robert Rich reported that they had "Clered the most peart of" their land.[39] They also built houses for their families. But the earliest Bermuda houses did not take long to erect, since they were rough-hewn wood frames with wattle-and-daub walls and palmetto-thatched roofs, typically with one or two rooms and no chimney. In Bermuda's mild climate most cooking was done out of doors, and many of the earliest houses did not have fireplaces. Dando and Smith would have marked off their lease with a palmetto fence, as a 1620 law required, or else "where the natural Palmetoe fence is failed and is found to be wantinge . . . there be planted a sufficiencye of Pomegranate and figg trees for a supplie thereof."[40] The "payled gardens" Robert Rich mentioned in his letter would have adjoined the houses and would have been planted, perhaps by the wives and children, with peas, potatoes, melons, and the like.

The exact size of the two families is not known, but the Dandos had at least one child, a daughter, Hannah, who would have been four or five years old in 1618. The Smiths may have had two children in 1618, both sons, whose names and ages cannot be determined from existing records. Next to William Smith's name on a list of workers is the notation "2 boyes." They were presumably under 16 but old enough to work. They were very likely Smith's sons, although they might have been two of the earlier-mentioned boys sent from London. Along with Marmaduke Dando and 17 other men, they worked Nathaniel Rich's 12 shares of land in Southampton Tribe.[41]

---

38. Robert Rich to Nathaniel Rich, May 25, 1617, in Ives, *Rich Papers,* 25.
39. Robert Rich to Nathaniel Rich, February 22, 1617/1618, ibid., 56.
40. Lefroy, *Memorials,* 1:176.
41. Hannah Dando's birth date is not recorded. She married in 1632. See A. C. Hollis Hallett, comp., *Early Bermuda Records, 1619–1826: A Guide to the Parish and Clergy Registers with Some Assessment Lists and Petitions* (Pembroke, Bermuda: Juniperhill Press, 1991), 19. The list of workers is in Robert Rich's letter to Nathaniel Rich, March 1617/1618, in Ives, *Rich Papers,* 81–82.

Besides working the land, Nathaniel Rich's tenants, like Bermuda's other tenants, also had to contribute their labor to the colony's public workforce. Dando and Smith wrote to Nathaniel Rich on February 23, 1617/1618, that they were "greatlye opprest and trobled about the generall woork as in makinge of hye wayes and makeinge of forts and such bisnesses for 3 or 4 weeks togeather."[42] But 1618 would be a good year for tobacco in Bermuda. That year the colony produced its first sizeable crop, 30,000 pounds, which, as one colonist observed, "gave great contentment and incouragement to the undertakers to proceed lustely in their plantation: for the most part, without some such sweet sence and quickenings now and then they grow dull and tyred."[43]

During the first year of their tenancy Dando and Smith bought a boat "for the use of the whole companye" (themselves and Rich's other tenants in Southampton Tribe). The vessel was probably a shallop, a small, open craft about 30 feet long, with one or two masts and lateen-rigged sails, used in the seventeenth century for fishing close to land and transporting goods from ship to shore. They could make good use of the craft, since their land was bounded by the ocean on two sides. Except for parts of Devonshire and Smith Tribes, the main island of Bermuda is no more than a mile wide, but it is 18 miles long, and for much of the islands' history, water provided the best transportation.[44] Every one of the colony's 400 occupied shares of land had access to the sea. In 1622, a decade after Bermuda's founding, Governor Nathaniel Butler estimated that the islands contained "one thousand five hundred persons with neere a hundred Boats."[45] There would soon be many more.

In their letter of February 1617/1618, Dando and Smith wrote for supplies to be sent them by the next ship from England. The items they listed were goods all Bermudians had to import; nothing was manufactured in the islands. From the list itself it is possible to reconstruct something of life in two modest households in seventeenth-century Bermuda.[46] Dando and Smith ordered "10 yards of Carsye [kersey, a lightweight woolen cloth] mixe Collered at 3 shillings or 3 shillings 4 pence per yard; 20 yards of ell-broad canvas [a coarse, unbleached fabric made of flax or hemp] at 14 pence per ell; 8 pr of shoues (2 pr of the syes of the eyghts and 6 pr of the tenns); 2 pr of Carsye

42. Marmaduke Dando and Willliam Smith to Nathaniel Rich, February 23, 1617/1618, in Ives, *Rich Papers,* 45. References to dates from January 1 through March 25, 1752, when the British adopted the Gregorian calendar, are given in both old style (Julian calendar) and new style (Gregorian) form. The Julian calendar began the new year on March 26.
43. Butler, *Bermudaes,* 110.
44. Land transportation, when necessary, was by horse and carriage, bicycle, and foot until 1931, when a railway was built. Automobiles were not used until 1946.
45. Lefroy, *Memorials,* 1:161.
46. For their list, see Marmaduke Dando and William Smith to Nathaniel Rich, February 23, 1617/1618, in Ives, *Rich Papers,* 44–46.

stockens; 1 lb. of black and broune threed." These were the essentials, for clothing was at a premium in the islands. The two wives would make kersey dresses for themselves, and they would make breeches and jackets for their husbands and the Smiths's two sons out of the canvas, with some yardage left over, perhaps, to sell or trade. The two pairs of kersey stockings and the two pairs of size eight shoes were probably for the wives, since some seventeenth-century footwear could serve either gender as well as either foot. The shoes in the larger size would have supplied their husbands, and perhaps William Smith's two boys; the two extra pairs of shoes were probably to lay up or trade off.

After the clothing came the luxuries. The list-maker (presumably Dando, since Smith was illiterate) then called for "6 gallons of aquavitie (I pray put it in toe [two] rundletts)." Aqua vitae was the name used for any strong, fermented liquor. Bermudians were fond of it. "Will it ever be believed," Governor Nathaniel Butler wrote in 1622, "that twelve hundred persons (whereof the one halfe almost are women and children) should in three moneths space only, consome and emptye two thousand gallons of this heart burning geare?" A few years later another governor, Roger Wood, wrote in praise of aqua vitae: "A dramme in a hott day when men have been to hear preach, or planting or hoeing, or other worke in the fields, tastes well."[47] Dando and Smith would each have a three-gallon cask of aqua vitae, to sell or to be enjoyed with a pipe of tobacco at the end of a long day's toil. (In contrast, Robert Rich ordered six gallons of aqua vitae, a hogshead of beer, and six gallons of "good sacke" [white wine]).[48] Dando and Smith also requested a gross of tobacco pipes, more than enough to supply them and their wives. The use of tobacco was neither age- nor gender-specific. One governor observed that "Men, Women, & Children are all Greate Smokers of Tobacco."[49]

Something of these planters' diets may be inferred from two other items in their order: "4 gallons of sallatt oil . . . 40 lb. of cheese." (Robert Rich ordered "one firkene [one-quarter barrel] of butter" along with his cheese.) Corn, potatoes, and fish, with perhaps some poultry, made up the bill of fare in the ordinary household, with "sallatt oil" and cheese used to enhance flavor, then as now. Salad, a "cold dish of herbs or vegetables," was a common dish by the late 1400s.[50] The order for 40 pounds of cheese indicates that Dando

47. Nathaniel Butler, quoted in Wilkinson, *Adventurers,* 307; Roger Wood, quoted ibid., 306.
48. Robert Rich to Nathaniel Rich, February 27, 1617/1618, in Ives, *Rich Papers,* 66.
49. "Report of Governor Robert Robinson to the Lords of Trade, 1687," *BHQ* 2, no. 1 (1945): 17. Early tobacco pipes were long-stemmed, small-bowled receptacles usually made of a white clay and not meant to last long. Twelve dozen of them would have kept the Dandos and Smiths for a year.
50. The *Oxford English Dictionary* has a reference to *salad* in 1481.

and Smith did not have a cow, and cheese, like oil, could be bartered for other goods. Fish, plentiful in Bermuda's waters, would have been a staple in the Dando and Smith families' diets. As for utensils, forks were not yet common, and they ate with spoons (they ordered a dozen), probably from wooden trenchers, the usual dishes of ordinary households in the seventeenth century.

One of the last items on the list was "2 elles of good holland [linen] at 3 shillings 4 pence per ell." (Robert Rich ordered "12 ells of good [H]olland at 2s 1/2d per ell to make me shirtts.") Dando's and Smith's small quantity of linen (about two and one-half yards of fabric by modern measurement) was for the females in their families. William Smith's wife and Dando's wife and daughter would be able to adorn a plain kersey gown with a collar, perhaps, or to make a new linen cap. Like all proper seventeenth-century matrons, Goodwives Dando and Smith would have covered their heads in public. "We do desier your worship," Dando and Smith wrote to Nathaniel Rich, "to send these things and to put it in a barrell and by the returne of the shipe yu shalbe paid for."[51] In June of 1618 Nathaniel Rich made a careful list of the items they ordered, and the shipment presumably arrived in due time. Although the Dandos and the Smiths lived modestly and dressed simply, they, like other Bermudians, ate better than their counterparts in England.

After the first few years of settlement, food was never in short supply in Bermuda. In 1621 such delicacies as "figgs, pomegranates, oranges, lemans, plantanes, sugar canes, potatoe, and cassada rootes" were shipped to Virginia, and the next year a larger shipment of "twenty thousand weight of potatoes . . . great store of ducks and turkeys, some few conyes, all kinds of plantes in great varietie and quantitie, as likewise store of the cassada roote, and a good proportion of corne" helped to supplement Virginia diets.[52] In 1631 Governor Roger Wood wrote, "I thanke God wee abound wth all kind of provision for our subsistance as corne, potatoes, hoggs, Turkeys, and foules in great plenty, besydes owr fruits. . . . God is thus mercifull unto us, that although [they] may have almost naked backes and bare feet, yet they have full bellies."[53]

---

51. Robert Rich to Nathaniel Rich, May 25, 1617, in Ives, *Rich Papers,* 66. Dando and Smith to Nathaniel Rich, ibid., 45. Nathaniel Rich made a memorandum of Smith and Dando's letter, dated June 29, 1618, ibid., 102–3.

52. Butler, *Bermudaes,* 277, 285. The sugarcane in 1621 was no doubt the result of a 1620 recommendation of Somers Islands Company investors that Bermudians give up growing tobacco for sugarcane. The experiment was short-lived. See ibid., 210.

53. Letter Book of Roger Wood, 1631–1634, Colonial Records of Bermuda (hereafter, CR), Fragmentary Book F, letter no. 10, February 2, 1631/1632. The Colonial Records manuscript collection of early Bermuda documents in nine bound manuscript volumes in the Bermuda Archives is now on microfilm. Its contents are described in Lefroy, *Memorials,* 1:v–xxix. Roger Wood's letter book is excerpted in Lefroy, *Memorials,* 1:531–44.

In 1623 a report from Bermuda to King James I noted that "a great parte of those Ilands (they beeing generally all over-growne with wood) hath with infinite paynes and industrie of men ben cleared, between 1500 and 2000 persons there now inhabiting who have built them houses, plantes stores of Corne, and live not only in health but in plenty of good provisions fitt to susteyne the life of man with comfort and delight."[54] Robert Rich planted "[grape]vines, figg trees, . . . pynes [pineapples] & all lemons" in the large walled garden he had built. Bermuda did indeed grow pineapples and exotic edibles, as is evidenced by an act of the Assembly in 1629 to prevent the "pilferinge and stealinge of . . . sugar Canes Grapes Corne Plantaines and Pynes Potatoes Pompions Oranges Limons and Pownegranads &c." In 1633 Governor Wood rhapsodized over his crop of pineapples: "I wish I could send 1000 in their season to the Queene," he wrote, "and 500 more to such as desire them, for I can well spare them and eat enough myselfe. I sent 4 boats lading this yeare unto the mayne [the main island], to give them to those good dames that love to eat them better than to plant them. . . . I assure you I love to plant and preserve them, and behould them in their beauty, more than to munch them alone without the companie of my friends."[55]

By the early 1620s, as the islands' surveyor, Richard Norwood, noted in his journal, the early Bermudians "built for themselves and their families, not Tents or Cabins, but more substantiall houses; they cleared their grounds; and planted not onely such things as would yeeld them their fruits in a yeare, or halfe a yeare: but all such, too, as would afford them profit after certaine yeares, &c."[56] Norwood's 1622 map of the colony, made from his survey of 1616–1617, gives some suggestion of the colony's development in the first decade. The map shows five churches and 138 houses scattered over the eight tribes. The five churches may be too many. According to other records there were four, not five, churches in 1617, and eight, not seven, forts.[57] Since the population in 1622 was about 1,500, 138 houses would have meant an average of more than 10 people per house. It is likely that some of these dwellings were shared by more than one family in the early years. St. George's, the center of government, had 11 houses; Hamilton Tribe had 14, Smith's, 10; Devonshire, 15; Pembroke, 19; Paget, 10; Southampton, 13; Warwick, 8; and Sandys, 16. In 1622 the Somers Islands Company provided for four ministers for the colony, with glebe land set aside for churches and parsonages. The churches were to serve St. George's; Harrington, Hamilton,

54. Draft of Commissioners' Proposal to James I, ca. June 1623, in Ives, *Rich Papers,* 269.
55. Letter Book of Roger Wood, letter no. 31, dated January 1633. The 1629 act of the Assembly is printed in Lefroy, *Memorials,* 1:308.
56. Norwood, *Journal,* lxxvii.
57. Hallett, *Colonial Church,* 12–13, 262; Lefroy, *Memorials,* 1:212, 299.

and Smith's Tribes; Pembroke, Devonshire, and Paget Tribes; and Southampton, Warwick, and Sandys Tribes. Bermuda's churches were all nominally Anglican, or Church of England, but with a strong Puritan bent. Bermuda's first two clergymen, George Keith and Lewis Hughes, were Nonconformists and established a presbyterian form of church government.[58] On the Norwood map, all of the tribes but Warwick, Paget, and Hamilton have churches; but the residents of these three tribes would not have had to travel more than three miles to attend church in a neighboring tribe.

There were apparently few, if any, horses in Bermuda in the first few years, but ordinary folk went about their visits and errands on foot, traveling on paths made and maintained by the various tribes. By 1620 the residents of the three most populous tribes—Sandys, Southampton, and Warwick—had already made "a sufficient path . . . from the narrows of Somersett unto the further end of Warwicke tribe," a distance of about seven miles. The Assembly ordered footbridges to be built at the west end of Bermuda, between Somerset Island and the mainland, and at the east end, between Coney Island and Hamilton Tribe. There was already a bridge between Hamilton and Smith's Tribes "at the flatts over the mouth of the little sound."[59] Thus it was possible to go on foot from one end of Bermuda to the other, a distance of about 24 miles by land, and 18 by water. A ferry made runs across the 125-yard water passage between the east end of "the main" and the island capital at St. George's.

Some of the grueling work of building ferries and bridges, constructing churches, erecting houses, and tilling fields was done by laborers whose racial characteristics and cultural origins would forever set them apart from the other Bermudians. Of approximately 11 million Africans brought to the New World from the 1500s to the 1800s, only about 5,000 arrived in Bermuda, but the history of the first blacks in this small island colony can be traced in considerable detail.[60] The history of blacks in Bermuda begins in 1616,

58. See Hallett, *Colonial Church,* 15–20. See also Peter J. C. Smith, "Presbyterianism in Bermuda," *BHQ* 26, no. 2 (1969): 36–53; Babette Levy, "Early Puritanism in Southern and Island Colonies," *American Antiquarian Society Proceedings* 70, pt. 1 (1960): 69–348; Arthur P. Newton, *Colonising Activities of the English Puritans: The Last Phase of the Elizabethan Struggle with Spain* (1914; reprint, Port Washington, N.Y.: Kennikat Press, 1966).

59. Lefroy, *Memorials,* 1:169–71. The bridge at Somerset, with a 22-inch draw to allow boats to pass between Ely's Harbor and the Great Sound, is said to be the smallest drawbridge in the world.

60. James Walvin, *Black Ivory: A History of British Slavery* (New York: Harper Collins, 1992), 36–37, puts the total number transported at 11 million; Philip D. Curtin, *The Atlantic Slave Trade: A Census* (Madison, Wisc.: University of Wisconsin Press, 1969), 88, places it at 10 million, with 5,000 to Bermuda. See also James A. Rawley, *The Transatlantic Slave Trade: A History* (New York: W. W. Norton Co., 1981). Two Bermuda authors chronicle the history of slavery in the islands: Cyril Outerbridge Packwood, *Chained on the Rock: Slavery in Bermuda*

three years before the earliest known evidence of blacks in Virginia. A census recorded 32 blacks in Virginia in the spring of 1619, and Virginia colonist John Rolfe noted the arrival of "20 and odd Negroes" on a Dutch ship in August of the same year.[61] A few blacks may have been brought to that mainland colony before 1619, but little is known about the initial contacts between blacks and whites in Virginia. In Bermuda, however, the coming of the first black can be precisely documented, and the individual histories of a handful of later arrivals can be followed.

At the beginning of the seventeenth century, when England began to colonize, blacks were already an integral part of the labor force in the Spanish Caribbean colonies of Cuba, Hispaniola, and Puerto Rico, as well as in the Spanish and Portuguese colonies on the mainland, and there the institution of slavery was already firmly established in law.[62] The legal status of the first blacks brought to the English colonies, on the other hand, is not clear from the existing records. The evidence suggests that they were not at once defined as slaves, and they were probably treated in a manner not very different from the whites who were sold as servants. In Bermuda and in England's other colonies, the institution of slavery developed slowly, through several decades of association between whites and blacks. Since the chronology and complexity of this fateful change cannot be definitely established, the origins of slavery in North America have provoked a rich and varied scholarly debate.[63]

In February 1615/1616 the Somers Islands Company's commission to Richard Moore's successor, Governor Daniel Tucker, informed him that the Company was sending a trader to the "Savadge Islands" (Lesser Antilles) for "sundrye thinges wch is hoped he shall there gett for the Plantacon, as Cattle Cassadoe [cassava, a nutritious, starchy tuber native to the West Indies and South America], Sugar Canes, negroes to dive for pearles, and what other

(New York: Eliseo Torres and Sons, 1975), and James E. Smith, *Slavery in Bermuda* (New York: Vantage Press, 1976).

61. On the census of 1619, see Thorndale, "The Virginia Census of 1619," 155–70. Rolfe's letter of August 19, 1619, to Sir Edwin Sandys is printed in *Records of the Virginia Company,* 2:243. See also Sluiter, "New Light on the '20 and Odd Negroes,'" 39.

62. See Alan Watson, *Slave Law in the Americas* (Athens, Ga.: University of Georgia Press, 1989). For comparative views, see Ira Berlin and Philip D. Morgan, eds., *Cultivation and Culture: Labor and the Shaping of Slave Life in America* (Charlottesville, Va.: University Press of Virginia, 1993), John Thornton, *Africa and Africans in the Making of the Atlantic World* (Cambridge, Eng.: Cambridge Universtiy Press, 1992), and Michael L. Conniff and T. J. Davis, *Africans in the Americas: A History of the Black Diaspora* (New York: St. Martin's Press, 1992).

63. See Betty Wood, *The Origins of American Slavery: Freedom and Bondage in the English Colonies* (New York: Hill and Wang, 1997), and note 2 above. See also Joseph E. Inikori and Stanley L. Engerman, eds., *The Atlantic Slave Trade: Effects on Economies, Societies, and People in Africa, the Americas, and Europe* (Durham, N.C.: Duke University Press, 1992).

plants are there to be had, wch we cannot write in pticulers."[64] That casual mention of "negroes" begins the multiracial history of the Bermuda colony, although at least one black and two American Indians had visited the islands earlier. In 1603 "One Venturilla, a Negroe," crew member aboard a Spanish ship, went ashore briefly, and in 1609, two Indians from Virginia were among the passengers of an English vessel shipwrecked on the islands.[65] It is worth noting that in 1616 the Somers Islands Company official sought blacks for their special skills as pearl divers, not as ordinary laborers. But the Lesser Antilles had been fertile ground for slave hunters since the early 1500s, when a Spanish decree of 1503 allowed enslavement of the region's native Carib Indians.[66] In May 1616, the *Edwin* arrived in Bermuda from the West Indies, and Governor Tucker noted that she "brought with her also one Indian and a Negroe (the first thes Ilands ever had)."[67] It is not clear whether the parenthetical observation applied to the black only, or to the Indian as well. The presence of the Indian, like the African, would have been a novelty in Bermuda, since that colony, unlike the Caribbean islands, had no indigenous peoples. The Indian was probably a Carib, one of a declining population that had numbered several million in that region at the time of Columbus's arrival. Presumably the Indian and the black were males brought to Bermuda "to dive for pearles." The Bermuda islands might not have gold or silver mines, but the Englishmen who settled there still cherished hopes of finding riches in Bermuda as the Spanish had done in Mexico and Peru.[68]

The Indian and the black may have been put to work diving for pearls, but their status—whether free or slave—is unrecorded, and their treatment—as highly skilled workers or common laborers—is unknown. Their labor was owned by the Somers Islands Company, and they would have lived and worked alongside the white servants on the Company's land. There are no more records of Indians until the 1640s, but the single black brought to the islands in May 1616 was soon joined by others. In May 1617 a letter from young Robert Rich to Nathaniel Rich mentioned the "good store of neggars

64. Lefroy, *Memorials,* 1:115–16.
65. See Wilkinson, *Adventurers,* 23; Barbour, ed., *Complete Works,* 2:350.
66. See Kenneth F. Kiple and Kriemhild C. Ornelas, "After the Encounter: Disease and Demographics," in *The Lesser Antilles in the Age of European Expansion,* ed. Robert Paquette and Stanley L. Engerman (Gainesville, Fla.: University Press of Florida, 1996), 54–55. Caribs were still "fairly numerous" in the first half of the seventeenth century.
67. Butler, *Bermudaes,* 84.
68. Hopes for windfall profits from pearls were never realized, though a few defective pearls were found in Bermuda oysters in the 1620s. Lefroy, *Memorials,* 1:159–60; see also Kenneth R. Andrews, *The Spanish Caribbean: Trade and Plunder, 1530–1630* (New Haven: Yale University Press, 1978), and Richard S. Dunn, *Sugar and Slaves: The Rise of the Planter Class in the English West Indies, 1624–1713* (Chapel Hill: University of North Carolina Press, 1972).

which Mr. Powell brought from the West Indies." Robert did not say how many there were, but they were apparently put to work in the tobacco fields. Confident of the new workers' skills, Robert told his elder brother, Nathaniel, "I doubt not but you will have from us good store of Tobaco, which will prove very vendable."[69] The number of blacks brought to Bermuda from the West Indies in the seventeenth century is not known, but some of them were placed there by privateers supported by the elder Robert Rich, second Earl of Warwick.[70] In the same letter that mentioned a "good store of neggars," the young Robert Rich also observed somewhat ruefully that "the negor that I have brought over is full of the frence pox [syphilis], and is under care. He hath had many provicions from mee." The care evidently effected a cure, for in February 1617/1618 Robert wrote to his brother Nathaniel, informing him that he had placed this "neger" on some barren land and that he planned to order "the negres planting of west endy plants, wherin hee hath good scill."[71] Such plants would no doubt have included tobacco, cassava, a plant native to the West Indies and unknown to English colonists, as well as melons, pumpkins, squash, and the like. In his letter to his brother the younger Rich also mentioned another skilled black: "I intreat you to procure mee a neger whose name is Francisco. Hee is one [of] the generall; his judgment in the cureing of tobackoe is such that I had rather have him than all the other negers that bee here. Hee is Captain Powells. I doubt not but you may obtayne him for . . . one hundreth pounds. I wish that you would redeeme hime for the aforesaid sum; you need not greatly to complayne." Captain John Powell was the master of the *Hopewell*, a small bark belonging to the Somers Islands Company. In 1617 Powell captured a Brazilian vessel whose booty was in turn taken from him by a French ship. Later that year Powell captured three other vessels of unknown nationality and brought them to Bermuda. Francisco may have been aboard one of these. Powell was paid by the Company to trade for livestock in the West Indies and later became a privateer for the Earl of Warwick.[72] Francisco's Spanish name suggests that he came from the West

69. Robert Rich to Nathaniel Rich, May 25, 1617, in Ives, *Rich Papers,* 25.

70. See W. F. Craven, "The Earl of Warwick, A Speculator in Piracy," *Hispanic American Historical Review* 10 (1930): 457–79. On Warwick's privateering and trading in blacks, see also CR, 2:107, 113.

71. Robert Rich to Nathaniel Rich, May 15, 1617, and February 22, 1617/1618, in Ives, *Rich Papers,* 17, 59.

72. Captain Powell also engaged in privateering for the Dutch. Robert Rich mentions him in the February 22 letter, in Ives, *Rich Papers,* 16. See also Lewis Hughes to Nathaniel Rich, February 12, 1619/1620, ibid., 167; Nathaniel Butler to Nathaniel Rich, March 15, 1619/1620, ibid., 178–82; and Lefroy, *Memorials,* 1:721. In 1617 Powell had lost some of Rich's cargo to a French pirate ship and was in debt to the Riches for £100. Robert Rich thought the transaction involving Francisco would satisfy the debt.

Indies, where he probably also acquired his knowledge of tobacco culture. In Bermuda in early 1618 he was working with an undetermined number of blacks and whites in the "general," an unassigned workforce or labor pool on the public lands near the capital, St. George's. In any case, Nathaniel Rich, upon receiving his brother's letter, made himself a note on June 29, 1618, to "procure Franciscoe a Negro: Powells servant now on the generall, to be upon our Tribe."[73]

In the meantime the younger Rich had somehow procured Francisco on his own, for this skilled black man is listed on Rich's March 1618 record of the men working on Nathaniel Rich's 300 acres in Southampton Tribe.[74] There are 19 workers in all, including two unnamed boys, the sons (or servants) of Marmaduke Dando's partner, William Smith. The names of Marmaduke Dando and William Smith head the list, and at the end of it are the names Francisco, "Antonye," and "James the negger," all without surnames. "James the negger," whose name appears last on the list, may well have been the same individual that Robert Rich had treated for syphilis. It is also possible that James's physical appearance set him apart from the other two blacks, who may have been lighter-skinned, though they were described elsewhere as "Negroes." This listing, which groups at the end the names of the three men without surnames, indicates that Rich perceived these three as certainly different from, but not necessarily inferior to, the whites. Moreover, the list is not in a discernible order of rank or status, since the names of men leasing "on halves" are intermingled with those of men who are servants in the Rich family's employ. In young Robert Rich's correspondence with his brother he made no distinction between the blacks and the other laborers, describing them all as "men that are now resident uppon your land in Southamptons Trybe." The blacks apparently held the land they worked under the same terms as the white laborers, and there is no indication that they were slaves.

Some of the whites, including Marmaduke Dando and William Smith, were leasing land "on halves," turning over half their annual profits to the owner. Others, including Francisco, Antony, and James, were laborers hired or assigned to the land by Robert Rich. Their status—whether bond or free— is not clear, but since the blacks were listed without a separate classification, it is reasonable to assume that these three shared the same status as their white co-workers. One of these was an indentured servant named Hugh Wentworth, who managed to buy out his indenture by 1620 and to become a member of the Bermuda Council by 1627. At his death in 1641 "Hugh Wentworth,

73. Ives, *Rich Papers*, 103.
74. Robert Rich to Nathaniel Rich, March 1617/1618, ibid., 81–82.

Gent." was an agent for the Earl of Warwick and one of the colony's leading traders in servants, both black and white.[75]

While other English colonists on the mainland in the seventeenth century seem to have preferred to use white indentured servants as long as the supply of such labor lasted, turning to blacks only when white servants became scarce toward the end of the century, Bermuda settlers seem to have preferred blacks from the beginning. In the first two decades of settlement, blacks were difficult to come by and highly coveted as a labor supply. In 1622 Governor Nathaniel Butler thought them to be "a most necessary commoditie for thes Ilands."[76] Besides Francisco, Antony, and James, who may have been among the "good store" of blacks brought in 1617 by the privateer Captain John Powell, other blacks soon arrived in Bermuda. At least 43 blacks from the West Indies were brought to Bermuda just prior to Governor Butler's arrival in 1620, and a series of references to them offers further proof of the scarcity and desirability of blacks in the colony's early years. In 1619 Captain Daniel Elfrith (like John Powell a privateer in the employ of the Earl of Warwick) brought 29 blacks to Bermuda. About the same time 14 blacks were presented to acting governor Miles Kendall by another privateer, a Captain Kirby, in return for Kendall's allowing him to provision his ship in Bermuda. Kendall wrote to Nathaniel Rich that some blacks had "accidentally happened uppon our Coast here, being in number 14, And were freely given unto mee." But Kendall was not permitted to keep these blacks, who finally became the property of the Somers Islands Company. On October 9, 1620, Nathaniel Butler wrote to Warwick that "Your Lordships Negroes are disposed of after your directions and the generall Letters." In a postscript about the 14 blacks, Butler wrote, "I humbly thanck your Lordship for my two." The 14 blacks, along with the 29 others brought by Elfrith, were apparently distributed on Rich's land. John Dutton, who managed the Rich family's land after the death of young Robert Rich in 1620, wrote to the Earl of Warwick on October 17 of that year that the "Negros which caime in" would be "placed at Christmas when they come into my hands."[77]

75. On Wentworth's background, see Wilkinson, *Adventurers,* 100 n, 108 n.

76. Butler, *Bermudaes,* 144. The English colonists who settled on Providence Island, founded in 1630, also turned eagerly to slave labor to cultivate tobacco. See Karen Ordahl Kupperman, *Providence Island, 1630–1641: The Other Puritan Colony* (Cambridge, Eng.: Cambridge University Press, 1993), 175–80. By 1633 there were enough blacks on Providence Island to cause apprehension in the white community. See also Newton, *Colonising Activities,* 150.

77. Miles Kendall to Nathaniel Rich, January 18, 1619/1620, in Ives, *Rich Papers,* 123; Nathaniel Butler to the Earl of Warwick, October 9, 1620, ibid., 184, 188; John Dutton to the Earl of Warwick, October 17, 1620, ibid., 202. See also Lefroy, *Memorials,* 1:281; Craven, *Introduction,* 418–20. In 1618 the Earl of Warwick had become a member of the Guinea

Where the first blacks in Bermuda had come from is a matter for speculation; what they did when they arrived is more easily established. Some
of them could well have been Africans taken directly from West Africa by
Spanish or Portuguese traders and later captured at sea by English or Dutch
privateers. Others, like Francisco and Robert Rich's unnamed black who was
skilled in "west endy plants," were West Indian blacks taken from Spanish
settlements in the Caribbean. Because of their seasoning in the West Indies,
these were considered by some to be "the better sort of Negroes." Some
of the blacks brought to Bermuda in the 1620s may have been "Atlantic
creoles," Africans who had developed a knowledge of trade and language
skills from years of contact with Europeans in the coastal towns along Africa's
west coast. In the Spanish colonies these individuals were sometimes called
"white Negroes" because of their acculturated behavior and speech. Many
of these multicultured blacks lived in the Dutch colony of New Netherland
between the 1620s and its takeover by the English in 1664.[78] Like them,
Bermuda's first blacks may well have been multilingual. Robert Rich, who
wrote copious and detailed accounts of his colonization experiences, would
surely have mentioned a language barrier if there had been one.

Whatever the origins of the blacks first brought to Bermuda, they were
much sought after as workers. The alacrity of the colony's whites in acquiring
blacks stands in marked contrast to the slowness of planters in the Chesapeake
to adopt a black labor force. While there is some debate as to why the change
to black labor took longer in Virginia and Maryland, in Bermuda the white
colonists' eagerness to use black workers is not hard to understand. Besides
being somewhat familiar with European ways, Bermuda's earliest blacks had
two skills that made them especially valuable to the English colonists: They
knew how to swim, and they knew how to grow tobacco. A seventeenth-
century English visitor to Barbados remarked upon the blacks' aquatic skills:
"Excellent Swimmers and Divers they are, both men and women."[79] Swimming and tobacco-growing were virtually unknown in England. As we have
seen, in 1616 the Somers Islands Company sought blacks to dive for pearls and
brought in an expert to show the colonists how to grow tobacco. Pearl-diving

---

Company, newly formed for African slave trading, and it is possible that some of these blacks
were newly purchased Africans. See Newton, *Colonising Activities*, 22, 35–36.

78. Berlin, "From Creole to African," 251–88, refers to an informal and largely undocumented network of connections between blacks in North America and the Caribbean by the
seventeenth century. Bermuda, where many vessels from those regions stopped, was also part
of that network. See ibid., 275–76.

79. Richard Ligon, *A True and Exact Account of the Island of Barbadoes* (London, 1673), in
*After Africa: Extracts from British Travel Accounts and Journals of the Seventeenth, Eighteenth,
and Nineteenth Centuries Concerning the Slaves, Their Manners, and Customs in the British West
Indies*, ed. Roger D. Abrahams and John F. Szwed (New Haven: Yale University Press, 1983), 62.

required a strong and practiced swimmer, and although pearls never became a source of income, underwater salvage operations did. Many passing vessels were wrecked on Bermuda's treacherous reefs, and shipwrecks (discussed in a later chapter) became a source of windfall profits for some Bermudians by the 1620s. Blacks who were skillful at swimming and diving were an integral part of such salvage operations. Tobacco growing, like swimming, was a specialized skill. Besides a knowledge of planting, tending, and harvesting, a practiced eye was needed to judge exactly when the tobacco was cured, that is, when the hanging bunches of tobacco leaves had dried just enough to pack into hogsheads for shipment.

By the end of 1619 the blacks Francisco and James were proving their worth as skilled growers and curers of tobacco. (Antony, their co-worker in 1617, disappears from the records.) After the harvest of 1619 a colonist named Thomas Durham wrote to Nathaniel Rich in some amazement that "the negroes made 1350 pounds of tobacco. He that made it up, seeinge it wayed [weighed], took accompte of it and will take his oth upon a booke there was so much." Indeed there was: A good yield for two shares in Bermuda was around 1,000 pounds of tobacco. In 1620 Durham reported that "Henry Wethersby hath 2 shares which ly towardes the east. Next to him the negroes 2 [shares], of which one is not imployed but I hear John Hammore hath taken one." John Hanmore, a friend of Robert Rich, had apparently taken a lease on one of the shares worked by the blacks. Perhaps Antony had died or had left and Hanmore took his share. Francisco and James's 1,350 pounds of tobacco seemed to amaze Thomas Durham, but it was similar to yields in Virginia. The average tobacco output per hand in that colony in the 1620s was about 710 pounds, or a little over 1,400 pounds for two workers. The output per hand in Virginia increased to 1,600 pounds by the 1670s.[80] Francisco and James had used their specialized knowledge of tobacco culture to good advantage and had obviously increased the value of their land. In 1621 John Dutton, who served the Rich interests after Robert's death in the fall of 1620, mentioned that another colonist was eager to lease the share of land that "ould Francisco and James, the Negros, with theire wifes, have and doe live upon."[81]

In the beginning, Robert Rich had placed tenants on his brother's land "by famylyes." "I intend to lett none [of the shares in Southampton] but to

80. See Thomas Durham's letter to Nathaniel Rich, ca. January 1619/1620, in Ives, *Rich Papers*, 82, 173 (quotation), 176, 205–6. On tobacco production, see Allan Kulikoff, *Tobacco and Slaves: The Development of Southern Cultures in the Chesapeake, 1680–1800* (Chapel Hill: University of North Carolina Press, 1986), 31.

81. The colonist who tried to lease the land was Daniel Elfrith, the erstwhile privateer. In 1621 he was leasing the share of land (owned by Nathaniel Rich) next to that worked by Francisco and James.

marryed men," he wrote, "by reason that single men are fickle and inconstant." Perhaps young Rich was thinking of the turbulent history of early Virginia, where women were scarce, single men far outnumbered married ones, and social order was fragile. His mention here of the benefits of marriage is one of the few references to gender roles in the early Bermuda records. A few years later colonist Thomas Durham complained that one of Rich's tenants, Thomas Downum, had planted some tobacco which he called his "wife's crop." Durham observed, "If he be sufferd to do this, every mans wife will do the like and have as great crops as theire husbands, and in tyme it will growe to a custome."[82] But Bermuda, unlike Virginia, had a stable society, with almost as many women as men, and families—black as well as white— soon flourished. Whether Francisco and James were already married in 1617 when their names appeared on the list of Southampton tenants is not known, but given Robert Rich's predilection for married tenants, it is likely that they were. Their wives may have been among the blacks brought by Captain Powell in 1617, or among those brought by other traders. In 1620, at any rate, the two women mentioned as wives of Francisco and James were tending to their households and helping their husbands in the fields. These two black couples were living and working independently of resident white supervision, turning over their tobacco crop to the lease holder or landlord, just as white servants would have done. They also lived very near white families.

As early as 1618 these Southampton tenants with their wives and children formed a biracial community, living and working side by side. It is likely that the blacks, skillful in the growing of tobacco and other plants unfamiliar to the English, shared their knowledge with their less experienced neighbors. Perhaps Francisco and James advised Daniel Elfrith, the erstwhile privateer who leased the share of land next to theirs in 1621, on how to grow tobacco. Elfrith's land was, according to John Dutton, "more than he and his two Negros can any way imploye."[83] Blacks probably also taught whites how to swim, and perhaps to sail, in Bermuda's clear blue waters. Whites and blacks would have sailed and fished together in the boat that Dando and Smith had bought for the use of all the Richs' tenants. A handful of recorded baptisms for blacks in the Southampton church register show that blacks and whites shared in the religious as well as the economic life of their community. Other

---

82. Robert Rich to Nathaniel Rich, February 22, 1617/1618, in Ives, *Rich Papers*, 50; Durham to Rich, ca. January 1619/1620, ibid., 172. Kathleen M. Brown, *Good Wives, Nasty Wenches, and Anxious Patriarchs: Gender, Race, and Power in Colonial Virginia* (Chapel Hill: University of North Carolina Press, 1996), finds that Virginia's white males lost no time in establishing their authority over women and slaves. Fragments of evidence suggest that Bermuda's gender and race relations developed differently.

83. John Dutton to Nathaniel Rich, December 4, 1621, in Ives, *Rich Papers*, 233.

scraps of evidence suggest that close relationships developed between blacks and whites in these first few years of settlement. James and his wife had a daughter born in the late 1620s and named her Hanna, the same name as the eldest daughter of their neighbors, Marmaduke Dando and his wife. In 1636, James and his wife gave this young daughter, Hanna, to one of their former neighbors and fellow tenants, Hugh Wentworth, to bring up. These three couples—James and his wife, the Dandos, and the Wentworths—had known each other since 1617.[84]

The Rich family's Southampton tenants were a small, close-knit community. In 1622 there were a total of 28 "able men" and 33 "women and children" living on the combined holdings of 15 shares (375 acres) belonging to Nathaniel Rich and Robert Rich, the Earl of Warwick, in Southampton Tribe.[85] It is not unreasonable to assume that other tribes had similarly close communities whose records have not survived. A census of the eight tribes in 1622 suggests that their demographic, if not their racial, makeup was similar (see table 1).

This census, taken prior to Governor John Bernard's arrival, was designed to show how many of the 50 shares in each of the eight tribes had been "furnished" with tenants. In 1622 Southampton and Sandys were the only tribes to have all their shares (1,250 acres) "supplied" with tenants. In all, 321 of the 400 shares were then occupied. The three western tribes, Sandys, Southampton, and Warwick, were the most populous as well as the most prosperous, and in 1623 the Assembly required them to pay one-third more in the annual levy than residents in the other five tribes, who had "great charge and little land."[86] According to the census of 1622 there were 806 men, women, and children living in the eight tribes. A note at the end of this document states that the total represents "Persons uppon the Tribes beside those which are uppon the publick Land beside the Negroes." Whether the "Negroes" referred to were only those working for the Somers Islands Company on the public land or all of those in the colony is not clear. Since Bermuda's population at this time was estimated at 1,500, there were approximately 700 men, women, and children, black and white, who were not residents of the eight tribes but who lived on the public lands called the "general." This land, which belonged to the Somers Islands Company, included the island of St. George's, where the seat of government was located, the island of St. David's, the land known as Tucker's Town, and various smaller islands totaling 1,890 acres. As table 1 indicates, women and children made up a considerable portion of Bermuda's

84. Of the tenants on Nathaniel Rich's land in 1617, only two—Marmaduke Dando and Henry Wethersby—would end their days there and be buried in the Southampton churchyard: Wethersby in 1664, Dando in 1668 (Hallett, *Early Bermuda Records*, 21, 23).

85. Census of 1622, MS in Bermuda Archives, printed in Ives, *Rich Papers*, 240–45.

86. Lefroy, *Memorials*, 1:300–301.

Table 1	Census of the Eight Tribes, 1622			
Tribe	# Shares	Able Men	Women & Children	Population
Hamilton	24	19	13	32
Smith's	35	41	39	80
Devonshire	15	55	59	114
Pembroke	40	74	52	126
Paget	37	24	30	54
Warwick	36	59	55	114
Southampton	51	71	73	144
Sandys	50	70	72	142
Total	321	413	393	806

"Island Census," 1622, in Ives, *Rich Papers,* 241–45.

population even in the early years of settlement. Even in Hamilton Tribe, the smallest in population, 13 of the 32 persons in listed in tenant households in 1622 were women and children. Southampton Tribe, with 144 people—71 men, 73 women and children—was Bermuda's most populous tribe, followed by Sandys Tribe with 142 in almost identical distribution: 70 men, 72 women and children. Bermuda thus stands in marked contrast to Virginia, where men outnumbered women by three to one in the early years of settlement and family life was slow to develop.[87]

While Bermuda and Virginia had markedly different demographic histories, the two colonies were similar in one important aspect: the ambiguous status of blacks in the early years of settlement. In Bermuda, as in Virginia, it appears that for a brief time at least, while blacks were still few in number, some of them enjoyed a measure of freedom and a status similar to that of white laborers.[88] During Virginia's first four decades (or, one could say, during the

87. On the demography of Virginia and the Chesapeake, see Russell R. Menard, "British Migration to the Chesapeake Colonies in the Seventeenth Century," in *Colonial Chesapeake Society,* ed. Lois Green Carr, Philip D. Morgan, and Jean B. Russo (Chapel Hill: University of North Carolina Press, 1988), 99–132. See also Kulikoff, *Tobacco and Slaves,* 32–36.

88. See Winthrop Jordan, *White over Black: American Attitudes toward the Negro, 1550–1812* (Chapel Hill: University of North Carolina Press, 1968), 71–82; Morgan, *American Slavery,* 154–57; Alden T. Vaughan, "Blacks in Virginia: A Note on the First Decade," *WMQ,* 3d ser., 29, no. 3 (July 1972): 470–71; Russell R. Menard, "From Servants to Slaves: The Transformation of the Chesapeake Labor System," *Southern Studies* 16 (winter 1977): 367–69; Sylvia Frey, "In Search of Roots: The Colonial Antecedents of Slavery in the Plantation Colonies," *Georgia Historical Quarterly* 68, no. 2 (summer 1984): 248–49. See also T. H. Breen and Stephen

first generation of contact between blacks and whites) at least one black man
testified in the trial of a white man, some blacks earned wages and acquired
land, and one black owned another black man as his slave. There are indications
that until almost the close of the seventeenth century in Virginia, free blacks
had access to the legal system and were subject to few restrictions except being
barred from service in the militia.[89] Likewise, the earliest court case involving
a black person in Bermuda makes clear that slavery was not the ordinary status
of that colony's first blacks and that the term *slave* was applied without regard
to race.[90]

In the Bermuda assize of October 1617, "Symon, the Negro for having to
do with a child in carnall copulation was condemned to be a slave to the Colony
during the Governor's pleasure."[91] It is significant to note that this sentence
was, not for life, but for an unspecified time to be determined by the governor.
The court record is silent on the race and sex of the child. It is possible that
there might have been a child or children among the blacks that Captain Powell
had brought to the island in May, just a few months earlier. If "Symon the
Negro" assaulted a white child, there is no indication that the severity of his
punishment was based on his race. In contrast to this early record of the trial of
a black in Bermuda, the earliest recorded disciplinary action involving a black
in Virginia was clearly based on race. In 1630 a white man named Hugh Davis
was "soundly whipped, before an assembly of Negroes and others for abusing
himself to the dishonour of God and shame of Christians, by defiling his body
in lying with a negro; which fault he is to acknowledge next Sabbath day."[92]

Innes, *'Myne Owne Ground': Race and Freedom on Virginia's Eastern Shore, 1640–1676* (New
York: Oxford University Press, 1980).

89. In 1624 "John Phillip, a Negro Christened in England" testified in a case involving the
debt of Symon Tuching, an Irishman. See H. R. McIlwaine, ed., *Minutes of the Council and
General Court of Virginia* (Richmond, Va.: Colonial Press, Everett Waddey, 1924), 33. In the
1650s Anthony Johnson, a free black in Virginia, owned both land and servants—at least one of
whom was black. See Breen and Innes, *'Myne Owne Ground,'* 10–15. A 1639 act ordered that
"all persons except negroes" in Virginia be armed. William Walter Hening, comp., *The Statutes
at Large; Being a Collection of all the Laws of Virginia* . . . (Richmond, Va., Philadelphia, and
New York, 1819–1823), 1:226.

90. Use of the words *slave* and *servant* was often ambiguous. McColley, "Slavery in Virginia,"
12–14, argues that in the seventeenth century *servant* meant both servant and slave.

91. Assize of October 1617. The surviving pages of this assize in CR, vol. 1, are now
unreadable. The record is in Lefroy, *Memorials*, 1:127–28 (quotation, p. 127). Beginning in
1616 Bermuda's criminal and civil cases were tried in biannual courts of assize.

92. Hening, *Statutes*, 1:146. In 1640 a Virginia colonist named Robert Sweet was made to
do penance in church for "getting a negroe woman with child." The woman was whipped. See
ibid., 1:552. In 1650 one William Watts and "Mary (Mr. Cornelius Lloyds negro woman)" were
ordered to do penance by "standing in a white sheete with a white Rodd in theire hands in the
Chappell." *Lower Norfolk County Virginia Antiquary*, ed. Edward W. James (Baltimore: The
Friedenwald Co., 1895–1906), 1:113a. Rape and adultery were capital offenses in Virginia, but
there was no statutory penalty for fornication. Hening, *Statutes*, 1:68–69.

The Bermuda case is curiously devoid of racial consciousness. Indeed, Symon the Negro received the same punishment that Nicholas Gabriell, a white laborer, received at the same assize. Gabriell, for publicly criticizing the autocratic Governor Daniel Tucker, was sentenced to be "a slave unto the colony." Most likely both Symon and Gabriell were placed in the "general"—the Company's labor pool—until the governor saw fit to pardon them. Nicholas Gabriell apparently served only a brief time, for an assize record of March 1625/1626 shows that he brought a civil suit against another colonist.[93] Unfortunately Symon disappears from the written record at this point, so the length of his term of servitude cannot be known.[94]

While black Bermudians may have occupied an ambiguous social status because of their race, there was no doubt of their desirability as laborers. Thomas Durham wrote to Nathaniel Rich, complaining that "Mr. Dutton will not lett me have above one negro, neither am I certaine whether I shall have him." Durham complained that John Dutton had evicted several white tenants from the Earl of Warwick's land and "to serve his owne turne hired negros." Since blacks were not "on halves" as white tenants were, Dutton, who as bailiff of Warwick Tribe supervised the labor and recorded the amount of tobacco grown, could employ the blacks and keep part of the tobacco profits for himself. John Dutton was not the only culprit in this matter. In 1620, when representative government was established, the first act of the Bermuda Assembly made it unlawful to hire out any "servant or apprentice" without written permission from the landlord, and in 1621 the Somers Islands Company abolished the office of bailiff, replacing it with two "overseers" for each tribe for better surveillance.[95]

On January 12, 1621/1622, Governor Butler wrote to Nathaniel Rich that "thes Slaves are the most proper and cheape instruments for this plantation that can be, and not safe to be any wher but under the Governours eye."[96] He may have been referring to the dishonest practices of Dutton and others using black labor. Butler's use of the word *slave* here is the first specific application of the term to blacks, but other evidence suggests that he used the word in a

93. Assize of March 1625/1626, CR, 1:28B. Gabriell served as a juror in the assize of July 1627, and in the late 1620s he was involved in some minor civil actions and worked as a house builder in Pembroke Tribe. See CR, 1:73B, 76B, 78B, 133A, 147A. The author is indebted to Dr. A. C. Hollis Hallett of Bermuda for the post-1617 references to Gabriell in the Colonial Records.

94. There is an undated memorandum, probably written about 1650, "that George the sonne of old Symon is to continue searvant upon the Land . . . at one hundred pounds tobacco wages to be paid to Mr. George Tucker and his assignes." CR, 2:188.

95. Thomas Durham to Nathaniel Rich, October or November 1620, in Ives, *Rich Papers*, 215 (first quotation); Durham to Rich, October 18, 1620, ibid., 212 (second quotation); *Memorials*, 1:165–66.

96. Butler to Rich, January 12, 1620/1621, in Ives, *Rich Papers*, 229.

figurative sense. The blacks he referred to were indeed "cheape": They were the earlier-mentioned 29 who had apparently been seized by Elfrith in his privateering ventures in 1619, and the 14 who had been given that same year as a gift to Governor Kendall. The disposition of these two groups of blacks continued to be a source of controversy for a number of years. In 1623 the new governor, John Harrison, ordered the island's sheriff to "make dilligent search for all those negroes that belonge unto the Earle of Warwicke wch have byn brought unto theis parts by Capt. Kerby & Capt. Elfrey, and them found, to cause to be disposed accordynge to the councells said determynacon."[97]

It would appear from this that a number of blacks were living independently, either on their own or with whites who had no right to their labor. In fact, these unaccounted-for blacks could well have been the ones who caused the Bermuda Assembly to pass "An Act to restrayne the insolencies of the Negroes." This act, passed in 1623, is the first law dealing with the presence of blacks anywhere in the English colonies. It states:

> Whereas the Inhabitants of the Somer Islands doe complaine and present unto this honorable and grave assemblie, that the negroes who are servents to divers persons inhabiting in theise Islands, having bene negligently looked unto, and suffered to goe abroad in the night and other unfitt tymes have committed many trespasses against us the inhabitants aforesaid, as stealinge of piggs potatoes, poultrye and other fruit and thinges to the great losse and damage of several persons who cannott possible have reccompence at theire hands who have nothing where with to make them any satisfaccon and that divers of them (to prevent such as should pursue to apprehend them,) have carried secretly cudgells and other weapons and working tools, very dangerous and not meete to be suffered to be carried by such vassalls. for Reform whereof be it ennacted by the authority of this present generall assemblie that if any negroe shall hereafter weare any weapon in the day tyme, or knowne to walke abroad at any undue houre in the night tyme or any other tyme or tymes go out of the way into any lands in the occupacon of any other person then the land of his Master that then the Master or owner of such negroe shall from tyme to tyme make full recompense to the person grieved for the value of all such things as the said Negroes or any of them shall purloyne steale or grable, or any other hurt or damage by them done. And shall within three dayes after demand and due proof made thereof upon pains of forfeiture of treble damage to such partie grieved to be recovered by accon [action] of debt, besides such corporall punishment to be inflicted upon such Negroes as the lawe in such case requireth, or as the officer to whom the complainte shalbe made shall thinke fitt. Last of all that it shall not be lawfull for any negroe to buy or Sell, barter or exchange for goods Tobacco or other thinges whatsoever, without the knowledge and consent of his Master for the goods and Tobacco he tradeth for, upon pains of punishment aforesaid.[98]

---

97. Lefroy, *Memorials,* 1:281.

98. CR, vol. 1, book A, printed in Lefroy, *Memorials,* 1:308–9. On slave laws in other colonies, see William M. Wiecek, "The Statutory Law of Slavery and Race in the Thirteen Mainland Colonies of British America," *WMQ,* 3d ser., 34, no. 2 (April 1977): 258–80.

Although this piece of legislation does little to define the exact status of blacks in Bermuda society, it is clearly a response to existing conditions, and as such deserves a close reading. It is clear that blacks stole food and livestock from whites and that they also traded illegally. If they occupied a markedly inferior status in white society, such behavior was either a subtle form of resistance to the discrimination of whites or a means of augmenting a meager existence, or both. It is important to note that blacks seem to have had the upper hand: They pilfered "piggs potatoes, poultrye" (one imagines them feasting on the incriminating evidence) and apparently intimidated their would-be captors. They also carried on a furtive trade of their own, with each other, with the crew members of visiting ships, and with white Bermudians.

Equally notable are the vagueness and perhaps the lenient terms of the pre-scribed punishment. In the early years of the Virginia colony, theft, regardless of the race or status of the guilty party, was a capital offense, as it was in England for the theft of goods worth over 12 pence. In Bermuda in 1627 a white man, William Hingson, was hanged for stealing a pair of shoes. In Virginia a slave who left home without permission, or carried a weapon, or dared to "lift up his hand in opposition against any Christian" was given 30 lashes "well layd on." Later, when Bermuda's lawmakers did specify the number of lashes for a given punishment, they did not use the phrase "well layd on," so common in Virginia laws. In Bermuda the usual modifying phrase was "upon the naked back."[99] Of course "as the lawe . . . requireth" could mean anything from whipping to ear-cropping or worse, but that was left to the official in each case to decide. The punishment apparently did little to prevent the crime: The 1623 act, slightly altered in wording, would be reenacted periodically for the next hundred years.[100] While Bermuda's white masters complained about their black servants' "insolencies" and tried to punish them, they also exhibited remarkable concern for the welfare of servants both black and white. In 1624 Governor Henry Woodhouse instructed the colony's overseers to watch out for "the hard usage of any maisters towards their servants" and to make sure that servants had adequate "victuall, apparell, lodgeing and necessaries convenient for them." By itself, of course, this could be read as an effort to correct a prevailing practice, but other evidence contravenes that interpretation. In 1627 the Bermuda Council admonished "indulgent masters who give leave unto their apprentices and hyred servants to keepe hogg." In

99. Hening, *Statutes*, 2:480–81. On capital crime in Virginia, see William Strachey, *For the Colony of Virginia Britannia: Lawes Divine, Morall and Martiall,* ed. David Flaherty (Charlottesville, Va.: University Press of Virginia, 1969), 11–13. The case of William Hingson is in assize of July 1627, printed in Lefroy, *Memorials,* 1:450.
100. See *Ancient Journals of the House of Assembly of Bermuda from 1691 to 1785* (Hamilton, Bermuda, 1890), 1:87, 196, 251; Miscellaneous Acts, 1711–1759, n.p., Bermuda Archives.

that same year Captain Thomas Jennings was reprimanded for "keeping of a hogge of a negroes, contrary to a statute in that case provided."[101] At another assize a few years later, a colonist named Symon Prosser was presented for "unseasonable correction of his servant."[102]

Besides the "insolencies" of the blacks and the nature of the prescribed punishment, the 1623 act is notable for what it reveals about Bermuda's whites. By requiring any master whose black servant was caught stealing to pay "treble damage" to the aggrieved party, the colony's lawmakers were controlling masters as well as servants. Severe penalties imposed upon masters might have been an attempt to induce them to provide better food and clothing for the blacks in their households, thus discouraging what appears to have been rampant petty theft. The "treble damage" rule may also have been an effort to prevent certain masters from looking the other way when their blacks made off with a neighbor's livestock or produce. Another law passed at the same time suggests a need for social control: "Boyes and negroes" could not take the ferry between the island of St. George's and the main island without written permission from their masters.[103]

Just how many blacks were in Bermuda when these first laws governing them were passed is difficult to determine. Up to 1623 only about 60 can be documented. They include the first black brought in 1616; "Symon the Negro," tried for a crime in 1617; Robert Rich's "neger" with the "French pox"; Francisco, James, Anthony, and their wives; the 29 blacks brought by Elfrith; and the 14 brought by Kirby. How many of these were women is not known. There were probably more blacks than these. In 1622 the Reverend Lewis Hughes complained that the Company's allowance to Governor Nathaniel Butler provided "no cloathing for the negroes," but he did not specify how many.[104] In a place as small as Bermuda, with a total population of 1,500, as many as 100 blacks would have been highly visible.[105] That would have been a ratio of one black to every 14 whites. Virginia, which had 23 blacks in a

---

101. Lefroy, *Memorials,* 1:337, 453, 451. On the harsh treatment of servants in Virginia, see Edmund S. Morgan, "The First American Boom: Virginia, 1618 to 1630," *WMQ,* 3d ser., 28, no. 2 (April 1971): 169–98.

102. Lefroy, *Memorials,* 1:555.

103. Ibid., 312.

104. Ibid., 231.

105. Philip Alexander Bruce, *An Economic History of Virginia in the Seventeenth Century* (1895; reprint, New York: P. Smith, 1935), 1:336, estimated that Virginia, with a population of 15,000 by 1649, had no more than 300 blacks. It is unlikely that Bermuda, a tiny island colony with much less need for a large labor force than Virginia, would have acquired a large number of blacks. For a refinement of Bruce's estimate, see Morgan, *American Slavery,* 395–405. In the 1630s English privateers in the Spanish West Indies brought an undetermined number of "captured Negroes" to Bermuda. See *Calendar of State Papers, Colonial Series, America and West Indies,* ed. Noel Sainsbury et al. (London, 1860–1953) (hereafter, *CSP*), 1574–1660:225.

population of approximately 1,200 in 1625, did not enact any laws to control the blacks' behavior until several decades later. With the exception of a 1639 law requiring "all persons except negroes" to possess arms and ammunition, it was not until the 1660s that Virginia's first laws mentioning race appeared. In any case, as Bermuda's first racially restrictive law suggests, there were enough blacks to cause concern in the white community.

Besides "insolent" blacks, by the mid-1620s Bermuda colonists had another cause for concern. It was becoming obvious that their tobacco could not compete successfully with the better grade of Spanish tobacco from the West Indies, and the Somers Islands Company urged the Bermudians to diversify their crops. However, the planters argued that they had "no other commodity to raise any benefit for livelihood but only tobacco." A few years earlier in 1617, the height of the tobacco boom, tobacco had sold for three shillings per pound. At that price, 25 acres yielding 500 pounds of the leafy crop would gross £75. Even after levies and customs duties, an ordinary man could earn two or three times what a laborer in England could earn in a year.[106]

For a brief time, even though their land was limited and the winds capricious, Bermuda planters were almost as tobacco-crazed as the Jamestown settlers. John Smith's *Generall Historie* (1624) observed that Bermudians "endeavoured so much for the planting Tobacco for present gaine, that they neglected many things [that] might more have prevailed for their good."[107] When the Somers Islands Company tried to impose quotas on tobacco in an effort to diversify the colony's economy, the planters protested. By 1625 the crown guaranteed Virginia and Bermuda a monopoly of the English tobacco trade, but a contract restricting Bermuda to 80,000 pounds of tobacco at one shilling and a penny per pound drew more complaints. In 1626 some of the "inhabitants," or heads of planter households, in each of the eight tribes put their names to letters protesting the Somers Islands Company's efforts to restrict the amount of tobacco grown there.[108] The Southampton Tribe letter, for example, pointed out the hardships such limitation would impose, complaining that by the time "the general charges of the Plantation, as food, salaries, Levies, provision of Powder, Servants wages, and divers other duties be discharged, the planter will not have (if his plantation go on) whereby to subsist."[109] Eighteen men, including Marmaduke Dando, signed the letter.

106. In 1625 Virginia tobacco was listed at 3s. per pound; in Bermuda, at 2s. 6d. *Considerations touching the New Contract for Tobacco* (London, 1625), 6.

107. Barbour, ed., *Complete Works*, 2:367.

108. Tobacco prices in the 1620s dropped sharply and declined more slowly for the next several decades, reaching a low of about one penny per pound by 1670. Kulikoff, *Tobacco and Slaves*, 5, 31. On the tobacco restrictions in Bermuda, see Wilkinson, *Adventurers*, 221. The eight tribes' letters are printed in Lefroy, *Memorials*, 1:379–84.

109. Lefroy, *Memorials*, 1:380.

The trouble was a shortage of land. To grow tobacco successfully, a planter needed to cultivate about 50 acres, but in land-poor Bermuda, the ratio was more like four acres of arable land for each planter. And after the first rush to plant tobacco (from 30,000 pounds in 1618 to more than 70,000 pounds exported to England in 1620), the quality of the crop began to decline, and apparently so did the care in packing it for shipment. Governor Nathaniel Butler observed that one crop in the early 1620s arrived in England "little better than starck rotten." The Somers Islands Company had ordered in 1622 that the colonists raise "other more stabile and solid Commodities," and in 1631 the Privy Council advised the Company to "prescribe a certen moderate quantitie [of tobacco] not to bee exceeded in these Islands."[110] While planters in the Chesapeake could afford to rotate crops, let the land lie fallow, or even move to new land, Bermuda's planters, holding an average of 25 to 50 acres (only a small fraction of which was suitable or consignable to tobacco) had no such luxury. Besides the worn-out soil, the islands' hot summers and harsh winds produced an inferior quality of tobacco, and some Bermuda planters were apparently careless in the curing of it. As early as 1620 the colony's assembly passed "An Act agaynst the makinge up of rotten and unmerchantable Tobacco." Bermuda's economic woes were accompanied by political wrangling between the Sandys and Warwick factions in the Somers Islands Company. From 1622 to 1629 there were four governors: Nathaniel Butler's successor, in 1622, John Bernard, died before the first year of his term was out; John Harrison, supported by the Sandys faction of the Company, lasted only one year; Captain Henry Woodhouse served from 1623 to 1626; Philip Bell, the Warwick group's choice, served from 1626 to 1629. Captain Roger Wood, who succeeded him, governed Bermuda from 1629 to 1637.[111]

By 1628 Bermuda tobacco sold for two shillings a pound, but planters grumbled that they made little more than "9 d. [pennies] the pound cleare."[112] The next year Governor Philip Bell wrote gloomily about Bermuda's economic prospects: "And as for this island, the strength and work of the land so much decrease and decay that in a short time it will be of very small value or profit, especially as so much tobacco now being planted and being brought home of better quality and from richer climates and plantations, and I make a question whether this will shortly be worth anything at all."[113] Not long afterward,

110. Butler, *Bermudaes*, 167.

111. Lefroy, *Memorials*, 1:168. For a list of Bermuda governors, 1612 to 1966, see "The Governors of Bermuda," *BHQ* 22, no. 4 (1965): 111–15. See also Newton, *Colonising Activities*, 23–25, 30–32.

112. Lefroy, *Memorials*, 1:479, 480. On Virginia and Bermuda tobacco prices, see Hening, *Statutes*, 1:462, and Wilkinson, *Adventurers*, 221.

113. Philip Bell to Nathaniel Rich, April 28, 1629, quoted in Newton, *Colonising Activities*, 33.

Governor Bell placed his hopes for a successful colony in Providence Island, where he became the first governor in 1629. He took a number of Bermudians, both whites and blacks, with him, and in 1631 "about eighty" more followed him to settle there. Some of the Bermudians who went with Bell to Providence were involved in religious disputes there, and were sent back to Bermuda. In 1637 Providence Island was thought to have too many blacks, and some were to be sent to Virginia and Bermuda.[114]

Bermuda's planters could not hope to match the individual fortunes made in the sister colony of Virginia, much less that colony's dominance in the tobacco market. By the late 1630s Virginia was exporting over 1,000,000 pounds of tobacco a year.[115] Most colonists were not as philosophical as Governor Roger Wood, who acknowledged that "Tobacco being of so low estimation it makes most of the Inhabitants weary of this Island and very desirous to transplant themselves elsewhere . . . , " but "no plantation can bee more secure and more safe than this where wee have . . . provisions enough for our subsistance . . . ." He thought that "if our endeavours would but furnish us with canvasses for our clothing and lockram for our shirts, and shoes for our feet we would think ourselves happie." Food was never a problem. In 1634 Governor Wood wrote to a friend in England, "I thanke god wee have good store of provisions and eate more fatt Hogges & Turkeys and fishe in varietie than they that have more money in their purses."[116] In 1639 the Somers Islands Company petitioned the Lords Commissioners for Foreign Plantations to grant their company more land in Virginia to accommodate Bermuda's growing population. The petition noted that some 500 persons were anxious to leave Bermuda "by reason of the increase of the people and the straitness of the place."[117] This was not idle rhetoric on the petitioners' part: by the 1630s Bermuda's population had grown to 3,000, with perhaps 1,500 able-bodied men, but it had only about 6,000 to 8,000 acres of arable land.

Of the original 19 tenants or lease-holders on the Richs' land in Southampton in 1617, all but two had apparently moved on, some to other locations in Bermuda, by the mid-1620s. Marmaduke Dando signed the Southampton Tribe tobacco protest letter of 1626, but none of the other names from Rich's 1617 list appear. William Smith, Dando's partner, had moved: The name William Smith appears on the letter of Paget Tribe. But it was a few

114. On the Bermudian connection to Providence Island, see Kupperman, *Providence Island,* 25–26, 28, 165; Wilkinson, *Adventurers,* 249; Newton, *Colonising Activities,* 59 ff, 118; *CSP,* 1574–1660:247.

115. On the Virginia tobacco trade, see McCusker and Menard, *Economy of British America,* 120–28, and Kulikoff, *Tobacco and Slaves,* 4–5, 31.

116. Letter Book of Roger Wood, letter no. 65, fragment, 1634, letter no. 45, fragment, 1634.

117. Lefroy, *Memorials,* 1:557.

months later, in the summer of 1626, that William Smith left Paget Tribe for points unknown, sailing away in his boat "with divers of his confederates," leaving three of his children and an apprentice named Peter Gates unprovided for.[118] Hugh Wentworth, the former indentured servant, had also moved; his name and mark are on the 1626 protest letter from Warwick Tribe.[119] As for the three black tenants, Antony's whereabouts are unknown, James remained in Southampton, and Francisco moved. In 1629 "two negroes called francisco and anthonia his wife, belonging unto the . . . Companie" were in the possession of Thomas Buckley, a member of the Governor's Council and a tobacco planter. But "at his goeing for England they were ymployed by the Governor to make up his number of 32 servants. . . ." The Somers Islands Company later gave the couple back to Buckley, who then "demanded and received the said negroes francisco and Anthonia and the Tobaco due unto them for their wages which was 180 lb . . ." for the year.[120]

Wage labor for Bermuda's first blacks was apparently not uncommon, although the existing records of it are sparse. In 1625 the overseers of Paget Tribe noted that 260 pounds of tobacco had been "taken out" of the amount payable to one planter, "for wages for two negroes and to another man."[121] While Francisco and Anthonia worked for wages, they were obviously not free. But there is no evidence to indicate that they were slaves, or that they were any less free than Bermuda's white indentured servants. Antony and James, Francisco's black co-workers, apparently shared the same status. Though Antony's whereabouts cannot be traced, James and his wife continued to live and work in Southampton, apparently independent of white supervision, until the 1650s. Their story will be taken up in the following chapter.

As for Marmaduke Dando, he, like other Bermuda planters, felt the effects of falling tobacco prices (a circumstance that would eventually force both whites and blacks to seek other sources of income). In 1629 Dando's income from his tobacco crop was among the lowest of Rich's tenants. A report of Southampton tenants' tobacco crop payments ("halves") to their landlord in 1629 lists Dando's payment at £3.05.08—a sum far short of the income of

118. Ibid., 392–93.
119. The 1626 letters of protests are printed ibid., 379–84. Wentworth, though apparently illiterate, had begun his rise to the rank of gentleman. In the letters of protest, a total of 128 planters' names appear; 95 signed their names, and 33 others, including Wentworth, made their marks.
120. Ibid., 483.
121. Ibid., 386. Under the terms of the Somers Islands Company the governor was allowed 32 servants (163). Thomas Buckley, as lieutenant of the governor's guards, received a yearly allowance of 200 pounds of tobacco in 1622 (162). In 1655 a reference to the Company's blacks being "hired" by other colonists indicates that some blacks regularly worked for wages. See ibid., 2:56.

£10 (Dando's half should have been £5) Robert Rich had predicted that share would yield in 1617. Dando could hardly have been supporting his family on what he cleared raising tobacco in the 1620s, when prices plummeted to five pennies per pound.[122] By 1629 he and his wife Joan had five children: besides Hannah, the eldest, there was Sarah, 8; Elizabeth, 5; Marmaduke, 3; and Martha, an infant.[123] With a growing family, Marmaduke Dando seems to have turned more to trading and fishing than to farming. In 1630 one "Goodwife Havard" noted that she paid 16 pounds of tobacco to Dando for "hooks and lines."[124]

Whatever his means of making a living, Marmaduke Dando seems to have been a respected resident of Southampton Tribe. Thomas Durham described him as "a painfull [painstaking, diligent] man as breathes."[125] When called upon, Marmaduke Dando served his government and his church. His name appears in early Bermuda records as a juror in the assize of 1616 and in 1652 as a member of a grand jury. For many years he was a "Reader" in the Southampton Church, and his wife Joan was listed as "Goodwife Dando," the occupant of a seat in the six women's pews of that church.[126]

On Sundays, Southampton's husbands, wives, and children would have joined those of the adjacent tribes of Warwick and Sandys for Sabbath services. There were some black families among them. One imagines them meeting each other as they walked along the pathway that ran through the center of the three tribes, from Somerset to Warwick. Two baptisms of black infants appeared in the Southampton parish register in the 1630s: In 1636 a black infant named Antonio was baptized. No father's name was given, but the mother's name was Phillass (Phyllis). In 1639 an infant girl, Susan, was baptized. No parents' names were recorded, but a marginal comment notes, "Negro living with Thos. Wells."[127] By the 1640s, or the second generation of blacks in Bermuda, there were more black baptisms, which eventually caused the Assembly to pass a law in 1647 excluding the baptism of "Bastards or Negroes children."[128]

---

122. Ives, *Rich Papers*, 302. The "halves" system, established in 1618, was discontinued in the 1630s (110).

123. In 1632 a sixth child, William, was born to the Dandos. A seventh child, whose birth is unrecorded, may have been a daughter, Anne. The marriage of Anne Dando to Henry Morgan is recorded in 1653. The marriages of three other daughters, Hannah (1632), Sara (1638), and Elizabeth (1640), are also in the Southampton church register. See Hallett, *Early Bermuda Records*, 4, 19.

124. Lefroy, *Memorials*, 1:519.

125. Durham to Rich, ca. January 1619/1620, in Ives, *Rich Papers*, 173.

126. On Dando and his wife, see Lefroy, *Memorials*, 1:126; 2:32; 1:524.

127. Hallett, *Early Bermuda Records*, 12.

128. The text of Bermuda's 1647 act regarding baptism is in William Golding, *Servants on Horseback, or . . . A Representation of the dejected state of the Inhabitants of Summer Islands*, a pamphlet reprinted in *BHQ* 9, no. 1 (1952): 182–213 (quotation, p. 200). On the debate over

Almost from the beginning of their arrival in the colony, Bermuda's blacks married and formed families. This stands in marked contrast to the experience of early blacks in the Chesapeake colonies, where masters "did little to encourage high fertility" among their black servants or slaves, and for most of the seventeenth century the black population of that region did not reproduce itself.[129] Such was not the case in Bermuda. Among the 25 blacks in Governor Roger Wood's household in the early 1630s, for example, there were at least four families and perhaps three generations. There are two records of these individuals, the first being an undated fragment of a memorandum of cattle and slaves on the flyleaf of Wood's letter book; the second, a similar list in Wood's 1632 letter to the Somers Islands Company. These lists contain the names of eight men, six women, and 13 children. The memorandum is a torn fragment with an incomplete list of names and is repeated in a partially unreadable copy in a letter in the letter book. These documents provide one of the earliest records of black families in the English colonies. Although some of the names are undecipherable or missing, it is possible to identify at least six married couples:

Saray	8 yeares	daughters of Maria a Negr[o] now
Dorothy	3 yeares	marryed unto Wylliam [of] the Compa[ny]
Susan	8 yeares	daughters of Maneno mayo[r]
Guindolin	6 yeares	whose wife Lucretia is
Priscilla	3 yeares	
William	8 yeares	children of Maneno
Saray	5 yeares	of Bridget his wife
Richard	3 yeares	
Maria	9 yeares	children of Sand. and
Penelope	6 yeares	Catale[na]
John	3 yeares	
3 yeares	daughter	

The rest of the first list is torn off, but the second list, incorporated in the letter, continues with the following:

| Justina | 3 yeares | daughter of [unreadable] |
| Anna | 3 yeares | daughter of Catalena whose husband is [unreadable] |

Mingo grando whose wife Polassa is dead

baptism in the 1660s, see Lefroy, *Memorials*, 2:291–92. On baptism in Virginia, see Morgan, *American Slavery*, 331–32; Hening, *Statutes*, 2:260.

129. Menard, "Servants to Slaves," 359.

Mingo and Isabella uxor
Anthonio ye long
Anthonio ye old[130]

The first couple listed may have been a mixed marriage: Maria "a Negr[o]" is listed as "marryed to Wylliam [of] the Compa[ny]." The race of the other individuals is not mentioned, but from the context it is clear that they were blacks and that they lived together as families.

Bermuda's race relations and the nature of slavery were both shaped by the unusually early growth of black families and their close relationships with the colony's white families. Early records from other English colonies suggest that black families developed much later than in Bermuda. In the Chesapeake, one of the first mentions of a black family is the 1644 inventory of a colonist named William Stafford. It lists four black children, ranging in age from two weeks to four years, along with four adults—a man and three women—but the parentage of the children is not indicated.[131]

Governor Wood's list and his accompanying letter to the Somers Islands Company offer a revealing glimpse of white attitudes toward blacks and of the status of blacks in Bermuda after nearly two decades of contact between the two races. It is interesting to note that most of the black parents listed have Spanish or African names, and all but one of the children, presumably born in Bermuda, have English names. One wonders whether names like Priscilla and Guindolin were bestowed by parents willing to adopt an alien culture, or by English masters eager to replicate the familiar given names of their homeland. While more exotic African or Native American names for blacks and Indians can be found in the West Indies and the English colonies on the North American mainland, the use of ordinary English given names for blacks, mulattos, and Indians in Bermuda sets it apart. African names such as Mingo, Sukey, Sambo, and Juba are almost nonexistent among the recorded names for Bermuda's early blacks, as are the fanciful names, such as Stormy or Jumper, and the classical, such as Hercules and Venus, found later among the slave names elsewhere. Most of Bermuda's other first-generation blacks bore names such as Mariah, Peter, Christopher, and Lucea.[132] One can only

130. "Rough memorandum of cattle & slaves," Letter Book of Roger Wood, letter no. 88, flyleaf, n.d.

131. On slave families, see also McColley, "Slavery in Virginia," 22. Oddly enough, the first black family whose names are recorded in South Carolina is one brought from Bermuda in 1670. See Peter Wood, *Black Majority: Negroes in Colonial South Carolina from 1670 through the Stono Rebellion* (New York: Knopf, 1974), 21. In North Carolina the first record of a slave family does not appear until 1709. John Inscoe, "Carolina Slaves Names: An Index to Acculturation," *Journal of Southern History* 49, no. 4 (November 1983): 529–30.

132. These names are taken from a collection of indentures and bills of sale in the 1630s. CR, 2:6, 8, 29.

speculate as to the individual histories and relationships of the blacks with non-English names on Wood's list. Were they fresh from Africa, captured from a Spanish or Portuguese slave ship by an English or Dutch privateer, perhaps?[133] Or were they seasoned blacks from the West Indies, taken in trade by some English mariner? It is very likely that Maneno mayor and Maneno, Mingo grando and Mingo, and the two Anthonios were fathers and sons.[134] Names, whether bestowed by owners or parents, are one key to cultural identity, and the fact that most of Bermuda's blacks bore English given names is a telling indication of their assimilation into the culture of that colony and of white attitudes toward them.[135]

Governor Wood's remarks about the blacks assigned to him reveal something of his own attitudes about race and class. To judge from his library, which contained volumes of Chaucer and Purchas, he was well read, and his perceptions would have been shaped by his larger knowledge of English literature and writings about the New World.[136] He refers to his servants as "this black crewe" and complains of the responsibility of caring for them. According to his letter he had 25 individuals under his care: eight men "among wch ould Anthonio is past service, 4 woemen negroes, and 13 children." Three of the children he had already put out to service, and he resolved to put out some others as soon as he could "fynd such masters as will be careful for their education."[137] Roger Wood's letters show him to be a devoutly religious man and a staunch Puritan. His concern for the education of the black children undoubtedly meant seeing that they learned to read the Bible. Other Bermudians voiced similar concerns, in marked contrast to another group of Puritans who settled on Providence Island in the 1630s. Karen O. Kupperman writes of the Puritans there: "Nowhere in their letters, formal or informal, does

133. Sluiter, in "New Light on the '20 and Odd Negroes,'" makes a credible case for these early Chesapeake blacks' coming directly from Africa, having been captured from a slave ship. It is not unreasonable to assume that some of Bermuda's blacks had similar histories. The incidence of a few African names, such as Sambo, Congo, and Mingo, lend credence to this.

134. Berlin, "From Creole to African," 251–52, notes the tendency of slaveowners to bestow diminutive, humorous, or classical names on the slaves in an effort to deprive them of their identity. See also Inscoe, "Carolina Slave Names," and "Generation and Gender as Reflected in Carolina Slave Naming Practices: A Challenge to the Gutman Thesis," *South Carolina Historical Magazine* 94 (October 1994): 252–63; and Elaine G. Breslaw's discussion of Barbados slave naming in *Tituba, Reluctant Witch of Salem: Devilish Indians and Puritan Fantasies* (New York: New York University Press, 1996), 12–14.

135. Bermuda was not unique in second-generation English names for blacks. McColley, "Slavery in Virginia," 22, notes that the 1644 inventory list of Chesapeake blacks suggests that the adults with foreign names (Anthonio, Conchanello, Palassa) were "almost certainly" born outside Virginia, but their children had English names (Mary, Anne).

136. His 1653 probate inventory is in Books of Wills and Inventories, 1648–1798, Bermuda Archives, vol. 1, pp. 26, 23.

137. Letter Book of Roger Wood, letter no. 85, 1634.

any discussion of religious education for slaves occur. These staunch puritans thus turned their backs on human beings in need, men and women who were in their power."[138] Bermuda's Governor Wood felt burdened by the 10 children and three women in his charge. "They [the women] doe little else than to looke to theire children for noe man wilbe troubled with them." This observation is somewhat puzzling, since three of the women—Maria, Isabella, and Bridget—had husbands, and Catalena, though not described as married, is paired with a man. In his letter to the Somers Islands Company, Wood declares that he is willing to support all of these individuals, nonetheless, "so long as you cloathe them as most nobly you have done this yeare."[139] Although Roger Wood listed the names of these blacks in the "Rough Memorandum of cattle & slaves," the word *slave* does not appear in Wood's accompanying letter.

It is important to note that *slave* was not synonymous with *Negro* in early Bermuda. Robert Rich, John Dutton, and Thomas Durham did not use the word *slave* to identify Francisco, James, and the other blacks in Southampton Tribe. Their status as laborers on Nathaniel Rich's land was clearly different from that of servants in the governor's household. Governor Wood's memorandum (which he describes in his letter as a "catalogue of . . . negroes") defines the status of the individuals given to the governor of Bermuda (along with livestock and land) for his personal use. By virtue of his office, a governor was allotted 32 "servants," 24 of whom were to work the 12 shares of land assigned to him. In these specifications the word *slave* was not used.[140] In 1629, when Francisco and Anthonia were employed by Governor Philip Bell, they were described as servants, not slaves. In 1618 Robert Rich had placed blacks such as "James the negger" at the end of his roster of Southampton residents, but he had not otherwise distinguished blacks from the rest of the laborers. In contrast, the English who settled in Barbados in the late 1620s not only used the word *slave* but were eager to apply it to the Indians they captured. Captain Henry Powell reported in 1627 that the Barbados colonists made "slaves" of 32 Indians he brought from Surinam, and that same year Henry Winthrop referred to "50 slaves" in Barbados.[141] Roger Wood's reference to

---

138. Kupperman, *Providence Island,* 179. In colonial Georgia more than a century later, slaveholders were reluctant to educate their slaves for fear they would become lazy or rebellious. See Betty Wood, *Slavery in Colonial Georgia, 1730–1775* (Athens, Ga.: University of Georgia Press, 1984), 116, 163–64. Early Bermuda indentures and bills of sale sometimes required that a black or mulatto child have Christian upbringing and be educated enough to read the Bible. See, for example, CR, 2:103, 145, 201.

139. Letter Book of Roger Wood, letter no. 85.

140. See Lefroy, *Memorials,* 1:202, 483, 540.

141. Dunn, *Sugar and Slaves,* 227. See also Breslaw, *Tituba,* 8–12. By 1629 Barbados had 1,600 English colonists who, as in Bermuda, were mostly tenants. On Henry Powell's role in Barbados colonization, see Wilkinson, *Adventurers,* 230, 260.

his black servants as "this black crewe" is ambiguous, since *crew* could be either an assemblage of persons for a specific purpose (e.g., the governor's servants) or a group so classified by common (racial) characteristics with a certain derogatory connotation. It is clear that Wood perceived the blacks assigned to him as different from himself, but those perceptions may have had as much to do with class as with race. The governor's blacks were given to him as servants to work his land, tend his livestock, and keep his house. He would naturally classify them far below him on the social scale.

Wood, like some other white Bermudians, considered blacks as individuals entitled to the benefits of education and religion, and respected their desires for stable family relationships and marriage. From the beginning, masters recognized marriage among Bermuda's black bondservants as a binding, if not a legal, institution. Marriages between slaves in other English colonies were also sanctioned by owners, but married slave couples were often separated by the sale of the husband or wife, and many couples were unable to live together because their masters lived far from each other.[142] In Bermuda, wherever possible, arrangements were made for couples to remain together. Sometime before 1631, for example, one of the Somers Islands Company's blacks, a man named Sambo, had married a woman servant (or slave) belonging to colonist Christopher Parker, and a woman in Governor Wood's household was married to one of Parker's men. In the letter accompanying his memorandum, Wood mentions this fact, remarking on "his [Parker's] man having married my woman, my man having married his." Wood, who disliked Parker, asked the Company to give him Sambo. Fragmentary documents prevent a full account of this transaction, but there was evidently a controversy between Parker and Wood over the ownership of Sambo and his wife and child. The question of ownership of a black bondservant's children was obviously at issue and had no legal precedent in Bermuda—another indication of the ambiguous status of black servants in a society where slavery was not yet fully defined.[143] Some years later the Bermuda General Court ruled on a similar case:

> Whereas this courte hath binne informed of a grievance in the behalfe of William Seamer concerning a negro woeman who is marryed to a negro man of Mr Paulson's whereby the said negro woman is deteyned from the service of the said William

142. In the Chesapeake colonies, on scattered farms and plantations, perhaps the majority of slave couples were obliged to live apart. See Kulikoff, *Tobacco and Slaves,* 353, 374–75. In the Danish West Indies Christian slaves could marry with their owners' permission, and under a 1755 law married couples were not to be sold or parted, nor children separated from their parents. This law, however, was not enforced until the 1800s. See Neville A. T. Hall, *Slave Society in the Danish West Indies: St. Thomas, St. John, and St. Croix,* ed. B. W. Higman (Baltimore: Johns Hopkins University Press, 1992), 60–61, 83.

143. Letter Book of Roger Wood, quoted in Lefroy, *Memorials,* 1:539 n.

Seamer by living with her husband; whereupon it is ordered that if the said Mr Paulson doth not give satisfaction to the said Seamer . . . as he hath promised to doe, That then the said negro woman shall remayne in her service with the said Will Seamer . . . And that her husband shall repayer to her every Saturday night, and so remayne with her till Munday morning.[144]

The respect for marriage ties and the strict punishment of fornication and adultery in Bermuda may be partly due to the influence of Puritanism in the colony. From the earliest years of settlement the church in Bermuda had been Puritan in its liturgy and sympathies. The Reverend Lewis Hughes wrote in 1617, "The ceremonies [of the Anglican liturgy] are in noe request, nor the booke of common praier, I use it not at all."[145] In the first few years the services were sporadic, since from 1617 to 1619 and part of 1621–1622 the colony had only one minister, Hughes, to serve the entire island group.[146] Hughes complained that he lived "more like a slave than a Minister . . . constrained to live comfortless alone, and to go up and down the Island for firewood, and bring it home upon my back, and then go from house to house for fire, and to go with my pitcher through the town to the pump for water. . . . Yet, I did (through the help of God) preach constantly every Thursday once, and every Sabbath twice, besides catechising."[147] In 1622 the colonists complained to the Company, declaring, "We are defrauded of the food of our souls, for, being not fewer than 1500 souls, dispersed into a length of 20 miles, we have at present only one minister."[148] That year, however, a new governor arrived, bringing four clergymen. The Reverend George Stirk came to serve Southampton. By 1627 the church was located on land near Marmaduke Dando's residence.[149]

Puritanism, with its strong emphasis on Bible reading, was almost certainly responsible for the early concern for religious instruction and public education in Bermuda. In 1622, when the colony was scarcely a decade old, Governor Nathaniel Butler ordered all the tribes to keep birth, marriage, and death records and to set aside time on the Sabbath for the religious instruction of children.[150] (Virginia, by contrast, did not adopt such a practice until 1632,

144. Lefroy, *Memorials,* 1:462–63. For other cases, see 2:107, 228–29.
145. Lewis Hughes to Nathaniel Rich, May 19, 1617, in Ives, *Rich Papers,* 10. Hughes served as minister in Bermuda from 1614 to 1623.
146. Hallett, *Colonial Church,* 26.
147. Lewis Hughes, petition to the Privy Council, quoted ibid., 26. It is interesting to note Hughes's figurative use of the word *slave* in this context, as an individual obliged to perform hard labor.
148. Royal Commission on Historical Manuscripts, ser. I, report VIII (London: H. M. Stationerey Office, 1881), 295, quoted ibid., 15.
149. On the early churches and church property, see Hallett, *Colonial Church,* 261–301. On Southampton Tribe, see 262–63. See also W. B. Hayward, "St. Peter's Churchyard," *BHQ* 11, no. 1 (1954): 41–43.
150. Lefroy, *Memorials,* 1:256.

25 years after its founding.) Marmaduke Dando's children's baptisms and the marriages of his daughters were recorded in the Southampton church register. Dando himself was a reader in that church, and he probably taught his children to read and write, since Southampton had no school. Fragmentary evidence suggests that many other Bermudians besides Dando were literate. By 1633, when the colony of Bermuda was little more than 20 years old, it had a free public school. Richard Norwood, the surveyor, served as schoolmaster in the colony for many years. One school could hardly serve a population scattered over the length of Bermuda, and in 1662 the Bermuda Assembly provided for building three schools "besides what is alreadye erected and settled." In Virginia, by contrast, after more than six decades of settlement Governor William Berkeley was to write that there were as yet "no free schools nor printing" in his colony.[151] In less than 30 years after its founding, Bermuda, unlike Virginia, was a settled society of families, many white and a few black, who lived and worked in close proximity. There were at least four churches and one school. A description of life in Bermuda by Juan de Rivera, a Spaniard whose ship was wrecked there in 1639, offers a view of the land and the people:

> The inhabitants of Bermuda . . . live in cabins made of wooden posts roofed with palm branches. . . . There seem to be about 290 households and each has its portion of land allotted to it and marked out; on this the planter sows tobacco, corn and potatoes, and yucca for making "cazabe" [cassava flour] according to his circumstances; the least competent is able to produce enough to live on, for as they have no expenses and no pretentions to pomp and authority, a little store of anything keeps each one independent of the other in time of need; the poorest is not without his patch of land for raising a crop of tobacco, which is the staple crop; by shipping it to England at the right season they live and maintain themselves. There is great abundance of potatoes and corn, which is the ordinary food of the working people. The potatoes are very large, I have seen and eaten many (sweet potatoes,) that weighted more than 2 lbs. each; they are good in taste and flavor, though the smallest are the best, like those in Spain.
>
> There are some cattle; every one breeds them and kills them to provide salt beef; he keeps what he needs for himself and distributes the remainder among his neighbours, who in due time will repay him in kind. They also raise pigs, for the same purpose. They make a very rich and delicious fresh butter; and have large quantities of cow's milk. No one fails to have a good number of chicken and capons, for these birds are raised without any of the care that is needed in Spain; they run about the woods eating wild berries, and sometimes the planter gives them a little corn. They roost in the trees. On some of the farms there are large flocks of turkeys. . . .
>
> In most of these farms there are orange trees and lemon trees, which bear very beautiful large fruit, in some places better than the Andalusian. There are many vineyards and rose trees and countless groves of fig trees we were able to pick fruit from the trees; the figs are small and all the more delicious because not cultivated.

---

151. Lefroy, *Memorials,* 2:188; Levy, "Early Puritanism," 175; Hening, *Statutes,* 2:517.

Numerous palms and junipers (sabinas), make the entire island a pleasant wooded retreat. There are also many flowers, plants and sweet-smelling herbs of the kind found in Spain; everyone has these growing in a little garden next to his home. . . . Considerable quantities of fish, usually abundant, are caught by the Islanders.

The observant Spanish visitor also remarked upon the devout religious practices:

On the Island there are 5 or 6 churches, which the people of each parish attend from their farms on Sunday morning and evening to hear the sermons preached by the ministers, the service lasting more than 3 hours. Men, women, youths, boys and girls and even children all carry their books to church. . . . The people listen very quietly, in silent devoutness. It is noon when the service ends, and after a meal the people return to their churches with the same punctuality. In the evening they have the same. Everyone dresses for the services in his best clothes. This day is observed most strictly; children are not even allowed to play the usual childish games.[152]

Records of the assizes and grand jury presentments from 1616 through the 1630s bear out Rivera's view of a society where religious and moral values dictated behavior and where infractions of the rules were punished. "Dycinge, cardinge and other unlawful playes and games" were punishable by fine; the number of "Tavernes or Drinking-houses" was limited by legislative authority. One husband and wife in 1618 were called to account for "comon Tipling." Moreover, such persons as were "given to Idleness pride gaming drunkenes or other unthriftines," according to a 1623 act, were to be taxed double in parish levies. The frequency of public punishments—whippings, stocks, and pillory—attest to the efforts of civil and religious authorities to punish moral transgressions. In 1626, for example, Margaret Heyling, the wife of planter John Heyling in Southampton Tribe, stole a turkey from Damon Knowles, a neighbor of Marmaduke Dando's. She was ordered to "stand in the church 2 sabbath dayes with a paper upon her breast written in great Letters *for stealing of a Turkey,* and to sitt behinde the church dore for the space of 6 monthes ensuing." The first jury found Margaret Heyling not guilty, for which they were fined and imprisoned; a second found her guilty and ordered her to have 12 lashes "upon her naked backe in private," but this part of the sentence was remitted. The following year the Somers Islands Company ruled that she was unjustly punished and ordered Governor Henry Woodhouse to pay her 100 pounds of tobacco. Another woman convicted, at the 1626 assize, of stealing a turkey was not so fortunate: Dorothie Whitteares, wife of Jeremy Whitteares of Sandys, received "30 lashes upon the naked backe which was privately executed." In 1629 Mary Frith, the wife of Henry Frith, was presented by

---

152. Juan de Rivera y Saabedra, "Shipwrecked Spaniards, 1639: Grievances against Bermudians," trans. L. D. Gurrin, *BHQ* 18, no. 1 (1961): 14–28. Rivera was a writer in the service of the Spanish crown and was also chief writer to the royal fleet on a voyage in the fall of 1639.

the grand jury "for breaking of the Sabbath by making of an Apron and one savegard [an outer skirt or petticoat to protect a woman's clothing]." She was "Admonished to reforme herself and her household."[153]

Observance of the Sabbath in private homes as well as in public was expected, and so was civil behavior in the public and private spheres. For example, in 1618 one Judith Bayley of Pembroke Tribe was censured for "raylings miscallings and all other uncivill speeches" in the Pembroke church. Apparently truculent by nature, this wife and mother was called to account some years later for "unreverent behavior in the church." On that occasion she was accused of "having her knife drawn" to threaten a fellow worshipper who tried to "still" her child.[154] At the assize of June 1639 one Henry Atwell of Pembroke Tribe was presented for "beatinge & abusinge his wyfe with insufferable blowes & vile speeches," but "it did appeare they were both faultie & therefore were censured." If either misbehaved again, "the husband to be bound to the good behaviour & the wyfe to be ducked." That was not Henry Atwell's last time in court: In 1651 he was fined "500 pounds of tobacco or five pounds stirl. in money" for "Incontinencie" with Dorothie Longbottome, the wife of Thomas Longbottome. She, "for conspireing to take away her husband's life, and committing adulterie, [and grossly slandering all the men of her tribe,] was censured to receave 39 lashes on the naked body at the comon whippinge post, and to be after tied to a stake with a fire before her."[155]

Marriage was the desirable state for couples, regardless of race, and fornication was a punishable offense for blacks as well as for whites in Bermuda. In 1638, for example, the assize court records reveal that "Maria a negro woman [was] presented for having a bastard & And she fathering it upon Fforce a negro man; were both censured to receive one and twentie lashies upon the naked backe, which was accordingly executed upon them at the comon whipping post." In 1639, Edward Bowley was accused of having fathered a child by "Anne a Negro woman." Bowley was found not guilty, but Anne received "21 lashes at the whipping post."[156] A few years later a black man named Daniel and a black woman called Mingo, both in the service of a colonist named Leaycraft in Southampton Tribe, were sentenced to 13 lashes apiece "for fornication before marriage." Maria, a black woman listed as "servant to Mr. Ballard," received 13 lashes for an "act of adultery with a Spaniard." Anthony, a black belonging to Thomas Durham, was convicted of adultery with Paraketa, another of Durham's blacks. Anthony was sentenced

153. For these transgressions, see the assize court records in Lefroy, *Memorials,* 1:132, 222, 309, 300–301, 367–68, 482.
154. Assizes of July 1618 and February 1628/1629, CR, vol. 1, printed ibid., 132, 482.
155. Assize of March [?] 1650/1651, ibid., 667.
156. Assize of June 1639, ibid., 555.

to 39 lashes, "he having a wife of his own in the house." Paraketa received 13 lashes.[157] It must be noted, however, that whites in Bermuda suffered similar punishments: In 1629 Lewis Evans and Alise Atkinson, a married woman, were accused of "Incontinencie." Evans received 39 lashes and Atkinson was made to do penance "with a white sheete in the Church." In 1640 Alexander Smythe was accused of adultery with Frances Ramsbotome, and both offenders were given 39 lashes.[158]

Early Bermuda had other sexual transgressions besides adultery. Besides the case of Symon, the black who assaulted a child, there are records of three other cases involving white male servants or laborers who were accused of the "criminal assault" of white female children as young as eight or nine, and one male servant who was accused of an "unnatural act." In each of these cases the accused was acquitted, although in 1633 a man who assaulted his ward and niece, an orphaned 16-year-old named Mary Carter, was hanged. There was another hanging for a similar crime in 1639, which was described by Rivera:

> A youth of some 16 years charged with assaulting a little girl of 5 or 6 (whom I saw) was condemned to death by hanging. Two days after the sentence was pronounced, they led him from the jail with his arms tied together above the elbows, and with a rope around his neck. Between the Sheriff and the Sergeant Major he was taken to the place of execution, which is a small island a stone's throw from the shore. The preacher and a large number of the English people accompanied him. Arrived there, they spent more than an hour in prayer, standing and kneeling. While this execution was taking place, the church was open and a bell tolled continuously until the execution was over.[159]

Blacks seldom appear in the early court records. In addition to Symon, only three blacks are mentioned in the assizes between 1616 and 1639. None of them is referred to as a slave, or even as a servant. It is possible that these individuals were free. Besides Maria and Force, mentioned earlier, "Phillip a negro woman" appears in the court records. She was one of the plaintiffs in a 1639 theft case against a white laborer named William Rookes. He was accused of stealing a pair of sheets, worth 12 shillings, from a white woman; a tablecloth, valued at 14 pence, from the household of Captain William Seymour; and a sheet, worth four shillings, from Phillip, who apparently lived on Seymour's land in Sandys Tribe. Rookes was found guilty of stealing the pair of sheets and the tablecloth from the whites, but not guilty of taking the other sheet. Thus the claim of Phillip, the black woman, did not stand.[160]

157. These three cases involving blacks are "Presentment by the Minister and Churchwardens," dated 1641 or 1647, a fragmentary and illegible record in CR, 1:193B.
158. Assize of November 27–30, 1638, Lefroy, *Memorials*, 1:550, 482; Assize of October 6, 1640, ibid., 563–65. For similar cases in Virginia, see *Lower Norfolk County*, 1:145.
159. Rivera, "Shipwrecked Spaniards," 26.
160. Lefroy, *Memorials*, 1:553.

These early court records lend credence to Rivera's observation that Bermuda had only "a few negroes" in 1639. "Some of them," he wrote, "have landed from vessels wrecked here, others have been left here by the Dutch who captured them."[161] Regardless of how they arrived, Bermuda's blacks were there to stay, and their numbers would increase rapidly. In the first three decades of settlement they married, had children, and some, at least, worked side by side with whites. There were enough of them to call forth legislation to control their "insolent" behavior toward whites. But slavery for blacks was not yet established in law, and *slave* was not synonymous with *negro* in the 1620s or 1630s. The fateful transition from freedom or servitude to slavery for most of Bermuda's blacks would begin in the 1640s, in the next generation.

161. Rivera, "Shipwrecked Spaniards," 26.

2 From Servitude to Slavery

Existing seventeenth-century records of the Caribbean and mainland colonies in North America do not permit a precise documentation of the transition from freedom or indentured servitude to slavery for Africans and Indians, but Bermuda's history provides some intriguing glimpses of the process as it affected individuals. In the experiences of the colony's first and second generations of blacks, for example, one can trace at least a partial outline of the emergence of slavery and, more important, the reluctance of whites to admit its legal implications. *Negro* was not synonymous with *slave* until the late seventeenth century, but bills of sale and indentures dating from the 1630s show that blacks' terms of servitude were markedly different from those of white servants. While white apprentices and indentured servants had lengths of service ranging from five to 10 years, blacks and Indians had, with a few exceptions, a single length of servitude: "four score and 19 years." In this earliest development of slavery, Bermuda colonists thus avoided by a technicality what must have been to all concerned a repugnant reality: the enslaving of an individual for life. Under the letter of the law, persons with 99-year indentures were not slaves and might become free at the end of service. Many of these indentures added the fateful phrase "if he [or she] shall live so long."

The hesitancy of at least some Englishmen to recognize lifetime servitude as an acceptable status for blacks is evident in two letters from the 1630s. In 1634 Robert Rich, Earl of Warwick, wrote to Bermuda's Hugh Wentworth (who was by then one of Warwick's agents in Bermuda) instructing him in making the best use of the blacks on the Rich property "with regard to my profit"; but in the same letter Warwick asked Wentworth to look into the problems of one of these blacks, a man named Sander, who had asked that his wife be allowed to live with him and had complained that his child had been sold by a white planter. Warwick instructed Wentworth to "help the poor man in all lawful office of favour," adding that for man and wife to live together seemed to him "a request full of reason." In 1638 Edward Montague, Lord Mandeville, a member of the Somers Islands Company, wrote to Bermuda's Thomas Durham, "For the negroes I see no reason why they should deserve freedom from their service, though I hope and pray that you do not over-use

them with intemperate labour, which as they be men ought to be avoided."[1]
In both letters the authors wrestled with the conflict between dealing with
blacks as exploitable property and as human beings with human needs. There
was an obvious reluctance to use the word *slave* as an identifying term for
blacks in public documents in Bermuda. Forthright use of that word does not
appear regularly in public records until the 1680s. One of the earliest usages
appears in a 1687 "Act to Regulate the Militia" in which "slaves" as well as
other men aged 15 to 50 are required to attend musters. Wills and inventories
in the last quarter of the seventeenth century also began to use the word *slave*
as well as *negro*.[2] Even then, most slaveholders preferred to use the word *Negro*
or *servant*.

Bermudians' reluctance to lock slavery into language and law stands in clear
contrast to other English colonies. In the short-lived (1630–1641) English
settlement on Providence Island in the Caribbean, colonists sought to purchase blacks as slave laborers (some as pearl divers) in the early 1630s, justifying
their enslavement as lawful because of their "strangeness from Christianity,"[3]
an issue never raised in Bermuda. On the contrary, efforts were made from the
beginning (by some Bermudians, at least) to impart religious instruction to
blacks, although by the 1640s others opposed baptizing blacks. In Virginia,
slavery was implicitly recognized in two laws in the 1660s. A 1661 law punishing English (white) servants who ran away with blacks (who were judged
"incapable of making satisfaction by addition of time") required the English
servants to serve for the time of the blacks' absences as well as their own—
the inference being that blacks were already serving for life. In 1662 another
Virginia law stated that "all children born in this country be bond or free,
according to the condition of their mother" and set double fines for whites
found guilty of fornication with blacks. In Maryland, a 1664 law stated that
"all Negroes and other slaves to bee hereafter imported into the Province shall
serve Durante Vita."[4] Legal recognition of slavery in Virginia and Maryland
came relatively early, when the ratio of blacks to whites in the Chesapeake
was still small. Virginia in 1660 had a population of about 26,000 whites and
fewer than 1,000 blacks, or one black to every 27 whites; with the addition of
Maryland, the population of the Chesapeake in 1660 comprised 33,738 whites

1. The letter from Warwick is quoted in Kupperman, *Providence Island*, 149; the Mandeville
letter is on p. 168.
2. CR, 9:49.
3. Kupperman, *Providence Island*, 168. See also 97, 106, 166–67. Enslavement of Indians
on Providence Island was prohibited (166). But there, as in Bermuda, the concept of lifetime
servitude for blacks was not yet firmly established, as Kupperman notes.
4. For the Virginia laws, see Hening, *Statutes*, 1:226, 2:26, 170. The Maryland law is quoted
in Willis Lee Rose, ed., *A Documentary History of Slavery in North America* (New York: Oxford
University Press, 1976), 24.

and 1,708 blacks, giving a ratio of one black to every 20 whites. In England's Caribbean colonies laws defining slavery also appeared by the 1660s, but in those colonies the ratios—and thus race relations—were dramatically different from either Bermuda or the Chesapeake. Barbados, for example, in 1660 had 26,200 whites and 27,100 blacks—nearly equal numbers.[5] As early as the 1640s, as the numbers of blacks in Barbados increased dramatically because of the labor demands of sugar plantations, the Barbados Council ruled that all blacks brought there to be sold must be sold for lifetime servitude unless a prior contract specified other conditions.[6] Barbados, not Bermuda, was the first English colony to become a slave society, and it has been called one of the most "nakedly racial and ruthlessly exploitative societies in Western history."[7]

Bermudians had yet to fully resolve the troublesome issue of the status of children born to a black or Indian woman with a 99-year indenture. Not all black servants in Bermuda were given 99-year terms of service, and the few blacks who received shorter terms were obviously special cases. So was the case of one white servant who had a lifetime indenture: On November 27, 1654, a man named Damian Pecke agreed to serve Nathaniel Waterman, a planter in Pembroke, for "all the daies of his life: to be ymployed in such service as he is able to performe: with condition that the said Nathaniell shall fynd him meate, drinke Cloathing Lodging And althings necessary for his body both in sicknes & in health."[8] This was an unusual case, most likely an adult male who was willing to give up a measure of freedom for lifetime economic security. Both parties—master and servant—signed the agreement. In a collection of indentures and deeds of sale from 1636 to 1661 there are transactions involving a total of 118 blacks, all but 12 of whom appear to have served for life. Of the 12 who had shorter terms of servitude, ranging from

---

5. Jack P. Greene, *Pursuits of Happiness: The Social Development of Early Modern British Colonies and the Formation of American Culture* (Chapel Hill: University of North Carolina Press, 1988), 178. The population figures are taken from ibid., 178–79. On slave laws in the mainland colonies, see Wiecek, "Statutory Law," 258–80.

6. Larry D. Gragg, " 'To Procure Negroes': The English Slave Trade to Barbados, 1627–60," *Slavery and Abolition* 16, no. 1 (April 1995): 70. Barbados after 1643 was controlled by Puritans, who, like those on Providence Island, readily adopted slavery as a desirable labor system. But Barbados, unlike Providence Island, received a large number of blacks: 387,000 between 1640 and the end of the slave trade in 1809. See Stanley L. Engerman, "Europe, the Lesser Antilles, and Economic Expansion, 1600–1800," in *Lesser Antilles,* ed. Paquette and Engerman, 155–58.

7. Philip D. Morgan, "British Encounters with Africans and African-Americans, circa 1600–1780," in *Strangers with the Realm,* ed. Bailyn and Morgan, 173. See also Michael Craton, "Reluctant Creoles: The Planter's World in the British West Indies," in *Strangers within the Realm,* ed. Bailyn and Morgan, 316–28, for an account of Barbados as the first British island colony to become "creolized," with a well-defined class structure.

8. CR, 2:240. Nathaniel Waterman is listed as the owner of one share in Pembroke Tribe in the survey of 1663.

seven to 30 years, three were a man, woman, and child presented by Captain William Jackson to Governor William Sayle for the unusual term of seven years; four were children defined as "negro," and five were mulatto children fathered by white Bermudians.[9] Virginia legislators in 1662 harbored "some doubts . . . whether children got by any Englishman upon a negro woman should be slave or free" but resolved that doubt by making the child of a slave mother also a slave.[10] If the Bermudians were in any such quandary they did not record it by legislation. Although the children of an enslaved mother were often given lifetime servitude, the question of their status was never defined by law in Bermuda. In the first few decades of contact between whites and blacks, the disposition of children born to blacks and Indians in servitude was uncertain and was resolved on an individual basis. In Virginia a series of laws left loopholes for the children of white/Indian parentage, and a 1705 law ruled that no Indians brought into the colony after that year, or their children, could be held as slaves.[11] William Jackson was careful to specify that any children born to the black couple he gave to William Sayle in 1644 would become "wholy at the dispose of" Sayle if they were born within the couple's seven-year terms of service.[12]

By the 1640s, as the second generation of blacks began to appear, so did the fruits of interracial liaisons, and at least some of the children born to a black female bondservant and a free white father were given their freedom. In Charleston, South Carolina, a society with a larger and more clearly defined slave population than Bermuda's, mulatto children were occasionally freed or placed in white households in the eighteenth century.[13] In Bermuda the mother in most cases was serving a 99-year indenture but was not legally a slave. In 1649, for example, a mulatto child born to a black woman in William Johnston's household and a white man named John Browne was to remain in the Johnston household until age 30, then "to be free." Later, another

9. On these blacks and Indians, see CR, 2:134, 147, 149, 168, 171, 304.
10. Hening, *Statutes,* 2:170.
11. See Peter Wallenstein, "Indian Foremothers: Race, Sex, Slavery, and Freedom in Early Virginia," in *The Devil's Lane: Sex and Race in the Early South,* ed. Catherine Clinton and Michelle Gillespie (New York: Oxford University Press, 1997), 58–59, 65. In eighteenth-century Louisiana the children of Indian slave women and freemen were considered free. Daniel H. Usner Jr., "Indian-Black Relations in Colonial and Antebellum Louisiana," in *Slave Cultures and the Cultures of Slavery,* ed. Stephan Palmié (Knoxville: University of Tennessee Press, 1995), 151. See also W. Stitt Robinson, "The Legal Status of the Indian in Colonial Virginia," *Virginia Magazine of History and Biography* 56 (July 1953): 247–59.
12. CR, 2:103. See also the case of boatwright Lewis Middleton's black servant, Christopher, and the disposition of Christopher's children, in CR, 2:186, 239–40.
13. Ira Berlin, "Time, Space, and the Evolution of Afro-American Society on British Mainland North America," *American Historical Review* 85 (1980): 62–64. Since a number of Bermudians migrated to South Carolina in the 1680s, they may have brought this practice with them.

child "reputed to be begotten by Lewis Pratt" and the same black woman in Johnston's service was ordered by the governor to "be for Mr. Johnston and his Assignes untill that child attaines to the age of thirtye yeares and then to be free."[14]

In 1651 "an Infant Mallato named John, begotten by an Englishman of the body of one of the Companyes Negroes . . . in regard of the cares and paines, that Mr. John Turnnor, Councellor of Devonshire tribe hath taken in Noorishinge and preserveinge the said Infant . . . the said Mallatto is to serve the said Mr. Turnnor untill he attaines to the age of Twenty Eight yeares, as an Apprentice, And the said Mr. Turnner is to Nurture, and bringe him up in the feare of god, and to find him all necessaries dureinge the said tearme and at the expiracion thereof, to give him two suyts of Apparrell."[15] In 1655 John Turner's household also held a black man named Thomas, who was owned by the Somers Islands Company. "Susan a Mallatta child borne at Mr. Smith's house" was placed at age two in the household of Captain Thomas Turner to serve "untill shee shall come to the age of 20 yeares, to be brought up by him in the feare of god."[16] A few weeks later a "Mallatto child" named Thomas, born at the house of Henry Smith, was placed with Smith himself, until the age of 20, to learn the "trade of a weaver." Not all mulattos were so indentured. A "Malatto boye comonly called John" was sold to Anne Middleton in 1649 "for and during the tearme of these boyes Life."[17] In another case John Burrows agreed that John Bailey should "Injoye the Negroe child which was borne at his house," and Burrows then sold the child to Bailey for 18 shillings, "according to the agreement made with Mary Burrowes the wife of John Burrowes." This child may have been the "Negroe girle named Elizabeth" whom Bailey gave as a present to his married daughter five years later. He was careful to provide for the future, specifying that the gift included any children born to Elizabeth and that "her children when born . . . [were] never to bee sould from one another."[18]

In the Bailey case the father's identity was not mentioned, but in at least

14. CR, 2:168. Lewis Pratt's identity is unknown. William Johnson lived in Pembroke Tribe in 1649. He died in 1650, leaving his "cattle and chattels" to his wife and two sons. Books of Wills, vol. 1, p. 2; C. F. E. Hallett, comp., *Early Bermuda Wills, 1629–1825* (Pembroke, Bermuda: Juniperhill Press, 1993), 322.

15. CR, 2:201.

16. Ibid., 147. Thomas Turner was a ship captain who owned a total of 85.5 acres in Sandys Tribe in 1663. He died in 1684. See Lefroy, *Memorials*, 2:729; Books of Wills, vol. 1, pp. 318, 321. The "Mr. Smith" referred to was Samuel Smith, a Sandys landowner, a neighbor of Turner's. See Lefroy, *Memorials*, 2:727.

17. The Middleton case is in CR, 2: n.p., January 22, 1649/1650.

18. On Burrows and Bailey, see CR, 2:203, and Lefroy, *Memorials*, 2:70. At his death in 1668 John Bailey owned five slaves, a woman and four men. Books of Wills, vol. 1, pp. 119, 121.

one instance the mother of the child identified the father: In 1648 "One Sarah a negroe Woeman beinge nowe with child" affirmed that "Francis Jennyns is the trewe father of the said child and none other." Jennyns, who was then "outward bound" on a sailing vessel, agreed to give the child "forever" to Mr. John Hooper, provided that Hooper promised to "bringe and nurture upp the same in the faith of Christ."[19] Since Sarah's master is not mentioned, it is possible that she was a free black. The apparent toleration in Bermuda of sexual relations between blacks and whites stands in marked contrast to the attitude in Virginia, where interracial sex was a serious offense and whites found guilty of fornication with blacks were required to pay double fines.[20]

In 1655 Somers Islands Company officials complained to Governor Josias Forster that "divers Bastardes, children begotten . . . upon the Companyes negroe weomen" were being "disposed [of] by their fathers at pleasure." The governor and his council were ordered to preserve the Company's rights to such children and to place them "for the use of the Company only." Company officials also expressed their concern about the care of elderly blacks. By the 1650s a number of Bermuda's first generation of blacks had "growne past labor." Governor Forster had proposed to move these "unserviceable" individuals to Longbird Island (a small island of about 46 acres in Castle Harbor), but the Company opposed such a plan, declaring that those blacks who did not "freely desier the same" should not be required to move and that the Company would provide for those who chose to stay on the main island.[21]

While aged black servants were becoming burdensome, young ones continued to be highly valued. Thirty years after Forster had complained about the disposition of mulatto children, Governor Richard Coney wrote that "as to the Colonys Slaves born in privat mens houses of their females, when let out for term of years, noe man will well part with them."[22] Sometimes these children born to the Company's women were apprenticed, as was a four-year-old mulatto girl named Joanna, the child of Penelope, a mulatto woman in the service of the Company in 1663. Three years earlier, Penelope Strange had married John Davis, a mariner, on the condition that every other child of the marriage would belong to the Company. Davis had the option to "put in a negro child" as a substitute. He was also required to pay the Company 40

19. On the Jennyns case, see CR, 2:145. The existing records do not identify Francis Jennyns or John Hooper.

20. Hening, *Statutes,* 1:146, 170. The 1641 case of Virginia colonist Hugh Davis, who was punished for "lying with a Negro," is mentioned in chapter 1. It is possible that the Davis case involved a homosexual liaison. Interracial marriages in Virginia were prohibited by law in 1691. Berlin, "Time, Space," 69, estimates that one-quarter to one-third of the illegitimate children born to white women in the seventeenth-century Chesapeake were mulattos.

21. Lefroy, *Memorials,* 2:52.

22. Ibid., 547.

shillings a year to compensate for the Company's loss of Penelope's wages. It is possible that Davis, a mariner, was lost at sea in the interim, or for some other reason could not meet his financial obligations, and Penelope had no choice but to let her daughter be bound out. The child was to "live with and serve" a colonist named Thomas Shaw until she reached age 21. At that time, she was to be given "Two Suites of Apparell. One for Sabbath daie, and the other for working dayes."[23] Joanna's master, Thomas Shaw, resided in the tiny capital of St. George's (which had only 22 houses in 1663), where the Company's servants also lived, so that Joanna and her mother would still have lived close together. The Somers Islands Company kept black bondservants for its own use and for selling to various planters through its agents in Bermuda. The Earl of Warwick, whose privateers had been involved in the slave trade since the early 1600s, regularly distributed blacks and Indians in Bermuda.

In January 1644/1645, for example, one of Warwick's privateers, Captain William Jackson, arrived in Bermuda from Jamaica with a group of blacks and Indians he had taken from the Spanish.[24] The surviving narrative of Jackson's attacks on the Spanish possessions in the Caribbean from 1642 to 1645 does not mention the taking of black or Indian captives, although the narrator records in some detail the taking of other kinds of plunder, such as pearls, sack, ammunition (including Indian arrows), sails, cables, and pieces of eight. It is possible that the blacks and Indians Jackson brought with him to Bermuda were indentured servants under some prior agreement or that they were free people who, for reasons of their own, left Jamaica willingly. Whatever their original status, they were not sold by Captain Jackson but placed in the white community on unusual terms. For example, he gave to Governor William Sayle a black couple and their four-year-old son, the parents to serve only "to the end & terme of seven yeeres," the child until the age of 30. Jackson protected these blacks with a provision at the end of the indenture agreement: "And know yee also that I the said William Jackson doe by these presents fully & wholy acquit & for ever discharge the said three Nigroes from any other or longer servitude or bondage than is heerin expressed PROVIDED that the said Nigro boy bee able at the end of the said thirty yeeres to make a reasonable profession of the Christian Faith." Jackson, like his patron, the Earl of Warwick, was almost certainly a Puritan, and this proviso may reflect his religious bent. Apparently under instructions from Warwick, he distributed the other individuals in his charge, "dyvers Indians & Nigroes" among "dyvers persons" in Bermuda—all

---

23. Ibid., 141, 197.
24. *The Voyages of Captain William Jackson (1642–1645),* ed. Vincent T. Harlow, Camden Miscellany, vol. 13, no. 4 (London: Royal Historical Society, 1923), 34; Lefroy, *Memorials,* 1:591–92; see also Kupperman, *Providence Island,* 287–88, 316.

of them for the unusual term of seven years. What moved Captain Jackson to specify the length of servitude for these blacks and Indians, or how many he brought from Jamaica, is not known. They would have received their freedom in 1652. Perhaps one of them was the woman referred to in a memorandum, among the records of sales and indentures for that year, stating that "Katherine Buller a Negroe is a free woeman, and att her owne disposeinge to imploye her wages for her owne Maintenance; and to make Choice of her service."[25]

Besides the Indians brought from Jamaica, an undetermined number of other Indians were sold as servants in Bermuda, most of them in the first half of the seventeenth century. In the 1630s and 1640s, captives from Indian wars in New England and Virginia were consigned to be sold in Bermuda. In the summer of 1637, for example, when the Pequot War in Massachusetts had left many Indian prisoners, John Winthrop noted in his journal, "We sent fifteen of the boys and two women to Bermuda by Mr. Peirce, but he, missing it, carried them to Providence Isle."[26] Later another 80 Pequots were sent to Bermuda, where many were bought by colonists on St. David's Island. Thomas Hutchinson's history of Massachusetts records that Pequot Indian captives were to be "sent to Bermuda and sold for slaves."[27]

Bermuda records from 1636 to 1661 contain indentures or bills of sale for 28 Indians, besides those brought by Captain Jackson: seven men, one boy, and 20 women. Some of them may have come from the West Indies. Of these captives, all but three were to serve for life or, like most blacks, for the term of "4 score & 19 yeares" (see table 2).[28] As the table indicates, two of the Indians, a boy and a woman, had no terms of service specified, and one man, Christopher Marteene, was to serve an indenture of 25 years. A planter named Walter Nailor sold Marteene to John Devitt, a councillor from Warwick Tribe, in 1648. Devitt paid Nailor £16.2s. for the indenture, which reads in part: "I Christopher Marteene doe bind myself per these presents to live and dwell with Mr. John Devitt . . . as an Apprentice & Covenant Servant duringe the term & time of 25 yeares."[29]

Among the Indians listed are some brought by Captain Bartholomew Preston, owner and master of the 80-ton bark *Charles,* in 1645. Preston

25. CR, 2:102–3. The charitable Jackson also made a gift of £150 for a "School for the Edifying of poore Children." On Katherine Buller, see CR, 2:193.

26. Richard S. Dunn, James Savage, and Letitia Yeandle, eds., *The Journal of John Winthrop, 1630–1649* (Cambridge: Belknap Press, 1996), 227.

27. Thomas Hutchinson, *History of the Colony and Province of Massachusetts,* ed. Lawrence Mayo (Cambridge: Harvard University Press, 1986), 1:71; August 21, 1641, entry in *Journal of John Winthrop,* 355.

28. See, for example, CR, 2:114, 115. Records of the transactions involving Indians are ibid., 2:93, 96, 99, 100, 104, 105, 108, 109, 110, 111, 120, 121, 130, 183, 187, 238, 304, 358, 368.

29. CR, 2:304. Devitt, who owned 51.5 acres in Warwick Tribe by 1663, bought and sold a number of blacks in the 1630s and 1640s.

Table 2	Indian Indentures, ca. 1636–1661		
Indian	Age	Terms	Date
Mary and Joane	30, 50	99 years	n.d.
George	24	99 years	n.d.
captive Indian man		99 years	1644
Indian woman		99 years	1645
Elizabeth	40	99 years	1645
Mischall alias Michaell		99 years	1645
Megge	36	99 years	1645
Nall	20	99 years	1645
Sarah and Marye	28, 33	99 years	1645
Barbarye	30	99 years	1645
Indian woman		99 years	1645
Marye	20	99 years	1645
Jane	40	99 years	1645
Joane	16	99 years	1645
Indian man		99 years	1645
Besse	24	99 years	1645
Elizabeth and Mary		99 years	1646
Anne		99 years	1648
Tomackin		life	1650
Ciscilly		99 years	1650
Francis (boy)		not given	1657
Christopher Marteene		25 years	1658
Maria		life	1660
Pedro		life	1660
Maria	20	not given	

CR, vol. 2, Indentures, deeds, bills of sale.

brought "30 or 40" Indian captives, whom he and various members of his crew sold on the same terms (99-year indentures) as blacks, at prices from £7 to £10 each.[30] The individual histories of a few of these Indians can be traced:

30. The sales of 19 of these Indian captives brought in 1646 can be documented; the terms of servitude were for life. Lefroy assumes that these Indians came from the West Indies, but they

Robert Dickinson, a Southampton blacksmith, bought Elizabeth, "aged about 40 yeares," for £10. Captain John Stowe, the Pembroke shipwright, paid £14 for Mary, age 30, and Joane, 50. These women, who may have been widowed by war in New England or Virginia or taken from their families in Barbados or Jamaica, were thus sold into lifetime servitude in Bermuda. Somewhere along the way they lost their Indian names and acquired English ones, perhaps given them by the individuals who sold them.

Elizabeth, Mary, and Joane came to live among an undetermined number of other servants in the prosperous Dickinson and Stowe households. Surviving records do not indicate how many servants Robert Dickinson had in 1646, but by 1663 he owned a "mansion house" and a 49-acre property in Southampton Tribe. The Indian Elizabeth, as did many newly arrived Indians, joined a biracial household of undetermined size and learned the ways of an alien culture. At John Stowe's residence, the Indians Mary and Joane became part of a large servant household of a dozen or more that included blacks, white indentured servants, and apprentices of both races. Between 1640 and 1658 John Stowe, who by 1663 owned 100 acres in Pembroke Tribe, contracted for two white apprentices and one black to be taught the trade of boatwright. Stowe already had two other white male apprentices (one a tailor, and one whose trade is not known). About this same time he also bought four young blacks—two boys and two girls. Additionally, an undated bill of sale shows that Stowe bought "three Negroes" during this period.[31] Another of the Indian captives of 1645, a woman named Nall, "aged about twentye yeares," was sold for £9 to James Stirrup, a weaver who lived on Longbird Island. The Somers Islands Company assigned that island to Stirrup and another weaver, James Wright. As "weavers of Dimity" (a lightweight cotton fabric), they were apparently given a special status and were not to grow any tobacco.[32] The young Indian woman would no doubt have had a knowledge of weaving, which may have been why Stirrup purchased her. In any case, Nall remained in his household for many years. When Stirrup died in 1665 his inventory listed "One Indian woman and one Indian girle" along with "Two Negros."[33] Nall would have been about 40 years old by then, and a mother. The identity of her child's father is unknown.

According to the existing records, many of the Indians brought to Bermuda in the 1640s were women, and it is unlikely that these women found mates

may have been brought from New England or Virginia. Lefroy, *Memorials,* 2:154, 154 n, 155. Bartholomew Preston bought the *Charles* from William Jackson. Ibid., 1:592, 716.

31. CR, 2:243. For Stowe's other transactions, see CR, 2:131 (the Indian women), 179, 92, 149, 180, 171, 214, 245, 308.

32. Lefroy, *Memorials,* 2:90.

33. Books of Wills, vol. 1, p. 100.

of their own race. Bermuda's English colonists apparently did not share their countrymen's aversion to sexual relationships with Indians (John Rolfe's marriage to Pocahontas notwithstanding).[34] The children mentioned in seventeenth-century wills and inventories as "Indian" may have been of mixed parentage, but their racial identity was that of their mothers. The record is silent on the racial preferences of Bermuda's Indian women and on the frequency of Indian-white or Indian-black liaisons. But the children born to an Indian woman were always identified as "Indian." By the 1660s the term *mustee,* like the Spanish *mestizo,* was used to designate the child of an Indian woman and a white man. In earlier usage, *mustee* referred to the child of a Spanish or Portuguese father and an Indian mother, but it could also mean a half-caste of any race.[35] Thus it could also have meant the offspring of an Indian and a black. Given the scarcity of Indian men in Bermuda, it is likely that a number of the latter mixed-race liaisons occurred and that *mustee* came to be used for their issue.

There is one instance in the existing records of an "Indian Negroe" child, and that was a daughter born to an Indian woman in the household of the surveyor Richard Norwood. In 1646 Norwood bought two Indian women, Elizabeth, 24, and Mary, 45, for £20, to serve for the customary 99-year indentures. Nearly 30 years later, an inventory of Norwood's estate lists 11 "servants" in all, including "an Indian Negroe girl" called Nan. The list, dated February 4, 1675, follows:

1	Negroe man called Argee	£25
1	Negroe man called Tom	£25
1	Negroe woman called Besse	£18
1	Negroe woman called new Besse	£22
1	Negroe woman called Marrea	£12
1	old Indian woman called Mary	£02
1	Indian Negroe girle called Nan	£13
1	Negroe boy called Dicke	£14
1	Negroe boy called Tom	£10
1	Negroe boy called Will	£08
1	Sucking Child a girle called Besse	£02[36]

34. On this peculiarity, which set the English apart from Spanish and French colonists, see Michael Zuckerman, "Identity in British America: Unease in Eden," in *Colonial Identity in the Atlantic World, 1500–1800,* ed. Nicholas Canny and Anthony Pagden (Princeton: Princeton University Press, 1988), 145–46; Bernard Sheehan, *Savagism and Civility: Indians and Englishmen in Colonial Virginia* (Cambridge, Eng.: Cambridge University Press, 1980), 114; James Axtell, "The White Indians of Colonial America," *WMQ,* 3d ser., 32, no. 1 (January 1975): 55–88. On mixed-race unions between Africans, Europeans, and Indians, see Jack Forbes, *Africans and Native Peoples: The Language of Race and the Evolution of Red-Black Peoples* (Urbana: University of Illinois Press, 1993), 181–89, 190–220.

35. *Oxford English Dictionary.* See also *mestizo.*

36. Book of Wills, vol. 1, p. 261.

Norwood's 1674 will mentions an "Indian Besse wch died in the Servise when shee had served from about Six yeares." This was probably Elizabeth, who would have been about 30 in 1652, six years after her purchase. The "Indian Negroe girl," Nan, living in Norwood's household 22 years later was probably the granddaughter of Elizabeth. (Mary was past childbearing age when she came to Norwood's household in 1646.) An infant born to Elizabeth between 1646 and 1652 would have been between 22 and 28 years of age at the time Norwood made his will and thus old enough to have been Nan's mother or father. The identities of the "Indian Negroe" girl's parents remain obscure, and no amount of examining the scraps of evidence will answer the obvious and vital questions: How did white Bermudians perceive the child of an Indian and a black? Was this an unusual combination in Bermuda? Was the mixed-race couple married? Did one of Nan's parents come from outside Norwood's household? There was at least one other married couple in Norwood's servant household: "Negro Tom & his wife called Besse" (described as "Bond Servants") and their two sons, Dick and Tom, were bequeathed to Norwood's daughter, Elizabeth, and his son, Andrew. The rest of Norwood's "servants," including Mary, "an old Indian woman" valued at £2 (she would have been 78 years old by then) were to be distributed "equally & indifferently" among his children—two sons and two daughters. Norwood and his wife had four children: Elizabeth, who married an Irish surgeon named James Witter; Anne, who married a man named Bowen and was accused of witchcraft in the 1650s; Andrew, a mariner with interests in Barbados; Matthew, the captain of the Somers Islands Company magazine ship.

There were other Indians among the Norwood family's servants. Norwood's son-in-law James Witter sold Norwood "one Indian man named George," about 24 years old, in an undated transaction, probably in the 1640s. This George was not in Norwood's household in 1674, but it is possible that he was the father of the Indian Elizabeth's child. George is mentioned in Norwood's will as his "man Servant called George" who served him for four or five years before the servant's transportation to Carolina at an unspecified date. In 1648 James Witter bought an Indian woman called Anne, age unknown. When Witter's wife (Norwood's daughter Elizabeth) died nearly 40 years later in 1691, she provided for an Indian boy, James, who was to be free at age 32 and be given "two good Suits of Apparel." It is possible that James was the grandchild of either Anne or George. It is also possible that the young James was the son or grandson of the master of the household, James Witter, who may have sired a child by an Indian woman. In any case, the naming of the Indian boy for James Witter suggests a close and perhaps affectionate relationship between master and servant families. Similar patterns of naming, as we shall see, occurred among Bermuda's white families and their black bondservants. The Witter family's other slaves, a black couple and four black children, were not freed but parceled out among Elizabeth Witter's adult children. Nan, the "Indian Negroe" girl of 1674, disappears from the records.[37]

Although most of the seventeenth-century Indian captives were sold under the same terms as blacks, the status of the Indians whom Captain Bartholomew Preston brought in 1645 was troubling to some Bermudians for many years afterward. In April 1655 the Somers Islands Company, at the behest of Bermuda colonist Richard Jennings, wrote to Governor Josias Forster concerning the Indians "taken by deceipt & brought unto the Somr Islands by Capt Preston & others about 11 yeares past."[38] These 30 or 40 Indians were "freeborn people And ther made perpetual slaves to the great dishonor of God & the pulling down his judgmt on the Inhabitants of the Islands to the prejudice of the Company." The Somers Islands Company officials were anxious that the "taking and Binding of such [Indians] for the future may be prevented." In the 1630s officials of the Providence Island Company forbade the enslavement of Indians by colonists there, although slavery for blacks (some of whom had been brought from Bermuda) was acceptable, and conditions for enslaved blacks became "increasingly exploitative" during the Providence Island colony's brief history. Although Bermuda's governor was instructed to restore "this freeborne people to their former libertyes," the record does not show that he took any action. Richard Jennings (who held 11 blacks and one mulatto, but no Indians, as servants at the time of his death in 1669) was not the only colonist who petitioned on behalf of the Indians. Six years later, in 1658, another letter from the Company noted it had "received severall complaints touching the Indians for soe manie yeares in bondage that were long since brought in by Captn Preston" and recommended that the Assembly "consider a way and manner for the enfranchiseing of these people."[39] What happened to most of these Indians is not known, but Nall was still in servitude to James Stirrup at the time of his death in 1665, 19 years after her arrival. Mary was listed as a servant in Richard Norwood's household in 1675, 40 years after he purchased her. James Witter's George, on the other hand, was sold into Norwood's household and eventually transported from there "to Carolina"—perhaps as a free man.

Other Indians appear in wills and inventories throughout the seventeenth and eighteenth centuries, most of them members of servant or slave households that also included blacks. The household of Richard Jennings Junior

37. Ibid., vol. 3, pt. 1, p. 136. For the sales of George and Anne, see CR, 2:238. On the Norwood family house, still in use, see Joyce Hall, "Norwood," *Bermuda* (December 1958): 19–27, 47–49.

38. Lefroy, *Memorials*, 2:54. See Kupperman, *Providence Island*, 166, 179–80.

39. Lefroy, *Memorials*, 2:55, 154.

(whose father had protested the enslavement of Indians in 1655), for example, included "One Indian man arrived from Carolina About Seven yeares to Serve called James."[40] The younger Jennings died in 1692. At the time of his death he had six black men in addition to the Indian, James. Jennings's estate inventory is one of a collection of 448 inventories from 1655 to 1777, of which 47 list Indians as slaves or servants.[41] There were 105 Indians in all: 32 men, 27 women, 20 boys, 21 girls, and three infants and two adults whose gender is not recorded. Of the 47 households with Indians, nine had Indians only, in numbers ranging from one to nine. More than half the households (27) contained only a single Indian servant or slave among other blacks. Only three Indians—Symon Harding's Anne, an "Indian lad" owned by Samuel Scrogham, and an Indian man in the household of John North—lived in a household with no other servants or slaves. Most of the other households were multiracial, containing Indian and black servants or slaves. Fifteen households contained Indian family groups with adults and children. The most significant thing about these inventories containing Indians is that only three of them are dated later than 1715. The last recorded Indian in these inventories is an "old Indian woman" in the 1761 inventory of merchant John Butterfield. By the late eighteenth century Indians disappear as a separate racial category of servants or slaves in Bermuda wills and inventories. This is not because they were manumitted, but simply because no new ones were brought in. Those Indians who managed to become free were, like free blacks and mulattos, required to leave Bermuda. In 1729 the Bermuda Assembly passed an "Act for Extirpating all free negroes Indians mulattoes such as have been Slaves (and freed or to be freed) so as they do not remain in those Islands."[42]

Wills and inventories show that by the early 1700s a number of Indians, both slave and free, lived in the capital, St. George's, and on St. David's Island, a narrow, 500-acre strip at the easternmost end of Bermuda. Three hundred acres of St. David's Island were part of "the general"; the remaining acreage was assigned to Hamilton Tribe until 1687, when these lands were included in St. George's Parish. Accessible only by water until 1895, St. David's remained somewhat isolated from the rest of Bermuda until the twentieth century. Many of its present residents claim Indian ancestry.[43] Some of them had been brought as captives from King Philip's War in 1676 in New England. Thomas Hutchinson's *History* records that after that conflict "most [Indians] . . . were

40. Books of Wills, vol. 3, p. 164. Jennings owned a plantation in Collington County, South Carolina.
41. These inventories are taken from Books of Wills.
42. Miscellaneous Acts, 1711–1759, March 12, 1729/1730.
43. See E. A. McCallan, *Life on Old St. David's* (Hamilton, Bermuda: Bermuda Historical Monuments Trust, 1948).

shipped off for slaves to Bermuda and other parts."[44] The 1688 inventory of Richard Jones, a cooper in St. George's, lists an Indian man, Dick, and an "old Indian woman." Two households, one in St. George's and one on St. David's, had nothing but Indians as slaves. The 1700 inventory of John Welsh Senior of St. George's lists two Indian men, Philip and Tony, an "old Indian" named Jane, and two Indian children, a girl and an infant boy. Captain Boaz Sharp of St. David's had nine Indians in his household: two men named Philip and Andrew, two women, Dinah and Sue, four girls, and a two-day-old boy. That two Indian men at this time bore the name Philip suggests a memory of the late King Philip, the Wampanoag ruler who died in King Philip's War in 1675. The will and inventory of another St. George's resident, Zachariah Briggs, tell a poignant tale of one Indian family. In January 1704/1705 Briggs's will bequeathed to his wife his "Indian man slave," Andrew, Andrew's wife, Jenny, and their daughter, Nanny, along with five blacks: a woman and her daughter, a man and his son, and a single black man.[45] At Briggs's death in the spring of 1706, his estate inventory lists "One Indian Man Andrew (Craisy)" and his daughter, Nan. In the seventeenth century, according to the *Oxford English Dictionary,* the word *crazy* (craisie, craisy) could mean either physical or mental deterioration. In that two years, Andrew's wife, Jenny, had died or been sold, and Andrew, perhaps because of the loss of his wife, had become "craisy."

Indians made up a small fraction of Bermuda's labor force throughout the seventeenth and eighteenth centuries, and the existing evidence offers only tantalizing fragments of their history. Were they perceived as different from blacks? Were they treated differently? In the mid-seventeenth century, at least, there is reason to believe they were.[46] Captain William Jackson's special terms of servitude for the Indians he brought from Jamaica in 1644 are a case in point, as is the concern about the Indians sold into slavery by Captain Preston. In 1651 a transaction between Philip Lea, a resident of Paget Tribe, and Captain William Williams of nearby Devonshire Tribe suggests that Indians had favored status as servants. "Uppon the Marriadge of their Servants: James and Francis [Frances], boath Indians," Lea and Williams agreed that Williams, as the owner of the woman, Frances, should have the first child born of this union; Lea, the second; and so on, as more children were born. Such

44. Hutchinson, *History of Massachusetts,* 1:71; Ethel Boissevain, "Whatever Became of the New England Indians Shipped to Bermuda and Sold as Slaves?" *Man in the Northeast* 21 (1981): 103–14.

45. Books of Wills, vol. 2, pt. 2, pp. 216, 226; ibid., vol. 3, pt. 2, p. 178; ibid., pp. 125, 127.

46. For a comparative view, see Douglas Deal, *Race and Class in Colonial Virginia: Indians, Englishmen, and Africans on the Eastern Shore during the Seventeenth Century* (New York: Garland Press, 1993).

arrangements became common practice as enslaved couples belonging to different owners had children. As a Bermuda governor explained it, "The people have a custom here . . . that if one Neighbor's Slave marrieth with another Neighbor's Slave, the children are to bee divided betwixt them."[47] This arrangement would eventually become a commonplace division for the children born to black as well as Indian servant or slave couples in Bermuda. But in this case Williams was also to pay Lea for the nursing and care of the second child for a year and a day. Lea, for his part, was "to pay for the Midwife and provide one Servant [to Williams] for the tyme the mother of the child Lyeth Inn for six weekes." Philip Lea and William Williams were prosperous sea captains, and their care of their servants may not have been typical. It is not likely that midwives and lying-in for servants were common in many households. What became of Frances and James is not known. Lea's 1674 estate inventory does not mention any Indians in his household, but lists "1 English man servant," "1 English maide servant," and "1 very old Broken Negro man whom wee Judge not fitt for appraisement."[48]

There is a sequel to the story of the Indian couple James and Frances: In 1657 Philip Lea sold one of their children to a planter, Lazarus Owen, who lived on Owen's Island in Crow Lane harbor, about half a mile from Philip Lea's property in Paget. Owen received "one Indian child Called by the name of Francis [Frances]," on April 17, 1657, with the provision that if the child died within a year and a day, Lea would refund the selling price of £8.6. The child lived, and on September 30, 1658, Lazarus Owen signed a document giving the Indian child, Frances, to his daughter on the day of her marriage "to be her owne for ever." Furthermore, Owen provided for any children born to Frances to be divided between his two daughters when each Indian child reached the age of a year and a half. The terms of service for these unborn children were not specified.[49] The elaborate arrangements for their disposition, however, reveal a degree of uncertainty on the part of their masters about their status, as well as a certain callousness at separating young children from their mothers. But at least Lazarus Owen's daughters, who were to receive the children of the Indian, Frances, were in the same family and may have lived near each other.

47. Lefroy, *Memorials*, 1:669–70. On James and Frances, see ibid., 2:547–48; CR, 2:195–96.
48. There is no surviving will or inventory for William Williams. On the Lea family, see Books of Wills, vol. 1, pp. 175, 178, 282, 648. Philip Lea's wife was the daughter of the dissident Puritan clergyman Patrick Copeland. Their only son, Copeland Lea, was apprenticed to Richard Norwood in 1665 to learn grammar, bookkeeping, and surveying. Their daughter, Susanna, married a grandson of Hugh Wentworth.
49. CR, 2:299–300. On the Owen family, see Books of Wills, vol. 2, pt. 2, p. 96; Lefroy, *Memorials*, 2:725.

Whether Indians were manumitted more often than were blacks is not clear from the existing records. Both Indians and blacks were listed in inventories, always identified by race, that is, "Indian" or "Negro," and both were held in lifetime servitude. After some doubt in the mid-seventeenth century about the justification of enslaving Indians, Bermuda slaveholders evidently had no qualms about keeping them in bondage. Some masters, however, freed their Indian servants and not their black ones in their wills. In 1674, for example, the estate inventory of Edward Sherlock, a cordwainer in Southampton Tribe, stated that "an Indian boy called John" was to be freed 30 years after Sherlock's death, but the two blacks, a boy named John and a "wench named Sarah," listed in the inventory were not freed. In 1684 John Wainwright of Warwick Tribe bequeathed his Indian woman, Dinah, to his son George, "to serve him thirtie yeares and then to be free."[50] Wainwright, however, did not free the rest of his Indian slaves; he bequeathed two Indian boys and an Indian girl (probably Dinah's children) to other members of his large family. The manumission of Indians, like the manumission of blacks, sometimes depended on the slave's economic value as well as the master's compassion. Whether Wainwright thought the Indian children were more valuable as slaves than their mother, or whether he thought they would receive better care as members of his children's households than with their mother, is a matter for conjecture. There is one difference in Indian manumissions, however: While both Indians and blacks were occasionally freed, and some masters freed their Indian slaves but not their black ones, there are almost no records of masters who chose to free their blacks but not their Indians.

A handful of Indians appear in early grand jury presentments and court records and, like blacks, apparently received equal treatment under the law. In 1653, for example, "John a Skotsman and servant to Jonathan Stokes, and an Indian woman of Edward Sherlocke's" were sentenced to be whipped. Their relationship was probably sexual; their punishment similar to the whippings meted out to other couples, regardless of race, who were found guilty of fornication. The two would have had to travel at least two or three miles to see each other: Jonathan Stokes, the Scot's master, lived in Paget; Edward Sherlock, in Southampton. Sherlock had purchased "Maria an Indian woman age 20" in 1645. She would have been about 33 in 1653. At Sherlock's death in 1674 the Indian boy named John, who was to be freed, was very likely the son of the Indian, Maria, and the Scotsman, John. In another case involving an Indian, "Anne the woman Indian servant unto Symon Harding" was accused of theft but was cleared by proclamation in an assize court in 1653. Harding, who described himself in his 1655 will as a "planter" on St. David's Island,

---

50. Books of Wills, vol. 1, pp. 177, 211.

had only the one servant, Anne.[51] She was probably one of the Indian women brought to Bermuda in the 1640s.

An Indian woman and three blacks figured prominently in a witchcraft scare in Bermuda's multiracial society in the 1650s, and their treatment offers further evidence that the colony's racial attitudes were still in flux. The alleged witches' victims included a mulatto woman, an Indian woman, and a "negro girle." Moreover, one of the witnesses against a white man was "a negro Boy called Symon." Between 1651 and 1655, 10 whites—eight women and two men—were indicted for witchcraft, and five of them—four women and one man—were hanged.[52] One would expect to find blacks, mulattos, and Indians—with their diverse African, Caribbean, and North American Indian backgrounds—as accused witches rather than supposed victims of witchcraft. In Salem, Massachusetts, in 1692, for example, a West Indian slave woman, Tituba, was the first to be accused of witchcraft. New England's popular culture associated Indians with savagery and satanic practices, and no doubt memories of Indian wars intensified the public's fears. When a number of Indian captives from King Philip's War in 1675 were taken to Barbados, the English colonists there were for a time possessed by a "bizarre fear of Indians." It is possible that Barbados's large black population, many of whom were newly arrived Africans whose unfamiliar culture was disturbing to that colony's whites, made the presence of Indians—yet another unassimilated group—cause for alarm. Barbados's whites had an additional reason to be afraid of Indians: Whites were a diminishing racial minority there. By the 1670s there were 44,000 blacks to 21,000 whites in the sugar island colony, compared to approximately 1,500 blacks and 4,500 whites in Bermuda.[53]

That persons of color were involved, both as victims and witnesses, in Bermuda's witchcraft trials suggests that the status of blacks, mulattos, and Indians was still uncertain and that all were perceived as possessing equal rights to justice from Bermuda's courts. In this aspect, Bermuda was not unlike some other English colonies in the seventeenth century. In New England,

51. On the relationship between Maria and John, see Lefroy, *Memorials,* 2:46. On Ann and the Harding household, see ibid., 2:45; Books of Wills, vol. 1, pp. 44, 45. Harding's entire estate, including Anne, who was valued at £20, came to £46.16.03.

52. There are records of eight more witchcraft cases scattered over the next half-century, but only one conviction, and in that 1671 case the colony's governor intervened with a pardon. Besides the 18 indictments, accusations were made against four other individuals, two in the period 1651–1655 and two in the later period, but none of these was sustained. CR, vol. 3 (1647–1661). This volume has no page numbers and is difficult to read. Witchcraft cases are excerpted in Lefroy, *Memorials,* 2:601–33.

53. See Elaine G. Breslaw, "The Salem Witch from Barbados: In Search of Tituba's Roots," *Essex Institute Historical Collections* 128, no. 4 (October 1992): 220, 230–33; Craton, "Reluctant Creoles," 318; Lefroy, *Memorials,* 2:432.

for example, blacks, who in 1660 numbered only 562 in a total population of about 33,000, were also considered equal under the law, testified against whites, and had access to legal counsel. In seventeenth-century Virginia the legal status of blacks was also on a par with that of whites until the early 1700s.[54]

For what Bermuda's witch trials reveal about race relations and racial attitudes, they deserve a closer examination. The witchcraft trouble began in May 1651, when Goodwife Jeane Gardiner, the wife of Ralph Gardiner of Hamilton Tribe, was accused of bewitching a mulatto woman named Tomasin. Jeane Gardiner was heard to say "that she would crampe Tomasin" and reportedly "used many other threatninge words tending to the hurt and *injurie* of the said mullatto woman." Gardiner's victim was then "very much tormented, and struck blind and dumb for the space of twoe houres or thereabouts." Jeane Gardiner may have been known in her neighborhood as the wife of Ralph Gardiner, a laborer who had come to Bermuda in 1612. A contentious man, he twice accused neighbors of stealing his poultry and was himself found guilty of stealing a fish gig.[55] The assize record mentions that Jeane Gardiner, in addition to practicing witchcraft on Tomasin, "at divers tymes in other places . . . did practice the said devilish craft of witchcraft on severall persons to the hurt and damage of their bodyes and goods."[56] A panel of 12 women, including the wives of several men who possessed black, Indian, or mulatto servants or slaves, found a witch mark, a suspicious "blewe spott" in Gardiner's mouth. As a further test, Gardiner was "throwne twice in the sea" where she was found to "swyme like a corke and could not sinke"—according to the lore of witchcraft, a sure sign of guilt. A white, middle-aged woman, wife of a laborer, Goodwife Gardiner was a typical candidate for witchcraft charges in Bermuda.

Of Tomasin, the mulatto woman who was Jeane Gardiner's alleged victim, nothing is known except her name. Since she is not identified as belonging to any master, it is possible that Tomasin was a free woman. Perhaps she was a neighbor of Gardiner's. Jeane Gardiner and Tomasin may have lived near

---

54. On population estimates, see Greene, *Pursuits of Happiness,* 178. On legal rights, see Robert C. Twombly and Robert H. Moore, "Black Puritan: The Negro in Seventeenth-Century Massachusetts," *WMQ,* 3d ser., 24, no. 2 (April 1967): 225–28; Breen and Innes, '*Myne Owne Ground,*' 13–15, 16–17.

55. The Gardiner case is in Lefroy, *Memorials,* 2:602–3. On Ralph Gardiner, see ibid., 1:61, 125, 525. On witchcraft, see Breslaw, *Tituba;* Larry D. Gragg, *The Salem Witch Crisis* (New York: Praeger, 1992); Carol F. Karlsen, *The Devil in the Shape of a Woman: Witchcraft in Colonial New England* (New York: W. W. Norton, 1987); John Demos, *Entertaining Satan: Witchcraft and the Culture of Early New England* (New York: Oxford University Press, 1982). See also Alan MacFarlane, *Witchcraft in Tudor and Stuart England: A Regional and Comparative Study* (New York: Harper and Row, 1970).

56. Lefroy, *Memorials,* 2:603.

each other, but nothing is known of their relationship. Did Tomasin, in word
or action, offend Jeane Gardiner? Did Gardiner, the wife of a laborer, feel
threatened by, or jealous of, Tomasin? On the connection between this white
woman and her mulatto neighbor the record is silent, but Bermuda's legal
system inflicted the full measure of punishment upon the mulatto woman's
malefactor: Jeane Gardiner was hanged "before many spectators" on May
26, 1651.

The next biracial witchcraft case—and the next conviction—occurred two
years later, when the assize of 1653 tried John Middleton, husband of Elizabeth Middleton, for bewitching a Scotsman by the name of Makeraton, who
lived at Governor Josias Forster's house. It is likely that both the victim and the
malefactor lived in Sandys Tribe at the far west end of Bermuda. The 50-year-
old Scotsman, unable to testify "by reason of strange fitts that he was fallen
into," was placed in prison, presumably to restrain him. Three inmates of the
jail testified on the victim's behalf.[57] Among these witnesses was "a negro Boy
called Symon," who said that, being in the room where the Scotsman was
sleeping, he "saw through a great hole in the wall a thing of black culler" that
"ran so swiftly that he could not well tell the shape of it, which thing went
out of the privy hole." He then heard the Scotsman "give a thump & make
a noyse."

Symon's age is unknown, but the fact that he was listed as a boy indicates
that he was under the age of 15. In 1647 Governor Thomas Turner gave
"Symon a negro child" to John Vaughan, the colony's secretary, "to serve
untill the said Symon Attaine to the age of 20 yeares." It is likely that this
Symon was that boy.[58] Why Symon was in jail cannot be determined from
the existing records. His description of a black creature could have come
from his own imagination, or perhaps it was inspired by something the victim
said. Jeames Blake, another prison inmate, reported that the victim, John
Makeraton, had told him he had been tormented by "a thing in the shape of a
man, black in culler." An unusual thing about Symon's deposition is that it was
signed—an indication of at least minimal literacy. Of the 52 witnesses whose
written depositions have survived in Bermuda's witchcraft cases, only nine
individuals were able to write their names.[59] Symon is the only black among

57. See Lefroy, *Memorials*, 2:604–10. The records for Middleton's trial and Christian Steven-
son and Alice Moore, two women he accused of witchcraft, are the most complete of the 18
Bermuda cases.
58. CR, 2:134.
59. CR, vol. 3. These were all males. Fourteen of the 19 women deponents signed their
depositions with a mark, and in the remaining five only the name has been copied, with no
indication of a signature. In this particular trial Symon was one of five males who signed their
depositions.

them. If this Symon was the same individual as the Symon in the household of John Vaughan, the colony's secretary, the boy may been taught to read and write. In any case, Symon's testimony, along with that of eight white men and two white women, served to convict and hang John Middleton.

In all the extant testimony in Bermuda's witchcraft cases, Middleton's is the only one containing descriptions of a black creature or a black man as the devil. Symon, the young black boy, described a "thing of black culler," and the victim, John Makeraton, described "a thing in the shape of a man, black in culler . . . who sate upon him very heveyley & asked him if he would love hym & he answered noe." Another deponent, Robert Priestley, reported that while herding cattle near Middleton's house he saw lying on the ground "a Black creatuer . . . in the shape of a catt but farre Bigger, with eyes like fier, and a tayle near as long as a mans arme." These depositions, taken with Middleton's confession of "adultery with English and Negroes," may also represent an undercurrent of concern about interracial sex in the colony at mid-century. There is evidence of a growing number of mulattoes in Bermuda by the 1650s, and by 1663 there was a law against miscegenation.[60]

The next witchcraft case involving a person of color was one with an Indian woman as victim. The accused witch was Grace Bedwell, a spinster (literally, a spinner of thread, a term that later came to mean an older unmarried woman), the wife of John Bedwell, a laborer in St. George's, Bermuda's capital. In 1655 she was said to have "mallitiously and unnaturally vexed and afflicted severall persons, most especially . . . Kate an Indian woman servant of Robert Powell."[61] Powell, who made the accusation, was a cooper, or barrel-maker, in St. George's. Both he and his wife had been involved in the earlier witchcraft cases. He had been a member of the panel that found witchmarks on John Middleton and sentenced him to hang in 1653. Powell's wife, Joane, had served on a panel in January 1654/1655 at the witchcraft trial of Elizabeth Page and Jane Hopkins, in which Hopkins was found guilty and sentenced to hang. Grace Bedwell and Kate, the Powells' Indian woman servant, lived in close proximity. The town of St. George's was a small place, and all the residents undoubtedly knew each other well. But the nature of the relationship between Grace Bedwell and the Indian woman, Kate, like that of Jeane Gardiner and the mulatto woman, Tomasin, is unknown.

Kate, like Tomasin, remains a shadowy figure in the records. She may have been among the Indians brought to Bermuda in the 1640s, and she may have

60. Lefroy, *Memorials*, 2: 190, 605.
61. The manuscript record of Grace Bedwell's trial in CR, vol. 3, is printed in full in Lefroy, *Memorials*, 2:627–28. Robert Powell is listed in 1663 as a tenant on a 24.5-acre share in St. George's, owned by the governor. See Lefroy, *Memorials*, 2:725.

had a family in the Powell household. Robert Powell's will, made in 1675, 20 years after the witchcraft trial, does not mention Kate, but does list three Indians: a man named Populo, a woman named Tabitha, and a child, Joane.[62] They were very likely a family and may have been related to Kate. Powell, who also owned a black man named Andrew, was one of the first to identify his servants as "slaves" in his will. "It is my Will," he wrote, "that all my Slaves that shall bee then liveing shall bee hired out to Service by the Church Warden." The annual wages earned were to be for the maintenance of Powell's son, Daniel. Powell bequeathed the Indian child, Joane, to his wife, Joane, "to dispose of as she pleases." One wonders if Joane Powell sold the child who bore her name, or if she kept her in the household along with the other slaves. Tabitha and the child disappear from the records, but Populo was still in Joan Powell's service years later. In the witchcraft trial of 1655, the white woman Grace Bedwell, the accused malefactor of the Powells' Indian slave, Kate, was indicted but "Found not guiltie" of witchcraft.[63] Unfortunately the record of Bedwell's trial is frustratingly brief. It indicates only that she was found to have "felloneously & wickedly had consultation and familiarity with the devell" and that a panel of women found "several markes & signes upon her body."

Bermuda's only other recorded biracial witchcraft case occurred some years after the trials in 1651–1655, and it may have had a connection with one of them. In 1684 the colony's sheriff, Captain John Hubbard, reported "having a negro girle strangely taken sick, wasting and pining away in such an unusual manner that he suspects she is bewitched by the said Elizabeth Ward." Elizabeth was the wife of Henry Ward, a planter who owned 16 acres on Round Hill Island.[64] Henry Ward himself had been twice accused of witchcraft, but never brought to trial, during the witch scare of 1651–1655. A panel of women was appointed to search Elizabeth Ward for witchmarks, but their names were not recorded, and there is no further account of her case. Her accuser was a man of some prominence, a councillor for Hamilton Tribe in 1663 and sheriff of the colony from 1677 to 1684. His servant girl, the victim, may have recovered from her mysterious illness. An undated inventory in the

62. Books of Wills, vol. 1, p. 227. Powell, who was illiterate and signed his will with his mark, may have had other slaves besides the four named. The inventory of his estate has not survived. Powell's will also mentions a grandson, "John Powell of New England," who was to inherit a share of his estate, including the slaves Andrew, Populo, and Tabitha.

63. Lefroy, *Memorials*, 2:628.

64. Ibid., 632, 654. The will of Henry Ward of Warwick Tribe in 1687 mentions a wife, Elizabeth, two grown children, and two grandchildren. Ward left a female servant, "the Negroe," to his wife, with the provision that any children born of this woman were to become the property of his grandson, Joseph Harris, and granddaughter, Mary Ward. Books of Wills, vol. 3, pt. 1, p. 13.

late 1680s for John Hubbard's estate lists five blacks, one woman and four men, plus an Indian man, all unnamed, and a "serving maid called Judith."[65] The multiracial nature of these witchcraft cases, in which the forces of evil were believed to have attacked a mulatto woman, an Indian woman, and a black girl as well as white men and women, suggest that whites, blacks, and Indians in Bermuda viewed each other with some ambivalence for much of the seventeenth century.

Although by the 1650s lifetime servitude was becoming the common state for most blacks and Indians, there were still exceptions. For example, in 1653 former governor Roger Wood made special provision in his will for a 27-year-old black man, "Roger the son of Louis and Maria." Wood was fulfilling a promise he had made more than 20 years earlier.[66] In 1631 Lieutenant John Crofts, the owner of Louis, the boy's father, had appeared before a council meeting to ask for "the half parte" of the children of Louis and Maria, a woman belonging to the Somers Islands Company and working in the household of the governor. It was not yet, but it would become, common practice when the parents of black or Indian children were owned by different masters, for the first child born to become the property of the mother's owner, the second child, the property of the father's owner, and so on, as in the case of William Williams and Philip Lea's 1651 arrangement. The fact that Crofts was obliged to go before the Governor's Council indicates that in the 1630s such divisions were not yet commonplace. Moreover, since one of Louis and Maria's four children had died in infancy, "It was questioned whether a dead child . . . should be accounted in the number of Halveing or nott." By a show of hands, the council members decided that "a negro child nott weaned from the mothers breasts shall not hereafter be accounted in the number of halveing in the Somer Islands." The practice of dividing a slave couple's children between two masters was not always evenly applied. For example, in a 1719 court case a slave named Jack, who belonged to Leonard White, married a slave woman, Bess, who belonged to Richard Johns. The record states that "they are permitted to be joyned as man & wife, the Owners of Such Slaves are to have an Equall dividend of the Children of Such Slaves begotten & born." Bess had five children; Leonard White and his wife sued for their share of the children, claiming that the second and fourth children belonged to them. Johns claimed that there was "no Such Custom in these Islands" and that the couple was not married. Johns won the case.[67]

65. Books of Wills, vol. 1, p. 154.
66. Ibid., pp. 23, 26. See also Lefroy, *Memorials,* 1:526–27.
67. For the 1631 case, see Lefroy, *Memorials,* 1:526. For the 1719 case, see Assize Court Records, AZ 102/4, 842.

In Crofts's case it was decided that to replace the deceased infant, Lieutenant Crofts was entitled to claim another of the couple's children, "one negro man child named Roger," then about five years old. Thereupon, Crofts "did assigne and freely bestowe all his said right and interest" in the boy to Governor Wood, "desiering . . . that he would be pleased that the said negro child should bee sett at liberty and made a freeman when he cometh unto the age of thirty yeares."

In 1649 Wood placed Roger, then about 23 years old, with John Stowe, stating that the young man was "to be in the Possession and Service of my Cousen John Stowe, and to be by him Instructed, and taught the trade he now useth, of boate makeinge." Roger was then to be freed upon reaching the age of 30 and to be given "twoe suyts of Apparrell, one for the holy daies another for the workeinge daies, and likewise such apporcion of Tooles as are usually delivered to Boate Wrights, or boate Carpenters Servants at the expiracion of their tymes of Service by Indenture."[68] There is more to this story: Roger Wood made his will in 1653, when the young Roger was 27 years old. In the will, Wood provided not only for Roger's freedom but for that of "Edward the son of My Negro Roger Wood and Anna his wife." Former governor Wood died in May 1654. On November 20, 1654, John Stowe paid "a valuable somme of money" to Lieutenant John Crofts to "acquitt & discharge Roger Lewis a negro man of & from all manner of service servitude or bondage." This Roger may have been Governor Wood's former charge. It is conceivable that upon receiving his freedom, he dropped the surname of his owner and took instead the name of his father, Lewis (Louis). Lieutenant Crofts, more than 20 years later, may have reneged on his 1631 agreement and may have tried to claim ownership of the said Roger, now a trained boatwright. In any case, one young black family—a man, his wife, and their son—were at liberty to make a place for themselves as free people in Bermuda.

Although Louis and Maria, the parents of young Roger, did not live together in the same household, many such couples did. Marriage between slaves was recognized in Bermuda, and married slaves usually lived together, often with the assistance of their masters.[69] In 1658, for example, when a black man belonging to the Somers Islands Company married a woman in

68. Memorandum signed by Roger Wood, 1649, in CR, 2:171. John Stowe had had at least one apprentice to the trade earlier. In 1640 a white man named John Chancellor bound himself to Stowe for five years to learn "the Arte and trade of A Boatwright." CR, 2:179, 243.
69. On Virginia slave marriages, see Kulikoff, *Tobacco and Slaves,* 356–57, 374–75; Philip D. Morgan, "Slave Life in Piedmont Virginia, 1720–1800," in *Colonial Chesapeake Society,* ed. Carr, Morgan, and Russo, 449–52. Among the slaves on plantations in the Caribbean colonies, slave marriages were unusual, and high mortality rates inhibited the growth of families. See David Barry Gaspar, "Ameliorating Slavery: The Leeward Islands Slave Act of 1798," in *Lesser Antilles,* ed. Paquette and Engerman, 252–55, on efforts to encourage marriage and family life.

the service of planter William Baseden, Baseden tried to purchase the man. Baseden argued that the "duties of Marriage cannot be performed to each other, which by the Lawes of God and man are comanded, by reason of the distance of their abode and the Lawes now in force . . . forbidding any negro man or woman whatsoever to be out of their masters plantation halfe an hour after sunsett upon payne of Death unless they shall have a ticket from their said masters for so doing." Since the Company's manservant resided at St. George's, at the northeast end of Bermuda, and Baseden's woman servant lived on his property in Warwick Tribe, on the southwest side, the couple was separated by a distance of about 12 miles. The Company refused to sell the man in question but agreed that Baseden should supply "a serviceable negro man" to work for the Company in his place, allowing the newlywed couple to live together on Baseden's property.[70]

Marriages, baptisms, and burials were recorded in church register books, but since Bermuda's church records are incomplete, it is impossible to determine the frequency of such ceremonies for blacks. Slave marriages, religious or not, were commonplace, as a Somers Islands Company report in 1676 suggests, with its estimated 30 marriages per year in the colony, "besides ye Blacks."[71] From records in two extant church registers for the seventeenth century with incomplete entries dating from 1619, the marriages of three black couples can be documented. The register of St. Anne's Church in Southampton Tribe lists a double wedding for "John Whan [Juan?] and Ellon Hernandries both Negroes" and "Antony & Amie Hernandries both Negroes" on July 21, 1643. Unfortunately nothing else is known about these couples except that on December 3, 1644, "Elon the daughter of John Whan Negro" was baptized. In the Pembroke church register the baptisms of two children of Katherine and Peter, a couple with no surname, are recorded. In 1647 their son, John, was baptized, and in 1648 a daughter, Sarah, was baptized. Both children were described as "Negro of married parents."[72]

In seventeenth-century Bermuda, as in other English colonies, uncertainty about the compatibility of Christianity and slavery eventually led to debates on the subject and sometimes resulted in legislation prohibiting baptism for blacks. Although an act of 1647 forbade the "baptizing of Bastards or Negroes children," this law, like some of Bermuda's other laws on the treatment of the colony's nonwhites, was not strictly observed. Some baptisms of black, mulatto, and at least one Indian infant did take place during the 1640s and

---

70. Lefroy, *Memorials*, 2:107. In 1663 William Baseden owned two shares of land (about 50 acres) in Warwick Tribe. See ibid., 698.

71. Ibid., 432.

72. For the Southampton record, see St. Anne's Church Records, 1619–1752, microfilm reel 19, Bermuda Archives; for Pembroke, see Hallett, *Early Bermuda Records*, 31.

1650s. In an unusual case involving Christianity as grounds for freedom, in 1653 a 15-year-old black or mulatto named Doll Allen, the daughter of one William Allen, petitioned the Somers Islands Company for her freedom. She claimed that on reaching "Woman's estate" she was about to become "a perpetuall slave." She argued that because it had "pleased God to set a distinction between her and heathen negroes," she deserved to be free to "dispose of herselfe in such service as she maie find most proper for her condition."[73] But Doll's father, a free man whose race is not specified, had petitioned the year before to keep her in his service until she reached the age of 20. The Somers Islands Company discounted the young woman's equation of freedom with Christianity and found in favor of Doll's father. Another debate over the baptism of blacks emerged in the 1660s, and Bermuda's whites, like Virginia's in 1667, at last decided that baptism did not alter a slave's legal status.[74]

The appearance of surnames for some blacks by the 1640s suggests a degree of privilege or difference in their status. Doll Allen is a case in point. A surname was generally an indication that its owner was not a slave, but a free individual or a bondservant, perhaps the mixed-race child of a white Bermudian. In the Southampton Tribe church records from the 1630s to the 1670s, for example, there are six black surnames: Simon, Simonson, Symons, Tucker, Whern (Whan? Juan?), and Hernandris (Hernandes?). It is tempting to speculate that the first three names, listed for baptisms in the 1640s through the 1670s, were derived from a relationship to "Symon the Negro," the first black to arrive in Bermuda. Tucker was the name of a prominent white family in Bermuda. In 1654 George Tucker listed "Three Negroes" for baptism as "Children of George." These were probably the offspring of his servant, "George the son of old Symon," mentioned in the preceding chapter. This George, who worked for wages of 100 pounds of tobacco per year as a "searvant uppon the Land," was very likely a free man. Sometime in the next two decades either he or his son adopted Symon as a surname. In 1673 the Southampton church register recorded the baptism of George Symon's twin daughters, Susannah and Martha, noting "Negro" after each infant's name.[75] The other two black surnames in the Southampton church records, Juan and Hernandes, indicate that these individuals, like Francisco, Nathaniel Rich's valued servant, came to Bermuda from the Spanish West Indies.

Of a total of 22 nonwhites whose names appear in the Southampton church register in the seventeenth century, nine were infants baptized with no

73. Lefroy, *Memorials,* 2:34–35.
74. Golding, *Servants on Horseback,* 200. On the debate over baptism in the 1660s, see Lefroy, *Memorials,* 2:291–92.
75. On "George the son of old Symon," see CR, 2:188. For the Southampton church register, see Hallett, *Early Bermuda Records,* 14.

surname. They were Antonio, born to a black woman named Philass (Phyllis) in 1636; Susan, of unrecorded parentage, born in 1639 in the household of colonist Thomas Wells; another Susan, whose father was a black named Simon and who was baptized in 1654. Others were James and Jane, both born in Thomas Wells's household in 1657, and Anthony, born in the Wells household in 1659. All of these infants were identified simply as "Negro" in the Southampton baptismal register. Besides these, there was a mulatto infant baptized as Ann in 1646 and belonging to colonist Richard Leacraft; Mary, a mulatto born to a woman named Penny (perhaps the Penelope mentioned earlier in this chapter) and baptized in 1648; and Richard, an Indian infant baptized in 1657. Besides the earlier-mentioned Ellen, the child of John and Ellen Whan, the other black infants whose names were recorded in the baptismal register were John Simon, born to Daniel Simon and an unidentified mother in 1642; Rebecca Simonson, born to Simon Simonson in 1649; Ann Simonson, born to Elizabeth Simonson, also in 1649. It is possible that Rebecca and Ann were twins, since their baptism was on the same day, July 29, 1649.

The inclusion of blacks, mulattos, and an Indian among the whites in the church records suggests that there was a viable, if limited, multiracial Christian community in Southampton Tribe. In Pembroke Tribe, besides the children of the above-mentioned Katherine and Peter, there is a record of one other baptism of a black infant: In 1660 Sarah, the daughter of one "Thomas, Snr." and an unnamed mother was baptized. If Southampton's and Pembroke's early church records are typical, blacks, mulattos, and Indians participated to some degree in the religious life of Bermuda's churches. Some of Bermuda's blacks were buried in parish churchyards, but timeworn gravestones and incomplete records leave only a suggestion of these individuals' participation in church and parish life. The early records from St. Peter's, Bermuda's oldest church, founded in St. George's in 1612, have been lost, but the separate graveyard where blacks were buried can still be seen behind a wall on the west side of the church. A number of worn tombstones still stand, their inscriptions now largely unreadable. It is possible that the blacks listed in church records and those buried in churchyards were accorded that status because they were literate enough to read the Bible and to participate in worship services. The congregations were small: In 1663 the number of households in each tribe ranged from 19 to 49 (see table 5 in the next chapter). Mandatory services, either with a lay reader or a minister presiding, on Sunday mornings and evenings drew all the residents of a tribe together. Bermuda's rural communities, each with a religious center, were not quite as close-knit as New England's towns and villages, but in the early years of settlement Bermudians had more in common with Puritans in Massachusetts in the 1630s than with the Puritans of another island colony, Providence Island. The English colonists who settled there in 1631 eagerly embraced slavery as an institution and apparently made no effort either to convert or to educate their slaves.[76]

In Bermuda as in other English colonies, the path from indentured servitude to slavery is not clearly marked, but the stories of two black families whose children were sold into slavery offer glimpses of a procedure that may have been all too common in the 1640s. The first is the brief history of the only black whose burial is recorded in the St. Anne's church register in Southampton Tribe in the seventeenth century. On August 13, 1648, "Sander a Negro of Damon Knowles" was buried. Sander, who may have been either a free black or an indentured servant at one time, appears in several earlier records. Knowles's servant may have been the same individual as the earlier-mentioned Sander who complained in 1634 that a colonist named Winter had sold his child. A few years later, in 1640, "Saunder a negro and his wyfe" received 39 lashes apiece for attempting to "run away with a Boat."[77] What became of the couple after their punishment is unknown, as is their status (free, bondservant, or slave) at the time. But by 1646, at least, Sander was not free. A bill of sale for that year shows that Damon Knowles, a tenant in Southampton Tribe, bought "one negro man, Sanders" for £14 from his landlord, colonist Richard Jennings, and his landlord's wife, Elizabeth, who lived in Smith's Tribe.[78] Sander moved to Southampton to serve Damon Knowles, and two years later was buried in the Southampton churchyard. Sander's wife disappears from the records, but Sander was survived by at least one child. "A Negroe child called Ellicke, the sonne of ould Saunders A negroe," was bound out in February 1647/1648 to Captain John Stowe of Pembroke Tribe. Ellicke was to serve Stowe until age 20, "to be brought upp by him in the feare of god and to readinge, as farr as the understandinge of the bible," and then "to be for the use of the Colloney."[79] Unfortunately, Ellicke died in August 1648—the same month his father was buried. Had Ellicke lived, he would eventually have become the property of the Somers Islands Company, either to work on the public lands at St. George's or to be assigned as one of the governor's 32 servants. Ellicke, for all practical purposes, was a slave, although the word *slave* was not used.

The second story of a family whose children slipped, as it were, into lifetime servitude is that of a family who had been in Bermuda at least since 1618. James, who worked with Francisco and Antony on Nathaniel Rich's land in Southampton in that year, was one of the first-generation blacks who acquired a surname and, presumably, the status of a free man. By 1644 he was referred to as "James Sarnando Commonly Called olde James the Nigro." James

76. Kupperman, *Providence Island,* 178–79.
77. See Hallett, *Early Bermuda Records,* 22; n 1 above; and the assize of October 6, 1640, in Lefroy, *Memorials,* 1:563.
78. See Lefroy, *Memorials,* 2:724.
79. CR, 2:149.

Sarnando's name appears several times in early Bermuda records, and from these fragments of evidence it is possible to piece together something of his and his family's history after the 1620s—a history that poignantly illuminates another path to slavery in Bermuda. After being mentioned as a Southampton laborer in the service of the Rich family in 1617, James next appears in the record of a transaction between himself and Hugh Wentworth, the same person who had investigated the sale of Sander's child in 1634. Wentworth, like James Sarnando, had been an indentured servant on Nathaniel Rich's Southampton lands in 1619, before he became an agent of the Earl of Warwick. By 1637 Wentworth had acquired a wife and children and had risen rapidly on the social ladder. He was a landowner and a council member from Warwick Tribe, and he put "Gent." after his name. Wentworth, although apparently illiterate when he came to Bermuda,[80] became a merchant, an agent for the Earl of Warwick, and one of Bermuda's leading traders. Somewhere along the way he also learned to write. His signature, scrawled in large, childish block letters, appears on documents indicating him as the seller of black servants to Bermuda colonists in 14 transactions: three undated, nine in 1637, and two in 1640, including three "for the Company" in 1637 and one for the Earl of Warwick in 1640.[81]

Hugh Wentworth and James Sarnando had known each other since at least 1619, when the men had worked Nathaniel Rich's land. Many years later, in 1637 or 1638, James Sarnando, his wife, and a young child appeared at Wentworth's house in Warwick Tribe and performed a touching ceremony:

> Olde James the Nigro with his wife & A Nigro Childe named Hanna about 7 yeeres of age came into the sayd [Wentworth's] house And the sayd James did take the said Childe by the hand & delivered it into the hande of Mr. Wentworth saying heere Master mee give you this Childe take her & bring her up & mee give her to you freely, And then in like manner hee did take the sayd Childe by the hande againe & putting the Childes hand into Mistress Wentworths hande sayd, heer Mistris mee give you this Childe take her & bring her up & mee give you her freely And then in like manner the Wife of the sayd James did take the sayd Childe by the hande, & put it into the hande of Mr. Wentworth.[82]

The reasons for this curious transaction are a matter of speculation. James Sarnando referred to Hanna as "this child," and in later records she is identified as Hanna Sarnando, his daughter. James Sarnando was very likely a free man. Hanna's mother (presumably James's wife) was also free; otherwise Hanna, as the child of a slave woman, would have been the property of that woman's owner. Why Sarnando and his wife would wish to give Hanna to the

---

80. Lefroy, *Memorials,* 1:381. In 1626 Wentworth signed a document with his mark. On his subsequent career, see ibid., 410, 430, 544, 549, 687, 689; Ives, *Rich Papers,* 81, 175, 318.
81. On Wentworth's transactions involving blacks, see CR, 2:6, 7, 8, 12, 27, 29, 36.
82. Ibid., 85.

Wentworths and have her brought up by them remains a puzzle. One likely explanation is that James, who was referred to as "olde James," felt that he and his wife were too old to bring up a young child. James, at least, would have been in his forties by then. He may have been even older, past the age of active labor and doubtful of his ability to support his family. What he did for a living at this time is not known. He lived near Herne Bay in Southampton, and may have subsisted, as did many Bermudians both black and white, by growing his own food, fishing, and perhaps keeping some livestock. If he raised tobacco, he shared the plight of other planters who, by the 1630s, suffered from falling prices and competition from better-quality Virginia tobacco. James may have believed that the prosperous Hugh Wentworth, his old acquaintance— perhaps his old friend—could provide a more secure future for young Hanna. It is remotely possible that Hanna was given to Wentworth in payment of some debt owed him by James Sarnando. The Sarnandos and the Wentworths lived close to each other, no more than a mile apart. The exact locations of their respective residences in Southampton and Warwick are not known, but for nearly 20 years the two families had maintained some connection, a relationship that caused James Sarnando to seek help from Wentworth when he needed it.

Hugh Wentworth appears to have been a man of good character, honest, hard-working, and upright. In 1619 colonist Thomas Durham, in a letter to Nathaniel Rich, described Wentworth as "a very true labouringe man." By 1628 Wentworth was a tenant on Rich's land in Warwick and a councillor for that tribe. Governor Philip Bell commended him: "Upon good proofe & knowledge I finde [him] to be not only of a very good witt & understandinge fitt for buisiness, but likewise a very honest & religious man as any is in the lande."[83] At the time Hanna Sarnando was given to them, Wentworth and his wife, Mary, had four children—John, Hugh, Mary, and Sarah—all of whom were under the age of 18 in 1637, when Hugh Wentworth made his will at age 46. No doubt James and his wife were consoled by the fact that Hanna would be in a household with children near her own age. But their hopes, and Hanna's future, were abruptly changed by the death of Hugh Wentworth a few years later.

The exact date of Wentworth's death is unknown. His will is dated December 9, 1637, and an inventory of his estate appears among other documents dated 1641 and 1642.[84] The Sarnandos' presentation of Hanna to the Went-

---

83. Ives, *Rich Papers*, 175, 318. According to Wilkinson, *Adventurers*, 101, 227 n, a son of the first Lord Rich had married a Wentworth.
84. Wentworth's will and inventory are in CR, 2:62–64. John Devitt was a witness to the will. The inventory is printed in Lefroy, *Memorials*, 1:567–69. Wentworth was listed as age 44 in a roster of passengers aboard the *Truelove* in 1635. Lefroy, *Memorials*, 1:689.

worths was not recorded until June 14, 1644, when Councillor John Devitt attested to having witnessed the incident "about foure or five yeares before" Wentworth's death. By Bermuda standards Wentworth was a prosperous man. His estate, not including the two shares of land he owned in Smith's Tribe, came to £329.14.11, including "2 servants" valued at £7 and "a Negro man, and Woman," valued at £20. Hanna Sarnando, who would have been about 14 or 15 at the time of the inventory, does not appear by name. She was probably the "Negro . . . woman." But her story does not end there.

Hanna's name next appears in 1645 as part of a transaction involving a £30 debt owed by the Earl of Warwick to the owners of a pinnace called the *Dymond*. Warwick ordered his agent, Stephen Paynter, a landowner in Southampton Tribe, to satisfy the debt by delivering "three of his Lordship['s] Nigroes" to the pinnace's owners. One of these three blacks was Hanna Sarnando. Rather than deliver this girl of 15 to the owners of the pinnace, Paynter arranged for her sale to the Reverend Nathaniel White, a Puritan clergyman who had been pastor of Pembroke and Devonshire churches from 1638 to 1642. White paid £10 sterling to the pinnace's owners for "one Nigro woman named Hanna Sarnando the daughter of James Sarnando alias: olde James the Nigro." Under the terms of this sale, White was "To have & to holde the sayd Nigro woman . . . from the day of the date heerof to the end & terme of fourescore & nineteen yeares If shee shall so long live." The date was January 10, 1645/1646. Thus it happened that by the unexpected death of Hugh Wentworth, Hanna Sarnando, who was very probably the daughter of a free man and woman, was sold into lifetime servitude. How she became the property of the Earl of Warwick after Wentworth's death is not recorded. Wentworth's widow, Mary, who did not remarry until 1650, may have been obliged to sell Hanna to pay her husband's debts.[85]

Stephen Paynter, who evidently had no choice but to sell Hanna, perhaps found the best home he could for this young woman. Paynter had worked as a tenant in Southampton in 1618, where he would have known both James Sarnando and Hugh Wentworth. An agent for the Earl of Warwick since 1622, Paynter had also served with Wentworth on the Governor's Council in the 1630s. Paynter was no doubt aware of James Sarnando's gift of Hanna to

---

85. CR, 2:113. On Stephen Paynter, see Ives, *Rich Papers,* 315 n; Lefroy, *Memorials,* 1:548. Paynter was a cooper by trade. He was in Bermuda as early as 1616, recorded as serving on a jury in that year. By 1618 he was living with "his wife and famyly" on land in Southampton Tribe. Robert Rich wrote to his cousin Nathaniel in 1618 that Paynter was "a very honnest discreete and paynful [painstaking] man and hath good judgment in tobackoe." By 1620 he was representing Southampton Tribe as a member of the Governor's Council. Paynter, a Puritan, was actively involved in various religious and political controversies in Bermuda. He died February 25, 1661, having been in Bermuda for more than 45 years.

Hugh Wentworth. And Paynter, a staunch Puritan, was also close to Nathaniel White, the leader of a group of Independents who formed a separate church in Bermuda in 1644. White and his wife had three sons and a daughter, all of whom would have been younger than Hanna Sarnando at the time she came to their household. Nathaniel White owned at least one other servant, a "negro man called Tony," whom he had bought from Hugh Wentworth in 1638. In the 1640s White was embroiled in religious and political controversies that took him to England at least once and confined him to jail in Bermuda at least twice. In 1649 White and about 60 other religious dissidents were banished to the island of Eleuthera in the Bahamas. Before he left, White sold his servant Tony to a Southampton planter, John Wainwright.[86] If Nathaniel White took his family with him to Eleuthera and back, he may have taken Hanna Sarnando as well. White did not return to Bermuda until 1657.

Hanna was still living in Nathaniel White's household when he made his will in 1666. She would have been in her late thirties by then. White wrote, "I give unto my dearly beloved wife Hannah my negro woman and Samuel her youngest sonne, withal all those children that shalbe borne of her bodie which belong unto mee after my decease."[87] That White felt it necessary to add this provision, effectively extending Hanna's 99-year indenture to her children, indicates the uncertain legal status of such children at the time. White's will mentions three other blacks, two boys, Nathaniell and Richard, who might have been Hanna's older sons, and a "negroe maid called Sarah," who was probably not related to the others. Nathaniell, Richard, and Sarah were left to three of White's grown children. White also made provision for his servants' religious training, ordering that his heirs "remaine faithfull in Catechizing their negroes," none of whom, it is interesting to note, was referred to as a "slave." Nathaniel White died in 1668. From 1657 until his death he and his family lived in the parsonage on the glebe land (about 50 acres) at the west end of Southampton Tribe. As for Hanna's parents, James Sarnando and his wife, they continued to live and work at Herne Bay on the east end of Southampton, not far from the place where they began as tenants on Nathaniel Rich's land in 1618. Hanna lived not more than two miles from them. These parents had given away their daughter with the best of intentions, only to witness her descent into slavery. One cannot help wondering what would have been the feelings between a slave daughter and her free parents, and between the Sarnandos and the Whites.

86. The sale is recorded in CR, 2:146. It is likely that Tony was the "Negroe man" White had bought from Hugh Wentworth around 1638, when White first arrived in Bermuda. See CR, 2:7. On White's career, see Lefroy, *Memorials*, 1:711–13, and Hallett, *Colonial Church*, 42, 47, 50, 54.
87. White's will is in Lefroy, *Memorials*, 2:278–80.

The story of the James Sarnando family has yet another chapter. In 1648 the Earl of Warwick gave "one Negro boy about the age of six yeeres called John Sonn unto James the Negro" to Stephen Paynter.[88] There is nothing in the record of the transaction to indicate the terms of John's servitude, if any. Oddly enough, the boy was already living with the Paynters at the time. Perhaps the Sarnandos gave the child to the Paynters, as they had once given Hanna to the Wentworths. The Paynters also had in their household a one-year-old black child named Margret, the daughter of Margret, a black woman owned by the Earl of Warwick. It is possible that the mother was also living in the Paynter household, although she was the wife of a man belonging to another planter, Solomon Middleton. In 1648, at the same time that the Earl of Warwick gave the six-year-old John Sarnando to the Paynters, he also gave them Margret's one-year-old daughter. Three years later, in 1651, Paynter bought Margret (the mother) from the Earl of Warwick for £10. A few years after that, in 1658, Paynter paid Warwick £15 for "one Negro man named Josias Simon." The terms of service are not given, and it is possible that Josias Simon was sold, not as a slave for life, but as a bondservant with an unspecified term. That he had a surname suggests he was not a slave. He may have been related to the black family with the same surname in Southampton Tribe.

At the time of Stephen Paynter's death in 1661, the inventory of his estate listed Josias Simon, "Black Bess," and "Black Peg." Peg was very likely the adult Margret whom Paynter had bought 10 years earlier. His 1659 will refers to these individuals as "my servants."[89] There is no record of young John Sarnando and Margret, who would then have been ages 19 and 14, respectively. Of Josias Simon, Paynter wrote, "It is my will that in case my Negro Josias Simon doe honestlie & faithfully demene himselfe during the life of my said wife, he shall have the oversight of the Land and familie untill my Grandsonne John Painter or his heires shall come to possess it . . . and then . . . that he be for ever freed." By this provision Paynter, whose only surviving son had died sometime prior to 1659, made his black bondservant, Josias Simon, the virtual head of his household and the overseer of his two shares of land in Southampton. Simon, who may have been literate and was obviously a capable manager, was accorded a position of unusual authority in his master's family. Unfortunately there is no documentation of when Josias Simon received his freedom, or what became of him. Like Hanna Sarnando, John, and young Margret, he vanishes from the record.

While Bermuda's seventeenth-century wills and inventories provide information about the histories and households of families such as the Paynters,

88. CR, 2:64, 326.
89. Books of Wills, vol. 1, p. 69.

Wentworths, and the Whites, the history of families like the Sanderses and Sarnandos must be gleaned in bits and pieces from unexpected sources. The last known record of the Sarnando family occurs in the council minutes for August 27, 1655. On that day "it was ordered by the Gouvner & councell upon the complaint of the wife of James the negro at Herne Bay" against four white male tenants "ffor abuse and damage done to her in a royetous way or manner" that the culprits be fined 10 pounds of tobacco apiece, with 30 going to the general levy and 10 pounds "to the Negro woman." One of the four men was the Sarnandos' neighbor, John Wainwright Jr., whose family leased two shares of land bordering Herne Bay in Southampton Tribe.[90] James Sarnando's wife, whose given name does not appear in any of the records, at least received a small measure of justice from Bermuda's legal system. The Sarnandos, husband and wife, apparently lived out their lives as free people, but at least one, and perhaps two, of their children—Hanna and John—ended their lives in bondage. Nathaniel White's widow died in 1673, and there is no record of the disposition of Hanna, who would have been in her middle forties by then, or her son, Samuel, who would have been a young man in his twenties.[91] One wishes for more than these fragments of the Sarnando family's history, for in that history lies part of the fateful story of their people's transition from freedom to slavery.

While Bermuda's whites still avoided using the word *slave* until the 1670s and seemed reluctant to admit that servitude for blacks was developing into full-fledged slavery, it is clear that the colony's blacks were all too aware of their condition. By the 1640s some were trying to run away. In a place as small as Bermuda, plotting an escape was not a matter of slipping away into an uninhabited area, as slaves on the mainland or in the Caribbean might be able to do. There are no records of maroons, or fugitive slaves in hiding, in Bermuda. Concealment in a place where individual landholdings averaged 35 acres, and virtually every inch of land was occupied, would have been of short duration.[92] And running away meant stealing a boat, setting out at night, and navigating the shallow, treacherous offshore reefs that surround Bermuda. Many Bermuda blacks were skilled sailors, but the nearest land was the Outer Banks of what is now North Carolina, a voyage of 600 miles—and at least six or seven days—on the Atlantic Ocean. That daunting prospect did not discourage

90. Lefroy, *Memorials,* 2:61 (quotation), 699.
91. Mrs. White's burial is recorded in the Southampton church register, July 17, 1673. Hallett, *Early Bermuda Records,* 23.
92. A 1663 survey lists a total of 454 individuals occupying 10,309 acres as owners or tenants, with the average individual holding at 34.9 acres. CR, vol. 6. This extraordinary document, with a detailed narrative of landholdings in the entire colony, is discussed in chapter 3. It is printed in Lefroy, *Memorials,* 2:645–731.

attempts to leave the islands, however, and the first recorded runaway plot took place in 1640. In May of that year "Black Will a negro" and four white men, "Edward Godwin, Robert Byshop and Edward Vincent, labourers," and John Hopkins, whose status is not recorded, apparently planned to run away together. Their plot is evident from the goods they were accused of stealing in three separate burglaries. Besides a boat, sails, anchor, and oars, these included "Seaven old shirts, on[e] skellet, one fryeing pann one cloth suite, one knife three pounds of candles three butter jar[s], twelve pound of rosem one cedar barrell one great iron pott one wooden traye one hatchet one musket, one Calyver," fish hooks and lines, "Two hogges . . . one pecke with salt," a bellows, and two Bibles and a prayer book. All were tried for burglary and found guilty. Burglary was a felony, a capital offense, and the culprits were sentenced to death. Governor Thomas Chaddock granted reprieves to Bishop, Vincent, and Hopkins, but Black Will and Edward Godwin were hanged on October 22, 1640. It may not be coincidence that a few months earlier, while this case was pending, another runaway attempt was made. Records of the assize of October 1640 show that "Saunder [Sander] a negro and his wyfe" were each given 39 lashes for their "Attempt to run away with a Boat."[93] After this punishment the assertive Sander, mentioned earlier, continued to live in bondage in Bermuda until his death in 1648.

Running away was one response to bondage; plotting to rebel was another. Accounts of runaways and rebels are scattered throughout the Caribbean colonies in the seventeenth century, in England's mainland colonies by the eighteenth century, and in the American South by the nineteenth century. Bermuda, on the other hand, has a somewhat different history. While other slave societies experienced more rather than fewer slave uprisings as time passed, and while the American, French, and Haitian revolutions spread ideas of liberty, Bermuda has no recorded slave rebellions after 1761. This island colony does have an earlier history of organized slave resistance, and the reasons for a relative calm after the 1760s have to do with the unique nature of Bermuda's multiracial society in the eighteenth century.

Bermuda's first recorded rebellion plot occurred in 1656, 40 years after the arrival of the first black in the colony. By then there were perhaps 200 or 300 blacks in a total population of approximately 3,000.[94] It is not known whether the instigators of the plot were creoles (second-generation blacks born in the islands) or recent arrivals from the West Indies. It is unlikely that they were Africans, since few Bermudian blacks came directly from Africa.

93. See assize of October 6, 1640, CR, 1:189.
94. A report to the Council of State, October 7, 1656, estimated Bermuda's population at 3,000, including 1,500 men able to bear arms. Lefroy, *Memorials*, 2:87.

In all probability the would-be rebels in Bermuda had heard tales of other revolts on other islands where there were many more blacks. In the sugar islands of the Caribbean, newly arrived Africans as well as acclimated ones were likely to plot violence against whites. The island colony of Barbados, for example, founded in 1627, had an attempted slave uprising in 1634 in which one slave was executed, and another rebellion in 1649 took the lives of 18 slaves.[95] The English settlement on Providence Island, founded in 1631, experienced an abortive rebellion in 1638, though it, like Bermuda, had only a few hundred blacks. The English on Providence Island were swift to retaliate: They executed 50 blacks. Afterward, some of Providence Island's suspected rebels were deported to the English colony of St. Kitts—and to Bermuda. Since an unknown number of Bermudian blacks had emigrated to Providence along with their masters when Governor Philip Bell took office there in 1631, some of the returning rebels could well have been Bermudians.[96] At any rate, Bermuda's blacks would certainly have heard stories of the Providence Island rebellion.

While Providence Island had a slave rebellion seven years after its founding, Bermuda's first recorded rebellion plot was much later, nearly four decades after the initial settlement. In the summer or fall of 1656, 10 black servants (their status, bondservant or slave, is not clear from the records) and a free black named William Force were accused of contriving a "conspiracy and plott" for "cutting off and the distroieing the English in the night." The plot "being cleerely manifested" (although the record does not say how), the 10 conspirators were tried by a court martial on November 2, 1656.[97] The accused men included Black Tom, belonging to Captain Thomas Burrows of Hamilton Tribe; Cabilecto, whose master was Gilbert Hill of Warwick; Frank Jeames (whose surname suggests that he was not a slave), belonging to John Devitt of Warwick; a man named Tony and one whose name is undecipherable in the records, who both belonged to Captain Christopher Lea of Warwick. Four of these conspirators lived close to each other, perhaps no more than half a mile apart, in Warwick Tribe. Three of the other conspirators may also have lived close to each other: Black Robin was the property of Joseph Wiseman of Devonshire; Black Harry and Black Jack belonged respectively to Jonathan Turner and a man named Longson (Longstone), both of whom lived in Devonshire Tribe in 1663, and who probably lived there in 1656. Black Anthony, a slave of Richard Hunt's (and thus a neighbor of Marmaduke

95. Carl Bridenbaugh, *No Peace beyond the Line: The English in the Caribbean, 1624–1690* (New York: Oxford University Press, 1972), 108.

96. Kupperman, *Providence Island,* 170–71.

97. CR, vol. 3. The record of the trial is printed in Lefroy, *Memorials,* 2:95–96.

Dando) lived in Southampton Tribe. The residence of the tenth conspirator, the free black named William Force, is unknown. He had been in Bermuda since at least 1638, when he was whipped for fathering a bastard child by a black woman named Maria. Black Jack may also have had a prior offense: He was probably the "Black Jacke a negro" who was sentenced to death in 1640 for stealing one silver dollar and one shilling "of current money," a fish line and hooks, and three tobacco pipes worth five shillings, sixpence. In that case the Governor remitted the death penalty and exacted a fine of 500 pounds of tobacco from his master.[98]

In the ensuing conspiracy trial, three of the men, Jack, Harry, and the one whose name is undecipherable, were found to be "instruments of the discovery of the plott in general" and thus judged "worthy of the favor of life."[99] Also reprieved were Frank Jeames, Tony, Robin, and Anthony. But "2 of the chiefe actors"—Black Tom and Cabilecto—and William Force were sentenced to hang. Their executioner may have been a black man: In 1652 a "negro man, servant unto John Young" was sentenced to death for stealing a piece of red cotton cloth from John Smith, another planter, but the council pardoned him and instead "made [him] common executioner upon his amendment of life." Although the prospect of slave rebellion frightened Bermuda's white community, and three blacks were hanged in this case, the response to attempted revolts and other acts of resistance was generally milder than in other slave societies. Whites in Virginia, for example, in retaliation for a 1663 slave rebellion, left an exhibit of "several bloody heads" on chimney tops, and in New York in 1712 the convicted slave rebels were burned at the stake, hanged, "broke on the wheel," and "hung a live in chains."[100]

In Bermuda the involvement of four blacks from Warwick Tribe, together with others from at least three different tribes several miles apart, suggests a network of clandestine communications whose extent cannot be known but whose existence invites speculation about the black community in Bermuda. Did blacks from several tribes often meet each other, with or without their masters' knowledge? Did they walk to such meetings, or did they use their masters' boats without permission? Did some know each other because they

98. The location of residences in this case are based on references in the individuals' wills and on Richard Norwood's survey of the colony, published in 1663. In some cases this study assumes that certain individuals' residences were in the same place in 1656 as in 1663 or earlier. Thomas Burrows's 1658 will, for example, places him in Hamilton in that year. Books of Wills, vol. 1, p. 51; Lefroy, *Memorials*, 1:563. On William Force and Maria, see assize of November 27–30, 1638, ibid., 550.

99. Assize of 1652, CR, vol. 1; see also Lefroy, *Memorials*, 2:35.

100. On the black executioner, see assize of December 7, 1652, CR, vol. 3, n.p., printed in extract in Lefroy, *Memorials*, 2:35. On the slave revolts, see Herbert Aptheker, *American Negro Slave Revolts* (New York: Columbia University Press, 1943), 165, 173.

routinely came into contact on business for their masters? It is likely that all of the above could be answered in the affirmative. As far as can be determined, all of the blacks involved in the conspiracy of 1656 belonged to men best described as Bermuda's emerging elite: sea captains, merchants, and traders, some of whom were active in public life as councillors, jurors, or holders of other minor offices. All of these men would have known each other; hence it is likely that their servants also knew each other. The servants no doubt ran errands and carried messages for their masters, who were connected to each other in the emerging network of trading and shipping interests.

The majority of the conspirators, with the exception of William Force, the free black, came from households where there were several other blacks—men, women, and children. Captain Thomas Burrows had at least five blacks at his death in 1658; Gilbert Hill had at least four at his death in 1667; John Devitt, whose will has not survived, is known to have purchased two blacks and an Indian (Christopher Marteene, mentioned earlier) prior to 1656; Captain Christopher Lea's 1664 inventory refers to his "6 Negroes"; Joseph Wiseman's 1671 will names five blacks—three boys and two "old Negroes" (Robin was not named). Richard Hunt's 1683 will mentions "servants" (the only one mentioned by name is Anthony, who may have been one of the 1656 conspirators).[101] Thus it is likely that some or all of the conspirators had families, yet they were nonetheless prepared to risk their lives in pursuit of freedom. At least one, and perhaps two, of them—William Force and Frank Jeames—were not slaves but men who willingly put their lives in jeopardy to join the rebels. The timing of their attempted rebellion may have been dictated by events outside their control but upon which they decided to act.

At the time of the rebellion plot, social order in the colony had barely recovered from the turmoil of the witchcraft scare. The last condemned witch had been hanged in January 1655/1656, 10 months before the slave conspiracy. Governor Josias Forster, who presided over the witchcraft trials, was also the presiding judge during the conspiracy trial. The witchcraft hangings had all taken place at the capital, St. George's, but in the conspiracy case Forster ordered three separate locations for the executions, perhaps to send a colony-wide warning of the punishments awaiting rebels—or perhaps to avoid a large, unruly crowd at one site. Tom was hanged in St. George's, and Cabilecto's execution took place at a gibbet set up on nearby Cobler's Island. For William Force, however, a third gibbet was erected at Herne Bay in Southampton Tribe, some 15 miles from St. George's. James Sarnando and his wife, who

101. Burrows's will is in Books of Wills, vol. 1, p. 51; for Hill, see ibid., 111; on Devitt, see CR, 2:304. Lea's will is in Books of Wills, vol. 1, p. 92; Wiseman's is in Books of Wills, vol. 1, p. 195; Hunt's, in Books of Wills, vol. 3, pt. 1, p. 1.

lived at Herne Bay, were probably witnesses to William Force's ordeal. The free black was taken there for questioning, "wher yt was hoped he would have confessed the plott amongst the negroes." Force may have lived in the Herne Bay neighborhood.[102] Although he was threatened and perhaps tortured (the record states that "he was putt to it to the uttermost"), Force refused to confess any details of the plot. The governor, perhaps impressed with his fortitude, granted him a reprieve, banishing him to the island of Eleuthera.[103]

What became of William Force, or any of the other free blacks reportedly shipped to this island in the Bahamas, is not known. The history of Bermudians at Eleuthera began in 1649 when the royalist faction in Bermuda banished about 70 Puritans, including the dissident clergymen, Nathaniel White and Patrick Copeland, to that island under the leadership of William Sayle, a former governor of Bermuda. A number of free blacks were sent there as well. Some of the Eleuthera group returned to Bermuda in 1650, and Bermuda acknowledged Cromwell's Puritan Commonwealth in 1652. In 1655 Nathaniel White and some others were invited back. A few Bermudians remained at Eleuthera in the 1650s, and others joined them later. In the summer of 1660, for example, three couples (two with children) and two single men, all whites, and "Allen a Molatto," apparently a free man, sailed to Eleuthera aboard the Bermuda ship *William*.[104] The Puritan faction held sway there until the Restoration.

Despite his clemency toward William Force, Governor Forster took stringent measures in response to the November 1656 conspiracy. On November 6, four days after the trial, he issued a proclamation whose wording suggests the government's unsuccessful efforts at social control:

> It is knowne . . . that ther hath bin great care taken . . . by the Government here, for the suppressing of the insolencies of the negroes amongst us, and for restreineing them from night walking and meeting together . . . hoping that every man would have bin a fellow helper in such cases as these: but falling out otherwise And these negroes seeing a general neglect, hath taken courage thereby to conspier the ruin of the whole body of these Islands, had not the Lord out of his goodnes and mercie opened the mouth of some amongst themselves to the discovery thereof.[105]

In an effort to prevent such conspiracies in the future, the governor issued a proclamation stating that blacks out at night ("halfe an hour after the setting

102. A free black woman named Anne Force lived in Southampton in 1672. She was very likely related to Force and may have been the child he fathered in 1638. See Lefroy, *Memorials*, 1:550.

103. Ibid., 2:95. On the history of the Eleuthera venture, see 2:10–12, 20, 84, 89, 98; *Journal of John Winthrop*, 351–52. See also Michael Craton and Gail Saunders, *Islanders in the Stream: A History of the Bahamian People* (Athens, Ga.: University of Georgia Press, 1992). See also Wilkinson, *Adventurers*, 280–89, 290–96.

104. CR, Fragmentary Book G, Shipping Register, 1656–1671, n.p. See also CR, 2:350.

105. Lefroy, *Memorials*, 2:95–96.

of the sunne") without a pass or a ticket from their masters could be killed "then & thiere without mercye."[106] In an attempt to discipline whites as well as blacks, the governor further decreed that any white person who came upon a fugitive black after dark and did not pursue him or her, or report the incident to the authorities, was to be fined 100 pounds of tobacco. No blacks were to trade with any "merchant or other man or woman," and all "owners of negros" were to see that they attended church on Sundays. Moreover, all free black men and women were to be banished from the colony. Clearly the influence of free blacks such as William Force was perceived as dangerous. Like him, a number of other free blacks were banished to Eleuthera in the 1650s.

One of the conspirators of 1656, Anthony, a slave belonging to Richard Hunt, may have been given his freedom more than 30 years later. Richard Hunt's 1683 will leaves an undetermined number of slaves to his wife, Frances, during her lifetime, who were to be divided among his three sons at her death—all but his "Negroe Man Anthony," who, he wrote, " shall bee sett free at the Expiration of Six Months after my aforesead wife's decease." Hunt died in 1687; Frances Hunt was still living in 1688. If the slave Anthony was in fact the conspirator of 1656, he would have been an old man by the time he received his freedom—if, in fact, he did. Ironically, Thomas Burrows, whose slave Tom was executed, freed two of his other slaves: On March 12, 1658/1659 he wrote in his will, "My Negro Francis & his wife to be freed" upon the death of his wife, Ellen. Captain Thomas Burrows died a few days later. In April 1659, about a month after her husband's death, Ellen Burrows was drowned near the family residence. Her death took place under somewhat mysterious circumstances, but a coroner's inquest ruled that the death of Thomas Burrows's widow by drowning was accidental. Under the terms of Burrows's will, the slave Francis and his wife would then have received their freedom.[107]

The man known as Frank Jeames, who was another of the conspirators of 1656 and who belonged to John Devitt of Warwick, was probably the "black ffranke a negro servant to Mr. John Devitt" who was involved in a later runaway attempt in 1658 with three other blacks and four whites. In September of that year, Frank joined Tomakin, Clemento, and Dick, blacks belonging to a widow in Paget Tribe, Mrs. Anne Trimingham, along with four white men (including two Irishmen and a Scotsman) in stealing a boat and two sails. The whites are identified as "servants," but their masters are not named. The blacks belonged to prominent white masters: Devitt was a

106. Ibid.
107. For Richard Hunt's will, see Books of Wills, vol. 3, pt. 1, p. 1. On Thomas Burrows, see ibid., vol. 1, p. 51; CR, 2:317.

former councillor from Warwick Tribe; Anne Trimingham was the widow of John Trimingham, "Gent.," a wealthy landowner in Paget Tribe, who had died in 1656. Like the earlier conspiracy plot, this runaway plan involved at least four men who lived near each other: Tomakin, Clemento, and Dick lived in Paget Tribe near Crow Lane harbor; Frank, in Warwick, lived less than a mile away. The residences of the four white men are not known. In the trial that followed, the accused were found to be not guilty. Yet the governor and council, "knowing them to be night walkers, and out of their masters and mistresses House that night," voted unanimously to give the offenders, blacks and whites, each 31 lashes "upon their naked backes." This punishment was administered on the following day.[108]

John Devitt's slave, Frank, had failed in both a rebellion and a runaway attempt, but he was not the only rebellious slave in Devitt's household. In December 1658 "John a negro man servant" belonging to Devitt was accused of murdering a white man named John Harper. He was tried and found guilty, but his sentence is not recorded in the existing trial record.[109] One cannot help wondering what John Devitt's other slaves or bondservants thought of Frank and John. Devitt had bought a boy, Peter, from Hugh Wentworth in 1637, and a woman, Grace, from John Stowe in 1648. That year Devitt had also purchased the aforementioned Indian, Christopher Marteene.

In 1659 another of the Trimingham family's blacks was involved in a runaway scheme: Plenthento, a man belonging to Anne Trimingham's son, Paul, was one of seven black sailors who, on a voyage to England, managed to escape from a vessel owned by Bermuda merchant Anthony Peniston. How they accomplished this remarkable escape is not recorded. One account says that they "ran away from the Islands and landed in England." Four of the blacks—Salvadoro and his son, Samuel, "whan (qu. Juan) als. John," and John Devale—belonged to Peniston; another, Anthonie, was the property of Bermuda colonist Thomas Griffin. Anthony Peniston, from whose vessel they escaped, petitioned the Somers Islands Company to aid in their capture in England. The runaways were apprehended near Plymouth, returned to London, and sent back to Bermuda. There is no record of punishment for these men, but their masters were obliged to pay the Somers Islands Company £20.12s per man (as much or more than the price of an able-bodied male slave) to cover the expense of capturing the runaways.[110]

The attempted runaway schemes of 1640, 1658, and 1659, as well as the 1656 rebellion plot, suggest not only a network of communication between

108. Lefroy, *Memorials*, 2:115.
109. Ibid., 115–16.
110. *CSP*, 1574–1660:476; Lefroy, *Memorials*, 2:127–28, 153.

slaves and servants belonging to different masters but also a knowledge of the wider transatlantic world outside Bermuda that in itself could inspire resistance to slavery. The blacks who served as sailors on Bermuda vessels making voyages to the English colonies on the mainland and in the West Indies as well as to England had access, albeit limited, to knowledge gained from other slaves and from sailors—white and black—in the ports they visited.[111] News from other colonies, as well as from the mother country, circulated easily in Bermuda, which was becoming an important part of trade between the growing English settlements on the mainland of North America and in the Caribbean. News from the mother country also came by sea to Bermuda, along with an undetermined number of Irish captives from Cromwell's conquest of Ireland. During the English Civil War between 1649 and 1655 some 12,000 political prisoners from England, Scotland, and Ireland were sent to English colonies in the Lesser Antilles. Some of these, sold into servitude in Bermuda, mingled with blacks and exacerbated whites' fears of another rebellion plot. That fear, as it turned out, was not unfounded.[112]

Anxieties over the prospect of a collaboration between Irish and black servants prompted several actions by Bermuda's officials in the late 1650s. At an assize court of 1657 the grand jury warned all owners of Irish servants to "take care that they straggle not night nor daie, as is too common with them." That same year Bermuda colonists were forbidden "to buy or purchase any more of the Irish nation upon any pretence whatsoever." Masters and mistresses of Irish servants were ordered to bring them to church on the Sabbath, where they should be "made to stay eyther abroad or in the church during the time of exercise." Like the Irish, some of Bermuda's blacks were newly arrived as well and may have caused further apprehension. A shipping register shows that in September 1659 Captain John Stowe's ship, the *Elizabeth and Anne,* brought "from Barbados 32 negroes"—presumably to sell in Bermuda. A year later the *Elizabeth and Anne* made another run to Barbados, this time bringing more blacks, with their disposition clearly stated. The shipping register for Stowe's vessel December 1660 carries the notation, "sells 3 negroes."[113] What became of these Barbadian blacks in Bermuda is not recorded, but some of them may have been involved in a rebellion plot the following year.

---

111. The network of transatlantic communication among black sailors in the seventeenth century has been largely unexplored. Ira Berlin suggests some of its implications in "From Creole to African." Jeffrey Bolster, *Black Jacks: African American Seamen in the Age of Sail* (Cambridge: Harvard University Press, 1997), makes a good beginning. See also Julius S. Scott, "Crisscrossing Empires: Ships, Sailors, and Resistance in the Lesser Antilles in the Eighteenth Century," in *Lesser Antilles,* ed. Paquette and Engerman, 128–43.

112. On the Irish, see Lefroy, *Memorials,* 2:103, and John Appleby, "English Settlement of the Lesser Antilles in War and Peace," in *Lesser Antilles,* ed. Paquette and Engerman, 86–104, esp. 101.

113. Shipping Register, 1656–1671. See also Lefroy, *Memorials,* 1:728–29.

In October 1661 an unnamed informant told Governor William Sayle and his council of "a dangerous plott or combination by the Irish and Negroes." Upon hearing of the suspected plot, Governor Sayle issued a proclamation declaring that "if the said Irish cannot have their ffreedom their intentions are . . . to cutt the throats of our Englishmen." Sayle's proclamation did not reveal the details of the Irish and black conspirators' plot, and there is no record of any trial. But the governor ordered night watches to be kept in every tribe, instructed militia officers to disarm the Irish in their trained bands, and "likewise to find out what armes anie Negroes have in their custodie, and to disarm them." Negroes and Irish found meeting together, "if but to the number of two or three," were to be "whipped from Constable to Constable whilst they run home to their Masters houses."[114]

Not until the 1660s, after several runaway attempts and two slave rebellion plots, did Bermuda' lawmakers attempt to define the slave's position. By that time the institution of slavery was well established in Bermuda's sister colonies in the Caribbean: St. Christoper (St. Kitts), settled by the English in 1624, Barbados (1627), Nevis (1628), Montserrat and Antigua (1632), and Jamaica (1655). By the 1660s slave codes in Barbados and Jamaica set forth the conditions that would bind both masters and slaves for nearly two centuries.[115] In Bermuda, when circumstances called for more stringent laws governing blacks, the language used by Bermuda's legislators shows little of the racial bias evident in the slave laws of the other English colonies. While the Barbados slave code of 1661 defined blacks as "an heathenish, brutish and an uncertaine dangerous kinde of people," and a South Carolina law defined them as having "barbarous, wild, savage natures," the worst that Bermuda's lawmakers could say of blacks was that they were "insolent" and "not ffree."

In 1663 the Bermuda Assembly, still avoiding the word *slave*, drafted a series of laws dealing with the colony's blacks. The first is an expanded version of the "Act to restrayne the insolencies of the Negroes," passed 40 years earlier:

> Wee the Generall Assembly having received severall Complaints of the insolent carriage of Negroes Molattoes & Musteses, have enacted . . . for the time to come that such persons as count themselves ffree because noe pticler masters claymeth

114. Lefroy, *Memorials,* 2:159, 160.
115. On the Barbados slave code, see Dunn, *Sugar and Slaves,* 238–46 (quotation, p. 238). See also Hilary Beckles, *White Servitude and Black Slavery in Barbados, 1627–1715* (Knoxville: University of Tennessee Press, 1989). The South Carolina law is quoted in John Boles, *Black Southerners, 1619–1869* (Lexington, Ky.: University of Kentucky Press, 1983), 23. On the history of the Caribbean colonies, see David Watts, *The West Indies: Patterns of Development, Culture, and Environmental Change since 1492* (Cambridge, Eng.: Cambridge University Press, 1990); Bridenbaugh, *No Peace beyond the Line;* Alan Cuthbert Burns, *History of the British West Indies* (London: Allen and Unwin, 1965); A. P. Newton, *The European Nations in the West Indies, 1493–1688* (1933; reprint, New York: Barnes and Noble, 1967); Vincent T. Harlow, ed., *Colonising Expeditions to the West Indies and Guiana, 1623–1667* (London: Hakluyt Society, 1925).

their service, yet in our judgments are not ffree to all nationall priviledges: If any such persons shall carie themselves and behave themselves mutinous or proudly against his Majesties Subjects: after conviction of the same, it shalbe lawfull for the Governor & Councell to Subject them to the service of the Colony or perpetuall banishment.[116]

After nearly two generations of contact among whites, blacks, and Indians, the reference to "molattoes & musteses" testifies to the frequency of their mixed-race unions. Bermudians apparently used *mustee* to identify the children of an English father and an Indian mother, although it could also have referred to the issue of an Indian/black union. In 1663 the Assembly at last found it necessary to draft a law against miscegenation: "If any of his Majesties free borne subjects . . . shall presume to Mary with, or have any carnall Copulation with any Negroes, Molattoes or Musteses, then after conviction, they are to bee subjected to the Colony, or be banished."[117] In stronger language, a Virginia law of 1691 "for prevention of that abominable mixture and spurious issue which hereafter may increase in this dominion," forbade the marriage of any English colonist to any "negro, mulatto, or Indian, bond or free."[118] In Virginia an English woman who bore a child of mixed race was to be fined £15 or, in the case of an indentured servant, to serve five years more. In Virginia, as was sometimes the case in Bermuda, such children were bound out until the age of 30. Another Bermuda law required all blacks "that have bin heretofore servants to any of the Inhabitants, and are now out of their times" (that is, free from servitude) to leave the colony after one year or "become Colony servants for ever." Some of those individuals may have been the blacks Captain William Jackson had brought in 1644. With terms of seven years, they would have been free in 1651 and may have been living as free people in Bermuda for more than a decade. Now some of them were liable to become servants "for ever." After nearly a half-century of contact between blacks and whites, and at least two decades of issuing 99-year indentures to blacks, white Bermudians were still reluctant to adopt the word *slave* to define the status of such individuals.

Two other acts passed in 1663 are reiterations of the 1623 legislation, and they are also indicative of the wide perimeters of activities engaged in by blacks in the islands. One act forbids whites to barter or trade with blacks and fines masters who "give lisence to their negroes molattoes or musteses To plant Tobacco & trade or barter awaie the same." The other act is an attempt to

116. CR, Fragmentary Book H, Acts of the General Assembly, January 27, 1662/1663, n.p.

117. In the British West Indies there were no laws against miscegenation. See Jordan, *White over Black,* 139–40. In Massachusetts racial intermarriage was not illegal until 1705, but there was apparently no practice of it earlier. See Twombly and Moore, "Black Puritan," 230.

118. Hening, *Statutes,* 3:86–87. In 1644 a similar law in Antigua forbade "Carnall Coppullation between Christian and Heathen," with the children born to such unions to be freed at age 21. By 1672 such children were enslaved for life. Dunn, *Sugar and Slaves,* 228.

restrict the "evill events of Negroes, Molattoes or Musteses walking abroad on nights and meeting together, Notwithstanding many Proclamations made for restraint." The authors of this legislation complained that "execution which is the life of the law" was "often omitted." Blacks abroad at night without a "ticket from their masters or mistresses" were to be "well whipped" (the number of lashes is unspecified), and officials who failed to enforce this law were to be fined 10 shillings.[119]

Even after the passage of racially restrictive laws in the 1660s, the status of Bermuda's blacks, and the attitudes of whites toward them, remained ambiguous. For example, after taking action to disarm all blacks in 1661 when some were reportedly plotting rebellion with the Irish, the Assembly ordered five years later, in 1666, that "Negroe men and Boyes . . . with what Weapons they think meet, or with Hoes, hachetts, axes, bills or the like," were to serve with the militia.[120] In Massachusetts a 1656 law prohibited Indians and blacks from serving in the militia, and in Virginia and the other mainland colonies blacks were forbidden to carry weapons and generally barred from military service except in dire emergencies. In Bermuda, as some of the runaways and rebellion plots and the witchcraft trials involving whites and blacks suggest, class, not race, was often a defining factor as servants, slaves, and sometimes free men plotted ways to resist bondage. But slavery, whether by name or by a 99-year indenture, was by the 1660s as firmly established in Bermuda as it was in England's other colonies. Meanwhile, white Bermudians' behavior toward the growing number of blacks, mulattos, and Indians, not to mention the Irish and a few Scots in their midst, varied with individuals. Enforcement of the law, as always, was lax: Mulatto infants continued to be born; blacks continued to engage in trade; free blacks, mulattos, Indians, and mustees continued to reside in the islands. The reasons for these conditions may be found in a further exploration of the colony's economic and social history in the seventeenth century.

119. Lefroy, *Memorials*, 2:190, 191.
120. Ibid., 242. A bill was a long staff with a curved blade or hook at the end.

3 Too Little Land, Too Many Slaves

By the middle of the seventeenth century, as England's other colonies promised vast reaches of land for settlement, Bermuda, whose strategic location in England's colonial empire had moved John Smith to call it "an excellent bit, to rule a great horse," was all but forgotten. By the 1630s all of the available land was taken up, and some English settlers moved to other colonies in search of better opportunities. Besides those who went to Providence Island in 1631, about 130 moved to St. Lucia in 1638. Other colonists, "straitened for want of land and liberties," planned to move to St. Lucia in 1639 but were prevented from doing so by the Somers Islands Company, whose officials claimed that the migrants to St. Lucia had left "without provision or Ammunition befitting a Plantation" and had been "Assaulted by the Savidges." There were some 400 or 500 more Bermudians eager to move, and the Company petitioned for land for them in Virginia.[1]

Although it had ceased to attract new colonists, Bermuda had something that no other seventeenth-century English colony had: a thriving creole, or native-born, acculturated slave population that was growing larger through natural increase.[2] Unlike the mainland and Caribbean colonies, Bermuda alone had a population of healthy blacks who began to establish families and bear children in the first generation. Although Bermuda's fragmentary sources do not allow a demographic analysis of any precision, records in the Southampton church register, beginning in 1619, testify to the growth of families. From 1619 through 1630, or roughly the first generation of colonists, 45 births were recorded. According to the census of 1622, Southampton Tribe had 71 able-bodied men and 53 women and children. For the first 40 years, from 1619 through 1659, the births of 113 white infants—52 females and 61 males—were recorded in Southampton Tribe, as well as 14 black infants—10 females and four males—and one mulatto infant, a girl.[3] Besides a substantial

1. John Smith's observation is in Barbour, ed., *Complete Works*, 3:220. On the migration to St. Lucia, see Golding, *Servants on Horseback*, 189, Lefroy, *Memorials*, 1:557–58, and Wilkinson, *Adventurers*, 261–62.
2. Craton, "Reluctant Creoles," argues that Barbados was the first "creolized" colony in the British Caribbean, but Craton's argument is applied to whites, not blacks, and does not take into account Bermuda, settled some years before Barbados.
3. Southampton church register, in Hallett, *Early Bermuda Records*, 2–16.

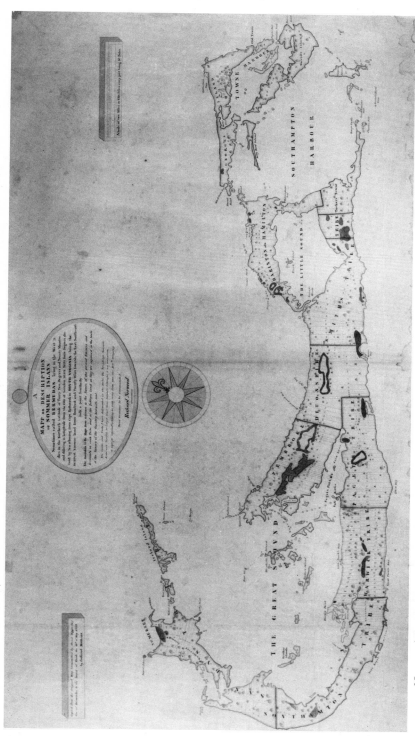

Norwood Survey Map, 1663 (Bermuda Archives: Collection).

number of creoles the rest of Bermuda's black population came mostly from the West Indies, not directly from Africa, and thus were already familiar with European ways. They did not come as outsiders to an unfamiliar culture as did the thousands of Africans who were brought to the Caribbean and to North America. The fact that Bermuda's acculturated population of blacks, Indians, mulattos, and mustees—nearly 3,000 by the 1670s—lived almost elbow to elbow with over 4,000 whites in an area of only 21 square miles would make · the history of slavery and race relations in Bermuda quite different from that of England's other colonies. More than most places, Bermuda's history has been shaped by its geography.

For whites and blacks alike this island colony was one of the most healthful places in the New World. Bermuda's water came from fresh-water wells and rainwater; it had no rivers to be contaminated by sewage and other organic waste. The warm climate and proximity to the sea encouraged swimming and bathing, fostering personal hygiene in an era when bathing, especially by immersing the body in water, was not a common experience for Europeans. Bermuda's remote location kept the colony free of malaria-bearing mosquitoes and contagious diseases, and its mild weather mitigated fevers and agues. Early observers of Bermuda commented upon its salubrious environment. In 1622, for example, Governor Nathaniel Butler wrote of the curative powers of the climate for a shipload of sickly immigrants: "In a fewe weekes . . . this dreadfull infection wholy ceased . . . for well knowne it is, that diseases (unless meerely accidentall) are strangely and, indeed, wonderfully rare and uncommon here." John Smith, writing in 1629, found the air "very healthfull and apt for the generation and nourishing of all things, so as many things transported from hence yeeld a farre greater increase, and if it be any living thing it becomes fatter and better."[4]

In contrast to the high mortality rates among settlers in the early Chesapeake and Caribbean colonies, people in Bermuda generally lived long and healthy lives. Bermuda colonist Richard Stafford remarked upon that fact in a report to the Royal Society in 1668: "As to the Age of our Inhabitants here . . . many live till they are nigh a hundred, but few above: And when they dye, 'tis age and weakness, that is the cause, and not any disease that attends them. The general distemper that is yearly amongst us, is a Cold; and that is most gotten in the hottest weather." In 1669 Governor John Heydon reported an outbreak of smallpox at St. George's, forcing the Assembly to hold its June meeting in Paget, but the disease apparently did not spread.[5] In 1687 Governor Robert Robinson reported to the secretary of the Lords

4. Butler, *Bermudaes*, 205; Barbour, ed., *Complete Works*, 2:340.
5. Stafford's letter is in Lefroy, *Memorials*, 2:265. Heydon's report is in CR, 7:209.

of Trade and Plantations, "There is no accustomary Disease here. . . . Here are no Venomous creatures nor Poisonous herbs known to grow."[6] Except for a brief outbreak of smallpox at St. George's in 1669 and a yellow fever epidemic in 1692, Bermuda was free of contagious diseases until the end of the seventeenth century and, despite the occasional epidemic, remained a notably healthier place than Britain's Caribbean colonies. In 1724 Governor John Bruce Hope wrote that the "air of this place alone cures those very distempers of the most virulent nature" common to the West Indies.[7]

The healthy effects of Bermuda's environment can be measured by the high birthrate and by the colony's low mortality rate. A 1679 report to the Privy Council estimated that for the previous seven years "about one hundred and twenty of Whites, Blacks, and Mulattos" had been born each year and "about twenty persons a year" died, in a total population of approximately 8,000.[8] In contrast, a similar report for Barbados in 1679 recorded 630 baptisms and 1,058 burials in a population of approximately 43,000.[9] The Bermuda census of 1698 shows a death rate of 13 deaths per 1,000 population; Barbados for the same period had a death rate of 33.7 per 1,000. Among England's mainland colonies, New Jersey, the only colony with comparable census data for this period, had a mortality rate of 15 to 20 per 1,000.[10] Bermuda's demographic history is strikingly different from that of both the mainland and the Caribbean colonies. In the seventeenth-century Chesapeake colonies, slave women bore few children. The low birthrate was due either to poor health from the hardships of African migration and the Middle Passage or to a conscious effort on the part of slaves to limit childbirths as a protest against enslavement. Similarly low birthrates in South Carolina and Georgia impaired the formation of slave families.[11] In the Caribbean colonies, hard labor, malnutrition, unsanitary living conditions, and a fragmented family life kept the slave population from reproducing itself. In the Caribbean, death rates for blacks and whites far exceeded the birth rate,

6. Letter of Governor Robert Robinson to William Blathwayt, Secretary, Lords of Trade and Plantations, June 11, 1687, printed in Council minutes, *BHQ* 2, no. 1 (1945): 14–19 (quotation, p. 16).

7. Governor John Bruce Hope to the Council of Trade and Plantations, January 14, 1724/1725, in CO 37/11: 46.

8. Lefroy, *Memorials*, 2:432.

9. *CSP*, 1677–1680:508. On the population growth in Barbados, see Walvin, *Black Ivory*, 105, and Engerman, "Lesser Antilles," 157–59.

10. Robert V. Wells, *The Population of the British Colonies in America before 1776: A Survey of Census Data* (Princeton: Princeton University Press, 1975), 141–42, 181, 196, 239, 250–51.

11. See Kulikoff, *Tobacco and Slaves*, 11, 69; Wood, *Slavery in Colonial Georgia*, 105–6; B. W. Higman, *Slave Populations in the British Caribbean* (Baltimore: Johns Hopkins University Press, 1984), 397. For a general discussion of slave population growth in the mainland colonies, see Peter Kolchin, *American Slavery, 1619–1877* (New York: Hill and Wang, 1993), 34–40.

and in Virginia the mortality rate remained high throughout the seventeenth century.[12]

In Bermuda, births far exceeded deaths in both the black and white populations. In 1691 Governor Isaac Richier reported a white population of 4,331 whites and 1,917 blacks. Of these, 960 whites and 562 blacks were males over the age of 15. The white population figure dropped sharply in 1692 when a yellow fever epidemic struck the islands, and it was reported that "a violent and Malignant ffeavor tooke away more then one fourth part of ye people."[13] The epidemic appears to have been far more devastating to the whites than to the nonwhites. A census of 1698 reports 3,615 whites, a loss of over 16 percent, while the nonwhite population stood at 2,247, an increase of 17 percent.[14] By the end of the seventeenth century nonwhites—"Negroes, Mulattoes, and Indians"—made up 38 percent of Bermuda's population.

On the North American mainland, blacks were a decided minority in the seventeenth century, while in the Caribbean islands the reverse was true. In 1660, for example, the total population of England's mainland colonies—New Hampshire, Massachusetts, Connecticut, Rhode Island, Delaware, New York, New Jersey, Virginia, Maryland, and North Carolina—was approximately 75,500, but blacks numbered only about 3,000, or less than 4 percent of the population. Of an estimated 2,920 blacks in North America in 1660, some 1,708 lived in Virginia and Maryland, the tobacco-growing colonies of the Chesapeake. Until the eighteenth century, white indentured servants far outnumbered blacks in the mainland colonies' labor force. On the other hand, England's Caribbean colonies—St. Christopher (St. Kitts), Barbados, Nevis, Montserrat, Antigua, and Jamaica—had far more blacks than whites by the 1670s. Barbados was the fastest-growing of England's island colonies. In 1643 it had a population of approximately 31,000: 25,000 whites and 6,000 blacks; by 1660 the population stood at 53,300, with 26,200 whites and 27,100 blacks.[15] By the turn of the century there would be more than 130,000 blacks in the Caribbean colonies, with whites a small minority: a ratio of one white to every four blacks in Barbados, one to seven in the Leeward Islands, and one to 10 in Jamaica.[16] At this same time, according to the 1698 census, Bermuda had approximately three whites to every two blacks. The

12. For a discussion of mortality rates in the West Indies, see Dunn, *Sugar and Slaves*, 300–334. For Virginia, see Morgan, *American Slavery*, 158–63.

13. Report of Thomas Burton, June 25, 1700, Colonial Office Papers, Public Record Office, Kew, Eng. (hereafter, CO), CO 37/3: 136. See also Lt. Col. C. M. Hughes-Hallett, "Yellow Fever," *BHQ* 11, no. 2 (1954): 101–4.

14. Richier's 1691 report is in Council minutes, *BHQ* 3, no. 1 (1946): 15–24. See also *BHQ* 3, no. 2 (1946): 63–73.

15. See Greene, *Pursuits of Happiness*, 178.

16. Dunn, *Sugar and Slaves*, 316.

black population grew to 47 percent of the total by the 1770s, but whites remained a narrow majority until the next century. Bermuda did not have a majority of blacks until the early 1800s.[17]

The surviving seventeenth-century records allow a portrait, albeit a fragmentary one, of a multiracial society where land was scarce but slaveholding was widespread, and slave families, like white families, were the normal order of society. Whites and blacks, mulattos and Indians, masters, slaves, and servants shared the same economic pursuits, obeyed the same laws, worshipped in the same churches—and lived together in the same houses. Some of these early Bermuda households contained not only slaves but also young white persons, male and female, who had come to the colony as apprentices or indentured servants. The Somers Islands Company decreed that all children or young people under 21 must live with "Masters of families; there being found to them diet, lodging and apparell convenient, with some other yeerely allowance of profit, according to their abilities and deserts." When the young men reached age 21 they could become tenants, living on their own, hoping to make their fortunes growing tobacco. Some were apparently reluctant to put any acres into corn, and a grand jury in 1653 requested an order that "whosoever doth lett Tobacco land to any young men shall also lett them corne ground as well." Other young men who had a "resolve to work abroad as labourers" were required to enter their names "in the counsellors booke where they entend to abide for that yeare" and "not to exact above 6d a day for their labours."[18] But land was so scarce in Bermuda that, with a few exceptions, most of the indentured servants and apprentices in Bermuda's first few decades served their time and moved on.[19] For example, of 199 males who sailed to Bermuda aboard the *Truelove* and the *Dorset* in 1635, only 18 were still there in 1663. What happened to all the rest? Of these 181 males who disappear from the records, most were young and presumably able-bodied; only two of them were over 40. Untimely deaths may have accounted for a few, but Bermuda had a remarkably low mortality rate. The majority of these young

17. Population figures are based on Bermuda census records, CO 37/2: 194; 37/39: 31. The percentages are based on the totals calculated by Hallett, who has corrected some arithmetical errors in the originals. See Hallett, *Colonial Church*, 118, 141. See also Dunn, *Sugar and Slaves*, 489 n; *CSP*, 1732:287–88.

18. Lefroy, *Memorials*, 1:203 (first quotation), 2:45 (second and third quotations).

19. Just how many bondservants—white or black—there were in Bermuda in the 1660s is impossible to determine. Darrett and Anita Rutman's study of a comparable society in Middlesex County, Virginia, finds that bound labor made up about 45 percent of the population in 1668. See Darrett B. Rutman and Anita H. Rutman, *A Place in Time: Middlesex County, Virginia, 1650–1750* (New York: W. W. Norton, 1984), 71–72. At the turn of the century there were 270 families and a total of 1,771 people in Middlesex County, and black servants or slaves outnumbered white servants by 4 to 1.

men and the boys would have been bound out as indentured servants when they arrived. As for young single women aboard the *Truelove* and the *Dorset,* there were only five: Elizabeth Aldworth, age 15, Jane Dart, 17, and Elizabeth Clark, Marie Goffe, and Katherine White, all 18. They were probably bound out as indentured servants, but their names disappear from the records.[20] They either married, died, or left the islands.

Many of the boys were among those described by the Spanish visitor, Rivera, in 1639: "Labour in the fields and in the farm-houses is performed by boys, who are either orphans or have been abandoned [in England] and most of them, expecting betterment, have been brought to the Island in the ships that call here. They serve for ten years at a very miserable wage, which is paid in tobacco. . . . They are clothed on the same mean scale, and thus live poorly and practically in a state of slavery. On completion of their time, however, they are freed; no force or violence is employed, a point to which much attention is given."[21] Some of these boys ran away to New England in 1641, as John Winthrop noted in his journal in June of that year: "About this time three boys of Summers' Islands stole away in an open boat or skiff, and having been eight weeks at sea, their boat was cast away upon a strand without Long Island, and themselves were saved by the Indians."[22]

The fortunes of some of the young men and boys who came on the *Truelove* and the *Dorset* in 1635 can be traced. Eight of them were still living in Bermuda nearly three decades later, at the time of a 1663 survey. Of these eight, five had become tenants on land owned by someone else, but at least three of these young men who came to Bermuda in 1635 with nothing but their labor had become landowners by 1663, and at least two of these had become wealthy slaveholders. They had managed to acquire land of their own in a colony where almost all the land had been parceled out and the path to upward mobility was growing very narrow indeed. The majority of the young white men and boys who came to Bermuda after the first generation of settlement left the islands, perhaps to try their luck in the English colonies on the mainland or in the Caribbean. There was simply no room for them in Bermuda.

In the 1660s, after Cromwell's forces had captured Jamaica from the Spanish, some 200 Bermudians—men, women, and children—emigrated there. In 1669 other Bermudians entertained the notion of moving to New York

20. The passenger lists for the *Truelove* and the *Dorset* are in Lefroy, *Memorials,* 1:687–90. Barbados also had a number of young white Englishmen as migrants in the 1630s, and most of them, like those in Bermuda, moved on. See Allison F. Games, "Opportunity and Mobility in Early Barbados," in *Lesser Antilles,* ed. Paquette and Engerman, 165–81.

21. Rivera, "Shipwrecked Spaniards," 26.

22. June 21, 1641, entry in *Journal of John Winthrop,* 92.

and sent agents to invest in land for "some hundreds of people." In 1670 Bermudians John Darrell and Hugh Wentworth wrote to Lord Ashley, one of the founders of the new colony in Carolina, that many Bermudians would be interested in emigrating there. Darrell and Wentworth wrote that Bermuda was "over peopled" and that the natives were "much straitened for want of land." A number of Bermudians emigrated to Carolina, taking with them certain Bermudian skills, such as the weaving of palmetto into baskets and hats and the use of palmetto in thatched roofs.[23]

There was a density of approximately 286 persons per square mile in Bermuda by the end of the seventeenth century. Bermuda, with 21 square miles, was a more crowded place than England's most populous colony at this time, Barbados. That colony, with 166 square miles, had a population density of about 259 persons per square mile in the 1670s. But there was another difference: Barbados by that time was covered with large sugarcane plantations, and Bermuda was dotted with small plots of tobacco and a little corn. Of Bermuda's approximately 6,000 arable acres, only about 2,000 were under cultivation by the late seventeenth century. Even if all of this acreage had been put to growing edible crops instead of tobacco, Bermuda could not hope to feed its people. The colony was vastly overpopulated for the amount of land it possessed, and some wanted to possess more than others. In 1652 a grand jury noted

> the great discontent that is in many of the Inhabitants of theis Islands Being that . . . we are increased and multiplied to a great people, insomuch that now here is no livinge for us whch comes to pass chiefly by the covetousness of some amongst us who labor and strive to get as much land into their hands as they can . . . as sone as any foote of land comes to be voyd, there is some that have 2 or 3 shares already seeke to take yt And being able to give a larger income then a poore man can they have yt, so that divers poore men their wives and children have not where to sett their foot.[24]

In 1659 the Somers Islands Company asked Richard Norwood to update his 1617 survey of Bermuda, recording the landlords and tenants for every share of land in the entire colony. In the next few years this redoubtable surveyor/scholar, then age 72, paced the lands of the entire island group with his surveyor's chain and constructed a narrative describing the size and location of every individual property. He recorded the names of landlords and tenants, drew new property lines, and made a map (see p. 95) showing the

---

23. On migrations, see Wilkinson, *Adventurers,* 301. Wilkinson notes that "many from Bermuda and Barbados intend to move" to New York (324). On the uses of palmetto, see p. 332. See also *CSP,* 1669–1674:32, 56, 278, 406–7, and Lefroy, *Memorials,* 2:289.

24. Grand jury presentments, assize of June 1652, CR, 3: n.p., printed in Lefroy, *Memorials,* 2:30.

boundaries of each plot of land. Norwood's "Book of Survey" has served as the basis for Bermuda land claims and deeds from that day to the present.[25] It is an extraordinary document that offers a portrait of the colony shortly after midcentury. According to the Norwood study there were 378 households in the colony in 1663, 325 of which were situated on 12,000 acres in the eight tribes and the public lands near the capital at St. George's. The other 53 households in the survey were located on various small island properties. From Juan Rivera's estimate of "about 290 houses" in 1639, the number of households in the colony had grown to about 380 in 1663, an increase of about 30 percent in less than a generation. The majority of Bermuda's individual properties were incredibly small compared to the size of landholdings in other British colonies (see table 3).

As table 3 shows, in 1663 only nine landowners in the entire colony possessed holdings of more than 200 acres. Of the 154 landowners (78 absentee and 76 resident), 104 owned less than 50 acres—at a time when Britain's other colonies offered a "headright," or a minimum of 50 acres, to individual settlers. Moreover, 50 (about one-third) of the landowners in Bermuda in 1663 held the equivalent of half a headright: one share (25 acres) or less. The average size of an individual holding was 29.5 acres, with an average of 35 acres for landowners and 24 acres for tenants. By comparison, the size of an average farm in the Chesapeake colonies of Virginia and Maryland was between 200 and 300 acres, with large plantations in the thousands of acres, and vast reaches of undeveloped land awaiting the cultivation of tobacco, the cash crop. A part of Virginia south of the Rappahannock River, for example, had an estimated 500 acres available for every worker in 1700, and in the tidewater area there were 100 acres of taxed land for every worker.[26] With abundant land at their disposal, Chesapeake planters could afford to rotate their tobacco fields, as Bermudians could not. A Virginia laborer, for instance, could work three acres for three years, then let them lie fallow for several years while moving to another three acres—a system impossible in Bermuda. The Chesapeake colonies' plentiful land also meant that households were naturally far apart. Calvert County, Maryland, for example, had two or three families

25. The Book of Survey is in CR, vol. 6, and is reprinted, along with an index of names, in Lefroy, *Memorials*, 2:645–731. See William Sears Zuill, "Norwood's Second Survey," *BHQ* 32, no. 3 (1975): 53–56. See also Terry Tucker, "Bermuda Tribes or Parishes as Placed on Norwood's Maps," *BHQ* 32, no. 4 (1975): 75–77, and Tucker, *The Islands of Bermuda* (Hamilton, Bermuda: Island Press, 1970).

26. Carville V. Earle, in *The Evolution of a Tidewater Settlement System: All Hallow's Parish, Maryland, 1650–1783*, University of Chicago Department of Geography Research Paper 170 (Chicago, 1975), has argued that tobacco planters needed a minimum of 20 acres per laborer, but if other crops are considered, the minimum acreage per worker is about 50 acres. See Kulikoff, *Tobacco and Slaves*, 48.

per square mile of taxed land, while Bermuda, with 378 households on 21 square miles, had a density of approximately 18 families for every square mile. Bermuda was indeed, as its residents claimed, a crowded place. In 1660 the colony had a total population of about 3,500 inhabitants. Using these figures with Norwood's record of households, that would give an average of about nine individuals per household, including apprentices, servants, and slaves.

Not surprisingly, the heads of households in 1663 were predominantly male, and most of them were tenants, not landowners. Of 378 households in Bermuda, only 20, or 5.3 percent, were headed by women. As table 4 shows, two of the eight tribes, Warwick and Sandys, had no women householders at all. Of the 20 households headed by women, 19 were tenants, mostly elderly widows living on the property of relatives. Only five women were listed as owners of property in Bermuda in 1663, and of these only one, Mrs. Hannah Dunscomb, the matriarch of a family in Pembroke Tribe, actually resided on her property. The same approximate ratio of absentee to resident owner holds true for men: Of 358 households headed by men, only 75, or approximately 21 percent, were also the property of the resident. As table 5 shows, tenants, not landowners, made up the majority of Bermuda's population in the mid-seventeenth century: Only about one-fifth of the heads of households, male or female, in the Norwood survey owned the property they lived on. But a great many people, landlords and tenants alike, held slaves.

Of a collection of 107 wills and inventories belonging to heads of the 378 households in Norwood's 1663 survey, 86, or slightly over 80 percent, mention blacks, mulattos, and Indians as servants or slaves.[27] It is reasonable to assume that there were more slaveholders whose records did not survive. Many persons of humble means owned a slave or two but did not make a will or have an estate inventory. From the selection of 107 wills and inventories a total of 346 slaves—293 blacks, 20 mulattos, and 33 Indians, most mentioned by name—can be verified as living in the households of colonists listed in the 1663 survey between 1663 and 1707 (the latest date of their wills or inventories).[28] But there were many more slaves whose presence cannot be documented and

27. This data is drawn from the readable wills and inventories made between 1663 and 1713. Bermuda's records do not allow a full demographic portrait such as Russell R. Menard's "The Maryland Slave Population, 1658–1730: A Demographic Profile of Blacks in Four Counties," *WMQ*, 3d ser., 32, no. 1 (January 1975): 29–54. Menard's study of more than 2,000 slaves finds that before 1710 most slaves were immigrants, most of them from Africa. The experience of these Maryland slaves was similar in one respect to that of Bermuda's creole slaves: the small sizes of slave households. More than half of the Maryland slaves lived on plantations with ten or fewer slaves, nearly one-third on plantations with fewer than five (34). Bermuda's slaves lived in households of comparable size, but much closer together than Maryland's farms and plantations.

28. These figures do not include slaves in the households of individuals who moved to Bermuda after 1663, many of whose residences are unknown. Few, if any, slaves came to Bermuda

Table 3	Size of Landholdings, 1663
Acres	Owners
0–24.5	50
25–49	54
50–99	28
100–200	13
Over 200	9

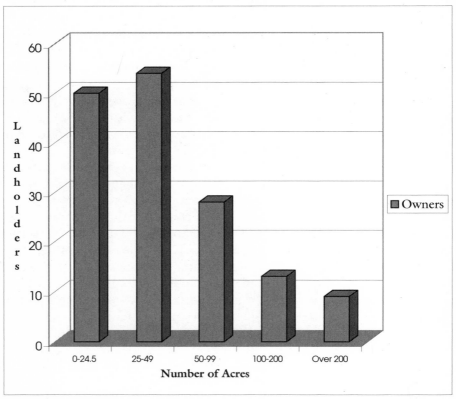

"Norwood's Book of Survey of 1662–1663," in Lefroy, *Memorials*, 2:645–717 (appendix 15).

after 1674, when a law forbade the "bringing in" of more blacks, mulattos, or Indians. This provision is discussed later in this chapter.

Table 4	Heads of Households by Gender, 1663	
Locale	Men	Women
St. George's	20	2
Hamilton	24	4
Smith's	31	2
Devonshire	34	4
Pembroke	41	1
Paget	41	3
Warwick	33	0
Southampton	32	4
Sandys	49	0
Islands	53	0

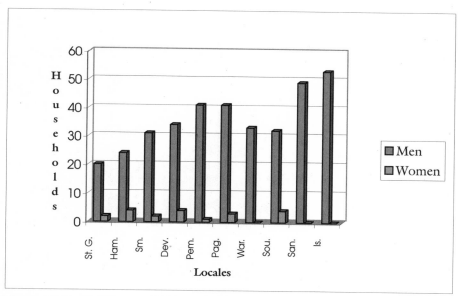

"Norwood's Book of Survey of 1662–1663," in Lefroy, *Memorials,* 2:645–717 (appendix 15).

Table 5	Tenants and Resident Owners, 1663	
Locale	Tenants	Owners
St. George's	22	0
Hamilton	19	9
Smith's	20	13
Devonshire	28	10
Pembroke	33	9
Paget	37	7
Warwick	24	9
Southampton	25	11
Sandys	41	8
Islands	50	3

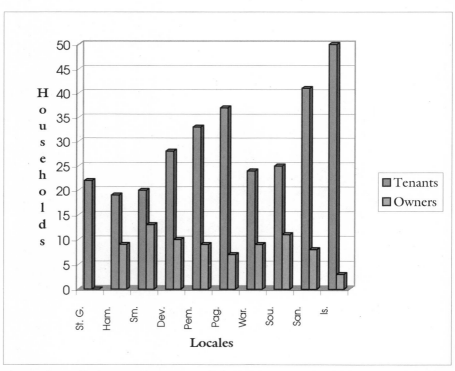

"Norwood's Book of Survey of 1662–1663," in Lefroy, *Memorials*, 2:645–717 (appendix 15).

some slaveholding households whose number of slaves cannot be ascertained. The Reverend Sampson Bond, for example, wrote in 1692 that he wished his wife to have "all my Indian & Negro slaves . . . both male & female young & old."[29]

Only six white servants—three women and three men—appear in these wills and inventories. Indentured servitude was declining in Bermuda by the latter part of the seventeenth century, as it was in other English colonies. But from Bermuda's earliest years, even when white servants were available, colonists eagerly sought "Negro" (black) rather than "English" (white) servants.

The use of *Negro* and *English* served not only to describe color and race but to define cultural identity. For white Bermudians, as for all English settlers in the age of New World colonization, to be *English* meant to worship a Christian deity, to know one's place in the social hierarchy, to defer to one's betters, to wear several layers of clothing, to be a subject of a monarch, to be represented in Parliament and possessed of certain political rights—and, above all, to be free. For black Bermudians, what it meant to be called a *Negro* was a far more complex question. Although the majority of Bermuda's blacks did not come directly from Africa, they shared African memories, without a doubt. To be a *Negro* was to carry burdens of beliefs, attitudes, and behaviors no longer useful and sometimes harmful in a new world where few blacks were free and where whites held power.[30] For Bermuda's blacks, as for the thousands of others brought to the American mainland and the Caribbean islands, fashioning a new identity depended on the nature of the white society in which they found themselves. Valued for their skills and labor, Bermuda's blacks lived and worked so closely with whites that adapting to white culture came easily. At the same time, in ways largely undocumented but obvious, Bermuda's blacks helped to shape that colony's white culture. Eating and drinking (such as bread made from cassava roots and "bibby," a fermented beverage made from palmetto tops), farming and livestock-raising, fishing and whaling, swimming and sailing, woodworking and basketry in Bermuda owed much to the knowledge of the blacks. In the occupations of everyday life the colony's blacks could use skills and strategies long familiar to them, and in the satisfaction of emotional and personal needs they could form relationships with the opposite sex that remained stable if not formal. They could also form families and bring up children.

---

29. Books of Wills, vol. 3, pt. 1, p. 186.

30. Many scholars have grappled with the problem of defining African and African-American cultural identities. See, for example, the pathbreaking study by Sidney W. Mintz and Richard Price, *The Birth of African-American Culture: An Anthropological Perspective* (Boston: Beacon Press, 1992), and Palmié, *Slave Cultures.*

Using wills and inventories, along with court records, it is possible to recon-struct something of the hidden history of Bermuda's non-English population in the latter half of the seventeenth century. Unfortunately Richard Norwood did not take note of the number of persons—white or black—living on the various properties he surveyed. His aim was to record real estate, not to conduct a census. While his narrative notes the size of each property and the buildings on it and names the head of each household, the record gives no indication of the number of people living on that property. The fact that by 1663 a substantial number of those residents were blacks, mulattos, and Indians apparently did not seem important to Norwood or, for that matter, to the Somers Islands Company officials, who might have ordered a household census along with the survey.

The vast majority (about 90 percent) of Bermudians lived in houses Nor-wood described as "tenements." Of the 378 households, 338 were tenements; another 30 were "dwellings," and 10 were "mansions." A tenement was a single-family house, usually a one-story, wood-framed, wattle-and-daub struc-ture with a palmetto-thatched roof. These houses thus combined traditional English (wattle-and-daub, a mixture of mud and twigs used to make a wall) and non-English (palmetto trees were native to parts of Africa as well as southern Europe and South America) building materials. Many of the houses were built by black laborers. Later in the seventeenth century, Bermuda houses would be built of blocks cut from the soft limestone found in the islands. A tenement, or ordinary house, generally had three or four rooms and consisted of a "hall," or main room where business, dining, and socializing took place, one or two "chambers," and a kitchen that was sometimes an outbuilding. Some of the houses Norwood classified as tenements, however, were commodious two-story residences of six or seven rooms, including porches, parlors, and other chambers. Some had cellars, and many tenement properties had out-buildings such as milk houses, cornhouses, and butteries used for keeping food cool.

The surviving inventories seldom mention separate housing for slaves. Most slaves slept in the slaveholder's house, usually in the kitchen, sometimes in another room. Edward Sherlock's 1674 inventory mentioned a "Porch chamber" containing "One old canvas bedtick such as ye Negroes Lyeth on." The majority of seventeenth-century inventories listed a householder's slave property in either the kitchen or in the "yard," placing slaves and servants in a separate grouping at the end of the inventory, either before or after the livestock—an indication both of inferior social position and, in the case of slaves, their legal status as chattels—personal property. Some slaveholders, like George Ball of Hamilton Tribe, resisted defining their human property in legalistic terms, listing his "Goods, Cattle, Chattels and Slaves" in his 1682 will.[31] But until the end of the seventeenth century, most Bermudians who wrote wills and made inventories avoided the use of the word *slave*, using *Negro* or *servant* instead. As the practice of 99-year indentures suggests, Bermudians could assuage their consciences by viewing persons with these indentures as servants, which, legally, they were, since at the end of 99 years they would be free. Meanwhile the word *Negro* gradually became a euphemism for *slave*.

By the 1660s land was scarce, but blacks were plentiful, and even the most modest Bermuda household might count a slave or two among its properties. For example, Martin Wellman, a tenant on 36 acres in Warwick Tribe, lived in a three-room "tenement" with a buttery and another outbuilding at the time of his death in 1669. His entire estate inventory totaled £53.08.01, but it included "one old Negro woman called Joane," valued at £10. Wellman's neighbor, Gilbert Hill (whose slave Cabilecto was executed for his role in the slave plot of 1656), occupied a tenement of five rooms on property that included a cornhouse and a buttery at the time of his death in 1667.[32] In his estate inventory his three slaves are listed, along with linens and clothing, under the contents of the buttery. The total value of £118 included "One Negro man" valued at £25, "Oldest Negro girle" worth £10, and "youngest Negro girle" at £8. Bermuda slave prices were roughly the same as those in the Chesapeake colonies. In the 1680s, with tobacco at 12d. per pound, the Virginia planter William Fitzhugh paid a top price of 5,000 pounds of tobacco, or about £25, for an adult male slave.[33]

Most slaveholders lived in the 338 residences classified as ordinary houses, or tenements, but others resided in the type of house Norwood called a "dwelling," or sometimes a "faire dwelling house." There were 30 of these in 1663. For example, the dwelling of Thomas Burgess, a merchant who owned 49 acres in Hamilton Tribe in 1663, was a two-story house with a hall and parlor downstairs and at least two rooms upstairs. Burgess also owned a warehouse, another outbuilding, and at least three slaves. At the time of his death in 1665 his total inventory, including household goods and the contents of his warehouse (mostly fabrics and sewing notions such as needles, pins, and thimbles), came to £463.18.01. The inventory listed three blacks: a man, woman, and boy, very likely a family. Their combined value was £35.

31. Ball's will is in Books of Wills, vol. 1, p. 391; for Sherlock's will and inventory, see ibid., 177, 180. Sherlock had three slaves at the time of his death: the Indian boy named John, mentioned in chapter 2, a black boy named Jo [John], and a "wench" named Sarah.
32. Wellman's will and inventory are in Books of Wills, vol. 1, p. 164; for Gilbert Hill's inventory, see ibid., p. 111. Hill's will also mentions a "servant" named Daniel Slinger.
33. On Chesapeake slave prices, see Morgan, *American Slavery*, 305, and Menard, "Servants to Slaves," 373. Menard estimates that the value of slaves in the 1670s was about three times that of indentured servants.

They were listed, unnamed, at the end of the inventory, before a listing of Burgess's livestock.[34]

In Norwood's survey only 10 of Bermuda's 378 households qualified as mansions. These were not, as were the great houses in Virginia, the homes of wealthy tobacco planters, but the residences of Bermuda's emerging mercantile elite, whose careers will be discussed in the next chapter. Some of these men had been in the colony since the 1620s. They made their money, not from raising tobacco, but from trading, sometimes illegally, in the great transatlantic network that linked Bermuda with the North American mainland, the Caribbean, and the mother country. They also profited, sometimes handsomely, from "wrecking," or salvaging the goods of hapless vessels on Bermuda's treacherous reefs. They lived well by seventeenth-century standards, and their houses were grander than most houses in seventeenth-century America. The mansion of Stephen Paynter, the Southampton colonist mentioned in the preceding chapter, will serve as an example. Paynter died in 1661, and the inventory of his estate is long and detailed.[35] It offers a revealing portrait of the life of an affluent Bermuda planter about the time of Norwood's survey. Paynter's two-story house in Southampton, situated with a view of the sea from Bermuda's south shore, had a "Hall," where receiving guests, dining, business transactions, and entertaining were done, and a "Parlor" and a "Great Chamber," which served as sleeping rooms and sitting rooms. Besides these, there were two bedrooms on an upper floor, and a kitchen (which may have been in separate building) with a room above it. There was also a cellar, a buttery, a cornhouse, a two-story milk house, and a "Negro Cabin." In the main house there were Turkish carpets (used as table covers, not rugs, in the seventeenth century) and cushions, brass andirons, candlesticks and snuffers, feather beds, silver serving pieces, spoons and wine cups, and a looking-glass. A brass chafing dish, a spice grater, mortar and pestle, and an large assortment of pots, pans, spits, and skimmers in the kitchen testify that the Paynter household's diet was much more varied than the fish, corn, and potatoes that ordinary Bermudians ate.

Paynter's inventory is one of the few in Bermuda that describes slave housing and furnishings. The "Negro Cabin" contained one bedstead, one bed with bolsters (pillows), two blankets, and one "long chest" for storage. In addition, a "room over the kitchen" contained two "halfe hedded bedsteds," which would also have been for slaves. At the time of his death Paynter had the

---

34. Books of Wills, vol. 1, pp. 95, 98.
35. Ibid., p. 69. Stephen Paynter's rise to affluence will be described in the next chapter. His grandson and heir was very likely the John Paynter who died intestate in 1707. See ibid., vol. 4, p. 4.

three blacks mentioned in chapter 2: his trusted overseer, Josias Simon, and two women, Bess and Margret. Simon probably occupied the cabin, and the two women, the room above the kitchen. Paynter called these three individuals his "servants" in his will.

Dwellings such as Thomas Burgess's and mansions like Stephen Paynter's made up a total of 40, or slightly over 10 percent, of the 378 households in Bermuda in the middle of the seventeenth century. These residences of Bermuda's rising economic elite were scattered over the entire colony, but the concentration of nine of the 30 dwellings in Hamilton Tribe and five of the colony's 10 mansions in Southampton Tribe did not happen by coincidence. By the 1660s a number of the most enterprising and resourceful colonists, faced with a shortage of land and a declining market for Bermuda tobacco, had managed to locate their residences in areas that were admirably suited for maritime interests such as trading and "wrecking." A choice property might include some acreage devoted to agriculture, but that was by no means the major occupation of the residents. Property in Hamilton with access to the Flatts (a small secluded inlet that connected Little Sound with the Atlantic Ocean) was highly desirable, as was land on the south shore of Southampton where many shipwrecks took place. But given Bermuda's geography, no place was far from the sea, including the capital at St. George's.

The seat of government was located at the eastern part of Bermuda, on the island also called St. George's. Unlike the land in the colony's tribes, St. George's 706 acres were owned by a single landlord: the Somers Islands Company. Thus all of the residents of St. George's, including the governor, were tenants, and in 1663 the town, although it was also the colony's official port, was the least populous part of Bermuda. There were 22 households, mostly the residences of craftsmen such as shipwrights, coopers, and blacksmiths. The land allotments of certain government officials, such as the sheriff, marshal, and secretary, were also here, as was the 50-acre glebe, where the minister resided. This property also included the 300 acres on the east end of the island allotted to the governor. Florentius Seymour, governor at the time of the 1663 survey, kept his residence in Southampton Tribe and did not live in St. George's.

The town of St. George's, like the rest of Bermuda, was populated by a mixture of races (white, black, Indian, mulatto) and an amalgam of classes (public officials, craftsmen, tradesmen, laborers). Only two of St. George's 22 households were headed by women. One was a tenant named Hannah Holloway, who lived on a 50-acre plot of the governor's land with six other tenants, all male. The other woman listed in the 1663 survey was Mrs. Ann Stalvers, who operated the ferry between the island of St. George's and the mainland. She was the widow of Captain George Stalvers, who for many years ran the ferry, carrying passengers and goods across the 125 yards of water that separated the colony's capital from the main island. After the captain's death in 1655 the Somers Islands Company directed Governor Forster to keep Stalvers's widow as the operator of the ferry: "Wee do thinke fitt that the wyfe of George Stalver the old ferryman be continued in the place of her late husband she undertaking and performing all such attendance & service as the quality of the place doth requier."[36]

The widow Stalvers had servants to help her. When she made her will in 1671 she left "One Negroe Man" to a married daughter with the stipulation that he was not to be alienated or sold (though she did not refer to him as a slave). Her "Indian servant boy," named Nicholas "or Nicke," she left orders to "manumitt & for ever sett free" upon her death.[37] An elderly widow, Ann Stalvers died in 1673, leaving a personal estate of £91, including several items of apparel, rarely listed in Bermuda inventories. Among her possessions were two silk coats, two gowns, and two gold rings. Stalvers lived in a four-room, two-story house with a kitchen and a buttery. Her "Negroe Man" apparently lived in the kitchen, since he is listed with that room's contents. Nicholas, the Indian servant boy, is not listed, since he was to gain his freedom upon the death of his mistress.

Nicholas may have remained in St. George's, joining a community of other Indians, mulattos, and blacks among St. George's residents. Some, like Nicholas, were slaves who had been promised their freedom. For example, the will of a householder named Thomas Sparkes, who died in 1672, left to his granddaughter "the time that my Mulato shall have to serve after my wifes death." The 1678 will of John Vaughan, who served as the colony's secretary in the 1650s, left to his wife, Ann, a "little girl Ann" to serve until the age of 21 and then to be manumitted and baptized. Vaughan also had three Indians—a woman, a girl, and a boy—whom he did not free but bequeathed to his children.[38]

Most of the blacks, Indians, and mulattos in St. George's were slaves, but some were free, and all would have been familiar to each other. In a place so small (the town proper covered an area of less than half a square mile), houses and public buildings were close together on narrow, winding streets and lanes. Masters and mistresses, servants and slaves, going about their daily business would have come to know each other well. Perhaps Tomasin, the mulatto victim of an alleged witch in 1651, still lived in St. George's. Robert

36. Lefroy, *Memorials*, 2:54. A George Stalvers served on a jury in 1616 and as an overseer in Devonshire Tribe in 1626. See ibid., 1:124, 127, 129, 382, 388.
37. Books of Wills, vol. 1, p. 172.
38. For Sparkes's and Vaughan's wills, see ibid., pp. 159, 274.

Powell, the cooper who was involved in the witchcraft trials in the 1650s, was still living there in 1663 and had black and Indian slaves in his household. At the time of his death in 1676 he counted as his slaves the black man named Andrew and the three Indians—Populo, Tabitha, and a child named Joane—mentioned earlier. It is interesting to note that Powell's will refers to "all my slaves." By the 1670s a few slaveholders had begun to use the word *slave* in their wills, but the majority still avoided it.[39]

Although they lived on an island, the people who lived at St. George's were by no means isolated from other parts of Bermuda—or from the transatlantic community. Town Harbor, on the south side of the island, was Bermuda's major port, where vessels from England, the Caribbean, and the North American mainland stopped to provision and trade. The residents of St. George's were also linked to a local network that furnished them with news of the whole of Bermuda. At least once a year the Assembly met in the statehouse at St. George's, and twice a year, usually in July and December, the Assize Court met. On these occasions people from all of the eight tribes visited the tiny capital. The members of the Assembly and the judges and jurors, accompanied by their servants and slaves, sojourned at St. George's for several days at a time. There would have been talk about the Assembly's business and, when the Assize Court was in session, gossip about various grand jury presentments and trials. On the Sabbath, blacks, mulattos, and Indians along with whites would have attended services at St. Peter's Church near the center of the town. From time to time a multiracial audience witnessed the public punishments, such as whippings, duckings, and serving time in the stocks, that took place in the market square at the edge of the water. Executions, another occasion for public gatherings, generally took place on Cobler's Island (later called Gallows Island), a tiny islet in Town Harbor across from the market square, in full view of the main part of the town. Interment of whites and blacks (albeit in separate sections) took place in the burying ground behind St. Peter's Church. In short, residents of St. George's 22 households, living and working on an island of approximately 700 acres, formed a small and close-knit multiracial community with ties to a much larger world.

A number of other islands were included in Norwood's survey. On Longbird Island, for example, the multiracial servant household of the weaver James Stirrup contained "Two Negroes" as well as the Indian woman and Indian girl mentioned in chapter 2. Stirrup also had an indentured servant named Thomas Atkins, who in 1665 had served all but "halfe a yeare of his tyme." Stirrup died on September 27. He left a widow, Elizabeth, and at least one son, John, to whom he left "3 thousands wt of silk." The inventory of his

39. Ibid., p. 227.

estate came to £243.15.01, besides two trading arrangements pending: an "Adventure sent by his sonne to Barbados" and a small chest of tobacco sent on the Somers Islands Company ship. This weaver who lived on an island also left two sailboats. No doubt his servants knew how to sail them.[40]

Across Town Harbor, south of the island of St. George's, lies St. David's Island, where, as noted in chapter 2, a considerable number of Indians lived. Most of them had been transported to Bermuda and sold as slaves, beginning in the 1640s, but there is evidence that Indians continued to be sold in Bermuda later in the seventeenth century. For example, a meeting of the Governor's Council in January 1687/1688 expressed concern over a group of Indians that Captain Boaz Sharp had brought to Bermuda. They were reportedly "subjects of the King of Spain" and may have been illegally sold.[41] What became of these Indians, who were probably from the West Indies, is not known. Some of them were no doubt among those listed in Sharp's inventory 20 years later. At his death in 1707 he had only Indians as servants in his household:

Phillip	£18
Dinah	£19
Andrew	£34
Sue	£28
Indian Childe two daies old	£1.5
Indian girl Jude	£2.8
Indian girl Ruth	£17
Indian girl Dinah	£19.10
Indian girl Rose	£6.10[42]

The four adults—two men and two women—and five children suggest at least two family groups among these Indians. Their status—whether servant or slave—is not recorded. They were very likely slaves, and Captain Sharp may have acquired them by nefarious means. As the years passed, these and other Indians on St. David's formed families, sometimes mixing races but still preserving stories of their ancient Indian origins, if not their tribal cultures, to pass down through generations into the twentieth century. Members of the Pequot, Mohican, Wampanoag, and Narragansett tribes from New England are the most likely to have been brought to Bermuda, but their tribal cultures did not survive. Many of the modern residents of St. David's claim Indian ancestry, but their identity is derived from their long association with the island of St. David's rather than recollections of tribal culture. For most of the seventeenth and eighteenth centuries these Indians, some free, some

---

40. Ibid., pp. 99, 100.
41. Minutes of a council meeting, January 7, 1687/1688, CR, 7:209.
42. Sharp's inventory of March 13, 1706/1707, is in Book of Wills, vol. 3, pt. 2, pp. 179–80.

slave, continued to live on St. David's Island, out of the busy mainstream of colonial life.

As for the rest of Bermuda, the eight tribes—Hamilton, Smith's, Devonshire, Pembroke, Paget, Warwick, Southampton, and Sandys—each only 1,250 acres, form a long, narrow strip of land 18 miles long and less than one mile wide, on average. The terrain is gently rolling, the highest point only 250 feet above sea level. Lush with vegetation, partly wooded, Bermuda in the seventeenth century was a rural space dotted with small plots of land under cultivation, all close together and marked off by stone walls or hedges, and fields where cattle and sheep grazed. And no place in Bermuda is farther than a mile from the Atlantic Ocean. Fish and shellfish, of course, made up a large portion of the colony's diet, and water, not land, was the preferred mode of transportation. It is safe to assume that by the 1660s, or almost the third generation of settlement, Bermudians of all races (and both genders) knew how to sail a boat.

At the time of Norwood's survey each of the eight tribes had its own social and political structure, not unlike that of an English parish. At the top in each tribe was a handful of prominent, affluent merchants or sea captains who held public office, served on vestries and juries, and drilled the militia. Next came the small planters and farmers; last came the servants and slaves. Among the slaveholders in this group whose slaves can be counted, the largest number of slaves held by one individual was 17. In the selection of 107 wills and inventories belonging to persons listed in the 1663 survey and dating from 1663 to 1707, 86 mention slaves. The numbers they held were small: about one-third of the slaveholders (24) owned only one or two slaves; 14 had three or four slaves; 12 had five or six. Of the owners with larger numbers of slaves, six owned seven or eight, and only five held nine or more. Only three of these had 12 or more slaves.

At first glance these statistics appear to reflect the patterns of slaveholding in the mainland English colonies in the seventeenth century: small numbers of slaves with resident (rather than absentee) owners. On closer examination, however, Bermuda's slaveholding proves quite different. While most of the slaves counted in the mainland colonies were adults, many of them newly arrived from the West Indies or Africa, most slaves in Bermuda's 1660s households were native-born—and many of them were children. Family life was as widespread among slaves as among slaveholders in seventeenth-century Bermuda, and families would continue to shape slavery and race relations until emancipation in the nineteenth century. Of the 86 slaveholding households in the sample, 49 contained slave children as well as adults.

If these households in the latter half of the seventeenth century are representative, they suggest close bonds between master and slave and a concern for the slave's individual welfare and personal morality beyond the cares of most slaveholders in other colonies. From one end of Bermuda to the other, slaveholders of ordinary means as well as the affluent recognized and approved of slave marriages, often named slave children for themselves or for members of their families, usually bequeathed slaves to relatives, avoided breaking up slave families, sometimes manumitted individuals, and almost never sold them. Sales of slaves are rare in the records. They usually took place because of financial stress, as in the case of Devonshire resident John Hariot, a widower, who left a will providing for the sale of his late wife's apparel, two gold rings, and "one Negro man called Jack," with the proceeds of the sale to be divided equally among five of his children.[43] In two households in the 1663 survey there is documentation of slave couples who remained together in the same slaveholding families for 20 and 30 years, a testimony, of sorts, to both longevity and the stability of slave life in Bermuda.

The wills and inventories for some slaveholders afford glimpses, some more detailed than others, of households with slaves and of the relationship between master and slave. The inventory of Samuel Stone, one of the richest men in Hamilton Tribe, reveals something of slavery and life in an affluent household in seventeenth-century Bermuda. Stone left a personal estate of £707.11.09, including seven slaves, at his death in 1668. He died intestate, but the inventory of his estate is fairly detailed. In the 1663 survey his house is described as an ordinary one, or tenement, on 37 acres. He lived there with his wife, Elizabeth, and their children. The number of children is not known, but the Stones' household furniture included a trundle bed, a cradle, and three small chairs. The Stones' slaves (although they were called "Negroes," not slaves, in the inventory) lived in a "Negroes Cabin" on the property. There were six blacks—three women, one man, two children—and one Indian boy "sick of the small pox." The Stones' concern for the welfare of their slaves is evident from the record of expenses around the time of Stone's death. The Indian boy with smallpox received medical attention: One of Stone's expenses was a payment of three shillings to a Mr. Moldredge "for seeing the Indian boye." The boy apparently lived; an Indian boy named Gregorie was listed in an inventory three years later. There was also a payment of nine shillings to a George Collins "for tending a sick Negroe," and another payment of five shillings to a Thomas Ireland "for burying the old Neg: woman." The names and ages of Samuel Stone's blacks are not recorded, but it is very likely that the man was the husband of one of the women and that the two children were their offspring.

43. See ibid., vol. 1, p. 196.

Among the Stones' other expenditures were those for their own family: payments for a tutor for their children and payments for children's shoes and hats. The list of expenses includes other payments to individuals for weaving, for making clothes, for binding a Bible, for killing and dressing "4 beefes." Stone's widow, Elizabeth, also recorded an expense of four shillings for "A straw hatt for myselfe," along with a payment for "Rum spent in the house 3 gall.1/2." The Stones paid 14 shillings to Captain John Stowe for "freight for the beef."[44] Stowe, who owned 100 acres in Pembroke Tribe, raised some cattle and probably sold the beef to Stone. Samuel Stone did not own any livestock, but he did raise some tobacco. The outbuildings on Stone's property included a storehouse containing a tobacco wheel, and a tobacco house for curing and storing tobacco. He may also have processed tobacco for his neighbors.

The one black man in the Stones' slave household, perhaps assisted by one or two of the women, cultivated some of the land in tobacco, but growing tobacco on 37 acres was definitely not Samuel Stone's major source of wealth. Like many of Bermuda's rising elites in the 1660s, Stone was not a tobacco planter but a merchant. The land that he leased was located less than half a mile from the Flatts. With easy access to the Atlantic as well as the interior of Bermuda, Samuel Stone made his money by importing and selling items that his fellow Bermudians did not manufacture: fabrics such as linen, canvas, and flannel, and items such as "25 pr. Mens Stockings, white," needles and pins, silver thimbles and bodkins, bottles, buttons, and rum.

The 1677 will of another prosperous merchant, John Darrell, of Warwick Tribe, also leaves a record of a family that cared for its slaves. Captain Darrell was one of the wealthiest residents of Warwick, a shipowner and merchant who owned three shares of land. Darrell and Hugh Wentworth, the son of the Hugh Wentworth mentioned in chapter 2, were joint owners of a trading vessel, the *Recovery*, in 1669. They also financed the settlement of some Bermudians in New Providence in the Bahamas in 1670.[45] Like many Bermuda merchants, Darrell was active in public life, serving as a member of a grand jury in 1656 and as councillor for Warwick in 1669. With William Sayle, Philip Lea, George Tucker, and Paul Trimingham, he was involved in whale fishing and various trading ventures. In 1657 Darrell bought "seventeen servants" for £238. Since they are not defined as "Negroes," it is likely that they were Irish captives, a number of whom were brought to Bermuda in the 1650s, and that he sold them there. Darrell also owned a number of slaves, and his 1677 will provided

44. Ibid., pp. 131, 133, 135, 143.
45. See *CSP*, 1669–1674:56.

for three adult slaves—Black Moll, Black Nan, a man named Jefferie—as well as three younger blacks—Black Laddie, Black Hester, and Black George. All of these were to be given Darrell's wife, Sarah. Sarah's date of death is not recorded, but 20 years later, when the Darrell's eldest son, John, died in 1689, the inventory of his estate named Laddie and Hester as two of his four "Negroe Slaves."[46] Laddie and Hester might have been siblings, but it is also possible that they met as young people and married somewhere along the way. In any case, they remained together in the same white family for more than two decades.

Jerome Ewer, an affluent Warwick slaveholder with two shares of land and a "faire dwelling house," was the owner of another long-lived slave couple in the 1660s. A longtime Bermuda resident, he had bought two blacks—Maria and Christopher—from Hugh Wentworth Sr. in 1637. At Ewer's death 30 years later, in 1667, "One Negro Man called Christopher and his Wife" were still in his household inventory along with five other slaves, including another slave couple, Frank and Moll. A record of expenses against Ewer's estate, kept by Henry Harvie, one of the executors of Ewer's will, offers yet another glimpse of a planter's care of his slaves and of life in seventeenth-century Bermuda. For "Clothing 7 Negroes one yeare, and 6 Negroes 2 yeares at 20 p. head," Harvie charged a total of £19. To "Mr. Goodwin Chirurgeon for . . . medicine to the Negroes," there was a charge of £2.16. Ewer's personal estate came to £307.15.08.[47] He owned only 50 acres, but he lived well by seventeenth-century standards. By comparison, Robert Cole, a contemporary of Ewer's in Maryland's St. Mary's County, owned six times as much land (300 acres) but left a personal estate of only half as much (£154) as Ewer's in 1662.[48]

The will of Nicholas Thornton, a tenant on two shares of land in Paget Tribe in 1663, made careful provisions for eight slaves a few days before his death in 1691: His "old slaves Queen & Frank" and an "old woman slave Huba" were left to Thornton's son, Benjamin, provided that Benjamin freed them within 12 years if he carried them out of the islands. If not, Benjamin was to "provide for them if they will not live with him." Thornton left a boy, Job, to his son, John; a girl, Sue, to his daughter, Rebecca; and three other girls—Hanna, Rachell, and Sarah—to three of his other daughters. Of the last-mentioned slave, Sarah, Thornton wrote that she was to be kept in his

46. Books of Wills, vol. 1, p. 258. On Darrell's various activities, see Lefroy, *Memorials,* 1:717, 736, 2:86, 100, 142, 146, 286, 302, 309, 437. The will and inventory of Darrell's son, John, are in Books of Wills, vol. 3, pt. 1, pp. 79, 149.

47. Books of Wills, vol. 1, pp. 113–14. Part of the will is torn and illegible.

48. See Lois Green Carr, Russell R. Menard, and Lorena S. Walsh, *Robert Cole's World: Agriculture and Society in Early Maryland* (Chapel Hill: University of North Carolina Press, 1991).

married daughter's family and given to her children. "If my said Negro be abused," Thornton wrote, the executors of his will were to "take her away and to take care of her."[49]

There are a number of manumissions in this sample of wills, some of which reveal the interracial ties that bound slaveholder and slave families. The will of Thomas Wood, an affluent Hamilton slaveholder and planter who raised cattle on his 147 acres, is one such example. Wood made his will shortly before his death in 1662, the year before the survey. Of Thomas Wood's slaves, only one, a young mulatto man, is mentioned by name in his will. This individual bore the same surname as Wood's trading partner, Captain William Williams, who in 1663 lived in Devonshire Tribe about a mile west of Wood's property. Wood wrote that "Onely my Molatto Phillip Williams, I will that he be freed at the age of thirtie one yeares." Wood's will also left to his son Joseph "two thousands [pounds] of beefe, 1600 in the hands of Capt William Willliams & 400 to be paid him [Joseph] by my daughter Ruth Willis." Some of Wood's other slaves may have passed to his widowed daughter, Ruth Willis, who also lived in Hamilton and was the executrix of her father's estate. At her death in 1692 she held six slaves.[50]

John Wainright of Southampton Tribe wrote in his 1684 will that his son, Thomas, was to have a "Negro man Francis if he is willing to live with him, If not to let him chuse him a master among my children." Wainwright, who had six children, had eight slaves besides Francis—four blacks and four Indians, all of whom he bequeathed to specific children. The only adult Indian woman, Dinah, he left to his son, George, "to serve him thirtie yeares and then to be free." Josias Forster, a mariner of Sandys Tribe and the son of Bermuda's governor of the same name, wrote in his 1679 will that his mulatto man, Obediah, should serve his wife and children "for 15 years and then be free." At Forster's death in 1680 Obediah was listed in the estate inventory as worth £28.10, with the notation that he was to have three shillings and 10 pence per year for "his clothing, being fond of it."[51] Forster had two other slaves, "Black Hanna" and "Young Lewis," whom he did not free, presumably because they were needed in his household: he had four children, and his wife was "with child" at the time he made his will.

Richard Stafford, a merchant who wrote "Esq." after his name in 1704 when he made his will, left his "mulatto man Whan" to his two grandsons for one year after his death, but thereafter Whan was to "have his Liberty"

49. Books of Wills, vol. 3, pt. 1, p. 144.
50. For Thomas Wood's will, see ibid., vol. 1, p. 71. Ruth Willis's will is ibid., vol. 3, pt. 1, p. 176.
51. Wainwright's will is ibid., vol. 1, p. 211; Forster's, ibid., vol. 2, pp. 280, 288.

and to live with either grandson he chose.[52] Of the 86 slaveholders whose wills and inventories are in this sample, Stafford held the largest number of slaves: 17. He lived well by Bermuda standards. His estate inventory included a rapier, several guns, a boat with a grapple, and considerable quantities of silver. Although he lived in a tenement in 1663, he lived in a luxuriously furnished mansion when he made his will in 1704. Part of his money came from selling rum. At an assize court in 1676 he was one of four colonists presented for selling strong drink and keeping a "disorderly house" without a license. Besides Stafford's mulatto slave, Whan, there were other mulattos among the 17 slaves in Stafford's household, including a man named Natty, a woman named Libby, and a girl, Ruth, none of whom Stafford freed. All the slaves but Whan were bequeathed to Stafford's children and grandchildren.

Another wealthy Bermudian, Perient Trott, a London merchant who became the largest landowner in Bermuda, freed three Indian slaves in his 1690 will. Trott served as "husband" of the Somers Islands Company for 15 years and bought the Bermuda holdings of the Earl of Warwick after Warwick's death in 1658. At the time of the 1663 survey Trott owned 713.5 acres scattered across the entire colony from Ireland Island to St. David's. In 1690 he also owned one-third of a 770-acre plantation in Carolina, along with its "Servants and stock." It is possible that some of his Indian slaves came from Carolina. Two of the Indian men, Sander and Ralph, and one Indian woman, Ruth, were to be put out to work for wages for 15 years after Trott's death, and then his executors were to "give them their freedom." Trott bequeathed his 10 other slaves—three men, two women, four boys, and a girl—to members of his family.[53]

Two other slaveholders who manumitted their slaves in this period deserve mention. They were neighbors in the affluent west end of Pembroke Tribe. In 1697 Henry Ford Jr. wrote a will freeing all eight of his slaves. Ford's will is unusual for another reason: It clearly identifies family groups and, in one instance, the marital status of a mulatto woman slave. Her name was Sarah Blackman, and the will refers to her as "als. the wife of James Eaton." To this woman and her two children Ford bequeathed not only freedom but household goods, including a cedar chest, an iron pot, a bedstead, and "some pewter." Henry Ford gave the same essential household goods, but no pewter, to another slave. Henry, or Harry, as this slave was called, was also ordered to take care of his two brothers. Ford's other slaves, a woman named Diana, two boys, John and David, and a mulatto boy "commonly called Nathaniel Sanders," were also to be given their freedom. Nathaniel was no doubt related

52. On Stafford, see ibid., vol. 3, pt. 2, p. 24, and assize of January 18, 1676/1677, CR, 7:5.
53. Books of Wills, vol. 3, pt. 1, p. 119. See also Wilkinson, *Adventurers,* 299.

to the family of Richard Sanders, who in 1663 occupied one-half share of land adjacent to Ford's residence. Sanders was buried in 1692, at the age of 103.[54] In her will in 1703 Dorothy Wood, widow of Thomas Wood and neighbor of Henry Ford, freed a "mulatto man called Stephen." He was the only one (and the only mulatto) among Wood's 12 slaves to be manumitted. She bequeathed Stephen to her eldest son, Thomas, to serve "till he shall come to fourty years of age and then to be free." Her other slaves, including five others to her son Thomas, she bequeathed to her children. The bequests were made according to family group: A man named Tony, two women, Moll and Beck (one of whom was probably Tony's wife), and a boy and a girl were given to Thomas; a man called Sam, "a wench called Joan," and a boy, Dickey, were to go to Benjamin, another son; to the family of a third son, Samuel Wood, went a woman named Hannah and a boy named Peter.[55]

The will of Richard Jennings, made in 1669, likewise made careful provision for his 11 slaves, mentioning them all by name. They were "Old Peter," with his daughter, Bess, and her son; Rabb and Beck (a husband and wife?), Marie and her daughter, "Peter the Mulatto" (a son of Old Peter?), Hanna, Sissie, and Little Bess. "And as for Old Peter," Jennings wrote in his will, "hee shall have his own libertie to do what he shall think good and to be kept with clothing fitting for him." Like many masters, Jennings acknowledged the importance of marriage and family ties among his slaves. His will provided that the black family groups—at least three in his slave household—were kept together in bequests to three of his adult children.[56] Jennings's neighbor, former Governor William Sayle, also had three families among his slaves: Sambo and his wife; Lucea and her two daughters; and Ned and his two sons, one of whom was an infant "at nurse at Richard Joneses of Devon. Tribe." Merchant John Somersall, another of Jennings's and Sayles's neighbors in Smith's Tribe, was also a slaveholder, although the exact number of his slaves is not known. His 1674 will does not use the word *slave* but makes specific reference to one black family: "Old Negroe Man Antony & Katherine his now wife and John his oldest son shall live with wch of my two Sonnes they please," to have "meate Drinke and all maner of necessaryes," or "to be free as they wish."[57]

Many slaveholders made special provisions for elderly slaves in their wills, providing for their maintenance, sometimes allowing them to choose which member of the master's or mistress's family they would live with, sometimes

54. Henry Ford's will is Books of Wills, vol. 2, pt. 2, p. 167; the probate documents are ibid., pt. 1, p. 219. On Richard Sanders, see Hallett, *Early Bermuda Records*, 38.
55. For the wills of Thomas and Dorothy Wood, see Books of Wills, vol. 1, p. 249, and vol. 3, pt. 2, p. 3.
56. Ibid., vol. 1, p. 128.
57. Ibid., vol. 1, p. 183.

freeing them. Occasionally, as in John Somersall's will, an elderly slave was given freedom as an option. Christopher Smith, a Hamilton resident who died in 1668, left a black woman, Frances, and an Indian woman, Kate, with the provision that "if Indian Kate desire to be free at the decease of my wife" she was to have her freedom, or if not, to choose which of his children she "would dwell with." Such open offers raise intriguing questions about the relationships between slaveholder and slave: Were the ties so strong that remaining in the master's household or that of a member of his family was preferable to freedom? In many cases, the slaves offered such options were elderly, and freedom would have been a daunting prospect. Thus many slaveholders provided a choice. In the Hamilton Tribe household of Francis Watlington lived an Indian called Sam, who was not as fortunate as Christopher Smith's Indian, Kate. Sam was not freed and was described in Watlington's estate inventory in 1688 as "Indian man Sam discontented who pleads for his freedom."[58] One can only wonder in what ways Sam manifested his discontent and what his fellow slaves, a black man and woman and four children, thought of his unhappy state.

Slave voices are silent in Bermuda's history, and the richness and variety of black, mulatto, and Indian lives must go largely undocumented, barely touched by public records. But sometimes, as with the description of the discontented Indian, Sam, a fragmentary notation in a will can speak volumes. The same is true of court records. Grand jury presentments at the semiannual assize courts, for example, offer glimpses of some of the personal relationships and perhaps the bonds of affection that mitigated lifelong servitude. For example, the name of Populo, the Indian man who belonged to Joane Powell, the widow of the St. George's cooper, Robert Powell, appears in a court record in the summer of 1679. He and an Indian woman belonging to St. George's resident Edward Lee were presented by a grand jury for having a bastard child. They were named along with two other St. George's couples. Peter, an Indian man belonging to the widow Elizabeth Sparkes, and Joane, a woman of unspecified race and status belonging to militia officer Lieutenant Edward Brangman, had a bastard child, as did a mulatto couple who also belonged to different owners. Elizabeth Sparkes's Indian man, Peter, had probably come from St. David's Island. His mistress was the wife of Thomas Sparkes, a tenant on 12 acres on St. David's. After his death in 1672, his widow apparently moved to St. George's, bringing Peter with her.[59] The number of sexual

58. For Christopher Smith's will, see ibid., p. 117; for Watlington's, see ibid., vol. 3, pt. 1, pp. 62–63. Indian Sam was listed last, after the blacks, and valued at £16; David, the black man listed first, was valued at £20.

59. Assize of January 18 and 19, 1676/1677, CR, 7:5; Books of Wills, vol. 1, p. 159.

liaisons between individuals who lived in different households suggests some degree, however small, of personal freedom. Servants and slaves were able to create private spaces for themselves and to enjoy relationships unsanctioned by their masters.

As in the case of one of the St. George's couples just mentioned, sexual relationships were sometimes mixed-race. An estate inventory and another court record offer documentation of another such liaison. The estate inventory of William Peasley, a wealthy Hamilton merchant who died in 1672, lists seven servants, including an Indian man and a white woman.[60] All, in the order below, are listed after the livestock under the heading "Without Doors." That designation notwithstanding, they probably lived in Peasley's house. His two-story residence (classified as a tenement in the survey of 1663) included a cellar and a kitchen as well as a milk house and buttery. Peasley's servant household, listed below, was one of the few that contained a white servant.

Indian man	£18
Negro woman	£20
Negro boy Michaell	£15
Black Tom	£10
Black Besse	£06
1 boy Sam	£06
1 Serving maide called Judith	£02

Peasley's household is also one of very few in which a sexual relationship between a white woman and a black man can be documented. At the assize court of June 6, 1670, Peasley's maidservant, a woman named Judith Porter, was "Censured by the Vote of the Court to be whipped in Hamilton Tribe Church yarde after the Evening Sermon" because she had "bin delivered of a Black Childe"[61]—not mulatto, but black. Here the mother's race or status did not determine the child's. What became of this mixed-race child is not known. He could well be the boy, Sam, listed next to Judith in Peasley's inventory two years later. The father could have been Peasley's slave, Black Tom. Judith is listed in the inventory with a value of only £2, which suggests that her indenture was almost up and she had not much longer to serve in the Peasley household. Did this white woman later live with or marry the black father of her child? White men in Bermuda fathered mulatto children with impunity, but white women had no such latitude. What social price did Judith Porter pay for having crossed a forbidden racial barrier? One can only wonder what became of her.

60. Books of Wills, vol. 1, p. 153.
61. Assize of June 6, 1670, CR, 5B: n.p., printed in Lefroy, *Memorials*, 2:314–15.

Another mixed-race liaison emerges from the records of John Casson, a Paget resident. Casson, a tenant on one share of land in 1663, made his will in 1688, giving his "Malato man called Diego, his freedome from slavery or bondage." "I hereby release him," Casson wrote, "from his slavery & servitude forever after the decease of Abigail my wife."[62] But that is the end, not the beginning, of Diego's story. Some years earlier, in 1671, a "mulatto man named Degoe" identified as "now or late the Servant of Mr. John Wilson of Pagets Tribe Planter," was convicted of theft and sentenced to death but was granted benefit of clergy, an action signifying that Diego could read and write. Instead of suffering the death penalty, Diego was made "Comon Executioner."[63] Diego's master at that time was Casson's father- in-law, John Wilson, age 80, who owned 50 acres and styled himself "gentleman" in his 1673 will. In that will, Wilson bequeathed his "mulatto man called Diego" to his daughter and son-in-law, Abigail and John Casson, who lived about a quarter of a mile from Wilson's property. How long Diego served as the local executioner is not known, but he was still in that position five years later when his name appears in the records in another context. In January of 1676/1677 "Diego the Hangman" and a woman named Mary Bolton were sentenced to be whipped for fornication: He was to receive 31 lashes; she, 21.[64] Since Mary Bolton's race is not specified, she was probably white, and since her master is not identified (as was the custom in public records) she was probably free. As with the case of Judith Porter, one wishes for more of the story. Who was Mary Bolton? How and where did she and Diego meet? Who initiated the relationship? What did the people of Paget Tribe, where Diego's master lived, think of these mixed-race lovers? And did the literate mulatto, Diego, ever receive his freedom?

Although many individual histories cannot be completed from the existing records, threads of other lives can be picked up at various points in time and some followed to a conclusion. Such is the case of Marmaduke Dando, the Southampton tenant whose early efforts to establish himself were traced in chapter 1. By using Norwood's "Book of Survey," Southampton church records, and the extant wills and inventories it is possible to reconstruct something of seventeenth-century Southampton Tribe's network of community and relationships and to complete the story of Marmaduke Dando's life some 40 years after he settled there.

---

62. Books of Wills, vol. 3, pt. 1, p. 48.
63. Lefroy, *Memorials*, 2:345. On black executioners, Wilkinson, *Adventurers*, 310, notes that the position of executioner was usually "delegated to a Negro," and "if the victim were colored" the executioner was always a black.
64. Assize of January 18 and 19, 1676/1677, CR, 7:5.

Southampton Tribe was one of the more prosperous Bermuda tribes in the seventeenth century. The 1663 survey of Southampton lists a total of 36 households, including five mansions, inhabited by 11 owners and 25 tenants. Among the heads of these 36 households were several individuals mentioned in earlier chapters: Stephen Paynter, the Reverend Nathaniel White, James Sarnando, and Marmaduke Dando. In 1663 Dando and his family still lived on the same 25-acre property they had occupied in 1617, and their fortunes do not appear to have changed much. If Marmaduke Dando ever acquired a servant, black or white, the records do not show it. The households on either side of his, however, were slaveholding households. On one side, Dando's neighbor was his landlord: Richard Hunt had a mansion house and four shares of land (almost 100 acres) due east of the Dandos' modest tenement. Hunt owned several slaves by the 1660s, one of whom, Anthony, had participated in the abortive rebellion plot of 1656 and was still living in his household in 1663. Hunt had moved to Southampton from Warwick Tribe sometime in the early 1640s. Hunt's wife, Frances, was the niece of Sir Nathaniel Rich, and the Southampton land the Hunts lived on was formerly Rich's property.[65] When Richard Hunt took up residence next to the Dandos is not clear from the existing records, but the Hunts and the Dandos would have come to know each other well. Frances Hunt bore eight children between 1646 and 1662. As a close neighbor, Joan Dando, Marmaduke's wife, would have been in attendance, perhaps assisting at the births of these children. Of Frances Hunt's eight children, six—three sons and three daughters—survived.[66] In 1653, when the Hunts buried their infant son, Richard, in Southampton churchyard, the Dandos would have been among the mourners, and again in 1658 when one-year-old Martha Hunt was buried. The church and churchyard were only a short walk, less than a quarter of a mile, from the Dandos' house. Dando and his wife were active in the religious life of the Southampton church. Dando was a lay reader in that church for many years, and Joan occupied the sixth-best seat in the women's pews.

While the Hunts' mansion house lay to the east of the Dandos' residence, a slaveholder of more modest means lived to the Dandos' west. Thomas Wells, a tenant on 50 acres, had been living in Southampton since at least 1620, almost as long as Dando. Wells, like Dando, had raised a family there. According to the Southampton parish register, between 1622 and 1640 Wells and his first wife, Alice, had seven children—one son and six daughters. In

65. See Ives, *Rich Papers*, 332 n.
66. Hallett, *Early Bermuda Records*, 8. See also Hallett, *Early Bermuda Wills*, 298. Richard Hunt died in 1687; his wife's death is not recorded. One of their daughters, Sarah, married Thomas Gibbs, who by the 1690s was one of the richest men in Bermuda.

1645 John Wells, the son, married a young woman named Jane Grimsditch, who bore him four daughters—Hester, Mary, Hannah, and Anne—between 1646 and 1656. In 1663 John Wells and his family lived on a half share of land adjacent to his father's land. That land also contained the church and the churchyard. Both the Wellses, father and son, lived on land owned by Perient Trott, the wealthy merchant of Hamilton Tribe.[67] Two of Thomas Wells's daughters—Hannah and Sarah—bore the same names as the daughters of their neighbors, the Dandos. No doubt the Wells children and the Dando children had grown up playing together, and no doubt the black children in the Wells household joined in their games. The most notable thing about Thomas Wells, an ordinary colonist, a tenant on someone else's land, is that he owned six slaves. In Bermuda, however, that was not unusual. Of the 36 householders in Southampton Tribe in 1663, 15 can be documented as having bought, sold, or bequeathed blacks, mulattos, and Indians between the 1630s and the 1670s. Of the 15 slaveholders for whom records exist, only five were landowners. In Southampton Tribe, as in the rest of Bermuda, slaveholding was not related to land ownership. Thomas Wells's will, made in 1673, the year before his death, made provision for James, "a negro man," John a "Mulato woeman," Jane, a "negro girle," and three boys, Thomas, Peter (a mulatto), and Matthew. It is possible that these individuals were all members of the same family. Black infants named James and Jane belonging to Thomas Wells had been baptized on November 30, 1657. Another black infant, Anthony, was baptized in 1659 but was not in the Wells household in 1673.[68] Thomas Wells bequeathed his slaves separately to his married son and married daughters. The girl named Jane, who was probably named for and related to the older Jane, he left to his granddaughter of the same name.

Next to Thomas Wells, and about half a mile from Marmaduke Dando, lived Damon Knowles, another tenant who had been in Southampton nearly 40 years. The baptisms of three Knowles children, Ann, John, and Robert, are recorded in the Southampton register from 1629 to 1633. Knowles was a tenant on 75 acres owned by Richard Jennings of Smith's Tribe. Like Wells, Damon Knowles was a slaveholder. Only one of Knowles's slaves can be documented: the man named Sander whose burial was recorded in the Southampton church register in 1648. The church register also records the Knowles family's close ties to the Dandos and the Wellses: In 1638 a Daniel Knowles (age unknown, but a son of Damon Knowles) married Sarah Dando, the 16-year-old daughter of Marmaduke Dando, and in 1656 another of

---

67. See Ives, *Rich Papers*, 28, 143, 173.
68. Southampton church register, in Hallett, *Early Bermuda Records*, 12.

Damon Knowles's sons, Robert, age 23, married Hester Wells, the 16-year-old daughter of Thomas Wells.

Southampton church records of the Dando family over the years suggest something of the intimate relationships among Southampton's white families. All of the Dandos' daughters married young men who resided in Southampton Tribe: Hanna, the eldest daughter, married John Ingham in 1632. Six years later, in 1638, Sarah married Daniel Knowles, and in 1640 16-year-old Elizabeth married John Richardson, also of Southampton. A 1653 record shows that Anne Dando, who was most likely another daughter, married Henry Morgan of Southampton. Martha, the remaining daughter, died unmarried at age 32 in 1661.[69] Marmaduke Dando Jr., the only son, married in 1655 and had three children—Elizabeth, Frances, and Marmaduke, born between 1656 and 1661. Since Dando Jr. is not listed separately in the survey of 1663, it is likely that he and his family were living on the same land as his father. Land was scarce in Bermuda, and unless he wished to leave the islands, there was no place for him to go. The shortage of land is probably the reason that Thomas Wells's adult son, John, lived on the church property next to his father's residence. The Dandos, the Wellses, and the Knowleses were a close-knit group, but they were not unusual in their intermarriages. The surviving records indicate that not only the residents of Southampton, but those of other tribes as well, tended to intermarry, and that sons-in-law and daughters-in-law as well as sons and daughters were often provided for in wills. Wills in Southampton, as in other tribes, testify to the close relationships between slaveholding families and their slaves. Slaves were usually bequeathed by name to specific family members.

While bequeathing a slave to a specific family member was not unusual—slaveholders in Virginia and other colonies on the mainland often followed the same practice[70]—Bermuda slavery was unique in the naming of slaves. Scholars wrestle with the origins (African or other) of slave names and with deciding who (the slaveholder or the slave parent) usually chose a slave child's name. No matter who made the choice, slaves in other slave societies almost never bore the same given names as members of their masters' families. In South Carolina, for example, female slaves infrequently shared the given names of their female mistresses, but male slaves and the males in the master's family did not.[71] Bermuda slaves and slaveholders, in striking contrast, did exactly the

---

69. Hallett, *Early Bermuda Records,* 4, 9, 12, 17, 19, 21.

70. See Kulikoff, *Tobacco and Slaves,* 11–12.

71. Cheryl Ann Cody, "There Was No 'Absalom' on the Ball Plantation: Slave-Naming Practices in the South Carolina Low Country, 1720–1865," *American Historical Review* 92 (June 1987): 563–96. Inscoe, "Carolina Slave Names," 539, observes that "one is struck by how rarely slaves took the given names of their master or his family for their own children." See

opposite: Many slaves, both male and female, in seventeenth-century Bermuda households bore the same given name as the master or a member of the master's family. For example, John Todd's 1678 estate inventory lists two slaves, Bess and Sarah. These two women, whose ages are not recorded, bore the same names as Todd's wife and daughter. Devonshire resident Joseph Wiseman bequeathed to his son Jeames a slave boy named Jeames, and to his son Samuel, a boy named Sam. The will of another Southampton resident, Thomas Kersey, bequeathed "a negro called Sarah" to his grown daughter, Sarah, in 1675. Whether the household was affluent or modest, with many slaves or a few, the practice was the same. The prosperous merchant Jerome Ewer bequeathed a girl named Jane to his grandniece, Jane. John Vaughan of St. George's had a slave called Jonny Boy, and Vaughan bequeathed to his wife, Ann, a "little girl" named Ann. Of a collection of 96 wills in the Bermuda Archives dating from the 1660s to the early 1700s and listing both the given names of slaveholding family members and the names of that family's slaves, 32 contain one or more pairs of namesakes, with males and females almost equally distributed (11 households had male namesakes; 15 had female namesakes, and six had both male and female pairs of namesakes). Josias Forster had a daughter named Hanna and a slave named Black Hanna; Richard Gilbert had a son named Thomas and a slave boy named Thomas; Edward Hinson and his wife, Elizabeth, had among their 10 slaves a man named Ned and a woman named Bess; Willliam Keele had a son named Daniel and a mulatto slave named Daniel; Thomas Dunscomb, a mariner of Pembroke Tribe, bequeathed a slave named Mary to his daughter, Mary. A Southampton tenant named Thomas Murrell left a "Negro woman Frances aged 19" to his unmarried daughter, Frances, and a "Negro girl Sarah" to his wife, Sarah.[72]

By the unusual terms of Murrell's 1675 will, these young black women, along with Joan, age 13, and Luke, a "molatto boy" of 10, were to be freed when they arrived "at the fortieth yeare of their respective ages." A "Negro servant William," however, was not to be freed. This part of the will is illegible but ends with the words, "to be given to my young children." William was probably needed to continue to work the few acres of tobacco and corn that Murrell would have grown on his 50-acre property. Murrell's widow could also have hired out William to work for wages to help support her and the children.[73]

---

also Inscoe's "Generation and Gender." Inscoe disagrees with Herbert Gutman's argument that slave children were frequently named for their fathers.

72. The location of these wills can be found in Hallett, *Early Bermuda Wills.*

73. Books of Wills, vol. 1, p. 216. Murrell was a tenant on two different plots of land in Southampton: a 15-acre property owned by Captain George Hubbard of Devonshire Tribe, who also owned land there and in Hamilton Tribe, and a 49-acre tract owned by another

The will and inventory of Thomas Kersey, who owned two shares of land at the east end of Southampton, afford a more detailed picture of a slaveholder's modest estate. Kersey, who died in 1676, owned at least two blacks at the time he made his will in 1675. One, a young woman named Sarah, mentioned earlier, he left to his daughter of the same name. The other, a boy named George, he left to his youngest daughter, Charity. Kersey and his wife, Mary, had five children: Henry, Sarah, Ruth, Thomas, and Charity, born between 1643 and 1658.[74] When Thomas Kersey died, he left a household inventory worth only £69. Kersey's worldly goods were few, and they were probably typical of many Bermuda households. Besides the two slaves, they included linens for both beds and tables, a variety of cooking utensils, and laundry equipment. Kersey also had "two old decayed Bibles and some other Books." There was a spinning wheel, and Kersey had two ewes and a lamb among his livestock, which suggests that his wife and daughters produced their own woolen cloth or, at least, woolen thread. The Kerseys, the Murrells, and other Bermuda families like these were slaveholders, but they lived simply, farming a few acres, keeping some livestock, living and working along with their slaves. Some of them also lived alongside free blacks. For example, Thomas Kersey leased a house, presumably on his 50 acres, to a free black woman named Ann Force. Her father may have been William Force, the free black who was involved in the 1656 slave conspiracy. Under the law of 1674 Ann Force was required to apprentice herself to "some man or other" or else to leave Bermuda. What became of her is not recorded.[75]

A few Southampton residents lived in grander style than the rest: Of the 10 houses in the 1663 survey described as mansions, five were in Southampton Tribe, and three of the five were on adjacent properties on the western shore. One of these, described earlier, belonged to Stephen Paynter, who had died in 1661. On either side of the Paynter property were the mansions of Captain Thomas Richards and Richard Leacraft. To the east lay the four shares of land owned by Richards, who, like Paynter, was a first-generation Bermuda colonist and had been there for 40 years. The two were apparently close friends, and Richards was an executor of Paynter's will.[76] As we shall see in the next chapter, Thomas Richards was also one of Bermuda's wealthiest merchants. He and his wife, Ann, had at least five children—three sons and two daughters—born

---

Thomas Murrell, probably his father, who lived in Paget and owned land there as well. Murrell's Southampton lands illustrate the complexity of landholding patterns in colonial Bermuda, where it was not unusual for a landowner to have property in more than one tribe, or for a tenant to be responsible for lands in more than one location.

74. Hallett, *Early Bermuda Records*, 9.
75. Lefroy, *Memorials*, 2:364.
76. Ibid., 2:569.

between 1626 and 1646. One of their sons would become chief justice of Bermuda in 1687. The mansion to the west of Stephen Paynter's was occupied by the widow of Richard Leacraft. Leacraft, like Paynter and Richards, had been in Bermuda since the 1620s. According to the Southampton church records he and his wife, Jane, had six children—four daughters and two sons—born between 1624 and 1637. Leacraft died in 1648, but in 1663 his widow lived on in the mansion, with her two grown sons, Richard, 31 years old, and Thomas, 27, residing nearby in two tenements on the family's 73-acre property.

Of the other two mansion-dwellers in Southampton, one, Robert Dickinson, was a blacksmith who had been in Bermuda at least since the birth of his son, John, in 1640. The child's baptism was recorded in the Southampton church register. Dickinson was also a slaveholder, although the number of his slaves is not known. As noted in chapter 2, he had purchased an Indian woman named Elizabeth in 1646. The remaining Southampton mansion was the property of Marmaduke Dando's neighbor to the east, Richard Hunt, who was almost a generation younger than Southampton's other wealthy residents. By the 1660s these first-generation colonists, some of whom had started out as tenants on someone else's land, had turned to means other than tobacco growing to make their fortunes. As we shall see in the next chapter, they looked to the sea and to trade for their livelihood.

One wonders what men such as Richards, Leacraft, Dickinson, and Hunt thought of their neighbor Marmaduke Dando, who had taken up his lease on land in Southampton Tribe in 1617 and lived contentedly as a tenant there for most of his life. Perhaps some of them, and surely his landlord, Richard Hunt, came to comfort his family when he died on October 29, 1668.[77] They may have been present at his funeral the next day at Southampton Church. Marmaduke Dando was buried near the church where he had served as a reader and close by the place where he had lived for more than 50 years. He never owned any land and probably never had any slaves or servants, but as his fellow colonist Richard Norwood wrote, "May it not justly be accounted happinesse and prosperitie, for men to live where they enjoy the meanes of true religion and salvation . . . where the government is good without rigour and opression, the place healthfull and temperate? where they are freed from all extreame care and toyle? where they have food in abundance, and very good, with other things needful to the body?"[78]

Marmaduke Dando probably would have agreed.

77. Hallett, *Early Bermuda Records*, 21.
78. Norwood, *Journal*, lxxvii.

Bermuda at the time of Dando's death was a colony whose economy was undergoing a transition from agricultural to mercantile and maritime pursuits, and where men of ambition situated themselves on property—either leased or owned—to take advantage of trade connections. As the survey of 1663 shows, Bermuda was not a wealthy colony, but about 10 percent of its householders were members of a rising economic and social elite. It is useful to identify some of them and to complete a bird's-eye view, as it were, of the colony in the latter half of the seventeenth century. Immediately to the west of the island of St. George's, accessible by ferry, is Hamilton Tribe, a narrow strip of land that curves around a large inland lake called the Little Sound. In 1663 Hamilton had 28 households, only nine of whose residents owned the land they lived on. The landowners' properties ranged in size from 25 to 75 acres, with only one landlord, John Hubbard, owning as much as 75 acres. Resident tenants' properties were also quite small, ranging from eight to 49 acres, with only two—one of 75 acres, the other of 147 acres—held by tenants. The 147-acre property was occupied by Ruth Willis, the widowed daughter of Thomas Wood, its late owner. Even so, Hamilton was a prosperous tribe. Nine of its 28 households were dwellings, not tenements. At least 13 of Hamilton's residents in the survey of 1663 left wills or inventories, and of these, at least 11 owned slaves. In all, 34 slaves, including five Indians and five mulattos, can be documented as living in Hamilton between 1663 and 1705, and there were undoubtedly many more.

At least 41 slaves—38 blacks, one mulatto, and two Indians—can be documented as residing in Smith's Tribe, which lies south and slightly to the west of Hamilton Tribe. The two tribes share the small inlet called the Flatts, which connects the Little Sound with the Atlantic Ocean. Much of Smith's Tribe is higher in elevation than neighboring Hamilton and Devonshire, with hills of 150 to 200 feet above sea level. In 1663 its 1,250 acres were divided among 33 householders: 13 owners and 20 tenants. Among these households were three mansions and three dwellings, with the other 27 being ordinary tenements. Of 12 extant wills or inventories for Smith's Tribe, all but one contain references to slaves—but only one uses the word *slave*. The will of William Sayle, a former governor of Bermuda who died in 1671, refers to his "Monie, Plate, Slaves & other Goods & Chattels." In the inventory of his estate, however, his nine blacks are listed as "The Negros."[79] Like Hamilton, Smith's Tribe was the home of a number of affluent merchants, three of whom, including William Sayle, lived in mansions. The other mansions belonged to Captain Richard Jennings and John Somersall. Sayle, Jennings, and Somersall all lived near the Flatts and less than a quarter of a mile from each other. Somersall owned the

79. Books of Wills, vol. 1, pp. 145, 149.

most land, 122 acres. All were engaged in maritime and mercantile ventures, and all held slaves.

Continuing along the main island's north shore, after St. George's, Hamilton, and Smith's, one comes to Devonshire and Pembroke, two of the least-prosperous tribes in seventeenth-century Bermuda. About one-eighth of Devonshire's land is a low, marshy section known as Devonshire Marsh. In 1663 this tribe had 38 householders, of whom 10 owned the land they lived on. Among the more affluent residents of Devonshire Tribe was George Hubbard, who had come to Bermuda in 1635, at age 16, aboard the *Dorset*. By 1663, he owned two shares of land in Devonshire as well as two more shares and two houses in Hamilton Tribe as rental property. In 1658 he was captain of the militia for both Devonshire and neighboring Pembroke, and in 1663 he was a councillor for Devonshire. When he died, in 1688, at age 69 he left a mansion and at least six slaves to various members of his family.[80] As for the numbers of blacks in Devonshire's households around the time of the 1663 survey, the records are fragmentary. There are 13 surviving wills or inventories for Devonshire between 1663 and 1705, with seven mentioning or listing slaves or servants. (The 1662 will of Ann Dawes, a widow, mentions one "English Maide servant.") Thirty-one blacks and one mulatto—none listed as "slaves"—can be identified in the existing records.

West of Devonshire lies Pembroke Tribe, a peninsula almost a mile wide and nearly two and a half miles long, whose north shore is a ridge of hills ranging from 100 to 200 feet above sea level, ending in a narrow neck of land known as Spanish Point. In the southeastern part of the tribe is Pembroke Marsh. A ridge whose highest point was once called Mount Hill lies almost in the center in the parish and rises to a height of 200 feet, isolating much of the windy north shore from the sheltered lands bordering the waters of the Great Sound and Crow Lane to the south. The only lands suitable for farming are in the central part, where the modern capital of Hamilton is now located, and western part, which is now the affluent neighborhood known as Fairylands. Pembroke in 1663 had 42 households, of which only nine were occupied by resident landowners. Of the 33 resident tenants in Pembroke, 22 had one share of land and 11 had only one-half shares. Most of Pembroke's land was divided into acreages barely large enough for subsistence farming. But this tribe's nearly five miles of shoreline with numerous coves and inlets made it ideal for seafaring and shipbuilding. By the middle of the seventeenth century many of Pembroke's residents made their livings from the sea, not the land. A total of 59 slaves, including four Indians, can be documented in

---

80. Books of Wills, vol. 3, pt. 1, p. 29. Hubbard's will mentions two grandchildren named Stowe, who may have been related to Captain John Stowe of Pembroke.

the Pembroke wills and inventories, with Richard Norwood's 11 being the largest number in one household. The nature and extent of Pembroke's black community can only be imagined, but evidence of its existence is the fact that slaves from at least four neighboring households in Pembroke, as we shall see, were among the leaders of a slave rebellion plot in 1673. The involvement of slaves belonging to John Stowe, Richard Norwood, John Squire, and the Reverend Sampson Bond in slave conspiracies is discussed later in this chapter.

Due south of Pembroke Tribe, across the sheltered harbor near Crow Lane, lie the gently sloping hills of Paget Tribe. In 1663 Paget, like Pembroke, was a populous tribe, with 44 households. Only seven of these, however, were the households of landowners, including the owners of one mansion and four dwellings. All the rest were tenants, most with small holdings of one share or less. The mansion belonged to Captain Philip Lea, the owner of 98 acres stretching from Crow Lane on the north to the Atlantic Ocean on the south. One of the dwellings belonged to Captain John Wentworth, the eldest son of Hugh Wentworth Sr. of Warwick. His younger brother, Hugh Jr., owned and lived on the family property in Warwick, but in 1663 John, a sea captain, was a tenant on his four shares in Paget Tribe.

West of Paget, lying on a narrow, curving strip of land that averages about half a mile in width, are the three remaining tribes: Warwick, Southampton, and Sandys. At the time of the survey Warwick, like Paget, its neighbor to the east, was composed of many small individual holdings. Of 33 Warwick households, 17 were on one share or less and only nine were occupied by the owners. There was one mansion, a "faire dwelling house," and three dwellings among its residences. The mansion belonged to Captain John Darrell, who lived about one-quarter mile from Jerome Ewer's dwelling; Hugh Wentworth's dwelling was about one-half mile from Ewer's. The other two owners of dwelling houses in Warwick were John Wainwright, who occupied 75 acres next to Ewer's property, and James Witter, the son-in-law of surveyor Richard Norwood. Witter, a surgeon, his wife, Elizabeth, and their seven children lived on, but did not own, 50 acres at the west end of Warwick in 1663. There are 11 surviving wills and inventories for Warwick Tribe, eight of which mention more than 39 slaves, including two Indians.

As table 5 shows, Sandys Tribe, at the far west end of Bermuda, was the most populous of the tribes, although its hilly terrain and many bays and inlets gave it far less arable land than the other tribes. Sandys Tribe's economy was based, obviously not on agriculture, but on maritime pursuits. These included the Bermuda pastime known as "wrecking," or salvaging goods and equipment from wrecked ships, which will be taken up in the next chapter. Many of the shipwrecks that occurred in Bermuda's waters took place on the hidden reefs off the Sandys coast. Sandys Tribe's 1,250 acres are situated on a narrow, curving peninsula and a scattering of small islands, two of which are named: Somerset and Ireland. The 1663 survey lists 49 householders on these 50 shares, but only eight of these residents owned the property they lived on.

Sandys had no mansions, but it did contain five dwelling houses that belonged to five of the largest landholders—all of whom bore the title "captain." Christopher Burrows, who owned a total of 92 acres and lived on Somerset Island, also owned a share of land in Pembroke Tribe, which he rented to two tenants. He was a sea captain, militia officer, and a councillor for Sandys. Josias Forster, a former governor, owned eight acres on Ireland Island and lived on his 42-acre property at Hog Bay in Sandys. His active role in the witchcraft trials and the slave conspiracy plot in the 1650s has already been noted. Florentius Seymour, governor from 1662 to 1668 and from 1681 to 1682, owned 4.5 acres on Ireland Island and 10 acres at Hog Bay and lived on his 18 acres on Somerset Island. Thomas Turner, also a former governor (1646–1649), lived on 14 acres at Somerset and owned 11 acres on Ireland Island and 18 acres at Hog Bay. The fifth resident of a dwelling in Sandys was William Waylett, who lived on his 34-acre property at Hog Bay and owned another six acres nearby. He also owned 3.5 acres on Ireland Island and 3.5 acres on Somerset Island. Owning or renting property—however small in acreage—on Ireland Island, a narrow island that stretches northeast of the rest of Sandys Tribe, enabled the owner or tenant to share in the spoils of wrecking and perhaps also to share in the division of any buried treasure found on the island. There were rumors of a Spanish treasure that had been hastily buried on Ireland Island in the late 1500s, a possibility that intrigued Bermudians for the next hundred years.[81]

The survey of 1663 laid out property lines for Bermuda's 378 households, which contained nearly 4,000 people. An undetermined number of them were blacks, mulattos, and Indians, and most of those were slaves. While the surviving records suggest that Bermuda's slaveholders looked after the welfare of their slaves, cared for them when they were ill, often named them for family members, sometimes manumitted them, and almost always bequeathed them

81. A series of depositions from various Bermudians in 1692 described a long-buried Spanish treasure on Ireland Island. The testimony involved several prominent colonists: Richard Stafford, who lived near Ellen Burrows, recalled her mention of a conversation with a man in England who claimed to know the whereabouts of the treasure. Joseph Ming, grandson of Edward Carter, one of the three Bermudians who found the ambergris in 1609, testified that his grandfather chose Cooper's Island as his land portion because of rumors of buried treasure there. Thomas Walker had heard that the Reverend Sampson Bond was taken by a Dutch privateer into a Spanish port called the Groine, where he heard tales of treasure on both Ireland and Cooper's Islands. Richard Leacraft, John Hurt, Samuel Brangman, Jonathan Stokes, William Keele, Edmund Evans, and Captain William Seymour also testified to hearing rumors of treasure. For an account of these stories and excerpts from the depositions, see Williams, *Historical & Statistical Account,* 301–23.

to relatives, keeping them in families rather than selling them, that by no means suggests that Bermuda's slaves were content under what appears to be a milder form of slavery than that in most other English colonies. As the slave population grew, there were undercurrents of unrest in black Bermuda society and a resulting unease in white Bermuda society. The records of slaveholders' care must be weighed against records of continued slave resistance and the white community's response to it.

A year after the 1663 legislation to control the behavior of Bermuda's blacks, both slave and free, Governor Florentius Seymour issued a proclamation whose language reveals the anxieties of the whites over the "insolent languages & cariages of the Negroes."[82] All able-bodied free blacks were ordered to depart from the colony, and Captain John Stowe of Pembroke Tribe was ordered to transport them—perhaps because some of them were the blacks he had brought from Barbados in 1659. Those who refused to leave were to be assigned to "Masters or Mistresses" chosen by the governor and council and would be, for all practical purposes, slaves. As for blacks who were too old to work, their "last Master" was ordered to "provide for them such accommodations as shall be convenient for Creatures of that hue and colour until their death." But, the governor continued, "for such Negroes as shall bee soe hardie & audatious as to dare to rise upp against their Masters, or any English person or ysons whatsoever, (as som of late have dared to doe both in words & deeds.) It is unanisly concluded. That such Negroe or Negroes shall be speedily tryed, Convicted & Executed by a Councell of Warr." The last recorded slave uprisings had been in 1656 and 1661. But, as Governor Seymour's language makes clear, there had been other instances of black assertiveness in "words & deeds" since then. The 32 blacks that John Stowe had brought from Barbados in 1659, some of whom may have been involved in the abortive 1661 plot, may have continued to demonstrate their discontent. In the 1660s there were other acts, individual and collective, of resistance to slavery.

Documentary evidence of runaways is fragmentary. On July 24, 1664, for example, Peter, a "servant" belonging to Captain William Waylett of Hog Bay in Sandys Tribe, and John, a "Negroe servant" of Mrs. Anne Kennish's of neighboring Southampton Tribe, stole a boat belonging to William Burch, a tenant on the property adjoining Waylett's. Waylett's household contained other blacks, some of whom may have been related to Peter. When Waylett died in 1679 he left three blacks—"Black Will," "Black Bess," and "Black Nan,"—and a mulatto girl named Rachel to his three daughters. To his wife he left a mulatto woman called Judah. In the summer of 1664 Waylett's man,

82. Lefroy, *Memorials*, 2:216.

Peter (aided by John, Peter's "Consort"), "by force of Armes" boarded the boat lying at anchor in Hog Bay and "did steal, take, and convay away" the craft, a two-masted vessel valued at 50 shillings. How Peter and John were apprehended is not recorded, but if they sailed out of Hog Bay, a small bay that opens onto the Great Sound, not the Atlantic Ocean, they would have had to take the purloined vessel to open seas through the narrow, crooked passages of the waterway that separates part of the mainland from Somerset Island or else sail it across the Great Sound for about four miles. Either way, they were bound to be discovered. At the trial an evidently defiant Peter refused to plead either innocent or guilty, but he was found guilty and sentenced to death. Mrs. Kennish's slave, John, was also found guilty and given the same punishment, but Governor Seymour gave him a reprieve. The reprieve itself, however, carried another, perhaps crueler punishment: Instead of being condemned to hang, John was made "executioner for Negroes for the time to come." And so, on August 22, 1664, John was forced to hang his friend, Peter.[83]

John was the executioner for another black that same day. A few days earlier, "Black Mathew, a Negroe servant youth of John Welch of St. George," had been convicted of breaking into the house of Mrs. Hannah Holloway. Welch, a boatwright, had paid £24 for Matthew in 1660, buying the youth from the commander of the *Abigail*. Welch had at that same time purchased a black youth, named Salvadore, from an English merchant, paying £20.[84] Salvadore apparently was not involved in Mathew's crime. John Welch was Hannah Holloway's neighbor. They and five others were tenants on 50 acres at St. George's. One of these tenants was John Bristow, marshal of the colony, who may have apprehended young Mathew. Hannah Holloway "was much affrighted" by the incident. And when Mathew was incarcerated to await his trial, he "did, by force of Armes . . . feloniously break out of the Comon Goale [jail]." What weapon or weapons Mathew used to accomplish his escape, or how he managed to come by them while in jail, is not recorded. But he was tried, found guilty, and sentenced to hang. After the execution Governor Seymour ordered Mathew's head to be "severed from his bodie & fixed upon a poles end at Stocks Point," a small promontory on St. David's Island, about 400 yards across Town Harbor from St. George's. The governor also ordered Peter's head to be severed and "fixed upon a spicke uppon the topp of the Island to the terror of all slaves that shall hereafter attempt the like feat and offence."[85] The placing of heads on poles, unusual for Bermuda, was no doubt

83. For the account of the runaway, see Lefroy, *Memorials,* 2:217–18. Waylett's will is in Books of Wills, vol. 1, p. 267.

84. CR, 2:372.

85. Records of the trials and executions of Peter and Mathew are in Lefroy, *Memorials,* 2:217–19.

ordered because of the seriousness of the crimes: Both Peter and Mathew had used "force of armes" against whites. It is also possible that the actions of these slaves and the whites' response to them were inspired by a slave rebellion in Gloucester County, Virginia, the previous year. As a result of that incident, several slaves were executed and their bloody heads were displayed from chimney tops.[86]

Not long after the executions of Peter and Mathew, Florentius Seymour's successor as governor, Sir John Heydon, had to cope with a different kind of resistance by some of Bermuda's blacks. In an extraordinary bid for freedom in 1669 a number of slaves petitioned the governor for their liberty on the grounds that they were baptized Christians. As we have seen, early church records show a few slave baptisms, but a Bermuda law of 1647 forbade the "baptizing of Bastards or Negroes children." The question of whether baptism was compatible with slavery provoked debates elsewhere in the English colonies during the seventeenth century, with varying results. In Virginia, for example, slaves were seldom baptized. In the Caribbean colonies, likewise, little effort was made to spread Christianity among the slaves, although some blacks appear in church records. In Barbados, for example, from 1670 to 1687 there were 34 baptisms of slaves recorded in the register of St. Michael's Church in Bridgetown.[87] In 1661 the Somers Islands Company had ordered Governor William Sayle to see that the colony's blacks and Indians received instruction in the Christian faith, and at least one of Bermuda's four clergymen, the Reverend Samuel Smith, favored baptizing slaves.[88] Although the extant records for Bermuda do not allow a precise account of either the 1669 petitioners or their petitions, these blacks may have been responding to rumors of freedom that circulated in the spring of 1669. When Governor Heydon arrived on May 15, 1669, there were rumors in at least one tribe that the colony's "Negroes"—still not officially referred to as slaves—were to be freed at the next muster, "when the Governor should cum upp."[89]

Oddly enough it was a white colonist who allegedly started these rumors. On June 9, one George Garrett, a resident of Southampton Tribe, was summoned to a meeting of the Governor's Council and questioned about the

86. Aptheker, *Slave Revolts,* 164–65.
87. Walvin, *Black Ivory,* 188–90.
88. See "Act for enforcing such as . . . neglect the Sacrament of the Lords Supper . . . ," in Golding, *Servants on Horseback.* For the 1661 instructions to Sayle, see Lefroy, *Memorials,* 2:154–55. On Smith, see 2:291. On slave baptism in seventeenth-century Virginia, see Morgan, *American Slavery,* 332.
89. The account of this episode is in Lefroy, *Memorials,* 2:289. A similar rumor circulated in Virginia in 1729 when it was reported that Colonel Spotswood had come with the king's authority to free all baptized slaves. Afterward, when a number of slaves were found plotting a rebellion, four were executed. See Aptheker, *Slave Revolts,* 179–80.

matter. He claimed that two other colonists, residents of Smith's Tribe, had told him that all of Bermuda's blacks were to be freed by order of the new governor. Garrett named Nathaniel Sayle, a son of the former governor, and a planter named Thomas Griffin Jr. as having started the rumor. But Sayle was not called to testify, and Griffin swore under oath that he had no knowledge of the rumor and even denied knowing Garrett. After some consideration the council voted "by pluralitie" that George Garrett, for spreading this rumor, should have 21 lashes at the whipping post in Pembroke Tribe "immediately after the Evening Sermon, the next ensuing Lord's Day." Garrett was also made to wear a paper pinned on his back with the following text: "George Garret Censured to be whipt, for falslie reporting that the native Negroes are to be freed by the Kings Majesties Comand."

In the next few days many people—both blacks and whites—in Southampton Tribe would have seen George Garrett wearing this sign. Talk of his punishment may well have spread across Warwick, Paget, and Devonshire to Smith's Tribe, where Garrett claimed he had first heard the rumors of freedom. Certainly the residents of Pembroke Tribe, where Garrett was whipped, would have discussed it thoroughly. Why Garrett's whipping took place in Pembroke rather than Southampton, his place of residence, is not stated. It may have been because Pembroke's church customarily had a large evening service that would guarantee a large audience, or simply that Southampton did not have a Sunday worship that week.[90] But as a result, the shocking rumor of freedom for Bermuda's slaves—and its denial—would soon have spread all over the colony, among blacks and whites alike. The summer of 1669 was an unsettling time for many Bermudians. Smallpox had struck the town of St. George's, and the Assembly was obliged to conduct its meeting in Paget Tribe. In late July or early August a hurricane described as the "most violent known by any alive" brought several days of winds and torrential rains.[91]

It may have been in the ensuing weeks that some of Bermuda's blacks decided to petition the new governor for their freedom, believing themselves entitled to it as baptized Christians. There was probably some public discussion of slave baptisms that summer, for in October 1669 the Reverend Samuel Smith, pastor at St. George's from 1663 to 1671, petitioned the council for permission to baptize "Molattoes, Indians, (and more especiallie) Negroes." The motion was tabled, although the reason was not stated. Whether the blacks submitted their petitions before or after this council meeting is not clear, but

90. Colonial Bermuda seldom had more than four clergymen for its eight tribes. In 1669 Sampson Bond and Samuel Smith were the only ministers in the islands. Hallett, *Colonial Church*, 345.

91. Lefroy, *Memorials,* 2:635; *CSP,* 1669–1674:45.

on November 13, 1669, Governor Heydon issued a proclamation responding to "divers petitions" submitted to him. Unfortunately none of the petitions has survived, so their substance must be inferred from the governor's text. Heydon avoided using the words *slave* or *slavery,* choosing instead an oblique reference: "The petitioners not well weighing the just Interests of their respective Owners and Masters to their persons, being purchased by them without condition or limitation. It being likewise so practised in these American Plantations and in other parts of the world."[92] Leaving the antecedent of "It" unspecified, the governor went on to argue in favor of baptism for servants and to condemn "heathenish Masters, that know not the Scriptures," who "would keep them in ignorance and blindenes, enslaveing the soules as well as the bodies." Here slavery is clearly understood to be the condition of the petitioners. But Christian baptism, according to the governor, does not mean liberty. Although some petitioners argued that "the Gospel allowes no bondmen," that is, according to Governor Heydon, "a gross mistake." He quotes from chapter 6 of Saint Paul's letter to the Ephesians: "Servants bee obedient unto them that are your Masters in the flesh, with feare and trembling, in singlenes of heart as unto Christ, not with eye service as men pleasers, but as the servants of Christ, doeing the will of God from the heart . . . knowing that whatsoever good thing any man doth, the same shall hee receive of the Lord, whether hee bee bond or free." The governor also cites, by chapter and verse, several other Bible passages in support of submissiveness to masters.

The conclusion of this proclamation is a plea for peace and order:

Now in consideration of what hath bin said, Masters and Servants are hereby advised, and in the kings name required to live in peace, mutuall love and respect to each other, Servants submitting to the condition wherein God hath placed them. And such Negroes as formerlie, or lately have bin baptized by severall Ministers, should not thereby think themselves more free from their Masters and Owners, but rather, by the meanes of their Christian profession, obliged to a more strict bond of fidelity and service. And if all persons professing Christianity would be careful in the discharge of their duties, living in the feare of God, and in due obedience to His Majesties Laws, complaints of this nature would be prevented, true religion, and civill conversation would be encouraged, the service of God would be esteemed the greatest freedome.[93]

While it is important to note that the governor carefully avoided using the words *slave* or *slavery,* the most remarkable aspect of this proclamation is the petitions that called it forth. The fact that the petitions were created means that some of Bermuda's blacks were literate and, moreover, were learned enough to put their demands into written form. How widespread literacy was in Bermuda

92. The proclamation is printed in Lefroy, *Memorials,* 2:293–94 (quotation, p. 293).
93. Ibid., 293–94.

for both whites and blacks is impossible to determine. There is no evidence to suggest that any blacks attended schools in seventeenth-century Bermuda, but there were never any laws forbidding the teaching of blacks to read and write. In fact, as evidenced by the efforts of Governor Roger Wood to see to the education of the black children in his charge in the 1630s and the provisions of various masters for young blacks to be taught to read the Bible, literacy for blacks as well as whites was obviously a desirable goal in Bermuda society. Persons who could read could claim benefit of clergy if convicted of a crime and thus avoid the death penalty. The trial of the mulatto slave, Diego, who claimed benefit of clergy in 1671 is a case in point.

Governor Heydon's plea for order was soon to be tested in another incident involving behavior of a slave. On August 12, 1671, Sambo, "the Negroe-man of Mr. William Baseden," was accused of "stubborn Cariage in Warwick Tribe Church Yard towards Capt John Darrell, Counsellor of that Tribe." William Basden and John Darrell were neighbors: Darrell's 75 acres lay immediately to the east of Basden's 50 acres, and both properties were less than one-quarter mile from the church. Since the incident occurred in the churchyard, it probably took place before or after a church service. One wonders what passed between Sambo and John Darrell that caused Sambo to draw his knife, "frighting the Wife of Capt Darrell." This incident was reported (no doubt by Councillor Darrell) to the Governor's Council. Apparently Sambo had a reputation for insubordinate behavior toward whites, and the council ordered him to "bee for the aforesaid and other outragious Carriages, carryed to the Galloes, and there stand thereunto tied, some short tyme, and there Whipped with Eleven stripes upon the naked back."[94] In this instance a black man who threatened a white man with a knife seems to have had a relatively light punishment, but perhaps one designed to frighten a valuable servant into more submissive behavior. What became of Sambo after this incident is unknown. When William Basden made his will more than 20 years later, in 1685, he had six slaves. He left to his wife Margery a "Negro woman Sarah," who was to "bee free from servitude" at his wife's death. The other slaves—a girl named Sarah, a woman named Nell, and three children—were bequeathed to Basden's children. Sambo, who may have been the husband of Nell and the father of her children, was not listed.[95]

The insubordinate Sambo may also have been among a group of slaves who plotted to seize their freedom in 1673. They numbered 15 or more, and they devised an elaborate plan: Two of them were to ride horseback through all the tribes, giving the alarm for a general insurrection, with the rest of the rebels

94. Ibid., 349.
95. Books of Wills, vol. 3, pt. 1, pp. 3, 5.

waited for other slaves to join them in the center of the colony at Crow Lane, near the harbor opening onto the Great Sound. This seems an ill-conceived plan, since the horseback riders would have had to cover about 24 miles and in all likelihood would have been discovered before a general uprising could take place. That may in fact have been what happened.

Perhaps the conspirators were moved by the failure of the 1669 petitions, for freedom and by the political turmoil in the colony. Governor Heydon and the Assembly were at odds over trade and other policies of the Somers Islands Company (the colony would pass under the control of the crown in 1684) and on August 23, 1673, the governor dissolved the Assembly. It did not meet again until 1683.[96] The conspirators may also have been inspired by news of several abortive slave plots in Virginia in 1672.[97] It is obvious that the transatlantic trade network brought far more than cloth and trinkets to Bermuda. Virginia vessels came often to Bermuda, and Bermuda ships were no strangers to Chesapeake Bay. Black sailors and black dockhands would have had ample opportunities for furtive exchanges of news. In more than one instance, as we shall see, organized acts of slave resistance in the English colonies in the late 1600s and early 1700s seemed to follow close upon each other, spreading from colony to colony, perhaps set off by clandestine conversations among black seamen. It is also possible that some of the conspirators were newly arrived Africans. At an unspecified date in 1673, in fact, a Bermuda vessel had brought about 125 blacks from Calabar, on the Guinea coast, half of whom were sold in Bermuda, and the rest in the Caribbean and mainland colonies.[98]

In Bermuda's 1673 conspiracy, one of the slaves, a black named Robin, gave away the plan, although the record does not say how. As a result, he and 14 other suspects were seized and put in jail at St. George's, where a grand jury presented them as "Guilty of a Daingerous plott."[99] A discussion of their punishment was the subject of a council meeting on December 24. Governor Heydon recommended that since there was "noe blood shed," the slaves not be tried by a court-martial, as ordered by the preceding governor's proclamation of 1664. Instead, Heydon proposed that the leaders of the plot be taken to the gallows, tied there, whipped, and "burned in ye fforhead with

---

96. Lefroy, *Memorials*, 2:384.

97. Aptheker, *Slave Revolts*, 166.

98. See *CSP*, 1708:59. Bennett reported that no blacks "directly from Africa" had been brought in since 1698, but that the 125 from Calabar had been brought in "about 36 years ago," which would have been around 1673.

99. The records of the 1673 conspiracy are in CR, 5B:249–50, printed in Lefroy, *Memorials*, 2:388–92. See also Michael Craton, *Testing the Chains: Resistance to Slavery in the British West Indies* (Ithaca, N.Y.: Cornell University Press, 1982), 335–36.

ye letter R"[100] (for rogue). The rest of the conspirators were to be "whipped and sent home."

The council members disagreed. Their responses are perhaps indicative of the varying racial attitudes among Bermuda's white elites. Secretary Cornelius White was of the opinion that the accused should have a jury trial.[101] The confessions of those who had pleaded guilty, White said, should be used against them, but the rest of the conspirators should not be allowed to testify against each other "because they are Incertaine." The other council members disagreed. Thomas Leacraft of Southampton agreed with Governor Heydon; John Wainwright (also of Southampton) and Henry Tucker of St. George's recommended a modified version of the governor's proposal: that the 15 conspirators be "Tied up to ye Galloes with their toes touching to ye ground and burnt in ye fforhead." Thomas Wood of Pembroke thought there should be a trial by a council of war in which "Black to Black shall be good evidence one against ye other." Councillors William Peniston of Smith's, Henry Moore of Pembroke, Captain John Hubbard of Devonshire, and Sheriff Anthony Jenour all agreed with Wood. Although five of the 10 favored a trial, either civil or court-martial, the council finally decided against such action, and the governor's initial recommendation was carried out, with the additional punishment for the six leaders of having their noses slit.

The punishment took place a few days later at Crow Lane, "where they intended the plott." The council ordered a gibbet erected there, where presumably each man in turn would be tied, branded, and whipped (the number of lashes was unspecified). In addition, "ye two Negroes that rid ye horses are that day to ride upon the said Gybitt." Crow Lane was an area easily accessible from all parts of the islands, and such a sensational event no doubt drew a large crowd of blacks and whites alike. A few days after the punishments at Crow Lane, Governor Heydon issued a proclamation that reveals something of the public's reaction to the incident: "And forasmuch as divers heathenish Negroes . . . have by examination and ye Mutuall impeachment of one an other, bin convicted of a Barbarous and bloudie designe, tending to the destruction of this plantation . . . . And because (since that) I have bin Informed that some disorderly ysons, doe threaten those Negroes being stigmatized for their wicked intentions, to ripp them upp, or otherwise to kill them at their pleasure. I would have such person to know that such a bloudy fact is against ye Law of God & ye King."[102]

100. Lefroy, *Memorials*, 2:388.
101. Cornelius White was very likely the son of the clergyman Nathaniel White, who died in 1668. See ibid., 278.
102. Ibid., 391–92.

There are no records of violence against the marked slaves, but one cannot help but wonder how they fared after the branding. How did whites treat them? How did other slaves treat them? Were they "stigmatized" (as the council members termed their branding) as rash and foolish? What were the feelings of master and slave toward each other after this episode? What was the value of a slave marked as a rebel? These men bore scars, but there is no mention of any other identification sometimes used elsewhere to mark rebel slaves. A Maryland slave named Sam, for example, accused of leading several slave plots, was made to wear an iron collar around his neck for life, with death the punishment for removing it.[103] The existing fragments of evidence afford a glimpse—but no more—into the lives of some of the conspirators.

The identity of nine of the 1673 conspirators is unknown, but the six ringleaders—those who had their noses slit—are mentioned by name. All belonged to prominent men in the colony. Four belonged to wealthy merchants: Frank, a slave of Captain John Stowe; Kitt, who belonged to John Squire; Hercules, a slave of Hugh Wentworth; and Tom, a slave of John Darrell. The other named conspirators were Robin, a slave of the Reverend Sampson Bond; and Argee, who belonged to Richard Norwood. All of the would-be rebels came from households with from five to 10 slaves, including some women and children.[104]

Frank, Kitt, Hercules, and Tom may have been seamen, since their masters either owned or had interests in vessels that traded with the Caribbean and mainland colonies outside Bermuda. In serving their masters' interests at sea, these blacks would have had opportunities for contacts with other blacks in seaport towns along the Atlantic coast and in the Caribbean islands. Men like Frank, Kitt, Hercules, and Tom were part of an extensive but largely undocumented network of black sailors who served aboard ships that sailed in Atlantic and Caribbean waters. Robin and Argee, being in the households of masters with interests outside Bermuda, were also part of that transatlantic network. Robin's master, Sampson Bond, had contacts in England and New England; Argee's master, Richard Norwood, also had contacts in England and in the Caribbean. Robin and Argee were probably house servants, but they, like most Bermuda slaves, undoubtedly knew how to sail a boat and catch fish. They would have had ample opportunity to hear news of places outside Bermuda.

Robin and Argee may also have been literate, since they lived in the households of a clergyman and a former surveyor/schoolmaster, where reading and

103. Aptheker, *Slave Revolts*, 167.
104. The information on these slaves' households is taken from the wills and inventories of their owners, and from the records of slave sales in CR, vol. 2.

writing and book learning were common pursuits. Richard Norwood started a school in Bermuda in 1638 and kept up his scholarly interests until his death in 1675.[105] It is also possible that Robin and Argee, along with Kitt and Frank, all of whom lived near each other in Pembroke Tribe, were among the slaves who petitioned for their liberty a few years earlier in 1669. With petitions rejected and peaceful manumission thus denied, they may have sought other means to attain their freedom.

It would have been only a short walk for Robin to meet with Argee, Frank, and Kitt in the wooded hills of Pembroke that lay between the glebe, where Robin's master lived, and Mill Shares, where the masters of Argee, Frank, and Kitt lived on adjacent properties. And at the time of the 1673 conspiracy Robin may have felt somewhat freer than the others to move about Pembroke, since his master, Sampson Bond, was in England. The other co-conspirators, Hercules and Tom, who lived a mile apart in Warwick, would have had to walk four miles or sail about three-quarters of a mile across Crow Lane harbor to reach Pembroke. The council minutes, however, state that the conspirators' main meeting place was the east end of Crow Lane. In that case each of the six ringleaders would have had to walk no more than a mile or two. There they and the other nine co-conspirators planned to assemble at some prearranged time—for a rebellion that never came to pass.

Of the six leaders, at least three remained in their masters' households, and one of these, Richard Norwood's Argee, was bequeathed to Norwood's grandson nearly 20 years later. When Norwood made his will in 1674 he mentioned "a Negro man called Argee" as one of five slaves living in his house. The other house slaves were an "old Indian woman," an "Indian Negro girl," a black woman, and a "Negro boy called Will of about a year & halfe old." It is possible that the woman and the boy were Argee's wife and son. Norwood had 10 slaves in all; besides the five house slaves, a family of four lived in an out-building, and one slave woman lived at a neighbor's house. Norwood died in November 1675. The inventory of his estate dated July 15, 1676, lists Argee, a known leader of a slave rebellion plot, as the first of 11 slaves (their number had increased by one: a "sucking child") in Norwood's possession. Argee was not sold, but remained in the family. In 1691 Norwood's daughter, Elizabeth Witter, bequeathed "A Negro man called Argee and his wife" to her son.[106]

Like Argee, Sampson Bond's Robin was one of several slaves in a household and may have had a family. Bond's 1692 will refers to "all my Indian & Negro

105. Norwood served as schoolmaster from 1638 to 1650, when his political and religious controversies forced his removal during the English Civil War. He later opened his own school in Pembroke. See Hallett, *Colonial Church*, 328–31.

106. Norwood's will and inventories are in Books of Wills, vol. 1, pp. 213, 219, 261. For Elizabeth Witter's will, see ibid., vol. 3, pt. 1, p. 136.

slaves" but does not name any. When Bond's widow made her will in 1702 she mentioned five slaves—two women, two boys, and a girl. What became of Robin is not known.[107] As for Kitt, John Squire's slave, he was one of six—three men and three women—living in Squire's household 14 years later. Squire's 1687 inventory lists him as worth £15, which suggests that Kitt was getting on in years, perhaps past his prime as a worker.[108] Like Kitt, Hugh Wentworth's Hercules may have been among the older members of the conspiracy. Hercules was valued at £14 in Wentworth's 1674 inventory. He was one of 10 slaves— an Indian man and woman, three black men, three black women, and two children (a girl and a boy)—in the Wentworth household. As for Frank, John Stowe's slave, he may have been one of the "three negroes" Stowe bought in an undated transaction sometime between 1640 and 1667.[109] Stowe bought eight other slaves during this period, so Frank, like his co-conspirators, lived and worked among other black men and women and may have had a wife and family. The remaining member of the notorious six was Tom, who belonged to John Darrell. But Tom is not among the six slaves—two women, one man, and three children (two girls and a boy) named in John Darrell's will in 1677.[110]

For Bermuda's whites, the blacks whose foreheads had been branded with an *R* and whose noses had been slit were disturbing reminders of slave rebellion. As a result of the 1673 plot, laws governing slaves were tightened. The "Orders for ye Suppressing the Insolencies and abuses of ye Negroes" were to be read once each quarter in each parish church: Any slave found outside his master's premises without a "ticket" from the master could be whipped; a second offense would lead to the cutting off "a piece of his ear"; the third offense, a whipping and a branding with the letter *R* on the forehead; the fourth, jail and "punishment as ye Governor & Councell shall think fit." Similar physical punishments were common in other slave societies, but not in Bermuda. In South Carolina until 1833, for example, slaves were branded to identify their owners, and felons had their ears cropped.[111] Slaves were not to venture outside their own parishes on the Sabbath unless accompanied by their owners and were not to gather in groups of more than three "not being of ye same family." The tacit acknowledgment of the existence of slave families and their habitual gatherings on Sundays offers further proof that

107. Ann Bond's will is ibid., vol. 3, pt. 2, p. 22; Sampson Bond's is ibid., pt. 1, p. 186.
108. Ibid., pt. 1, p. 20.
109. CR, 2:83, 180, 214. The exact number of slaves in Stowe's household in 1673 cannot be determined from the existing records.
110. Books of Wills, vol. 1, p. 258.
111. CR, 5B:260–61, printed in Lefroy, *Memorials,* 2:390–91. On slave punishments, see Orlando Patterson, *Slavery and Social Death: A Comparative Study* (Cambridge: Harvard University Press, 1982), 59.

Bermuda slaveholders, who had always recognized marriages among slaves, also respected the importance of family ties in their slave households. In addition to being read aloud every three months, all of the aforementioned orders were to be published so "that none may plead ignorance." Such a provision suggests a certain level of literacy, perhaps for blacks as well as whites. How effectively such orders were obeyed is another matter: Similar orders had been in existence since the 1620s and would be repeated periodically for the next hundred years.

As long as slavery existed, laws to control and to punish blacks were passed repeatedly, but both whites and blacks continued to find ways to ignore or to circumvent such laws. As we have seen, white and black families in Bermuda lived in closer proximity than those in other colonies, and the harshness of slavery was constantly mitigated by the personal and individual nature of contacts between the races. Here were no overseers, no absentee landlords, no great numbers of slaves laboring on plantations under harsh conditions. In 1663 even the largest slaveowner in Bermuda had no more than 17 slaves, and the average household had two or three. But given the prevalence of slave families, Bermuda's slave population would continue to grow. That increase would have been welcome in England's other colonies, but Bermuda, with its 12,000 acres, already had more slaves than it could use.

As the black population grew, so did white anxieties about the colony's racial balance. Only a year after the slave plot of 1673, an apprehensive Assembly, noting "ye great Mischiefes & dainger wch may happen to the Somer Islands . . . by the great number of Negroes, Indians and Mallatoes the wch: are already upon ye sd Island and dayly are brought thither," passed a law "for the hindering of the bringeing of any more." Under the terms of this law any "Negroe, Indian or Mallatoe" brought in "either as a Slave or Servant" was to be seized and sold off the islands by the Somers Islands Company. At the time, it appeared to Company officials that blacks were being "brought in verie numerous, and yet not to be discovered." This was probably a reference to a controversial group of slaves brought to Bermuda in 1665 and sold without the Company's knowledge. During the war with Holland, Captain John Wentworth had visited the Dutch island of Tortola in the Virgin Islands and had taken 67 blacks. Whether or not they wished to leave is not recorded, but all were brought to Bermuda and sold there.[112] While other English colonies, perpetually short of labor, were purchasing slaves in

112. On the continuing controversy over the Tortola blacks, see Lefroy, *Memorials,* 2:231, 260, 266–67, 276, 305–6, 328, 351, 356. For the text of the law, see ibid., 404–5. On the results, see ibid., 432, 463, 506. A report to the Privy Council's Committee on Trade and Foreign Plantations estimated Bermuda's population in 1679 at "about eight thousand Men, Women, Children, and Slaves, about a thousand White people able to bear armes." This same

ever-increasing numbers by the late seventeenth century, Bermuda, with more slaves than it could use, was trying to put an end to such purchases. While Virginians, for example, would import more than 100,000 blacks from the end of the seventeenth century to the American Revolution, the Bermudians by the 1670s had closed the door to imported slaves. When the law went into effect in 1674 Bermudians who brought in new slaves were forced to part with them. In 1678, for example, a mariner named Daniel Johnson who brought an "Indian Man" to Bermuda was obliged to take him to Virginia because of the Somers Islands Company ruling that forbade the "bringing into thes Islands of Negroes, Indians, & Mulattos."[113] Despite official efforts to limit the colony's black population, however, natural increase ensured its steady growth. By the closing years of the seventeenth century slavery was flourishing in England's smallest colony, but Bermudians had yet to find sufficient gainful employment for the growing number of individuals they had enslaved.

---

report noted that only "About fifty Blacks have been brought in with seaven years past and sold at about fifteen pounds *p* head." Ibid., 432.

113. CR, 8:28.

4 A Living from the Sea

Bermudians realized as early as the 1620s that growing tobacco would not make them rich and that the way to wealth lay, not on the land, but on the sea. Even if a Richard Jennings or a Perient Trott had been able to amass enough land for a large plantation (holdings of more than 250 acres in one tribe were forbidden by law), the profits from a few hundred acres were negligible compared to those of a Chesapeake or Caribbean establishment with 1,000 acres or more. This fact was obvious from the beginning, and the shrewd and the ambitious among Bermuda's early colonists began to seek their fortunes, not in the produce of their fields, but in the ships that sailed the transatlantic trade routes between England, the North American mainland, and the Caribbean colonies. The transformation from an agricultural to a maritime economy in this slaveholding society took place gradually and incrementally over several decades in the seventeenth century, with profound effects on Bermudians, black and white. This economic transformation grew as the transatlantic community grew, as the rivalries between England, Spain, France, and the Netherlands for trade and territory waxed hot and cold, as privateers from these countries looted each other's ships, and as the demands for goods in the colonies on the North American mainland and in the Caribbean islands increased. As the years passed, Bermuda's change from farming to seafaring offered new roles for many of Bermuda's slaves and slaveholders, thus altering the nature of race relations as well as economic pursuits.

As Bermuda entered the last quarter of the seventeenth century it was all too clear that tobacco would not serve as the colony's staple crop. The annual yield was only about 400,000 pounds of tobacco per year—at a time when Virginia's annual crop was around 20 million pounds. Bermudian tobacco was not only small in quantity, it was of inferior quality. The Somers Islands Company complained to the governor and council, "Wee have often put you in mind of A Law made in July 1671, for the preventing of makeing up of evill and unmerchantable Tobaccoe, but doe not finde that it is minded, for that Tobacco comes over every yeare worse then other." But Bermuda's tobacco was not its only source of income. The Company reported exports to Virginia, Carolina, and the Bahamas of £6,000 per year from the sale of "Beef, Pork, Fish, Wax, Honey, Palmetto-hats, Baskets, and Woodden

148

ware."[1] Bermuda's total annual income from tobacco and other exports was about £11,000.

The 1679 report produced by the governor and council of Bermuda painted a picture of a modest economy, with the wealth of the entire colony about £20,000. There were reportedly "thirteen or fourteen ships belonging to the Island." The officials estimated that the "Estates of the Merchants and Planters may bee about a hundred pounds each." This was modest, indeed. In England's mainland colonies in the seventeenth century, a personal estate—household goods and cash—of over £200 represented a comfortable living, although the vast majority of ordinary English colonists, including most Bermudians, had far less.[2] Some colonists' estates around the time of the 1679 report, however, were worth considerably more than £100. In a sample of 33 Bermuda probate inventories for the period 1665 to 1677, 12 were valued at more than £200; of those, eight were valued above £300. Included in the 12 were five personal estates worth more than £500: Francis Watlington with £510; Jerome Ewer, £707; Samuel Whalley, £838; Samuel Stone, £707; and Anthony Jenour, £982. As the years passed, the level of affluence rose, and so did the standard of living. Bermudians lived as well as, and some lived better than, their contemporaries in England's mainland colonies. In a sample of 115 Bermuda inventories, including those just mentioned, for the period 1665–1699, 57 listed personal estates in the £100–£200 range.[3] Only 41 were under £100, and 17 had personalty valued at more than £490. Moreover, certain items listed, such as 770 ounces of silver, 1,856 ounces of bullion, and three "bags of money" worth £377, strongly suggest that the possessors of these estates did not make their livings growing tobacco or raising livestock on a few acres of land. The first generation of Bermuda's colonists had coveted land, but succeeding generations found ways to make their fortunes on the sea—sometimes legally, sometimes illegally.

From the beginning, Bermuda's founders had cherished hopes of windfall profits, but such profits eluded them. At first, ambergris, the precious substance found in whales' stomachs and used in making perfume, was looked to as the colony's source of wealth. But after the one "fortunate find," worth

1. Lefroy, *Memorials*, 2:429–34. The report estimated Bermuda's tobacco to be worth £5,000 worth of tobacco. At 3d. per pound, that would be about 400,000 pounds of tobacco.
2. On seventeenth-century levels of wealth as measured by consumer goods, see articles by Lois Green Carr, Lorena S. Walsh, Gloria L. Main, and Jackson Turner Main in "Toward a History of the Standard of Living in British North America," *WMQ*, 3d ser., 45, no. 1 (January 1988): 116–70. On the eighteenth century, see Cary Carson, Ronald Hoffman, and Peter J. Albert, eds., *Of Consuming Interests: The Style of Life in the Eighteenth Century* (Charlottesville, Va.: University of Virginia Press, 1994).
3. The sample is composed of the readable wills and inventories in Books of Wills for these dates.

£9,000, in 1610, whaling proved a disappointment: "Whether it was the swiftnes of the Whale in swimming, or the condition of the place, certain it is for all their labour and hazard, they could kill none, though they strucke many." In 1625 Governor Henry Woodhouse wrote to the Somers Islands Company, "I have made assay in chasinge the whales 3 or 4 dayes together but without good successe they were so shie that they will not abide our boats to come up with them." Efforts at whaling were sporadic and largely unsuccessful. In 1662 the Somers Islands Company appointed Hugh Wentworth Jr. as its agent for a whaling enterprise in Bermuda, to be financed by members of the Company and Bermuda investors. This joint-stock operation was launched the following spring with limited success. In 1667 Richard Norwood wrote to the Royal Society in London that as "for the killing of Whales, it hath been formerly attempted in vain, but within these 2 or 3 years, in the Spring-time and fair weather, they take sometimes one, or two, or three in a day."[4] The Somers Islands Company forbade Bermuda's tenants and landowners alike to engage in whaling without a license. In 1676 there was a dispute over the shares of a "Sperma-Cety Whale," and in 1685 Governor Richard Coney reported "about fourteene Whales" taken. The Bermuda colonists continued to complain of the Company's control of whaling in the islands, but they were not free to engage in whaling on their own until 1730, when the monopoly was broken. Despite hopes of another "fortunate find," whaling never provided a major source of income, although small amounts of whale oil supplied a portion of Bermuda's exports from time to time. In the 1720s Governor John Bruce Hope liked to sight the whaleboats as he rode horseback on Bermuda's shores and then gallop after them to be "in at the death of the whale."[5] A 1730 report estimated Bermuda's income from whaling at £100 per year.

Investors in the 1667 whaling venture included several of the more affluent residents of Bermuda: Captain Thomas Richards, Captain Florentius Seymour, and John Wainwright, all of Southampton Tribe, Captain John Stowe of Pembroke Tribe, Captain Richard Jennings of Smith's Tribe, and a dozen or so others who had risen to positions of prominence by the latter half of the seventeenth century. The rise of this colonial elite was largely due to the singular nature of Bermuda's geographic location and to individual enterprise, but it was not in whaling that these men found their profits. Whaling, like raising mulberries, figs, indigo, and grapes for wine, proved

4. Barbour, ed., *Complete Works*, 2:366; Woodhouse's quotation is in Lefroy, *Memorials*, 1:345. On whaling, see Lefroy, *Memorials*, 2:209–11, 303, 436–41, 443–44. For Norwood's comments, see Lefroy, *Memorials*, 2:254. See also Charles M. Andrews, *The Colonial Period of American History* (New Haven: Yale University Press, 1934), 1:240, and *CSP*, 1730:xxiv.

5. John Bruce Hope to Lord Carteret, April 12, 1723, in *CSP*, 1722–1723:249.

an unreliable alternative to growing tobacco, but other sources of wealth presented themselves.

In the first few years of settlement it was apparent that the treacherous underwater reefs surrounding the islands wrecked many a hapless sailing vessel, and "salvaging" such wrecks soon provided enterprising Bermudians with a welcome if irregular source of income. It did not take long to discover such opportunities. As early as 1615 some colonists happened upon a wrecked vessel and recovered goods to the value of £20. A blacksmith who helped in the salvage operations exulted that "it could not be but that his share in this purchase would amount to noe lesse than the makeinge of him a gentleman, if not with an improvement of a ladyship for his wife."[6] A shipwreck in 1619 prompted Governor Miles Kendall to write Nathaniel Rich about the unfortunate frigate "cast away on this cost [coast] but very poure."[7] As Kendall reported with some disappointment, "Onely some . . . dyeing stuffe was preserved with some ropes & sayles, cabbles & ancres." That wreck yielded little, but others were more lucrative. By 1622, after a Spanish ship was wrecked off the western end of Bermuda, the Somers Islands Company claimed for itself "the Moity of all lawfull wrecks." The other half would go to the recoverers, with the provision that "if the wrecke be driven within the bounds of any particular mans Land; the Recoverers shall yield to the Owner of the said Land the one halfe of their Moity."[8] Thus a landowner stood to gain at least one-quarter of any booty brought to his shores from a wrecked vessel, and if he himself was the recoverer, one-half the prize was his. No wonder Southampton and Sandys Tribes, where the reefs lay close to shore, were among the most desirable properties in the islands. Ireland Island, a narrow piece of land stretching out from the land's end in Sandys, was especially advantageous. The undersea reefs, some less than 500 yards from the shore, spelled doom for many an unsuspecting vessel passing too close to the islands. Bermuda is surrounded by treacherous shallows, many with depths of less than two fathoms (12 feet). Modern navigational charts for Bermuda are covered with cautionary statements and warnings that read, "Area to be avoided." Mariners are told to "navigate with extreme care in the approaches to the Bermuda Islands due to the extensive and dangerous fringing reefs. . . . The only safe approach to the island is from the south-east, preferably in daylight."[9] In the seventeenth and eighteenth centuries only native Bermudians knew the channels through the reefs to the safe harbors at the eastern and western ends

6. Butler, *Bermudaes*, 68–69.
7. Ives, *Rich Papers*, 122.
8. Lefroy, *Memorials*, 1:205.
9. *North Atlantic Ocean: Bermuda Islands*, navigational chart (Hamilton, Bermuda, 1996).

of the colony. Even today, with modern navigational charts, large ships have been known to run aground trying to enter St. George's Harbor, formerly called Town Harbor, through a narrow passage known as Town Cut.

In September 1622, when the settlement at Bermuda was barely a decade old, a hurricane drove a Spanish ship, the 300-ton *San Antonio,* against the reefs off the coast of Southampton Tribe. Bound for Spain, she was carrying a cargo that included 30,000 pounds of tobacco, 6,000 pounds of indigo, and gold and silver worth £5,000.[10] Bermudians helped to rescue 70 survivors, and Governor Nathaniel Butler came to meet them. He instructed his sergeant to "bring the woemen to Mr. Painter [Paynter] his bay by water, and lett the rest come by land on foote." Evidently the meeting was to take place at Stephen Paynter's house in Southampton Tribe, near what is now called Whale Bay. Governor Butler also reported that "some of the baser sort [of Bermudians] had been rifling some of them [the castaways] before the Governors arrival." The governor ordered the culprits searched, and £140 was recovered. Butler used the money to defray the expenses of the Spaniards, who were to spend "nine or ten weekes" in Bermuda. One of the female passengers, described only as a "Gentlewoman," gave birth to a son three days after her rescue. The grateful Spaniards made a gift to Governor Butler of whatever might be salvaged from their wrecked vessel, but according to the governor, "never had ship a more sudden death." At the time, he reported that only three cannons were recovered. Later salvage efforts recovered a few other items, including a gold ingot and a bag containing 150 pieces of eight. Whites and blacks alike shared in the arduous, sometimes dangerous labor of recovering goods from a wrecked vessel. Among the 20 or more men who worked on the Spanish shipwreck were "Two negroes."[11]

A few months later the Spanish ambassador in London sent a somewhat different version of this shipwreck to the Somers Islands Company:

> Some of ye passengers haveing saved themselves by meanes of ye Cocke Boate, and ye rest by what other waie theie could, the said cocke boate was taken from them by the English men there wthout p.mitting ye Spaniards in no case to retorne back to save and to benifite themselves of ye goodes wth wch ye saide ship was fraighted whc was great store of gold silver and marchandizes to ye value of more than 60,000 crownes All wch ye saide English tooke and seized upon even unto ye Artillery and the rest wthout givinge or restoring anie thinge to ye said Spaniards, not soe much as their aparell although theie [the Bermudians] shewed them [the salvaged clothes] unto them saying that they would sell those unto them because

10. On the controversy surrounding this shipwreck and the recovery of her cargo, see *CSP,* 1554–1660:27–28, 32, 33, 120; Lefroy, *Memorials,* 1:157–58, 254; Barbour, ed., *Complete Works,* 2:383–85.
11. The correspondence over the wreck is in Lefroy, *Memorials,* 2:241–60.

they were not made of ye English fashion, and knowinge that they had not one penie left being robed and spoiled by them of there verie cloths and of whatsoever they had saved and gotten to land.[12]

An official investigation produced a flurry of conflicting testimony, and Governor Nathaniel Butler was finally exonerated. The exact whereabouts of the alleged gold and silver, however, remained a mystery.

Wills and inventories for the seventeenth century as well as the records of the Somers Islands Company suggest that a perennial way to wealth in Bermuda lay in the salvaging of vessels wrecked on the dangerous reefs surrounding the islands. A few other examples of "wrecking," as it came to be called, will serve to illustrate the Bermudians' enthusiasm for this pastime. In 1623, when the British *Seaflower* exploded in a gunpowder accident at St. George's, there were so many scavengers that Butler's successor as governor, John Harrison, was obliged to issue a proclamation ordering the colonists to "bring forth all such goods as they have taken up at sea or found on shore wch . . . belong to this shipp and companie, or any passenger thereof." A few days later Harrison complained of "divers boats belonging to the mayne [main island] who use to scowt up and down the coast of St. Davids, Coopers Island, and other Islands neare adjoyning, to pillage such caske and chest as were driven on shore by the 'Seaflower.'" Some of the unfortunate ship's passengers, he said, were "left heare without apparel or provision" because their belongings had been "felloneouslye embesselled and stolne away." The governor ordered "all and everye Boat and master and gange of the same" not to go near the wreck or the coast near it without special permission.[13]

In 1639 the Spanish *La Viga* met disaster off the west coast of Bermuda. One of her officers was Juan de Rivera, whose impressions of life in the colony have been quoted above. He also set down his impressions of the Bermudians he sighted as he and his ship's company were building rafts to float ashore: "While the work was in hand," he wrote, "a great many small sailing boats with lateen sails were seen coming in our direction from the Island, like herons in flight twisting and turning as they cut through the restless waves towards us, for even though they were tiny craft they had to use great care to avoid the many shallows."[14] The vessels Rivera described were Bermuda-built boats similar to those known in modern times as the Bermuda dinghy, a small craft with a 14-foot keel and a 4.5-foot beam, with a single enormous lateen-rigged, or triangle-shaped, sail of some 780 square feet. Such a boat could skim the waves rapidly and, needless to say, required skillful sailors. Bermuda's blacks

12. Ibid., 1:240.
13. Ibid., 2:288.
14. Rivera, "Shipwrecked Spaniards," 15.

as well as whites built and handled these vessels, bailing (when necessary) with a calabash gourd cut in half and anchoring in shallow waters with a killick, or stone weight attached to a mooring line swung from a 5-foot wooden stick.

Rivera continued his description of the Bermuda boats:

> When they reached the tender [a smaller vessel that had also run onto the rocks] their crews clambered aboard and must have found the loot they were seeking. . . .
>
> Numerous small boats were gathered round her, and their crews were busy ripping her to pieces to steal whatever they could—like a flock of voracious vultures circling the sky in search of a cadaver and, finding one, pouncing upon it and tearing it apart. So these English troglodytes, coming upon that wooden hull, clambered up and down it in haste, their insatiable appetite not even sparing her stout timbers.[15]

La Viga had apparently struck the reefs somewhere off Bermuda's southwest shore, probably Southampton, for the master of the Bermudian rescue vessel informed the castaways that the port of St. George "lay six leagues [about 18 miles] to the north." Rivera was enchanted by what he saw: "We landed at a peaceful spot where a hill covered with wild palms [palmettos] in green fields looked so beautiful it seemed we were entering some pleasant and delightful gardens where young trees grew among golden flowers. . . . Some Englishmen with their wives came out of their houses to watch us and greet us. . . . [A]nd so we reached the house where we were to stay." Whose house this was is not recorded, but from Rivera's description it was very likely the residence of Richard Leacraft, Stephen Paynter, or Thomas Richards, all of whom lived close to each other on the southwest shore of Southampton. Paynter had played host to the victims of the 1622 shipwreck. The Spaniard described a place with "Lovely orange trees, intertwined vines and other fruit trees . . . a delightful setting; the rooms—living rooms, bedrooms and offices—were all well planned and furnished, in every way comfortable and clean." When at last he arrived at Bermuda's capital at the other end of the islands, he was not impressed. St. George's, he noted, had "only six badly built timber houses."

Rivera was even less impressed with the behavior of Governor Thomas Chaddock and the governor's friends. Rivera claimed that they "had set their hearts on finding ways of taking from us the money they had judged we had brought from the Indies, and since this was what they wanted, their every thought was directed to that goal." The Bermudians insisted that the shipwrecked Spaniards, 160 in all, purchase a ship then under construction at St. George's but refused to discuss the purchase price until the vessel was completed. The Spanish shipwreck had occurred in October; the new ship was not ready until February. The Spanish complained of their hosts' "unbridled

15. Ibid.

avarice." Said Rivera: "We had to make the payments for the people in lodgings at the end of each month . . . [T]he longer the delay the more money they made out of our expenses." After much haggling, and payment of 2,000 pesos to an interpreter who "sold . . . his words very dear," the Spanish agreed to pay 7,900 pesos for the vessel, which they christened *El Salvador.* "The wreck of a ship," wrote Rivera, "is a most happy event for the islanders, but it makes them covetous and overgreedy to possess the things which their deprivation has made them desire, when such occasions occur, their rapacity knows no limit."[16]

The practice of "wrecking" continued. In May of 1642 a "Spanish ship laden with silver fell on the rocks"[17] with predictable results. Much of that silver undoubtedly found its way to Bermuda coffers and made the islands' residents—especially those who lived near the coast and could sight vessels in distress—hungry for more. A 1645 petition to the Somers Islands Company noted that as for wrecks, "as it concerns those that live near the place of wrecks, so we leave each particular man to answer for himself." Some Bermudians involved in wrecking took a ship's valuables without much regard for the vessel's survivors. After the 1655 wreck of an English ship, the *Hopeful Luck,* the Somers Islands Company wrote to Governor Josias Forster condemning the "Rudenes of some of the planters . . . in cutting downe the Ridginge of the ship . . . And takeinge awaie goodes out of the hould not withstanding the Capt of the ship was on board and notwithstanding the Govrnors order to the contrary."[18] After a shipwreck in April 1658 the Governor's Council decreed that the "recoverers of the goodes" from the wreck of the *Anne* should have half of those goods, provided that "the ganges who have spedd best, doth take a proportionable number of the seamen to bed and board at a free charge."[19] At the June assize court, the grand jury deplored the "great voyelancey that was practiced by several ganges" that looted the *Anne* and asked for restitution to the ship's sailors.[20]

In 1655, when the *Hopeful Luck* was being salvaged, Governor Forster had asked for restitution to be made to a Bermudian. Forster issued orders to deliver up "all the proceed of the said goodes and all such goodes as came to ye hands yet unsould unto Mr. Thomas Richardes the Agent of Mr. Trott who hath bin a great sufferer by the said loss." Wealthy merchant Perient Trott, an official of the Somers Islands Company, employed Thomas Richards of Southampton Tribe as his agent. Richards was also his father-in-law: Trott's wife, Mary, was Thomas Richards's daughter. Trott had come to reside in

16. Ibid., 20, 23, 26.
17. Lefroy, *Memorials,* 1:724, 606.
18. Ibid., 2:60–61.
19. For accounts of other wrecks, see ibid., 1:634, and 2:5, 13, 124, 222.
20. Assize of June 1658, CR, 3: n.p.

Hamilton Tribe sometime before 1663. The matter of the *Hopeful Luck*'s looted cargo was not easily settled, and in January 1658/1659 Governor Forster, noting "the remembrance of the horrid and unparallelled abuses offered by our Islanders in and about the Hopefull-Luck wreck" issued a proclamation ordering the return of the contraband goods.[21] Whether Thomas Richards was able to recover any of the pilfered goods for Perient Trott is not recorded.

Richards himself was among Bermuda's first-generation planters who rose to affluence in trade and wrecking in the latter half of the seventeenth century. At the time of Richard Norwood's survey of 1663 Thomas Richards was the largest landowner in Southampton Tribe, with 171 acres there and another 73 acres in Pembroke Tribe. His Southampton property bordered the coast near Bermuda's western reefs, where many shipwrecks occurred; his Pembroke holdings gave him access to both the north coast and the secluded harbor known as Crow Lane in the center of the colony. He became one of the richest men in the colony. Richards apparently was also one of the most rapacious, as a presentment by a grand jury in 1655 suggests:

> Upon divers complaints made unto us by the Inhabitants wee doe present Mr. Thomas Richards . . . ffor that he when as Mr. Peniston brought in a vessell laden with salt, a comoditie wch the Iland had great need of, and would have been sold for hides, hay and basketts and such like trade as people had, he steps in and buyes yt all up and sells agayne for money and tobacco. . . . And also when the ship "Imployment" . . . brought over a parsell or cargo of goodes amounting by the report to the value of 50 or threescore powndes or thereabouts And this also Mr. Richards went aboard, and bought all up and carried to his house, and there sells them Doubtles at a greater rate than he payed for them.

If the "goodes had not been so bought in grosse," said the grand jury, they would have sold "at very reasonable rates for ready tobacco, and many people would have much bin releived by them."[22]

Thomas Richards is notable not only for his dedication to the pursuit of gain but also for his longevity: He lived to be 89 years old and was active until his last years. Little is known about his early life, or even when he arrived in Bermuda. A Thomas Richards was one of the signers of a letter protesting limitations on tobacco crops in 1626, and in that same year his wife, Ann, bore him a son. In 1629 Ann gave birth to a daughter, and in 1633 she bore another son. Thomas Richards's name next appears in early Bermuda records as a passenger returning to Bermuda aboard the *Truelove* in 1635. He was then 24 years old. Like his neighbors, Richard Leacraft and Stephen Paynter, Richards took an active role in the colony's affairs, serving

21. Lefroy, *Memorials,* 2:124.
22. Ibid., 62–63.

as a councillor and as an officer in the militia. In 1693, some time after the death of his first wife, Ann, Thomas Richards, then 84, obtained a license to marry the daughter of the Southampton minister George Stirk. "Agnes Stirke, a single woman, aged three score years and upwards," became the second Mrs. Richards. Richards had known Agnes all her life. Her mother was Stephen Paynter's daughter, Elizabeth, who had married the Reverend Stirk in the 1630s.[23] Thomas Richards died in 1698; Agnes lived until 1705.

Thomas Richard's neighbor Richard Hunt was also one of Southampton's major landowners, and he, too, participated in gathering spoils from the sea. Around midnight on March 26, 1661, a 300-ton British ship, the *Virginia Merchant,* was wrecked off the coast of Southampton "neere unto Mr. Richard Hunts House standing at Port Royall." The *Virginia Merchant* carried 180 persons, all but 10 of whom were drowned. The usual "wrecking" took place, and in this case Richard Hunt, as the nearest landowner to the wreck, would have been entitled to one-quarter of the salvaged goods. If he was also one of the recoverers in the salvage operation, he would have profited even more. In this case it was the sheriff of the colony who seized the salvaged goods from the *Virginia Merchant* and divided them half and half between the Somers Islands Company and the recoverers, but the matter did not end there. In August the Somers Islands Company received a petition from the widow of Thomas Atwood, a *Virginia Merchant* seaman who lost his life in the wreck. She complained that the vessel's goods, including items belonging to her late husband, had been wrongfully seized. Although his "goods had no marke," she demanded the return of them. The Company ordered that "all the goods that can be made appeare to be her husbands be granted & restored unto her (as to the Companies part)."[24] Whether Atwood's widow actually recovered any of his goods is not recorded. Brief notices of other wrecks are scattered throughout early Bermuda records. For example, a shipping register records that on January 12, 1658/1659, between 9 and 10 P.M., the *Eagle* of London was "cast awaie and became a wreck upon the North East breakers or Rocks of our Island." In 1664 another English vessel, the *Friendship,* was "by extremety of wether forsed uppon the sholes of Bermudas, and there unhappilie Cast away uppon the 16th day of October."[25]

Despite the efforts of the Somers Islands Company to regulate the salvaging of shipwrecked vessels, the looting continued year after year. In December of 1670, after the wreck of the *Truelove,* an English ship from Bristol, in Bermuda

23. Agnes was born in 1633; her father died in 1637. See Hallett, *Early Bermuda Records,* 14, and Hallett, *Early Bermuda Wills,* 476.
24. The notice of Mary Atwood's petition is in Lefroy, *Memorials,* 2:154.
25. Shipping Register, 1656–1671, n.p., abstracted in Lefroy, *Memorials,* 1:720. See also 2:733.

waters, a colonist named Jeremiah Burrows was accused of taking goods worth £20 "besides severall caskes of Brandy, cables, anchors, and other comodities, not as yet brought to light, or to S Georges." The exasperated governor of the colony then gave orders that only two boats in every tribe were to be authorized to go to the aid of wrecks: "In the first place they are to take care of the persons, Secondly of the Goods; Thirdly, that they doe not disable the shipp by cutting or destroying the Sailes, Cables, Shrouds, or Apparell."[26]

Richard Norwood was also involved in "wrecking," and his probate inventory places him among the affluent Bermudians of his day. He owned 49 acres in Pembroke Tribe, and at the time of his death (at age 84) in 1675 he had a seven-room house and personal goods and chattels worth £497, including 11 slaves. Also included in his personal estate was £133 in "Spanish money"— perhaps acquired from the wreck of a ship. In 1642 Norwood and Richard Jennings of Smith's Tribe were involved in the investigation of the wreck of a Spanish ship, but the disposition of the vessel's salvaged cargo does not appear in the existing records. Norwood was also connected to the wider transatlantic trade world: His elder son, Andrew, resided in Barbados, and his younger son, Matthew, was master of the Somers Islands Company's magazine ship, which made regular runs between Bermuda and England.[27]

Toward the latter part of the seventeenth century the Bermudians' practice of preying on shipwrecks came to the attention of the Lord High Admiral, James, Duke of York. He instituted a new policy on the recovery of valuable goods from wrecks off Bermuda and the West Indies, claiming that all such goods rightfully became the property of the Lord High Admiral. He authorized a London merchant, Edmund Custis, and Custis's business partners to "recover and sell such goods." No one else was to engage in "wreck fishing." The new policy was largely ignored, and throughout the colonial period Bermudians increased their fortunes by taking booty from wrecked ships in the Bahamas as well as in Bermuda waters. In fact, some Bermudian vessels bound for the West Indies carried divers especially for underwater salvaging. The crafting and repairing of iron tools for salvage work may account for the wealth of blacksmith Robert Dickinson, who was one of the five landowners with mansions in Southampton Tribe in 1663. More than 200 years later, Sir John Harvey Darrell, a native Bermudian and descendant of the seventeenth-century colonist John Darrell, wrote, "I myself remember two or three such vessels. Old Capt. Sears, of the Flatts, Bermuda, considered a rich man, was generally reported to have acquired his wealth in that way."[28] So

26. On the *Truelove,* see Lefroy, *Memorials,* 2:333.

27. On Norwood's estate, see Books of Wills, vol. 1, pp. 217, 219, 261. On the 1642 wreck, see Lefroy, *Memorials,* 2:6–7. On Norwood, see Lefroy, *Memorials,* 2:401, 424.

28. On wreck fishing, see ibid., 340–41. Darrell is quoted ibid., 1:717. On Dickinson, see Books of Wills, vol. 1, p. 177, and Lefroy, *Memorials,* 2:703.

did many other Bermudians. In January 1680/1681, for example, Governor Heydon issued a proclamation to forbid further looting of a French ship "unhappelie run upon the North-Side Sholes."[29] In 1712 Attorney General George Larkin registered his disapproval of the Bermudians' acquisitive ways: "Since my coming here," he wrote, "a vessell laden with logwood hath been unfortunately cast upon the Rocks, some of the Inhabitants went immediately and instead of affording their assistance cut away her boat from her sterne, cut up her Decks, broke open the Masters Cabbin, carryed away his best Clothes and great part of the lading. So barbarous are the people of this Country when anything of that nature happens, which is too often, I told the Governour [Benjamin Bennett] as he was Vice-Admirall he ought to inquire into the matter."[30] Wrecks were indeed frequent in Bermuda's waters. Many are unrecorded, but one indication of the continuing frequency of shipwrecks in Bermuda's waters may be read in a few matter-of-fact diary entries of the Reverend James Holiday in the 1740s: "December 25, 1746: Some people were taken up at at sea in a boat & brought into Town; their vessel having foundered agoing to Lisbon." January 26, 1746/1747: "A ship cast away on the North Rocks." February 12, 1746/1747: "A ship ran upon the rocks."[31]

Besides the profitable (if unsteady) occupation of "wrecking," Bermudians also went to sea to trade with other colonies, and as the years passed, they became adept at circumventing the trade restrictions imposed by both the Somers Islands Company and the crown. Bermuda, although it could not compete in the tobacco market, had from the beginning produced fruits and vegetables it could exchange for goods from other colonies, especially its sister colony, Virginia. In the 1670s a ship captain bound for Carolina was instructed to bring corn, cattle, and other foodstuffs from Bermuda and to find out the "way of planting and using cassatha [cassava] for bread and drink . . . and all other husbandry applicable" to Carolina. The captain was also to inquire at what rates "orange flowers and rose water, honey, and other rarities are to be had" from the Bermudians.[32] Rose stills, for making rose water, are listed in a number of Bermuda inventories. A visitor to Bermuda in the 1680s observed that the colony's ship captains often exported "Cattle, Swine, and Turkies

29. CR, 7:21.
30. George Larkin to the Lords of Trade and Plantations, August 19, 1712, in CO 37/4: 9.
31. The surviving fragments of Holiday's diary are reprinted in "Diary of the Rev. James Holiday, 1746–1747," *BHQ* 2, no. 2 (1945): 84–89. See also Jane Harris, "History under Siege: A Review of Marine Archaeology in Bermuda," *Bermuda Journal of Archaeology and Maritime History* 45, no. 4 (July 1990): 15–16, and "Shipwrecks Reveal a Wealth of Maritime History," *Bermuda* 31, no. 11 (October 1, 1996): 85.
32. On Carolina, see the letter of Shaftesbury to Andrew Percivall of the ship *Edisto*, May 23, 1674, *CSP,* 1669–1674:584–86. On the Virginia trade, see Lefroy, *Memorials,* 1:158–59. See also Daniel C. Littlefield, *Rice and Slaves: Ethnicity and the Slave Trade of Colonial South Carolina* (Baton Rouge: Louisiana State University Press, 1981).

for the Carribies, and Carolina."[33] Other Bermuda products, including salted beef, pork, fish, beeswax, honey, and palmetto ware, supplied English colonies on the mainland and in the Caribbean.

Until 1684, when Bermuda came under royal control, the colony's trade was controlled by the Somers Islands Company. All goods imported and all tobacco exported were to be carried in the Company's magazine ships that visited the islands twice a year.[34] The Company also forbade trade in Bermuda-built ships. In 1637, when "some of the Inhabitants to their great cost and hazzard had prepared a vessel for that purpose," the Company sent word that no persons, no cattle, and "no provision (but upon limited conditions, incompatible with merchandizing), should be sent away." As one of the outraged colonists wrote later, " 'Tis as though they had said, you shall build vessel (if you will) to look upon, and undoe your selves, but shall have no encouragement to employ her." Colonists chafed at the Somers Islands Company's rules and prices. "Consider the state of the Inhabitants who must trade with no ships but the Company, and must have [buy] their [the Company's] goods, or goe naked. . . . The truth is, had not providence put the inhabitants into a way of weaving Cotten, which they buy for Porke, Beefe, and Fish, of one ship or another (upon hard tearmes) trading between them and Barbadoes, the Inhabitants had long since turned Adamites out of necessity."[35] The Navigation Act of 1663 expressly forbade England's colonies to import goods except through England and in English ships, and to prevent such trade in Bermuda the Somers Islands Company forbade the building of any vessel over five tons, effectively keeping Bermudians off the high seas.[36]

Shipping lists for the seventeenth century are incomplete, but a partial compilation to 1656 and a shipping register from 1656 to 1671 show that Bermuda was a frequent stopover for ships bound to and from England's other American colonies, both mainland and island. For the years 1655 to 1671 (with the exclusion of 1663, which is missing from the record) the register records a total of 292 vessels arriving in Bermuda's Castle Harbor and Town Harbor, most at the latter.[37] The average number of ships per year in these records was 22. Vessels from Boston, Barbados, Virginia, Puerto Rico,

33. John Crawford, *A New and Most Exact Account of the . . . Colony of Carolina* (Dublin, 1683), 4, quoted in Wood, *Black Majority*, 28 n.
34. Regulation of the Somers Islands Quarter Court, 1628, in Lefroy, *Memorials*, 1:472. See also an order by Governor William Sayle, March 1661, ibid., 2:146.
35. See Golding, *Servants on Horseback*, 191 (first quotation), 193 (second quotation).
36. Somers Islands Quarter Court, November 25, 1663, in Lefroy, *Memorials*, 2:204. On the colonists' objections to restrictions on shipbuilding and trade, see also 2:193, 209, 472, 474, 475.
37. CR, Fragmentary Book G, Shipping Register, 1656–1671. An abstract of this register, with additional notes on shipping to 1685, is in Lefroy, *Memorials*, 1:726–39.

New York, and Jamaica, as well as England, testify to the widespread nature of Bermuda's contacts. For example, on August 16, 1658, the *Jeames,* "Captain W. Jeames," master, came from Barbados "with a prize taken in the W.I. Sugar chiefly." On January 30, 1658/1659, the pink (a small sailing vessel) *Hope,* Edward Stone, master, arrived in Town Harbor with a cargo of salt and departed April 14 with cattle for the Leeward Islands. On November 8, 1669, the *Matthew and Francis* came from Barbados and left on December 2, "filled up with oranges and potatoes." A 1676 report estimated "ten or twelve sail of small vessels yearly from New England, New Yorke, Barbados &c" came to trade for provisions, and "Besides eight, or ten more may touch at the Island in their passage to and from other places."[38] Repeated laws against illegal trading attest to the volume of surreptitious transactions that must have occurred when Bermudians, black and white, boarded those visiting vessels in Town Harbor. Other vessels dropped anchor in more secluded waters, which made clandestine transactions easier. A shallop called the *Fortune* from New York is recorded as visiting Bailey's Bay on the north shore of Hamilton Tribe from June 14 to October 23, 1669. What she did there is not recorded. Occasionally, the place of anchorage is left blank in the shipping register's notices of vessels, or the register includes enigmatic notations, as in the record of a ketch from New England, John Alden, master, that reportedly carried away 21,000 pounds of "contraband tobacco."[39]

The frequency of illicit trade outside Town Harbor or Castle Harbor is indicated by a proclamation of Governor William Sayle in 1661, reminding Bermuda colonists that it was "Contrary to the Lawes of the Kingdome of England, and the Honoble Companys Orders, that anie goods shall bee put aboard any Ship riding at an anker in any Creeke or other obscure place."[40] In March of that year (1660/1661) the governor had discovered that tobacco was being illegally shipped aboard the *Hopeful James,* then "at anker in Crow Lane." Sayle issued orders to her commander, Captain Philip Lea of Paget, and to two other residents of that tribe, Captain George Tucker and Paul Trimingham, to bring her "into one of our harbours soe soone as winde and wether shall possibly permit."[41] These orders were carried out and an inspection conducted. On April 23, 1661, "Mr. John Darrell, Merchant," of

38. Lefroy, *Memorials,* 2:432–33.
39. The note about John Alden is in the print version, ibid., 1:737. It is undocumented and does not appear in the original shipping register.
40. Lefroy, *Memorials,* 2:146.
41. Ibid. Philip Lea, George Tucker, and Paul Trimingham were members of families whose fortunes were made in trade and whose names are still prominent in Bermuda. On the Tuckers and Triminghams, see Hallett, *Early Bermuda Wills,* 583–86, 591–615. Paul Trimingham would be a witness to Philip Lea's will in 1673, and in 1689 Lea's son Copeland would be one of the executors of Trimingham's will.

Warwick Tribe registered an official complaint with his brother-in-law, colony secretary Henry Tucker, saying that the *Hopeful James* "is overcharged with severall chests and provisions uppon her deck, which will hazard the lives and estates of such as are to goe in her."[42] The record does not indicate whether the *Hopeful James*'s cargo (including the contraband tobacco) was lightened, but the vessel sailed for England the following day, April 24.[43] Philip Lea, who seems to have made at least part of his money from such clandestine trade, also cut and sold Bermuda cedar in violation of a 1622 law. In 1658 the Somers Islands Company ordered an inquiry into "what cedar hath bin felled and carried away from Captn Phillip Lea's land since September 1656 and by whom."[44] Like Thomas Richards, Richard Leacraft, and several other prosperous traders in Bermuda in the mid-seventeenth century, Lea was a member of the Governor's Council, an officer in the militia, and a man with a keen eye for a profit. Lea also saw the value of education. He apprenticed his son, Copeland Lea, to the surveyor Richard Norwood to be taught grammar, bookkeeping, and surveying, and he also made provision in his will for his grandson to be educated in "Reading Writing Arithmetick & Navigation." Lea was the owner of 100 acres in the center of Paget Tribe, with access to the Atlantic Ocean on the south shore and to the harbor near Crow Lane by way of the free school lands given to the colony by his father-in-law, the Reverend Patrick Copeland.[45]

Owning property near the offshore reefs where wrecks occurred, or property with a secluded access to the sea, away from the inquisitive eyes of government officials, was almost a prerequisite to the acquisition of wealth in Bermuda. Men like Stephen Paynter who managed to acquire land near the offshore reefs rose to affluence by the middle of the seventeenth century. Paynter, a cooper by trade, died February 25, 1660/1661. A prosperous resident of Southampton, with a mansion and 100 acres, he lived in Bermuda for more than 45 years.[46] How did he come by his money? Not through plying his trade of barrel making and not by cultivating tobacco. Although he was obviously a careful planter (his earlier "good judgment of tobackoe"

42. Lefroy, *Memorials*, 2:148.
43. Shipping register, April 24, 1661.
44. Lefroy, *Memorials*, 2:123. In 1655 another colonist, John Ball, had allegedly transported "cedar of a good value" in violation of the law. See ibid., 55. Bermuda's sailing vessels were made of cedar; so were the crates or boxes used to export such items as oranges and potatoes. *CSP*, 1669–1674:1126.
45. CR, 5A:120; Books of Wills, vol. 1, p. 175.
46. A surviving fragment of Paynter's will, undated, mentions a grandson, John, apparently residing outside Bermuda; a son, "Stephen Paynter deceased"; two daughters, Patience and Ruth; several grandchildren; two nieces; and his "deare and loving Wife," Jane, executrix of his estate. Books of Wills, vol. 1, p. 69.

was previously noted, and his will ordered his overseers to have his land "manured"—that is, cultivated), the profits from four shares of land could not have made him rich, even if he had been able to plant every inch of them with tobacco. But he lived on the west end of the main island, where undersea reefs surprised many a ship and where a place was aptly named Wreck Hill. Paynter may also have made and sold rum. One of the outbuildings listed in his estate inventory was a "still-house." In it were "1 still with the furniture," as well as a quantity of barrels and hogsheads. Paynter, with his knowledge of the cooper's trade, could have supplied not only the rum but the hogsheads and barrels to contain it. In 1653 the price of Barbados rum was set at four shillings per gallon. Imported rum was later taxed by the Somers Islands Company at 4 d. per gallon, and in 1669 the Company passed a law against "councillors selling drink."[47]

As an official report to the Council of Trade and Plantations noted, "The places of trade are the storehouses of the inhabitants."[48] Many Bermudians besides Stephen Paynter acquired prime waterfront property in the first generation and built considerable fortunes (by Bermuda standards) by the second generation. The career of John Stowe, the ship captain, pilot, and trader, is one example. His 100 acres in Pembroke, with two secluded inlets screened by low, wooded hills, offered an ideal location for loading and unloading vessels laden with goods, unseen by customs officers at St. George's. In 1651 the Earl of Warwick granted Stowe a license to build a shallop, and in 1652 Stowe was the owner of a larger vessel, a sloop called the *Elizabeth and Anne*. She carried family names: His wife and one of his daughters were named Elizabeth; another daughter was named Anne. In 1656 Stowe bought a two-thirds interest in a small ketch called the *Speedwell* from an owner in Bristol, England.[49]

By the 1660s John Stowe had widespread trade interests, with contacts in England, Barbados, and New England. His household was large, with a wife and six children—two sons and four daughters. As we have seen, his domestic servant/slave household was also large, containing white indentured servants and apprentices as well as blacks (at least one of whom had been taught the craft of a shipwright and given his freedom) and Indians (at least two of whom he bought in the 1640s). Stowe also traded in slaves. In 1648, for example, he sold "Grace a Negro Woeman," whom he had bought from council member John Hall, to another council member, John Devitt. In 1650 he bought "three yonge Negroes," a boy named Quicke, and girls named Black Bess

---

47. On rum, see Lefroy, *Memorials,* 2:42, 288, 421.
48. *CSP,* 1677–1680:394.
49. Lefroy, *Memorials,* 1:717, 725, 727.

and Maria, from a New England mariner, but then sold Maria to a colonist named Henry Sharp.[50]

John Stowe's *Elizabeth and Anne* made frequent voyages to Barbados and elsewhere. The shipping lists for the 1650s, for example, show that she left Bermuda for Barbados in November 1657, February 1657/1658, and June 1658. She also made a voyage there in 1659 and brought back 32 blacks, presumably to sell in Bermuda. Stowe acquired another vessel some years later, for a 1669 record shows that he took five shipwrecked Frenchmen to Barbados aboard the *Samuells Adventure* in August of that year, returning in December.[51] John Stowe was also an enthusiastic participant in Bermuda's public life, serving as a ship's pilot for the colony in 1648 and as marshal of the colony during the witchcraft trials of the 1650s. His wife, Elizabeth, served on a women's panel in several of those trials. In 1670 Governor John Heydon refused to accept the captain as a member of a grand jury, saying that Stowe was "apt to be inflamed with Drinke, being frequently subject to speake pationatlie." Richard Norwood, then a councillor for Pembroke, wrote to the governor that he did not intend to choose Stowe for the position of juror, but that Stowe "had spoken to many, and had so manie to give their votes for him, that I could not avoyd it." Governor Heydon later declared Stowe eligible to serve in any capacity "hee may be called to."[52] Captain John Stowe died in 1684, not long after he made his will, stating that he was "very Weake but in perfect memory." Unfortunately only a fragment of that will has survived. In it are mentioned his eldest son, Joseph, and four of his six daughters, of whom at least four married into affluent Bermuda families. They were Ann Rayner, Elizabeth Trott (wife of Samuel Trott, Perient's brother), Susanna Sayle (wife of James Sayle, a son of former governor William Sayle), and Martha Outerbridge (wife of the merchant Thomas Outerbridge).[53]

The family of Captain Richard Jennings, like the family of Captain John Stowe, found the way to wealth in Bermuda in the latter half of the seventeenth century and established a long line of descendants. Richard Jennings first appears in Bermuda records as one of those involved in the salvaging of the Spanish shipwreck in 1622. He next appears in 1635, when he was a passenger aboard the *Dorset,* sailing from England to Bermuda with his 18-year-old daughter, Sarah. He was then 35 years old. Jennings and his wife also had two sons, Richard and John, and another daughter, Elizabeth. In 1642 Jennings

50. Stowe's transactions are recorded in CR, 2:145, 180, 205. See also Lefroy, *Memorials,* 1:729.
51. See the shipping records in Lefroy, *Memorials,* 1:727, 736, 737. The 32 blacks from Barbados are noted in the shipping register.
52. Lefroy, *Memorials,* 2:7, 263, 312–13, 320.
53. Books of Wills, vol. 1, p. 314.

was again involved in wrecking, as he and Richard Norwood were ordered to examine the wreck of a Spanish ship laden with silver off the Bermuda coast. Eight years later the Somers Islands Company was still awaiting Captain Jennings's report on that wreck. What happened to the silver is not recorded. In 1650 Jennings was involved in political intrigue of some sort, rumored to be plotting with unknown persons in England to take over Bermuda. On the basis of these rumors he was removed from his command of King's Castle Fort.[54] The rumors were apparently unfounded, but two years later Jennings was again in trouble, accused of trading illegally with the Dutch. By 1653, however, Richard Jennings was back in public favor and was a member of the Bermuda Council. The survey of 1663 shows that he owned 10 shares of land (250 acres), three in Southampton and seven in Smith's Tribe, where he had a mansion on property bordering the Flatts on the north side and touching the open Atlantic on the south.[55]

The secluded harbor of the Flatts was ideally suited for a smugglers' haven. From there, lantern lights could be easily seen all along the north shore from Smith's Tribe to Pembroke Tribe and from Somerset and Ireland Islands at the far west end of Bermuda. Vessels riding at anchor in the calm waters at the Flatts were not visible from the open sea to the north or from the capital, St. George's, to the west. Smugglers could thus load or unload contraband goods without fear of discovery by customs officials. At the Flatts, and at other secluded inlets, a considerable and largely undocumented amount of illegal trade took place. As one governor noted in the 1720s, "Pyrates in former days, were here made very welcome, and Governors have gain'd estates by them."[56] When Richard Jennings died in 1669 at the age of 69, his will divided his land and 11 slaves among his four children. Jennings's total estate value is not listed, but he was clearly a wealthy man, and by the end of the seventeenth century his sons had become even wealthier. Families like the Stowes and the Jenningses were obviously a small fraction of Bermuda's population, but their activities, and those of their even wealthier descendants, shaped the economic and social history of seventeenth-century Bermuda.

An official report of 1679 estimated the total number of people in the colony, including blacks, mulattos, and Indians, to be "about eight thousand men, women, and children." Of this number there were "about foure hundred Planters" and "about a thousand White people able to bear arms."[57] The num-

---

54. On Jennings's early career in Bermuda, see Lefroy, *Memorials*, 1:254, 410, 689, and 2:6–7, 10, 38.
55. Ibid., 2:648, 663, 668, 703.
56. Hope to the Council of Trade and Plantations, January 14, 1724/1725, in CO 37/11: 46.
57. Lefroy, *Memorials*, 2:432.

ber of blacks, mulattos, and Indians is not separately estimated in this report, but their numbers, too, were increasing and their occupations, like those of the white Bermudians, were changing. By the last quarter of the seventeenth century most adult slaves in Bermuda did not work as agricultural laborers, as did their counterparts in the mainland and Caribbean colonies. Skilled trades for blacks had been common since the mid-seventeenth century, as tobacco-growing declined and slaveholders sought other occupations for their slaves. In 1661 the Somers Islands Company had ordered that "the negroe Boyes belonging to the company be put out as Apprentices to Carpenters, Smiths, Coopers, and other handycraft trades in ye Islands from 8 until they be 16 yeares of age."[58] A slave who was skilled in one of these trades not only could serve his master's needs but could also be hired out, with the master receiving most of the slave's wages. Besides working as carpenters, coopers, stonemasons, and in other skilled trades, Bermuda's adult male slaves served as crewmen on their masters' vessels, fished, kept the islands' forts, roads, and bridges in good repair, and traded. Slave men and women made saleable items from Bermuda's palmetto trees. From the broad leaves came "Cables, Ropes, matts"; from the fibrous tops of the trees they made "bongraces [sun-shades or hats], basketts broomes Sives Chaires."[59] The palmetto is a native plant in Africa as well as in the New World, and many blacks in the islands and in South Carolina, perhaps using their memories of skills handed down in Africa, made woven baskets and hats from the broad palmetto leaves. Hats, especially, were a popular trade item, and were, as one governor remarked, "of great use to the poor."[60]

Toward the end of the seventeenth century, many of Bermuda's "poor," blacks as well as whites, became involved in the salt trade, which was to become the mainstay of Bermuda's economy for more than a hundred years. In 1670 Bermudian John Darrell was aware of a salt pond on the Bahamian Island of Little Exuma, and Bermudians began to explore the possibilities of harvesting salt from Turks Islands in the 1670s.[61] The Turks Island group, lying southeast of New Providence Island in the Bahamas and due north of St. Domingue, derived its name either from the Turk's-head cactus, which grew in abundance in the West Indies, or from the shape of the largest of the islands, Grand Turk, which bears a vague resemblance to the head of a Turk with a fez atop it. By

58. Lefroy, *Memorials*, 2:155.

59. Robinson to Blathwayt, Lords of Trade and Plantations, June 11, 1687, in Council minutes, *BHQ* 2. no. 1 (1945): 17. Wood, *Black Majority*, 105, notes the widespread use of palmetto baskets, boxes, and the like by slaves in South Carolina.

60. Pitt to Lords of Trade and Plantations, in CO 37/12: 172–76.

61. The reference to Darrell and the salt trade is in Craton and Saunders, *Islanders in the Stream*, 197.

the 1670s Bermudan trading vessels were plying the waters between Bermuda and the Bahamas with some regularity, and it is likely that a Bermudian sloop visited the Turks Islands then. On the two largest of these islands, Grand Turk and Salt Cay, Bermudians discovered the product that would provide them the one thing their economy lacked: a staple crop. Salt, needed not only for seasoning food but also for preserving it, was a precious commodity in the age before refrigeration. Bermuda workers harvested the salt from the Turks Islands from the 1680s until 1710, when the Spanish drove them away. A Bermudian "privateering expedition" under Captain Lewis Middleton then evicted the Spanish, and Bermuda salt-raking continued undisturbed until 1764, when the French from St. Domingue captured the Bermuda salt-rakers. The French were later obliged to pay an indemnity.[62]

Best of all for the Bermudians, the Turks Islands salt was free for the taking. All they had to do was to provide the labor to collect it. Bermudians had some experience with harvesting salt by boiling seawater in large vessels, as a place in Paget Tribe still called Salt Kettle attests. An easier way to extract the salt was to channel seawater into a shallow "salt pond" and let it evaporate, which is what the Bermudians did on Grand Turk and Salt Cay. Salt-raking was heavy labor. Ponds had to be dug, and when the water evaporated the salt had to be shoveled into wheelbarrows, piled on the shore, and covered with palmetto thatch against rain. The salt was then shoveled into half-barrel containers (bushels) and loaded onto vessels—all under a hot tropical sun. Salt-raking was grueling work for both blacks and whites.[63]

Exactly how many Bermudians were engaged in salt-raking is difficult to determine, but it is estimated that as many as 1,000 men and boys, well over one-fourth of the population of the islands, were involved in salt-raking by the end of the seventeenth century. Each year from February to October or November, the salt-rakers left their families, sailed to the West Indies, and lived on the Turks Islands, harvesting the salt. It was a hard life, and some of the salt-rakers barely made a living from their labors. Edward Randolph reported that "some years" Bermuda vessels carried fish, onions, cabbages, and whale oil to trade in Barbados and the Leeward Islands, but that most small vessels sailed "in their Ballas" (ballast, empty of cargo) to the Bahamas for salt, which they then took to the Carolinas "from whence they Bring in

---

62. On the origins and history of the Bermuda salt trade, see Lefroy, *Memorials,* 2:465–66; William Sears Zuill, "Bermuda, Salt, and the Turks Islands," *BHQ* 8, no. 4 (1951): 162–68; and Smith, *Slavery in Bermuda,* 59. On the French attack on Turks Islands, see *Journals of . . . Assembly,* 1:780–81.

63. Williams, *Historical & Statistical Account,* 82, notes that Paget and Warwick were the tribes mainly involved in the salt trade. For a discussion of salt-raking in the Bahamas, see Higman, *Slave Populations,* 178.

Return provision and get but little by those voyages." That is, many owners of Bermuda sloops were barely making enough to feed themselves and their households. Other Bermuda shipowners, however, reportedly cut "Braselett wood" in the Bahamas and sold it in Curaçao, "with their Sloops makeing their return in peices of 8 and Holland Manufacture."[64]

Each year, in the beginning of winter, "before the salt season comes on," the owners of small sloops loaded their vessels with Bermuda produce such as cabbages and onions for a run to the West Indies, where they traded for cotton cloth, sugar, molasses, and rum. Later, they made a voyage with salt from Turks Islands to the "Northern Plantations," or mainland colonies, to trade for Indian corn, bread, and flour. Sometimes these voyages proved dangerous beyond ordinary hazards at sea: In 1705 Bermuda's governor, Benjamin Bennett, wrote that "att Turks Islands pirates frequently came & took vessels that were rakeing salt there on which is our chiefest dependence."[65] The Bermuda Assembly observed that salt-raking vessels were "often molested by the Spaniards in pursuit of this business, their construction is entirely calculated for Swift Sailing."[66]

As a means of preserving fish and meat, salt was a much-prized commodity in the mainland colonies as well as in Bermuda, and enterprising Bermudians who loaded cargoes of salt from the Turks Islands soon found a ready market in New England, New York, and the Chesapeake. Bermuda salt supplied the colonies on the North American mainland, and the proceeds from this trade supplied other wants of Bermuda colonists. Evidence of their increasing interest and involvement in the salt trade can be found in wills and inventories of the late seventeenth century. In 1670, before the salt trade at Turks Island began, the inventory of the Hamilton Tribe merchant Samuel Stone, for example, included 39 bushels of salt valued at £3.18. In 1690 the will of William Peasley of Hamilton Tribe left to his mother the proceeds from 225 bushels of salt, priced at three shillings per bushel, "sold to Samuel Carpenter of Philadelphia."[67] The 1705 inventory of Joseph Lightbourn shows that he owned two-thirds of a "new vessel," one sloop "worne and ould," and part of a sloop and "salt on board" that vessel. Two other items in the inventory reflect the rising price of salt since 1690: 800 bushels of salt valued at 19s. per bushel, and the money paid him for 1,720 bushels of salt, which came to £136.13.[68]

64. Edward Randolph to Lords of Trade and Plantations, November 15, 1700, in CO 37/3: 181–83 (quotation, p. 182).
65. *CSP*, 1705:20, 229, 634.
66. *Journals of . . . Assembly*, 1:780. For more on the salt trade, Bermuda sailors, and their encounters with pirates, see William Sears Zuill, *The Story of Bermuda and Her People* (London: Macmillan, 1973), 80–87.
67. Books of Wills, vol. 1, p. 153.
68. Ibid., vol. 3, pt. 2, pp. 117, 150.

The 1706 inventory of Philip Lea of Paget shows his interest in shipbuilding as well as salt: Among its contents, along with a firelock gun, a silver-hilted sword, and a bayonet, were 998 feet of cedar planks and "One percell [parcel] of salt." The Bermuda Assembly commented on the vital importance of the salt trade, noting that the colony had "no sort of staple, nor produce of any kind . . . to enable the Inhabitants to carry on Commerce, and should this small beneficial Trade be taken away, they are thereby disabled from employing their Vessels and Seamen to any sort of advantage, as they have no other resource whatever, their whole dependence being on Salt, Cedar and Sailors." As the enterprising Bermudians described their product, the Turks Islands salt was "made by the Sun on Salt Springs, and esteemed the best and wholsomest Table Salt in the World, and will much better answer the Purpose of preserving . . . being of a stronger Nature than any Salt whatsoever." By the middle of the eighteenth century the Bermudians were transporting 130,000 bushels of salt a year to North America.[69] In 1758 the Bermuda Assembly noted that about 80 vessels and "Not less that [*sic*] twelve hundred People" were employed in gathering and transporting Turks Islands salt.[70] That, in a population of somewhere between 9,000 and 10,000, was a considerable portion of the islands' able-bodied men and boys, both blacks and whites. By the end of the eighteenth century more than 100 Bermudians claimed "salt lots" in the Turks Islands. The holders of this property included well-known Bermuda names such as Wainwright, Darrell, Baseden, Dunscomb, Lightbourn, and Ingham.[71]

The rise of a merchant elite in Bermuda can be traced in some of the histories of the second generation, the sons of founding families. The careers of Captain John Stowe's two sons, Joseph and Benjamin, represent the widening mercantile interests among Bermudians. The will and inventory of the eldest son, Joseph, who died in 1692, illustrate something of the diversification of economic pursuits in the transformation from agriculture to trade. At his death Joseph Stowe owned three shares of the family's Pembroke land, two houses, two boats, and personal property worth £445.17, including 12 slaves with a combined value of £169. His two-story house was very likely the family home at Mill Shares that his father had occupied: a structure with

69. *Journals of . . . Assembly,* 1:780–81. Bermuda supplied a large portion of the English mainland colonies' salt needs. In 1750 Pennsylvanian Robert Hunter Morris petitioned the crown for the exclusive right to the North American salt trade. Colonel Henry Tucker, Bermuda's colonial agent in London, persuaded the agents from New England, Virginia, and the Carolinas to help scuttle Morris's proposal. See Williams, *Historical & Statistical Account,* 76.
70. *Journals of . . . Assembly,* 1:780. In 1790 there were only four vessels in the Turks Island fleet where once there had been 10 or 12. In 1792 salt was selling for 6d. per bushel. See Mary Alicia Juliette Arton, *Trade and Commerce of Bermuda, 1515 to 1839* (Hamilton, Bermuda: Island Press, 1965), 22, 25. In 1804 the Bahamas incorporated Turks and Caicos Islands, ending Bermuda's involvement in the salt trade. See Higman, *Slave Populations,* 44.
71. Maps of Turks Islands, 1790, Bermuda Archives, copies of two maps in CO 700.

seven rooms—a hall, an "old hall," a parlor, three sleeping chambers, and a kitchen. In addition there was a cellar and a cornhouse. In the storehouse, described as a "house below," near the water, there were casks, cables, and dredging equipment. Many Bermuda traders had similar storehouses close to the water and concealed from view by land. Joseph Stowe's household furnishings, while not luxurious, show a rising level of wealth. They included chairs with cushions, brass andirons and candlesticks, feather beds (one with creweled curtains and valances), looking glasses, pewter, glass, and earthen dishes, a substantial collection of linens for bed and table, and (rare for early Bermuda) a pewter chamber pot. There were 10 Stowe children: five sons and five daughters. One of the daughters, Elizabeth, married Richard Stafford, a prosperous merchant of Hamilton Tribe; another, Susanna, married a son of Richard Norwood, who lived not far from the Stowes. Stowe's five sons ensured that the family name would be carried on, as indeed it was.

The individuals in Joseph Stowe's slave household had no surnames, but they, too, were families whose descendants carried on to later generations. The inventory of Stowe's estate in 1704 lists them very carefully, according to age, and in family groups:

Francisco a Negro Man	£10
Frank a Negro Man	£10
Filea a Negro woman	£16
Hambro a Negro Man	£15
A Negro Child	£03
Harry a Negro Man	£25
Jane a Negro woman	£20
Jo a Negro boy	£10
Jane a Negro girle	£10
Joane a Negro girle	£08
Sue a Negro girle	£15
Saile a Negro Man	£25[72]

These 12 slaves—two elderly men, three able-bodied men, two women, a boy, three girls, and a young child—comprised at least three families. At the time of Stowe's death in 1704 they lived and worked on his Pembroke land, serving a white household of at least eight people—a husband and wife and their six children still living at home. Joseph Stowe's detailed estate inventory allows a closer view of how these closely connected whites and blacks lived. Like his father before him, Joseph Stowe was knowledgeable about ships and shipbuilding, and like his father, he taught the craft of shipbuilding to some of his slaves. Someone on the Stowe property was building a vessel in 1704: The inventory lists cedar boards, a tar barrel, and a partially built boat. Joseph

72. For Joseph Stowe's will and inventory, see Book of Wills, vol. 3, pt. 2, pp. 9, 11.

Stowe had "one great boat" and "one small boat," probably a sloop and a shallop or dinghy. The sloop, a trading vessel, would probably have sailed often to the West Indies, as Stowe's father's sloops had done. Some of his male slaves may have sailed with it. The others would have fished in the smaller vessel and ventured far out to sea: The inventory lists both "shore hooks" and "sea hooks." The slaves would also have planted some corn and potatoes and probably some tobacco on Stowe's 75 acres, and the women and children would have tended a vegetable garden to supply the needs of Stowe's large family as well as their own families. Some of the men would have worked at felling cedar trees to saw and plane for shipbuilding, and others—perhaps Francisco and Frank, with the older children—would have tended the livestock. Stowe's livestock inventory was large by Bermuda standards: seven sheep, five ewes, 10 young bulls, eight heifers, one old bull, three steers, eight "milch cows," 10 calves, five oxen, three hogs, one sow with a litter of pigs, and a "stock of bees." In addition there was a gray mare and her colt. Joseph Stowe, the son of the doughty Captain John Stowe, followed his father's footsteps. He built boats, and he raised sheep, cattle, and hogs and kept bees—to trade his wool, beef, pork, and honey abroad. While Joseph Stowe and his family prospered on the estate at Mill Shares, Captain John Stowe's younger son, Benjamin, went to sea. He may been involved in privateering, for he was reportedly a prisoner in Algiers at the time of his father's death in 1684. But somewhere along the way, Captain Benjamin Stowe married and had at least one child. He was a widower at the time of his death in 1701, and the guardianship of his son, Benjamin Jr., fell to his brother-in-law, Samuel Sherlock, a wealthy merchant of Devonshire Tribe.[73]

Another second-generation achiever was Richard Jennings's son, John, who described himself as a "Merchant" in his 1684 will. He lived in Southampton, where he had married a daughter of Southampton Tribe's Thomas Richards. His will leaves his "mansion house and out houses" to his son, John, along with two shares of land, a gold thumb ring, and "a pistole piece of gold." To his two daughters he left land, the rest of his gold rings, and money, including £300 to the eldest when she reached age 19 or married. To this same daughter he left a "Silke Mantle" (cloak) that her grandfather, the elder Richard Jennings, had given to her late mother. Jennings also willed to both daughters their mother's clothing and "all their mother's childbedd linnen."[74]

When John's brother, Richard Jennings the younger, made his will, he was even wealthier than his sibling, and his holdings testify to the widespread

73. Sherlock was married to Stowe's sister, Esther. Benjamin Stowe's Algiers imprisonment is recorded by a descendant, William Hall Darrell, in Genealogical Note Book, 1872, Bermuda Archives. See also Books of Wills, vol. 2, pt. 2, pp. 150, 159.

74. Books of Wills, vol. 3, pt. 1, p. 32.

nature of some Bermudians' connections. He owned not only a mansion house and land in Bermuda, but also a brick house in Boston (which he rented out) and a plantation in Collington County, South Carolina. In the inventory taken after his death in 1692 the younger Richard Jennings's personal wealth, not including the value of his land and slaves, was estimated at over £1,300. The contents of the inventory include £442 in cash and "1239 ounces Bullion at 6 s. per ounce," worth £371.17. The inventory also included "One Long Gun" and four pistols. Jennings's eight-room mansion boasted a "Dining Room Above Stairs" that could seat 12 on its cane chairs. The Jenningses and their guests drank from silver tankards and might have had chocolate from a "Copper Chocolate Pott" in the parlor with "2 Large Armed Chairs" and cushions.[75] The Jenningses' beds, not feather, but down, were warmed in winter with a brass warming pan, and chamber pots (an unusual amenity for Bermuda) were a part of the household furnishings. The Jenningses lived as well as, although they did not have the large landholdings of, their affluent counterparts in the mainland colonies. In Virginia, for example, the inventory of the wealthy planter Ralph Wormeley in 1701 lists a 10-room house with such luxuries as a clock, brass warming pans, and a "Crimson sattin quilt." Most Virginians, however, were far less affluent. In the early 1700s most households of the "middling sort" in Virginia had personal property worth an average of £137, and about two-thirds of all households were at the "bottom levels of society."[76] Richard Jennings passed on the bulk of his estate to his two sons, who bore the family names Richard and John. They in turn had sons of their own, thus establishing a line of Jenningses that runs through the history of colonial Bermuda.

By the closing decade of the seventeenth century, a number of Bermuda colonists had accumulated personal fortunes of more than £1,000—a substantial amount of wealth for settlers in any colony in that period. The first generation of settlers—men like Thomas Richards, John Stowe, and Richard Jennings—had laid a foundation of wealth for their sons to build upon. The inventories of the second generation of Bermuda colonists are demonstrable proof of a level of affluence, even opulence, among a small and interconnected merchant elite at the beginning of the eighteenth century. As one of the colony's governors remarked of the members of the Governor's Council, they were "all men who have visited most parts of the trading world in the quality of Commanders of vessels" and were "well respected in the country."[77] It is worth

75. Ibid., p. 164.
76. Rutman and Rutman, *A Place in Time*, 154–55, 188–89.
77. Governor John Bruce Hope to the Committee on Trade and Plantations, March 20, 1724/1725, in *CSP*, 34:69.

noting that these wealthy, well-connected men were also slaveholders and that their slaves also shared in their activities. Slaves loaded and unloaded goods from vessels; some slaves were sailors on those vessels. Slaves who served the households of these merchants heard talk of faraway places. The implications of such knowledge for Bermuda's blacks will be explored later in this chapter.

Besides Richard Jennings Jr., who died in 1692, five other men left personal estates worth more than £1,000 in the 1690s. Captain Abraham Adderley, who died in 1690, left an inventory of personal property worth more than £1,450, including 14 slaves—four men, five women, and five children—valued at £219. Among his slaves was a black man appropriately named Fortune. Adderley, a merchant, also owned a sloop. When he first came to Bermuda is not known, but in 1658 he left there for a time: "Abraham Aderly his wife and children" are listed among the emigrants to Jamaica with nearly 200 other Bermudians after the English conquest of Jamaica under Cromwell in 1655.[78] The group of prospective settlers did not all remain in the Caribbean, and sometime in the 1660s Abraham Adderley and his family returned to Bermuda. In 1665 his name appears as one of eight Bermudians censured by the governor and council for illegal whaling. These "refractory spirits" caught a whale "about 20 foote in length." Between 1671 and 1680 Adderly and his wife, Tabitha, had four children, including two sons named Abraham and Isaac. When Adderley died, in 1689, his estate included "1 great boat with her Masts, Sayles, Grapple,[79] &c," and an "old small boat with a grapple." He also had a store of "Merchants Goods": broadcloth, linen, ivory combs, scissors, and "3 pair of Silke Stockings Small." His adult slaves—the four men and five women—would have been involved in the operation of their master's sailing vessels and the disposition of their goods. Abraham Adderley had obviously profited by his West Indies connections and perhaps a fortunate wreck or two: He had 1,856 ounces of gold bullion at the time of his death.

Thomas Gibbs, who witnessed Adderley's will, and William Greene, who appraised his inventory, were themselves among Bermuda's very rich. Gibbs, who married a daughter of Stephen Paynter, lived in Southampton, although

78. Lefroy, *Memorials*, 2:223. The list of people who went to Jamaica is reprinted ibid., 1:718. One of them was Thomas Wiverley, the first husband of Tabitha Adderley. Abraham Adderley mentions her two sons by Wiverley in his will. See also Hallett, *Early Bermuda Records*, 2.

79. The *Oxford English Dictionary* defines *grapple* as "an implement for grappling or laying hold" and "to be at anchor." In modern Bermuda a grapple is a small anchor used to hold a fishing boat in place on a sandy bottom. In seventeenth- and eighteenth-century Bermuda *grapple* could also mean a device used to lay hold of another vessel so that goods or passengers might be transferred. The word *grapple* appears in several Bermuda inventories, mostly of men who were engaged in trade, not fishing. See, for example, Richard Jennings's 1692 inventory, Books of Wills, vol. 2, pt. 1, p. 160, and Thomas Outerbridge's 1694 inventory, Books of Wills, vol. 2, pt. 2, p. 83.

not at the time of the 1663 survey. Gibbs Hill lighthouse stands today on one of the highest points in the islands. Thomas Gibbs witnessed the will of Southampton's Richard Hunt in 1683, and Gibbs himself died intestate 10 years later. His inventory, taken in 1693, was valued at £1,145, including £777 in "cash," 119 ounces of "plate," and one-third of a sloop called the *Dove*. The inventory lists six slaves—a woman, two boys, and three young children. Gibbs also had six cattle, six hogs, four sheep, and two hives of bees. Among his other assets was "3 barrels of beefe adventured at sea," valued at £6.[80] Gibbs, like several other Bermudians, traded in beef to other colonies, and shared in the profits—and perhaps the plunder—of Bermuda's expanding maritime activities.

William Greene, who died in 1692, styled himself "Gent." in his will. He owned at least two shares of land in Paget Tribe, where he resided. His house had eight rooms, including a study that contained at least 50 or 60 books. Greene's library, rare for Bermuda in the colonial period, consisted of "a parcell of law books," works on history, mathematics, medicine, and religion, a Latin grammar, and three Bibles.[81] At the time of his death William Greene also had £750 in cash. The source of this wealth is not clear from his personal property, although he, like Thomas Gibbs, evidently traded in beef. He had a larger-than-average holding in livestock: 26 head of cattle, 10 hogs, six sheep, and four goats. To help tend them Greene also had 16 slaves—two men, three women, eight boys, and three girls. His will provided for his wife, Mary, to have six of these slaves, "such as shee shall make choice of," and for the rest to be sold—a rare provision in a Bermuda slaveowner's will. Apparently the couple had no living children who could keep the remaining slaves in the family, as was the custom.

Stephen Righton, who, like William Greene, wrote "Gent." after his name, also died in 1692, leaving an estate worth £1,771. His mansion in Hamilton Tribe had 11 rooms, and he had 13 slaves—four men, four women, and five children. One of his slaves evidently was a shoemaker, since the inventory also includes tanned hides, lasts, and "49 pr. of shooes & pumps." Righton also had 14 head of cattle, eight sheep, seven hogs, two horses, and nine beehives. He, like Gibbs and Greene, probably "adventured" in beef, and he obviously traded in honey and beeswax as well. The bulk of his estate was £1,357 in cash from the sale of his sloop and one share of land.[82] Among Stephen Righton's bequests was £5 to a friend, Thomas Outerbridge of Hamilton Tribe, whom he made one of the executors of his estate. Outerbridge did not need the money.

80. Books of Wills, vol. 2, pp. 41, 91.
81. Ibid., vol. 3, pt. 1, p. 193; ibid., vol. 2, pt. 1, p. 19.
82. Ibid., vol. 3, pt. 1, p. 197; ibid., vol. 2, pt. 2, pp. 101, 106.

When he died a month after Stephen Righton in 1692 he left an estate worth £1,550, including "One Greate Boate Masts Sayles and grappell," a canoe with mast, sails, and grapple, £736 in cash, and 583 ounces of bullion. There were 10 slaves in the Outerbridge household: three men, two women, and five children. In his will, Outerbridge left his slaves to his wife (the daughter of John Stowe) during her lifetime. He provided that his "old Negro Dick" was to have his freedom at Mrs. Outerbridge's death but was "to remain and live with one of my sons wch of them he likes best." Thomas and Martha Outerbridge had six children, five of them sons whose descendants would keep that name alive in Bermuda until the present day.[83]

These six men—Abraham Adderley, Thomas Gibbs, William Greene, Stephen Righton, Thomas Outerbridge, and Richard Jennings—were among the wealthiest individuals in late-seventeenth-century Bermuda. All six lived in large houses that were luxurious by Bermuda standards; all had slave households of six to 16 slaves that contained one or more slave families with children; all but Greene and Outerbridge had one or more Indians among their slaves—perhaps an indication that Indians were highly prized as servants, or merely that the owners had contacts with privateers who sold Indian captives.[84] All of these men had large amounts of cash at the time of their deaths, and except for Abraham Adderley, all of them had guns. All but William Greene had a boat or sloop in his possession, and all had varying amounts of bullion or plate among their effects. The presence of large amounts of cash, gold bullion, and silver plate in their probate inventories suggests that convenient discoveries of shipwrecks with valuable cargoes, as well as a clandestine and profitable trade in the Caribbean, were responsible for the wealth of these Bermuda colonists.

Families like the Jenningses and the Outerbridges represent the upper level of Bermuda society in the late seventeenth century. Such families continued to play prominent roles in Bermuda's public life and private society for centuries to come. Much like the affluent planter families of Virginia, these families were connected by ties of kinship and friendship that often stretched across tribe boundaries as well as binding neighbors within a particular tribe. The heads of these families witnessed each other's wills, appraised each other's inventories, and saw their children form new families through intermarriage. Thus William Greene was an executor of Abraham Adderley's will, and Thomas Gibbs a witness to it in 1688; Thomas Richards was an executor of Stephen Paynter's will

83. Ibid., vol. 2, p. 58. Thomas Outerbridge is not listed in the survey of 1663, but his father, William, was a tenant on 75 acres in Hamilton Tribe. A Thomas Outerbridge who was in Bermuda in 1626 and died in 1677 may have been his uncle. See Hallet, *Early Bermuda Wills*, 422, 423.

84. Adderley had 14 slaves; Gibbs, six; Righton, 13; Outerbridge, 10; and Jennings, six.

in 1661; Joseph Stowe was an executor of Thomas Outerbridge's will in 1692, and related to him as "brother-in-law," since Outerbridge had married John Stowe's daughter, Martha. As noted earlier, Captain John Stowe managed to marry four of his daughters to wealthy Bermudians, and Thomas Richards's daughter Mary married the merchant Perient Trott.[85] Sarah, another daughter of Thomas Richards, married Richard Jennings's son, John. By the last quarter of the seventeenth century these well-connected, wealthy families had interests and incomes that were largely outside the control of either the Somers Islands Company or, after 1684, the crown.

The colony passed from the Somers Islands Company to royal control in 1684, and acts passed by the colony's legislature in the 1680s and 1690s reflect a certain social turmoil, with efforts to control the behavior of whites and blacks alike. Part of that disruptive behavior concerned illegal trade. In 1682, for example, a colonist named Thomas Motton in Smith's Tribe was fined 200 pounds of tobacco for "dealing" (trading) in palmetto tops with a slave belonging to Edward Smith. The slave was whipped. Grand jury presentments complained against illegal trade between blacks and whites, and the Assembly passed an act to prevent the colony's whites from "Buying, Selling, Bartering with Negroes or Other Slaves." Some merchants bought goods precisely for that purpose, as one inventory's listing of "24 small bone Combs for Negroes" attests.[86] In 1686 the Governor's Council tried once again to prevent illegal trading with vessels entering Bermuda's waters. The council ordered that "no man, white or black, presume to go to sea, to speake with any shipp or shipping" without the permission of the local justice of the peace or militia captain. For the two races, however, the punishment was different: a month in prison for whites, a whipping or other unspecified punishment "with severity" for blacks.[87]

Trade, licit or illicit, was the foundation of Bermuda's economy, and sea-faring was becoming a way of life for many. Governor Richard Coney, who arrived in 1683, just a year before Bermuda passed from the control of the Somers Islands Company to the crown, reported that there were "about thirty Sail of trading vessels." He grumbled that "their Owners are wealthy and the

85. When Perient Trott died in 1691, William Green and Thomas Outerbridge were the executors of his will. Hallett, *Early Bermuda Wills*, 588. Outerbridge's will is in Books of Wills, vol. 3, pt. 1, p. 200. Martha Stowe Outerbridge is named in Stowe's will. Books of Wills, vol. 1, p. 314. Lefroy (*Memorials*, 2:475) remarked that many of the same names that appear in seventeenth-century Bermuda politics were still prominent some two centuries later, in the 1870s.
86. CR, 9:32. See also CR, 7:114, 116. The inventory, an unidentified fragment, is dated 1685, Books of Wills, 1.
87. Council minutes, July 22, 1686, *BHQ* 1, no. 2 (1944): 56.

most contentious yet pretend poverty."[88] When Bermuda at last became a royal colony, the colonists, no longer bound by the Somers Islands Company's trade restrictions, were free to build their own vessels and to sail them wherever they pleased. Bermuda shipowners regularly flouted customs regulations. For example, one irate official in the 1680s reported the illegal departure of the *Fortune*, a "small new built sloop of about tenn tunn . . . without Giving in any bonds, being searched, or taking their sea brief or passes to ye fortes (going in a clear contrary way) on any manner of leave, license, or clearing according to Custome—It seems they give out . . . [that] they are bound to ye Bahamahs but wth how many passengers, or what indebted here, [I] cannot yet learne, nor with what they are laden."[89] The *Fortune* belonged to Samuel Trott, son of Perient Trott.

Governor Coney (who, not surprisingly, was unpopular) fumed at the illicit trade, especially in tobacco: "As to the Customs on Tobacco they are soe farr from being willing to pay it, that they privately convey it in their own bottoms to other parts, as New England, Barbados &c pretending that from those parts it shall bee transported for Old England. . . . And the better to paliate the discovery they stow it in Cask lined with ffish." Governor Coney estimated that, according to "the Judgment of several persons," "at least one hundred thousand weight [of tobacco] hath privately been transported to Barbados and other parts this Spring." Coney also reported that "Timber is wholy destroy'd what with building Vessels and then selling them to Forreigners." Furthermore, said he, "And when I prohibit it then they cry out, What are you sent hither to enslave us? Wee are free-born-people, our Lands are our own, and we will doe with our own what wee please, And if wee doe not like the King's Government wee can desert the Country and live better elsewhere."[90] In an attempt to impose order, Coney recommended the appointment of a commission to search for smuggled tobacco or prohibited goods. He noted that the practice of "wrecking" continued unchecked, reporting that some colonists had recently set a stranded French vessel afire "for her Iron." A blacksmith, Francis Dickinson (very likely the son of Southampton blacksmith Robert Dickinson) was suspect in this case, but there was insufficient evidence to convict him. The Bermudians, said Governor Coney, "will not evidence against each other in any publique concern; for they are all of them a kin

88. Lefroy, *Memorials,* 2:548–49. On Governor Coney and the turbulent political history of Bermuda's becoming a royal colony, see Richard S. Dunn, "The Downfall of the Bermuda Company: A Restoration Farce," *WMQ,* 3d ser., 20, no. 4 (October 1963): 487–512.

89. Letter of John Jauncye, secretary, 1687, quoted in Council minutes, *BHQ* 2, no. 1 (1945): 14.

90. Lefroy, *Memorials,* 2:548 (first quotation), 555 (second quotation), 549 (third quotation).

both by Consanguinity and Villany." Moreover, said Coney, the colonists were planning "to choose one Thomas Richards to bee their Governor."[91] In April 1687 Governor Coney was replaced, not by Thomas Richards, but by Sir Robert Robinson, who served until 1690.

Upon his arrival in Bermuda Governor Robinson made a detailed report of the island colony he had come to govern.[92] The document provides an overview of Bermuda and its people toward the close of the seventeenth century. In 1687 there was a total population of 5,909: 4,152 whites and 1,737 blacks. There were 735 men able to serve in the militia, of whom 120 were "Verry Poore" and could not supply their own arms. Where in 1663 there had been 378 houses, there were now 579 residences scattered over Bermuda's 12,000 acres.[93] Of these, 29 were built of stone and 63 of shingle, but all the rest, 487, were humble houses like the tenements in Norwood's survey, made of wooden frames, wattle-and-daub, and palmetto thatch. Most Bermuda colonists were men like Marmaduke Dando, Thomas Wells, and the others who worked the soil, fished, and bartered a little for a living. Some were craftsmen: There were 151 of these skilled workers in 1687, with coopers, joiners, carpenters, and shoemakers being the most numerous, and the rest being sawyers, weavers, blacksmiths, plasterers, and cordwainers. Many Bermudians, both blacks and whites, were sailors. Governor Robinson estimated that about one-sixth of the colony's men were at sea at any given time. Robinson's 1687 report enumerated "sundry small Vessells," listing a total of 42: 31 sloops (small single-masted vessels generally under 20 tons) and 11 barks (vessels with 3 or more masts) ranging in size from 20 to 90 tons.[94] The nautical skills required to navigate and sail these vessels across hundreds of miles of open sea are eloquent testimony to the expertise of Bermuda's sailors, black and white. Governor Robinson paid tribute to them in his report.

In a detailed description of the colony's people and their occupations, Robinson wrote that the Bermudians were "generally of quick Growth & of pretty Easie tempers." The men were "generally Saylors . . . verry hardey but of unexperienced Courage." The women were "likewise of a large growth & Skillful in Swiming & Pilotting they are Comonly Good huswives & Verry amorous." Bermuda's children, the governor noted, had "but little Education their parents . . . neither Covetting nor affording it," since the colonists' main occupations were "Fishing Swimming Diveing Diging & ye Like Sciences to

91. Ibid., 2:564 (first quotation); 549 (second quotation).
92. See Robinson to Blathwayt, June 11, 1687, in Council minutes, *BHQ* 2, no. 1 (1945): 14–19.
93. Ibid., 16.
94. Ibid., 18.

be artists in wch they need no greate Instructions." The entire population, men, women, and children, were "all Great Smokers of tobacco."[95] Another governor, John Bruce Hope, also remarked upon the physical health and strength of the Bermudians. He found them a handsome people with "English countenances, but of a Browner Complexion; Tall, Lean, Strong-limb'd & well proportion'd . . . all of them can Swim."[96] Hope remarked that in fair weather "the whole Inhabitants are almost all out at Fishing, some of them four or five Leagues [12 or 15 miles] from the Shoar." He also noted that their fishing boats often overturned in violent winds, but "it rarely happens that any of them are lost." Bermudians also continued to augment their fortunes with "wrecking." Governor Robinson reported that the wreck of a Spanish ship in 1687, with its treasure of £48,000 in gold bullion, was shared by many, including the crown and the governor.[97]

The land in Bermuda was reportedly not worth much, Governor Robinson wrote in his report, "for want of Slaves to manure it." This is a curious statement, indeed, considering that Bermuda had at least 2,000 acres under cultivation and 1,700 slaves. Bermuda had more than enough slaves to work its small amount of arable land, but by the end of the seventeenth century, the majority of the colony's male slaves were not engaged in growing crops. As the years passed, agriculture fell into disrepute, and farming and gardening became occupations for children and old people. The decline of the islands' agricultural resources can be seen in the condition of fruit trees: In 1639 Juan de Rivera had admired the many "orange trees and lemon trees, which bear very beautiful large fruit," but by 1687 Governor Robinson wrote of the "Vast number of Orranges lemons Pongranats & Cytron trees wch for Sundry yeares Past have been Blasted [damaged by hurricanes] & all totally lost unless some few small & mostly withered Orranges."[98]

In 1691 Governor Isaac Richier complained that Bermuda's colonists were "generally very poor and positively resolved to continue so unless the sea will make them otherwise, for none will labour ashore either on land or trades."[99] But the Bermudians, wrote Richier, were "expert and industrious" in maritime pursuits and were "naturally stout and strong." According to Richier's report the colony's population in 1691 stood at 6,248, with 4,331 whites and 1,917 (44 percent) black. About one-third of the black population was age 15 or

95. Ibid., 17.
96. Governor John Bruce Hope, "A Description of the Bermudas or Summer Islands in America in the Year 1722," CO 37/10: 214–20 (quotation, p. 217).
97. Robinson to Blathwayt, 15. For an account of this wreck, which made the fortune of Sir William Phips, who discovered it, see Dunn, "Downfall of the Bermuda Company," 509.
98. Robinson to Blathwayt, 17; Rivera, "Shipwrecked Spaniards," 25.
99. Richier's report is in Council minutes, *BHQ* 3, no. 1 (1946): 15–24 (quotation, p. 16).

over. Bringing slaves into Bermuda had been illegal since 1674, but the slave population continued to grow through natural increase. Thomas Burton, the attorney general, wrote in 1700 that "The Island hath been very healthy since the yeare sixteen hundred ninety and two." Burton estimated the colony's population at the turn of the century to be "about four thousand Soules, more then one halfe of which are Negroes, one fifth capable to beare armes the rest women and children."[100] By the closing years of the seventeenth century the colony did not grow enough food for its own people—black or white. Maritime pursuits had become the occupation of choice, and food such as corn had to come mostly from the English colonies on the mainland. Edward Randolph's report on the produce and trade of the islands in 1700 clearly indicates that by the turn of the century Bermudians looked, not to the land, but to the sea for their livelihood:

> The first planters made great quantitys of Tobacco most part whereof was Brought to England. Some have made Sugar, most places in these Islands very proper for it they formerly sent great quantities of oranges Yearly to England and to the Northern plantations on the Continent. . . . But since the Orange Trees are blasted and their Ground Barren and Over Run in many places . . . they cannot Raise Indian Corn and provisions sufficient for their use but are forced to fetch it from Carolina & the Northern plantations and now they make but little Tobacco. So that they have no staple comodity growing upon their Islands.[101]

In 1700 Thomas Burton's report to the Council of Trade and Plantations stated that

> The Island decays yearly as to its Produce the Oranges and most of the other fruites carryed away wth a Blast the Ants alsoe destroying the Indian Corne in Several parts of the Island wch is their cheife provision in soe much that ye produce of the Island doth not maintaine the Inhabitants for last yeare the country bought above sixteene thousand bushells [of corn] and I believe this yeare will want more, and were it not for sundry small Vessells wch belong to the Islands wch bring in supplyes and for Fish of wch their is abundance Catcht, the Island could not Subsist.[102]

While many slaves learned skilled trades, especially those involved in the labor of shipbuilding, many others became sailors. Black crew members helped to man the sloops and larger vessels that plied the waters between Bermuda and the West Indies and mainland colonies. The number of sailors, black and white, and the number of Bermudian vessels at the turn of the century had dramatically increased since the 1670s, as an itemized report at the turn of the century shows:

100. CO 37/3: 136.
101. See Report of Edward Randolph to Lords of Trade and Plantations, November 15, 1700, CO 37/3: 181–83 (quotation, p. 183).
102. Thomas Burton to Lords of Trade and Plantations, in CO 37/3: 137.

170 Navigators able to take charge of Vessells and Carry them to most known places of Trade:

50 Shipp Wrights

5 Smith Forges for Shipp worke

76 Vessells Built in the Country and all of Ceder of which 4 are ships of about 100 Tuns

60 Sloops from 30 to above 40 Tuns 9 of which were lately taken by Ferdinando the pyrat.

3 or 400 small Two Mast Boats for Fishing and other occasion upon the Water

500 Saylers most of them are Natives of the Islands being about 400 White men and 100 Negros & molattos of which number above 60 sayle out of Jamaicia and above 30 out of Carasaio[103]

The number of black sailors increased over the next few years. At one time as many as four-fifths of a vessel's crew was black. In 1712, in order to ensure enough white men for defense of the islands in case of a French attack, the council had ordered that no master of any vessel should carry more than six to 10 white seamen, in the following ratio: vessels of 35 to 40 tons, six whites; 40 to 45 tons, eight whites; 45 to 50 tons, 10 whites. A report of 1733 listed 60 Bermudian vessels of 20 to 100 tons manned by a force that was more than half black: 200 whites and 150 blacks.[104] Although there is little documentation of the experiences of blacks in these maritime pursuits, it is obvious that skilled occupations such as helping to build ships and sail them offered far more personal satisfaction and provided much more self-esteem than did the repetitive drudgery of agricultural labor.[105] The craftsmanship of Bermuda's cedar sloops was known all over the Atlantic. The knowledge of winds and currents, the setting of mainsail, foresail, and jib, the dexterity required in sailing close to the wind and handling an intricate array of lines, spars, and sheets demanded skills far beyond those of land-bound laborers. Blacks and whites living and working together in the close quarters of a vessel at sea, sometimes in peril of their lives, and always under the hazardous conditions of a long voyage in a small craft, had to help and trust each other. Bermuda ships bound for the West Indies, for example, had to navigate nearly 1,000

103. Randolph to Committee on Trade and Plantations, November 15, 1700, in CO 37/3: 181–83.

104. Council minutes July 9, 1712, *BHQ* 5, no. 4 (1948): 161; Report of John Pitt to Board of Trade and Plantations, 1733, CO 37/12: 129–30. See also Walvin, *Black Ivory*, 113. A Virginia law of 1784 allowed as many as one-third of a vessel's crew to be black, and Robert Carter's two schooners had black masters.

105. On the complexity of sailing and the skills required of black seamen, see Jeffrey Bolster, *Black Jacks*, 68–84. Michael Mullin, *Africa in America: Slave Acculturation and Resistance in the American South and the British Caribbean, 1736–1831* (Urbana: University of Illinois Press, 1992), 230–31, points out the importance of a "good self image" for slave artisans and craftsmen who worked off the plantations.

miles of open sea in a voyage that could take two to three weeks. Every man had to stand his watch, and there would have been little leeway for slackers or troublemakers. Beginning in the 1680s, increasing numbers of blacks shipped out on vessels engaged in the salt trade.

By the early 1700s more blacks were engaging in the shipbuilding trade: cutting and hauling cedars, sawing, planing, and providing the labor necessary to build the sloops and larger craft. In fact, the sale of Bermuda vessels, small, fast, and well crafted, became a vital part of the colony's economy in the eighteenth century. From 1698 to 1708, according to a report to the Council of Trade and Plantations, Bermuda shipbuilders turned out 3 ships, 17 brigantines, and 217 sloops. Fourteen vessels registered in New York in 1700 were Bermuda-built.[106] By the 1730s skilled Bermuda shipwrights were turning out as many as 20 to 30 sloops a year, and shipbuilding had become a major occupation. Most of these Bermuda sloops first sailed to the Turks Islands for a cargo of salt, then continued to the mainland colonies to trade for other goods. The vessels themselves were sold on the mainland, and the owners returned to Bermuda to build more sloops. A 1735 report of the Council of Trade and Plantations noted that "this is the ordinary round of trade pursued by four parts in five of all the vessels that are sent out of the Summer Islands."[107]

Although by law all vessels were to enter and go through customs at either Castle Harbor or Town Harbor at St. George's, smuggling continued to exasperate colonial officials. One of them complained that "for a small present to the Governour . . . [customs clearance] is dispensed with, and they are suffered to go up into the Countrey where almost every Master of a vessell hath his Warehouse. . . . and herein brandy and other Commodityes brought frequently back from the French and Dutch Islands."[108] Besides goods illegally brought in, there were goods illegally shipped out. Outside the official harbors of Town Harbor and Castle Harbor at St. George's, there were several smaller, more convenient (and more remote) harbors scattered over the islands: Mangrove Bay and Ely's Harbor in Sandys Tribe; Herne (Heron) Bay in Southampton; Salt Kettle in Paget; Crow Lane, whose waters washed the shores of Pembroke, Paget, and Devonshire Tribes; and the Flatts, between Smith's and Hamilton Tribes.[109] In 1708 the Bermudians sent a petition with 462 signatures to Queen Anne, requesting that they be allowed to load and

106. *CSP*, 1685–1688:395; 1700:600, 658; 1706–June 1708:671. See also *Bermuda Statutes, Laws, and Acts of Assembly, 1690–1714* (London, 1719), 29.
107. Report of Council of Trade and Plantations to Parliament, 1735, *CSP*, 1734–1735:362.
108. George Larkin to the Lords of Trade and Plantations, August 19, 1712, in CO 37/3: 9.
109. Laura A. Bluck, "The Evolution of the Town of Hamilton, 1754–1857," *BHQ* 13, no. 3 (1956): 112.

unload their goods outside the official harbors at St. George's. The colonists argued that they must store salt from Turks Islands in their storehouses until they could sail with it to "Roanoak, Virginia, Maryland, Pensilvania, New York, and New England, and bring back Indian corn, bread, flower, pork, etc." These provisions would be ruined, they said, if they were transported from the official harbors in small open boats. Bermuda vessels also made regular runs to the West Indies carrying cabbages and onions to trade for "English goods, sugar, rum, melasses, and cotton."[110]

There were still "severall Thousand Weight" of tobacco produced annually in Bermuda in the early 1700s, but "a very small quantity of it" came to the attention of the customs collector who was supposed to collect the penny per pound due, "for the Negroes carry it aboard by night and a Negro . . . by an Act of Assembly here cannot give evidence against a White person."[111] In 1725 Governor John Bruce Hope mentioned the trial of one ship that had been seized by the customs collector "for having clandestinely put on shoar tobacco by negro slaves, with which she was navigated . . . So that tho' the fact was notorious, yet there cou'd be no evidence for the King."[112] The offending sloop in this case had only one white sailor, "and all the rest negro Slaves." Hope observed that it was the Bermudians' custom "to navigate their vessels with more negro's than the laws do allow of, but that is only in the same manner as pyracys and illegal trade has been the custom of these Islands." Hope also reported at length to the Council of Trade and Plantations on the illegal trade in Bermuda, noting that smuggled goods came in "by a channel at the West end of these Islands" and to "many convenient Creeks & Harbours, which are hid, or Land-lockd."[113]

Black and white seamen aboard Bermuda's vessels worked closely together, and shared not only the camaraderie of shipboard life, but opportunities for other occupations. Besides the salt, shipowners who made the long voyage to the Bahamas soon found that a sojourn in those waters could bring unexpected dividends. In 1703, for example, Governor Nathaniel Johnson of South Carolina wrote to the Council of Trade and Plantations that "persons may goe to such a maroone place as Turks Islands, and put their goods and merchandizes (which it may be are brought thither in an unqualified vessell)

110. Petition of Council, Assembly, Judges, Justices, Officers and Inhabitants to the Queen, 1708, *CSP,* 1708:176–77, iv.
111. Larkin to Lords of Trade and Plantations, in CO 37/3: 10.
112. John Bruce Hope to the Duke of Newcastle, September 30, 1725, in *CSP,* 1724–1725:442. For other examples of Bermuda's leading merchants and illicit trading activities, see Hereward T. Watlington, "The Bridge House, St. George's," *BHQ* 28, no. 1 (1971): 15; Council minutes, *BHQ* 5. no. 4 (1948): 157.
113. Hope, January 14, 1724/1725, CO 37/11: 46.

on board of a qualified vessell, and so import them into the Plantations." Governor Johnson was reporting a transaction involving a Royal African Company vessel from Gambia to Bermuda that put in at Turks Islands with slaves consigned to Daniel Johnson and Captain Tucker. Other slaves were put on a Carolina vessel then at Turks Islands and were later sold in that colony.[114]

When these trading vessels came into port, black and white crew members had opportunities to go ashore and engage in trade. Jamaica, for example, had slave markets where slaves could get licenses to buy and sell on their own, and in mainland ports in Virginia and the Carolinas there was also a thriving illicit trade among blacks.[115] Blacks who were able to procure goods for their own consumption, and perhaps to provide for their families, thus had a measure of autonomy.[116]

Governor John Bruce Hope (in whose honor some Bermudians named a ship, the *Bruce Hope,* at the end of his term in office in 1725), wrote a letter describing the illicit trading that Bermudians regularly carried on in the West Indies. If a Bermuda vessel happened to be lucky in "wrecking" or piracy, he said, "Curacao, St. Eustatia, St. Thomas's or the French Islands, are the ports where they are always well receiv'd without any questions ask'd; and if a good price is offered the vessel usually goes with the cargo; if not, they return and take in their white sailors with salt from the Turks Islands and under the covert of their old clearings from hence they proceed to some of the Northern Plantations." Hope observed that most Bermudians prized life at sea. What they liked best, he thought, was "wandering from one uninhabited Island to another (in their sloops), fishing for wrecks, and trading with pyrat's." Hope deplored the illegality of such trading but observed that "there is such a correspondence betwixt the pyrates [four of whom were in jail awaiting trial at the time] and those people that go from hence (as well as from the other Plantations)." On another occasion Governor Hope remarked, "Piracy and accessarys to piracy are crimes here just as epidemick as whoring and drinking, nor is it lookt upon by us here to be more enormous thatn smuggleing is in Brittain."[117]

In the early days of settlement, "Fishing upon the Wrecks" was a way of life for both whites and blacks. Hope noted that most blacks were good divers, and

114. Governor Sir Nathaniel Johnson to the Council of Trade and Plantations, July 1703, in *CSP,* 1702–1703:549.

115. See Mullin, *Africa in America,* 134–35, 153–54.

116. Betty Wood, *Women's Work, Men's Work: The Informal Slave Economies of Low Country Georgia* (Athens, Ga.: University of Georgia Press, 1995), finds a degree of autonomy for the slaves more important than the economic benefits they gained.

117. Hope to the Duke of Newcastle, September 30, 1725, in *CSP,* 1724–1725:443; Hope to Council of Trade and Plantations, ibid., 69; ibid., 1722–1723:220, 288.

credited their skills with much of the Bermudians' success in "wrecking."[118] This "maroon life," as the Bermudians called it, put black and white sailors together for weeks and months at a time. Governor Hope wrote that Bermuda vessels

> clear out a number of mariners sufficient to navigate the vessel anywhere; but they generally take three or four slaves besides, and this is a common practice at this day when they go agathering salt at Turks Islands etc., where when they arrive the white men (as they call their sailors) are turn'd ashore to rake salt where often they do continue for ten or twelve months on a stretch; and the master with his vessel navigated by negro's during that time goes a marooning; that is to say, fishing for turtle, diving upon wrecks, and sometimes trading with pyrates.[119]

If "three or four slaves" made up part of the crew of each of the 80 vessels making the run to Turks Islands, then somewhere between 240 and 320, or approximately one-fifth to one-fourth of the total number of sailors, were blacks.

For some black Bermuda seamen, the bustling Caribbean and mainland seaports with their large black populations offered the chance to escape. Such runaways are not often documented in Bermuda records, but a casual notation now and then gives a clue. Among the slaves listed in the 1705 inventory of Richard Lingar of Pembroke, for instance, is Peter, with no monetary value assigned, and a note: "The aforesaid Peter not being valued, being at sea."[120] One incident in 1710 is suggestive: The Bermuda sloop *Endeavour,* owned by Daniel Keele and commissioned as a privateer by Bermuda's Governor Bennett, encountered a French vessel in Musketo Bay off the coast of St. Thomas in the Virgin Islands, then part of the Danish West Indies. In the course of the encounter, six slaves, including one "Indian slave," jumped overboard and "swam safe on shoar."[121] Some of them later went aboard two other Bermuda sloops nearby, captained by George Frith and David Tynes. All six slaves were eventually seized by the governor of St. Thomas. Keele, who recorded the incident, petitioned for the return of the slaves. The Danish governor of St. Thomas had "seized and possessed himself of them," declaring that they were "Pyrates." The Indian and one of the blacks belonged to Keele; the other four had different Bermuda masters. These slaves were hired out by their respective owners to work on the *Endeavour* and no doubt to bring back a share of the privateer's gains. Their adventure in Musketo Bay leaves some

118. Hope, "Description of the Bermudas," 218.
119. Hope to the Duke of Newcastle, September 30, 1725, in *CSP,* 1724–1725:443. Co-operation between pirates and blacks from other colonies took place as well. Wood, *Black Majority,* 564, notes that in South Carolina "pirates occasionally conspired with Negroes to mutual advantage."
120. Books of Wills, vol. 3, pt. 2, p. 83.
121. The records of this incident are in CR, 9:170–72.

unanswered questions: Were these six slaves the only crew members of the *Endeavour* who jumped overboard? Was their swimming to shore a runaway attempt? If so, why did some of them go aboard two other Bermuda vessels? The results of Keele's petition have not survived, and the fate of the six slaves is not known. They are a part of the largely undocumented history of slaves involved in Bermuda privateering in the West Indies. There is evidence that slaves were experienced in salvaging wrecks and privateering ventures both in the Bahamas and in Bermuda waters.[122] One must remember that the region called the West Indies comprises about 100 islands forming a 2,100-mile arc from the tip of Florida to the coast of South America, and except for three straits, or passages, of about 100 miles, most of these islands are within 30 miles of each other—a day's sail for a good sailor in good weather. Once a slave reached the Bahamas, about 1,000 miles from Bermuda, the chances for running away were considerably enhanced.

In more than one instance a runaway Bermudian slave turned pirate himself. In 1733, for example, the Assembly recorded that Will, a black seaman belonging to Captain Lewis Middleton of Paget, who had "some time since absconded from his said master[,] hath in a piratical manner from time to time taken severall of our vessells and misused and abused the Inhabitants of these Islands in a Barbarous manner, to the great discouragements of the Trade and Navigation of this Colony, particularly at the severall salt seasons."[123] The Assembly resolved that a "certain person" should "go in Quest of the said negroe slave, and endeavour to take him or suppress his villainous proceedings." The outcome of this endeavor is not recorded, but it illustrates the opportunity for mobility among Bermuda's black seamen. In 1756 a Bermuda-born slave ran away from his master in St. Eustatias. He went from there to Bermuda, perhaps to visit relatives, and then moved on to South Carolina.[124] But compared with South Carolina and Virginia, where many of the runaways were black sailors who used their skills—and their transatlantic contacts—to escape bondage, Bermuda has few documented runaways. In the British Virgin Islands and Danish West Indies, slaves who ran away by sea were a common problem by the 1680s, drawing proclamations to control them in ports from Puerto Rico to Cannes.[125] Many of Bermuda's black sailors, unlike most of their counterparts in other colonies, were family men, and men with wives and children were not as likely as single men to seek freedom in a foreign port.

122. See Lefroy, *Memorials*, 1:252, 254.
123. *Journals of . . . Assembly*, 1:287.
124. Bolster, *Black Jacks*, 40. On the frequency of black sailors as runaways, see 21, 24.
125. Hall, *Slavery in the Danish West Indies*, 126–28, 133.

Ironically, some of Bermuda's black seamen participated, directly or indirectly, in the burgeoning transatlantic slave trade of the eighteenth century. Bermudians were not buying any blacks by the 1700s, but some Bermuda slaveholders were selling. Governor Bennett reported in 1708 that no blacks had been imported (the law of 1674 forbade that) but that Bermuda had for several years "been (by their great increase) over stockt." Of the surplus number of blacks, "many of them" had been "disposed of" in the Caribbean and North American colonies. Bennett reported that no blacks "directly from Africa" had been brought in since 1698, but that in the early 1670s a Bermuda ship sailed to Calabar on the Guinea coast and brought back 125 blacks, half of which were sold in Bermuda and the rest taken to Carolina and Virginia. In the 1680s a Bermudian, "Captain Stone," brought back 90 blacks from Calabar, but "most" were sold in North Carolina, Virginia, and "places on the Continent."[126] In the summer of 1716 a Bermuda sloop commanded by John Trott, son of Perient Trott, took six blacks from Bermuda to New York City, where presumably they were sold.[127] Trott was also the owner of a half-interest in the sloop. The other owner, Tobias Wall, was from the island of Nevis. Records of slaves brought by Bermuda-registered vessels to New York, Virginia, and Georgia from the early 1700s through the 1760s show that John Trott was only one of many Bermuda shipowners whose vessels carried slaves for sale—the majority of them from Bermuda (see appendix A). Bermuda, alone among the English colonies in the New World, by then had more slaves than it needed. By 1723 there were 8,435 people in Bermuda, 4,778 of whom were white, and 3,657 of whom (43 percent) were black, mulatto, or Indian. The ratio of blacks to whites in Bermuda did not approach the large majorities of blacks in slave societies such as Barbados, Jamaica, and South Carolina in the early 1700s. In 1710, for example, Barbados had over 52,000 blacks and 13,000 whites; Jamaica had 58,000 blacks to 7,200 whites.[128] Mostly one or two at a time, some Bermuda slaves were taken to be sold in a foreign port. The identities of these individuals, like the reasons for their sales, are unrecorded. Some may not have been Bermudian: It is possible that some were captives traded to Bermuda ship captains in the West Indies and brought back to Bermuda before being sold abroad. The vessels that carried them were mainly sloops. At least some, if not all, of the vessels that brought blacks from

126. Governor Benjamin Bennett to Council of Trade and Plantations, August 4, 1708, in *CSP,* 1708–1709:59.
127. "Negroes Imported into New York, 1715–1765," in *Documents Illustrative of the History of the Slave Trade to America,* ed. Elizabeth Donnan (Washington, D.C.: Carnegie Institution of Washington, 1932), 3:462–512. For the record of Trott's sloop, see p. 465.
128. Census of 1723, CO 37/11: 49. See Greene, *Pursuits of Happiness,* 178–79. In 1720 South Carolina had 11,828 blacks and 6,525 whites. Wood, *Black Majority,* 146–47.

Bermuda and other islands to sell in the mainland colonies would have also had black Bermudians as crew members.

Besides offering a partial view of Bermudian participation in the sale of slaves, the list of ships carrying slaves also suggests the widespread nature of Bermuda's trade connections. Bermuda-registered vessels brought slaves to the mainland colonies not just from Bermuda, but from St. Thomas, St. Christopher, Nevis, Antigua, St. Eustatius, Jamaica, Barbados, Turks Islands, and as far away as the Dutch islands of Curaçao and Bonaire. According to these records, between 1717 and 1742 more than 50 Bermuda-registered vessels carried a total of 166 slaves—60 or more from Bermuda and the rest from other islands in the Bahamas and the Greater and Lesser Antilles—to be sold in New York.

Most of the vessels were built in Bermuda, and some of them made repeated voyages. The Bermuda vessel that carried slaves to New York most often was a sloop built in 1729, owned by the Paynter family, including Stephen Paynter, a great-grandson of the first-generation Bermuda colonist Stephen Paynter who served as a dealer in slaves for the Earl of Warwick in the 1640s and 1650s.[129] The *Unity* arrived in New York on June 30, 1729, bringing three slaves from Bermuda. She made another four trips to New York between 1731 and 1738, bringing one slave from Jamaica, two from Barbados, one from Madeira, and one listed as being from "Curacoa and Bermuda." Among the shipowners' names are those of many of Bermuda's affluent families, such as Trott, Tucker, Stowe, Peniston, Burrows, Hunt, Leacraft, Jennings, Trimingham, and Darrell. Eight women are listed as part-owners of vessels carrying blacks to New York: Rachel Seymour, Elizabeth Walker, Angelina Hunt, Martha Forster, Ruth Evans, Mary Bassett, Mary Stiles, and Catherine Horton had interests under their own names, but all were widows of well-connected Bermudians. These women, like the men, profited from transactions that sold slaves not only from Bermuda but also from the far-flung islands in the Caribbean.

Partial records of slaves brought by Bermuda sloops to Virginia from 1710 to 1766 show much the same pattern as the records for New York (see appendix B) A considerable number (134 of 267) of the slaves were brought from Bermuda, with the rest coming from islands in the Caribbean. Of the 134 Bermuda slaves, 26 were carried individually, with the largest Bermuda group being the 23 slaves brought in August 1735 by the *Henry*, a 25-ton vessel captained by John Todd, no doubt a relative of the owner, listed as Edw. Todd. It is tempting to speculate that some of the slaves who arrived in New York and Virginia from Bermuda in the 1730s and the 1760s were

129. On the Paynter family members, see Hallett, *Early Bermuda Wills*, 432–44.

individuals whose behavior had made whites uneasy during the slave rebellion scares of those years. In April 1762, for instance, a year after Bermuda's last recorded slave rebellion plot, the *Molly,* captained by Samuel Peniston, carried a man and four women—the only women mentioned in these records—from Bermuda to sell in Accomack, Virginia.

It is clear from these scattered records that many of Bermuda's acquisitive ship captains and merchants took advantage of the lucrative slave trade, selling Bermuda slaves as well as West Indies slaves to the mainland colonies. Some of that trade was illegal, with merchandise and slaves changing hands at Turks Islands, where such transactions could and did go undocumented. A captain Daniel Johnson, for example, in 1703 was accused of transferring at least 13 slaves as well as a quantity of brass, pewter, beads, and other goods from the *Christopher,* a Royal African Company vessel, to a Bermuda sloop at Turks Islands, and carrying the contraband goods and slaves to Bermuda to be received by his father, Daniel Johnson Sr.[130]

Although the economic value of slaves in the English colonies in the Caribbean and on the mainland was growing, and a number of Bermuda traders did sell slaves abroad, most Bermuda families were reluctant to part with their slaves. In 1722 Governor Hope observed that "the Inhabitants have a Pride in keeping of them; nobody will sell a Negroe here that has been Born in his Family but upon the last extremity." In a telling comment, Hope remarked that "no slaves in the West Indies are us'd so well as the Negro's are here." Furthermore, the governor noted, "These Negroes are all sensible of the Happy Situation they are in."[131] That "happy situation" was due in large part to Bermuda's maritime economy, which involved many blacks in shipbuilding, seafaring, and trading. Men at sea were separated from their families for weeks or months at a time, but that was true for whites as well as blacks. The hardships of separation must be weighed against the rewards of a successful voyage and, for slaves, the satisfactions of a measure of independence in trading and providing for themselves and their families. Laboring to build a dinghy or a sloop or working as a crew member aboard a vessel put these blacks into relationships with whites that were quite different from the usual relationships between slaves and masters in agricultural labor. Maritime pursuits demanded special skills, often threatened danger, and depended on a level of mutual regard and trust between the master of a vessel and his crew. Although Bermuda's blacks achieved more autonomy in their everyday lives than did

130. The case of the *Christopher* is recorded in Donnan, *Slave Trade,* 4:253–55. The Johnsons, father and son, may have been related to a Bermuda ship captain named Daniel Johnson who transported an Indian from Bermuda to Virginia in 1678. See Lefroy, *Memorials,* 2:60, 461.

131. Hope, "Description of the Bermudas," CO 37/11: 217–18.

their counterparts on the American mainland and in the Caribbean islands, they, like slaves elsewhere, continued to seek freedom. But as Bermuda's whites and blacks turned more and more to maritime pursuits, the frequency of rebellion plots by slaves diminished. As we shall see in the next chapter, although individual acts of resistance continued, Bermuda, alone among New World slave societies, had only one recorded slave conspiracy in the eighteenth century.

5 Freedom and Control

As the generations passed, Bermuda was becoming a truly multiracial colony, with a proliferation of white, black, mulatto, and Indian residents whose behavior seemed to threaten traditional social mores. As whites and blacks often conspired together in acts of illicit trade, so did they in flouting religious and social rules. Blacks, especially, continued to express their desires for autonomy in acts of petty theft, insolent manners, and illicit sexual liaisons. Whites also disregarded the authorities of church and state, much to the dismay of the colony's governors. In a 1679 proclamation Governor John Heydon condemned the prevailing laxity in religious observances such as the neglect of the Lord's Supper, marriages not solemnized in church, baptisms and burials not recorded. Sabbath-breaking was rampant, with whites and blacks alike sailing, drinking, and carousing during "sermon-time."[1]

The surviving assize court records from the 1670s and 1680s suggest a determined effort at social control. Failure to attend church regularly brought public censure; fornication, adultery, and bastardy were regularly and publicly punished. Grand juries presented individuals of all races for such offenses as selling drink without a license, keeping a "disorderly house," and fornication. Some of the offenders were prominent citizens: In Pembroke in 1676, for example, three merchants, David Whitney, John Squire, and Richard Stafford, were all presented for selling drink and keeping a "Disorderly house" without a license. All were fined 20 shillings. Parents of bastard children, whether black or white, were punished, usually by whipping. In 1678 a black Pembroke couple described as servants—Black Moll, belonging to William Hall, and Black Tom, belonging to John Squire—were sentenced to be whipped for having a bastard child. In another assize some months later three Sandys women—Marie, an Indian in the household of William Burch, Bess, a black woman in the service of Mrs. Whitney, and Judah, a mulatto woman in William Waylett's household—were found guilty of fornication and sentenced to be whipped "as the sheriff shall appoint." In 1679 Sarah Wellman, the daughter of planter Francis Wellman of Paget, reportedly had a bastard child by colonist John Rawlings Jr. and both received whippings.[2]

1. "A Proclamation," January 17, 1678/1679, CR, 7:62.
2. Assize of January 18, 1676/1677, CR, 7:5; May 9–10, 1679, CR, 1:64; January 3–4, 1677/1678, CR, 7:42; Assize of January 1679/1680 (undated), CR, 7:84.

Class lines were no barrier to public censure for moral offenses, but the punishments were adjusted according to rank. When the wealthy merchant Perient Trott and his wife were among the couples accused of "incontinencie before marriage" in a grand jury presentment in 1676, they drew a fine of £3 or three months' imprisonment, while three other couples of lesser social standing accused of the same offense were fined only 20 or 30 shillings. Race, like class, presented no barrier to such punishments. Thus John Ford, a free black in Devonshire Tribe, was fined 50 shillings for incontinency before marriage, or, if he could not pay, he was to be "Taken upon the Colony Service" until the 50-shilling fine was "Satisfied." Ford was also given 30 lashes for "begetting a bastard"—presumably a result of the earlier transgression. A few years later "A Negro man of Daniel Ridlie of Pagetts Tribe" was whipped for "Bastardie with his Negro woman."[3]

The court records also contain information about a number of interracial sexual relationships. The 1663 law forbidding interracial sex evidently had had little effect, judging from grand jury presentments in the 1670s and 1680s. In St. George's, for example, a white man named George Williams, the "hired servant" of Mrs. Anne Vaughan, was presented for fornication with "Deborah the Indian" in the Vaughan household. Both were sentenced to be whipped. One Thomas Millson was fined £3 for having a bastard child with "Moll Turner a Molatto" in 1679. Since Moll has a surname and there is no mention of her owner or master, she was probably a free woman. She was sentenced "to be whipt," although the number of lashes was not stated. In 1682 Marie Harris, a white woman who lived in Smith's Tribe, bore a "Bastard Mulatto Childe" and was sentenced to be whipped or to pay a fine of 40 shillings.[4]

Although the 1674 law had prohibited the importation of blacks, Bermuda's growing black population, especially the free blacks, was cause for concern among the colony's officials. In 1676 a grand jury, voicing its concern "that all ffree Nigrowes and Mallattoes may depart the Island unlesse Such as are willing to be Servants to other men," ordered all free blacks to "depart the Islands Except they putt themselves under the Tuition of Masters."[5] Judging from continued references to free blacks in the colony, this order had little effect. In 1677 the Somers Islands Company observed that "Negroes . . . are grown more numerous then convenient."[6] Some of the increase was due to illegal trade in slaves. There is a report of a Bermuda vessel that sailed to Calabar on the Guinea coast in the early 1670s and returned with 125 blacks, about half

3.Assize of January 18, 1676/1677, CR, 7:5–6; Assize of July 16, 1679, CR, 7:67.
4.Assize of May 9–10, 1679, CR, 7:64; Assize of June 19–20, 1682, CR, 7:114.
5.Inquest, January 17, 1676/1677, CR, 7:4.
6.Lefroy, *Memorials,* 2:506.

of whom were sold in Bermuda and the rest taken to Carolina and Virginia.[7] In 1681 the Bermuda Assembly, considering the growing number of blacks, suggested that "noe Inhabitant should keep above three working servants for a share of land." No provision was made, however, for the enforcement of this rule, and anxieties over the number of slaves continued. So did sporadic plots of slave resistance and escape.

In the summer of 1681 the white community was shocked by the discovery of a murder plot conceived by an Indian slave named John, who belonged to the Maligan family of Smith's Tribe. John planned to set fire to Orange Grove, the family's mansion house, shoot Maligan and his family, and steal a boat to leave the islands. The plan failed; John was captured, tried, and found guilty. On June 30, 1681, he was hanged. Afterward his body was quartered, and the parts placed on exhibit in four different locations from one end of the colony to the other: Somerset Bridge in Sandys, Cobler's Island, the Flatts, and Stokes Bridge, near St. George's. His head was displayed at Stokes Bridge.[8]

The following year, race relations in the colony were disturbed by a rumor that all native-born blacks were to be freed at the king's command. It all began with the arrival of the Company's magazine ship *Resolution* in early March. Within a few days of the ship's arrival, a petition, dated March 12, was submitted to Governor Florentius Seymour declaring that the master of the *Resolution,* Captain Leonard Bushell, had "bin empowered by the Kings Majestie" to free "the Negroes born in these Islands."[9] But when the Governor's Council considered the petition at a meeting on April 6, the promise of freedom was declared to be "altogether falslie alleaged . . . By the Averment of Capt Bushell to the Contrary." The captain having denied it, the council found that the "petition was promoted by the assistance of English persons: John Dorsett the penner thereof and John Hamman the false Reporter of the promises." According to the testimony of another colonist, Nathaniel Tatem, John Hamman, whom Tatem identified as "Mr Samuel Trotts Smith" (blacksmith), came to Tatem's house and told him that he (Hamman) had just visited "Mr Rainers [Rayner's] Negroes Cabbin." Hamman had told the blacks at Samuel Rayner's that "there was good Newes for them: The King had sent to free them: and withall [Hamman] told them,

7. *CSP,* 1708–1709:59.
8. On the murder plot and the history of the owners of Orange Grove, see William Edward Sears Zuill, "John Somersall," *BHQ* 29, no. 2 (1972): 168; "The Second Mrs. Somersall," *BHQ* 29, no. 3 (1972): 203–12; "The Maligan Family," *BHQ* 29, no. 4 (1972): 246.
9. This petition, like the petitions of 1669, is not extant, but references to it, along with the testimony of persons involved in the rumors of freedom, are in the records of the council meeting of April 6, 1682. See CR, 7:111–12. Council minutes and subsequent quotations regarding the incident are in CR, 7:111–17.

That they must goe home and humble themselves to the King, and they said they would."[10] Evidently Hamman also spread that news among other blacks and, with the aid of John Dorsett and others, both white and black, composed a petition to present to Governor Seymour and the council when they met in April.

Besides John Hamman, the "false reporter," and the penman, John Dorsett, there were at least 17 others—four whites, 11 blacks, and two mulattos—who were involved in this bid for freedom, and they lived in different parts of the islands. Hamman, a blacksmith, was in the service of Perient Trott's son, Samuel, a wealthy merchant in Hamilton Tribe. Nathaniel Tatem's house, where Hamman reported telling a group of blacks about the promise of freedom, was very likely in Warwick Tribe, as was the residence of Samuel Rayner, a Warwick mariner. One of the other whites, John Casson, lived in Paget Tribe. Thomas Casson, also named as one of the "English persons" associated with the slaves in the petition, was a relative of John Casson and probably also lived in Paget. About Aron Ward and Thomas Nash, the other whites named, nothing further is known. Only one of the 11 blacks was identified in the council's records: "George the Negro of Mr. St. George Tucker" was a resident of St. George's. One of the two mulattos was identified as "Natt Master Places Mulatto." He, like George, was probably a resident of St. George's.[11] Thus, individuals from Warwick, in the western part of the main island, to Paget, located close to the center of the mainland, to St. George's Island, on the eastern end of Bermuda, a distance of some 16 miles, had been in close communication and had collaborated in drafting a petition for freedom for Bermuda's native-born blacks.

As in the case of the slave petition of 1669, a rumor spread by a white man raised false hopes among the blacks and disturbed white officials. Perhaps inspired by an offhand remark of Captain Bushell's, the rumored emancipation of "Negroes born in these islands" in 1682 would have set at liberty nearly all of the slaves in Bermuda. The official response was swift; the punishments for those involved in the petition were varied. John Hamman was to receive 39 lashes. The first 20 were to be given "under the Galloes forthwith"; and on the next "Lecture Daie" in Paget, "immediately after the Lecture," Hamman was to be taken to Mr. Rayner's house in Warwick, there to be "whipped with 19 lashes uppon the naked back," so that whites and blacks alike could look on and ponder the punishment of one who spoke falsely of freedom. After the Warwick whipping, Hamman was to be taken before Arthur Jones,

10. Ibid., 112.
11. Natt's master was probably the John Place who died in St. George's in 1692. See Hallett, *Early Bermuda Wills*, 460.

councillor for Hamilton Tribe, to be "put in Security for his good behavior." John Dorsett, whose only apparent involvement was to serve as the "penner" who copied out the petition, was to be bound over with "sufficient security" to appear at the next assize, or else to "abide in Prison" until that time. Three of the whites—Aron Ward and John and Thomas Casson—were to be "cleared out of Prison" and made to appear before the councillor of their respective tribes "ffor associating themselves with Negroes, and fomenting false Reports tending to the breach of the peace." Thomas Nash, who had disobeyed a constable, was also included in this order.

Ten of the blacks received 39 lashes "uppon the naked Buttocks," a specific and unusual punishment in Bermuda, where whippings were commonly administered "upon the naked back."[12] But the eleventh black, George, who belonged to St. George Tucker, a member of a prominent family in Bermuda, received only six lashes. Natt, "Master Places Mulatto," received 15. The other mulatto, unidentified, received the same punishment as the 10 blacks. Like John Hamman's whipping, the punishment was immediate, taking place on April 7, 1682—the day after the council meeting. With whippings in Warwick, Paget, and St. George's, news of the petition and its outcome would soon have spread all over the colony.

One can only speculate as to what conversations took place in Bermuda's black community, among the colony's whites, and between blacks and whites together over this affair. This incident reveals a bond between those at the bottom of the social scale: slaves, free blacks, and whites who were outside the dominant white power structure. These whites were the ones who traded illegally with blacks and who fraternized with them from time to time. At least one of the whites who collaborated with blacks in the petition of 1682, John Casson, was himself a slaveholder. John Hamman, the apparent ringleader, was a blacksmith, a skilled trade that some Bermudians plied with great financial reward, as the careers of the Dickinson family of Southampton blacksmiths illustrate. The scraps of evidence about the petition for freedom and the swift punishments that followed it raise a number of questions: Why would lower-class whites wish freedom for blacks who were below them on the social scale? And why would a slaveholder collaborate with slaves in search of liberty? John Casson owned at least one slave, the mulatto man called Diego, mentioned in chapter 3, whom he freed in his 1688 will. Was the literate Diego perhaps involved in the 1682 petition along with his master? Was he the unidentified mulatto who was lashed along with the 10 blacks? Another puzzling aspect of the 1682 petition is that John Dorsett and the other men whose cases were to be addressed at the next assize do not appear in the June 1682 assize. One

12. CR, 7:112.

of these men, John Casson, was mentioned in the June 19 assize, but only as the father of Maria Casson, one of several women accused of giving birth to illegitimate infants.[13] What further castigations they may have received are, like the text of the petition itself, missing from the historical record.

The dashed hopes of freedom in the spring of 1682 may have served as a motivation in the summer of that same year for the last reported slave conspiracy of the seventeenth century. This slave plot may also have gained momentum from a shortage of food. The summer of 1682 brought with it an infestation of insects in the corn, and "blast" (hurricane) and mildew damage to orange trees and cedar forests. Conditions were so severe that Governor Florentius Seymour ordered a prayerful "Day of Humiliation" on July 13, in which all Bermudians were to attend church services and do no work except necessary tasks.[14] Around that time (perhaps on July 13, when many people would have been in church) five black men met to form a daring plot: They would kill their masters and run away. Tom, who belonged to Thomas Smith of Smith's Tribe, conspired with four other men—three blacks and one Indian—to murder their respective masters and escape in a boat hidden at Spanish Point, at the west end of Pembroke Tribe. A vessel putting out to sea from Spanish Point would find safe passage through the dangerous underwater reefs surrounding most of Bermuda but would also be sailing in full view of the entire north shore. In daylight any boat on such a course would be quickly spotted, and after nightfall it would be too dark for the boat's occupants to see the reefs.

As the appointed time for the escape drew near, one of the would-be runaways apparently had second thoughts about the plan. Cuffe, a slave belonging to a "Mr. Hawkes," appeared before the Governor's Council on August 10, 1682, testifying that

> ever since the planting of Corne, Tom at Mr. Thomas Smiths has bin often with him [Cuffe] to have him rise to kill White ffolkes, And I [Cuffe] have beaten him off: And this last Sundaie he went to Crow Lane and came to mee afterwards, presently after Sunn: sett, and said hee had gotten Two or Three Companies at Crow Lane, and said next Sabbath Daie about Suppertyme hee will Rise up in Harrises Baie Tribe [Smith's Tribe], and kill Anthonie White, and Anthonie Peniston, and then he could drive all the others before him: And he would begin with his Master first, and bid mee kill my Master to And to have mee Rise first: And he could cum at three gunnes and A Box about 14 inches in length with Powder & Shott: But he would not tell me where it was, nor the names of them that were to Rise with him . . . And Crow:Lane Companie and his Company was to meete here and to fight up to Spanish Point, and after he had don fighting it was not to staie here, but to run

13. Assize of June 19, 1682, CR, 7:114–15.
14. CR, 7:115.

awaie in Boates. And those that would not fight with him: the English might kill them if they will; and threatened to kill mee if I told, and then if the English kill him he cares not: Mrs Breretons Negroe man Pimpro can declare as much as this, but he did still beat him off, and has no hand in the Riseing: And hee has Marked mee between the thum and the forefinger: And I likewise Marked him on the back of the hand with A Knife which is a Signe to us to be true and to the others: Tom said that when hee was in Jamaica he killed as many people as in this.[15]

Pimpro, identified as "Mrs Breretons Negroe," probably lived in Paget, near Crow Lane, where Breretons had lived since the 1650s.[16] Implicated in this plot, Pimpro also testified, saying that Tom invited him to join the conspirators when he (Pimpro) went to visit his wife, who lived in the household of Thomas Durham, a Pembroke planter. Pimpro refused to be a party to Tom's plan, saying that "he should cutt his throte before he would goe." Tom told Pimpro that he had powder, guns, and bullets, saying that he "had bin long enough in this Countrie to get them." He planned "to shoot the folkes when they came to catch him," and, said Pimpro, he "bid mee I should not tell Cuffee at Mr Hawkeses, ffor he would tell of itt."[17]

If Cuffe's and Pimpro's depositions are accurate, Tom may not have been in Bermuda long. It is possible that he had been involved in one or more Jamaican slave revolts a few years earlier. In 1673 and 1675, slaves on a few remote plantations in Jamaica seized arms and killed their masters. A number of these rebels escaped into the unsettled areas of the island. There was another, more organized Jamaican slave revolt in 1678, in which 20 or more slaves were executed. Tom may have been one of those who avoided capture.[18] Some of the Jamaican conspirators of 1678 had known each other in Barbados, where there had been a serious slave revolt in 1675. Such connections, taken with Tom's attempted revolt in Bermuda, suggest a network of slave contacts, or at least a flow of information through slave communities, between the Caribbean islands and Bermuda. The timing of slave revolts in Bermuda coincided with revolts in Barbados or Jamaica in 1673 and 1761; slave unrest in Jamaica

15. Council minutes, ibid., 117. Crow Lane, in the geographical center of the main island, appears to have been a central meeting place for slaves. In 1673 it had been the designated gathering place for the would-be rebels. Cuffe's telling the time of year by the time of planting corn, rather than naming the month, was common among African blacks. See Mullin, *Africa in America*, 71–72.

16. A Thomas Brereton occupied 50 acres of Company land bordering on Crow Lane in the survey of 1663. For other Breretons, see Hallet, *Early Bermuda Wills*, 57.

17. CR, 7:117.

18. Dunn, *Sugar and Slaves*, 259–60, finds native-born slaves more likely to rebel. Scholars differ on the role of newly arrived Africans in fomenting rebellions. For example, Hall, *Slave Society in the Danish West Indies*, 70–71, finds the sources of a slave uprising on the island of St. John in the Danish West Indies in 1733, and a more serious conspiracy in St. Croix in 1759, to be the work of African-born, not creole, slaves.

from 1725 to 1740 and in Antigua in the 1730s may have contributed to Bermuda's poisoning scares of the 1720s and 1730s. Unlike Bermuda, the Caribbean islands were fed by a supply of newly imported slaves from Africa. How Tom arrived in Bermuda, since the importation of slaves had been illegal since 1674, is not known. But on the testimony of Cuffe and Pimpro he was apprehended, tried by a "Council of Warr for Conspiracies" on August 24 and 25, 1682, and sentenced to death. The sentence, however, was not carried out. The reasons for that are puzzling, especially since this slave was, according to Cuffe, also a killer of whites in Jamaica. But Thomas Smith, Tom's master, petitioned to have him transported from Bermuda instead.[19]

In this instance, as in the 1656 and 1673 conspiracies and the 1682 petition for freedom, the involvement of slaves who lived in different tribes points to the continued existence and vitality of a slave community in Bermuda, one with an established network of communication. Tom, although recently arrived from Jamaica, was soon a part of this network. He met with Pimpro, who worked for the Brereton family in Paget, at least a mile away from Smith's Tribe, where Tom lived. Pimpro had a wife in Pembroke, where the rebels planned to hide their boat. It is likely that other slaves in Pembroke knew about the plot. The identities and residences of the other conspirators—an Indian and two other blacks—are not known. Cuffe's master, "Mr. Hawkes," probably lived in Smith's Tribe and may have been a neighbor of Thomas Smith, Tom's master. Anthony Peniston and Anthony White, the men Tom singled out as his first potential victims, were also his master's neighbors in Smith's Tribe. One can only speculate as to Tom's relationship with these men and on his particular reasons for wishing them dead.[20]

The incidents of slave unrest of the early 1680s obviously made white officials apprehensive. In 1685 Governor Richard Coney, noting the number of blacks in the islands, remarked that "there is so many of them that they grow dangerous." He recommended that "noe man in ye Island keep above ye number of ten slaves." Paradoxically, despite their uneasiness about a growing slave population and their memories of the abortive slave plot of 1682, the majority of slaveholders did not fear to put weapons in the hands of their slaves. Fears of a Spanish invasion of the colony in 1686 moved the Governor's Council to repeat an earlier law requiring all "men Negros" from ages 16 to 60 to serve in the militia, to be fitted with "offensive armes, or weapons

19. CR, 7:117.
20. A Richard Hawkes lived in Smith's Tribe in 1663, on land next to William Peniston's property. Anthony Peniston, a sea captain and merchant, was William Peniston's son. Anthony White was the son of another Anthony White, who lived in Smith's Tribe in 1663. Anthony White Jr. died there in 1709. See Lefroy, *Memorials*, 2:664; Hallett, *Early Bermuda Wills*, 439, 651.

as they may think most fitt," and to appear with their masters for training. Awareness of the possibility of slave uprisings lay close beneath this placid surface. When Governor Coney, in the course of a council meeting, expressed his admiration for a male mulatto slave belonging to the "Widow Birch" (Burch) and suggested that he would like to have that slave for his own use, Councillor Richard Jennings Jr. advised against such action, remarking that "such heathen rogues as he [the slave] was, if a course were not taken with them, would be our masters."[21]

Bermuda slaves were no less resistant to slavery than those in the Caribbean, where slave uprisings took place with fearsome frequency. It is not surprising that the history of the Caribbean islands, where blacks far outnumbered whites, is replete with accounts of slave conspiracies and rebellions for 200 years, from the seventeenth century to the end of slavery in the nineteenth. But such was not the case in Bermuda. Besides the seventeenth-century plots of 1656, 1661, 1673, and 1682 and the petitions of 1669 and 1682, there is only one other recorded episode of organized slave resistance in Bermuda's history. A planned uprising in 1761 never came to pass, but it alarmed the colony's officials and sent shock waves across the transatlantic trade network. So did a 1730 poisoning scare that resulted in the burning of a black woman at the stake. An examination of these eighteenth-century events offers further glimpses of the largely undocumented network of communication among slaves in Bermuda, the Caribbean islands, and the Americas. Bermuda was an integral part of that network, as Governor John Bruce Hope's 1724 report to the Council of Trade and Plantations makes clear. Bermuda, he wrote, was "the best place for intelligence of any in America . . . for the number of sloops . . . continually trading backwards and forwards from the Southern and Northern America . . . makes it, that we know much better, what passes in the western world, than any other colony in it."[22] For Bermuda's blacks, many of whom were sailors, that knowledge included information about slavery in other slave societies—including resistance and retaliation.

The history of the Caribbean islands is replete with slave uprisings, but that history is quite different from Bermuda's. A chronology of slave revolts in the English colonies in the Caribbean lists 75 from the seventeenth century through the 1830s, including seven in Barbados, 22 in Jamaica, five in Antigua, and four in the Bahamas. Most of those rebellions, however, took

21. Governor Coney's recommendation on the number of slaves is in Lefroy, *Memorials,* 2:563. For the other quotations, see Council minutes, July 22, 1686, CR, 7:150, and Council minutes, *BHQ* 2, no. 4 (1945): 160.
22. Hope to Council of Trade and Plantations, January 14, 1724/1725, in CO 37/11: 46–47.

place after 1700. Of Jamaica's 22, for example, 16 occurred between 1700 and 1832. In the Bahamas, all four uprisings took place between 1734 and 1834.[23] Besides the chronology of rebellion, there are some other significant differences between slave rebellions in the Caribbean and in Bermuda. First, Bermuda's population, enlarging by natural increase rather than immigration, grew more slowly and was always much smaller than those of its sister colonies in the Caribbean, where slaves far outnumbered whites by the mid-seventeenth century. Barbados, for example, settled in 1627, comprising about 166 square miles (roughly eight times the size of Bermuda), had 46,602 blacks and 19,568 whites by 1684.[24] Bermuda, by contrast, with 21 square miles, had 1,737 blacks and 4,132 whites in 1687. Bermuda's slave population, being mostly native-born, was more stable and did not have the continued influx of unacculturated newcomers from Africa. There are some other notable differences: All of Bermuda's slave conspiracies were discovered before they occurred, and no whites lost their lives. Moreover, retribution for attempted slave revolts in Bermuda was somewhat milder than in other slave societies, either on the mainland or in the Caribbean. In Antigua, for example, a slave rebel was "burned to ashes," and in New York in 1712 the convicted slaves were burned at the stake, hanged, "broke on the wheel," and "hung a live in chains." In New Orleans in 1730 eight slaves were "broke alive" after being tortured with burning matches.[25] There were hangings in Bermuda and one burning at the stake (perhaps two), but there are no slave executions to equal the mutilations and deaths by torture recorded in slave revolts elsewhere. In the southern mainland colonies, as slave resistance rose in the 1750s, so did the number of executions, many with mutilated bodies displayed. In the newly founded colony of Georgia, a slave code of 1755 forbade excessive punishments such as castration, mutilation, and burning, suggesting the tendency of masters to administer severe punishments. Punishments in the Danish West Indies

23. For a detailed chronology, see Craton, *Testing the Chains,* 335–39. Aptheker, *Slave Revolts,* estimated 250 attempted slave revolts on the mainland of North America. Aptheker defined a plot as one involving ten or more people, aimed at acquiring freedom, and referred to as a plot by contemporary witnesses (162). In the decades since Aptheker's work, a rich literature on the history of slave resistance has developed. See, for example, Eugene D. Genovese, *From Rebellion to Revolution: Afro-American Slave Revolts in the Making of the Modern World* (Baton Rouge: Louisiana State University Press, 1979), and John Lofton, *Denmark Vesey's Revolt: The Slave Plot that Lit a Fire to Fort Sumter* (Kent, Ohio: Kent State University Press, 1983). More recent studies of slave resistance include Mullin, *Africa in America;* Sylvia Frey, *Water from the Rock: Black Resistance in a Revolutionary Age* (Princeton: Princeton University Press, 1991); and Norrece T. Jones, *Born a Child of Freedom, Yet a Slave: Mechanisms of Slave Control and Strategies of Resistance in Antebellum South Carolina* (Hanover, N.H.: Weslayan University Press/University Press of New England, 1990).

24. Dunn, *Sugar and Slaves,* 87.

25. Aptheker, *Slave Revolts,* 173, 182.

involved the use of red-hot pincers and branding irons and the amputations of hands.[26]

Although organized slave rebellions in Bermuda were less violent, and slavery there was in some ways less brutish than in other English colonies, Bermuda's slaves, like those on the North American mainland and in the Caribbean, found a variety of ways to demonstrate their resistance. Bermuda's small size and the close relationships among slaveholders and slaves were no deterrent to slave initiative and risk-taking in pursuit of freedom. Individuals regularly pilfered goods of all kinds from whites; they carried on a clandestine trade aboard visiting ships; they flouted laws that confined them to their masters' premises. Bermuda's first generation of blacks had defined their identity by insolent behavior toward whites, and in succeeding generations, patterns of black assertiveness continued to disturb white society. In 1669, for example, the Somers Islands Company enacted a law repeating earlier legislation about stealing, especially "theft of fruits, roots, poultry &c. by negroes."[27] Such acts of larceny were obviously committed to produce a tasty supplement to everyday diets of corn and fish, but stealing was also a means of asserting autonomy and challenging white authority. Such assertions took other forms as well. Sambo, who drew his knife on Captain John Darrell in the Warwick churchyard in 1671, was not the only slave accused of "stubborn carriage" toward whites. Many such incidents no doubt went unrecorded, but the repeated use of the words *insolent* and *independent* in various public documents referring to blacks is suggestive. In 1724, for example, the Governor's Council complained of "the independent behavior of negroes & other slaves to white people, and the miserable state of the country is in by their thieving, the reason of which being that the laws against Negros and other slaves are not duly just in execution by the magistrates who are empowered to do it."[28]

Law enforcement was a perennial problem in Bermuda, with many rural areas remote from government supervision and tribes, or parishes, as they came to be called, with local officials who often held office year after year. Each of the eight parishes had a justice of the peace, appointed by the Governor's Council, who served as the principal officer in the parish, calling meetings, conducting elections for the Assembly and for jury service, and presiding over courts to decide parish disputes and petty crimes. Each parish also had two churchwardens and two constables, chosen by the parish vestry.

26. On rebellions and punishments in other colonies, see Frey, *Water from the Rock*, 17–18. See also Wood, *Slavery in Colonial Georgia*, 113–14. On mutilation, torture, and executions in the Caribbean, see Walvin, *Black Ivory*, 248–49, and Hall, *Slave Society in the Danish West Indies*, 56–57.

27. Lefroy, *Memorials*, 2:288.

28. Council minutes, January 7, 1724/1725, *BHQ* 8, no. 1 (1951): 3.

The churchwardens were responsible for reporting crimes and misdemeanors to the civil authorities. Churchwardens and constables thus had primary responsibility for keeping order in a parish and for bringing offenders, both black and white, to the attention of the justices of the peace or the assize courts, which met twice a year in St. George's.[29]

Despite an established procedure for law enforcement, local officials were uneven in their application of justice to their neighbors. After all, accusing a neighbor's slave of a crime and carting that slave off to jail to await trial might mean subjecting the neighbor to economic hardship. The slave's owner not only would be deprived of a worker but also would have to pay jail fees—in effect, room and board—for the incarcerated slave until the legal system at St. George's reached a verdict. Moreover, if a slave accused of a felony were found guilty and executed, the owner would have to petition the court for reimbursement for the value of that slave. It is no wonder that churchwardens or constables were sometimes reluctant to press charges or that government officials viewed law enforcement as lax. In 1698 Governor Samuel Day observed, "Although several Criminals be among negroes and other slaves, yet the same are not duly prosecuted according to Law in Compassion to the masters of such slaves."[30]

There were increasing efforts to control both white and black Bermudians' activities on the Sabbath—the one day when slaves as well as free blacks and whites were not obliged to work, and thus a day when some might turn to mischief. An "Act for ye Strict Observation of Ye Lords Day" passed by the Assembly in 1691 echoed earlier pronouncements from Somers Islands Company in the 1660s. The Assembly complained of "Disorder & Lewdness" on the Sabbath, resulting from the "unlawfull Sports, Pastimes or worldly affaires on the Day as Fishing, unnecessary Sailing in Boats, Gaming, Idle Wandering from house to house, & several servile works of Imployment." In contrast, slaves in South Carolina in the early 1700s worked Sundays on their own gardens and in other ways to provide for themselves and their families. But they, like Bermuda slaves, had their "ffeasts, dances, and merry Meetings."[31] In Bermuda, Sabbath violators were to be fined five shillings; those without funds were to be placed in the stocks for two hours or publicly whipped, at the discretion of the local justice of the peace.[32] This act further ordered church attendance for all Bermudians "with their Children, & Servants,"

29. On parish government, see Hallett, *Colonial Church,* 358–66.

30. Assembly session of November 1, 1698, in *Journals of . . . Assembly,* 1:16–17.

31. Quoted in Wood, *Black Majority,* 139. Wood (136) also records instances of the brutality of Carolina slaveholders—a record strikingly absent from Bermuda.

32. CR, 9:19–20. In 1701 this act was repeated, with the provision that guilty slaves' masters be punished as well. Council minutes, May 13, 1701, *BHQ* 4, no. 2 (1947): 46.

with a one-shilling fine or an hour in the stocks as punishment. This law, however, was not as restrictive as it might appear. It did not apply to those who stayed at home "out of Conscience, & to keep good Order in their Families . . . or to such as stay at home for dressing of meat in Familyes, or dressing or selling of meats in Licensed Victualling Houses." In 1691 the Bermuda Assembly passed a series of laws prohibiting whites from "buying, selling or bargaining with Negroes and other slaves" and regulating the trials of "Negroes and Slaves," and repeated an "Act to prevent the Insolency of Negroes and other Slaves."[33]

Despite an apparent reluctance to bring slaves to justice, early Bermuda court records, as noted in an earlier chapter, contain cases of slaves accused of crimes ranging from petty theft to murder. Although the evidence is fragmentary, such cases provide another view of race relations in this small multiracial society. In at least a few instances, the crimes of whites against blacks reached the courts. In Southampton Tribe in 1693, for example, two young white men, Thomas Weaverley and John MacKenny, were accused of assaulting a black girl named Betty, who belonged to Thomas Walmesley, Esquire. The details of their actions do not appear in the court record, but they were accused of burning her so severely that she died. A jury found the two young men (who may have been adolescents) not guilty. There is more to this case than meets the eye: Thomas Weaverley, one of the defendants, was Thomas Walmesley's stepson and probably lived in his house. Weaverley's mother, Tabitha, had been twice widowed: Thomas Weaverley Sr. died in 1688, and Tabitha then married Abraham Adderley, a wealthy merchant who died in 1689.[34]

In another case, two young white men were convicted of severely beating a black man. When Daniel Hinson and William Burrows attacked a black man named William Furblow in the spring of 1731, Furblow's master, a wealthy Sandys mariner named Jeremiah Burch, brought suit for damages, claiming the two "did assault beat wound & Evill treat him the said Will soe that his Life was dispaired of." Burch won the suit. The punishment of the guilty parties is not recorded. It is likely that young Hinson was the son of Daniel Hinson of Sandys; Burrows may have been the son of a mariner, William Burrows, also of Sandys. Presumably Will Furblow survived: A slave named Will was listed in Jeremiah Burch's inventory 20 years later.[35]

33. *Bermuda Acts, 1690–1883*, comp. Reginald Gray (London, 1884).

34. Assize records, August 1693, AZ 102/1, n.p. On Tabitha Weaverley Adderly Walmesley, see Hallett, *Early Bermuda Wills*, 635, 642. John MacKenny, the other defendant, was probably the son of a John MacKenny who died in 1662. Hallet, *Early Bermuda Wills*, 364.

35. Assize records, May 29, 1731, AZ 102/6, 291–94; Hallett, *Early Bermuda Wills*, 286; Books of Wills, vol. 8, pp. 129, 138. A William Burrows, mariner, died in 1778. *Early Bermuda*

A black man who had been assaulted by a white man might win a jury's sympathy, but a black man who raped a white woman was another matter. Some years earlier, when "Ben a Negro man Slave belonging to Mrs. Francis [Frances] Astwood of Paget Tribe widow" was found guilty of "Ravishing Martha Stoks [*sic*] of Pagets Tribe Single Woman," he received a death sentence. The record of this case does not provide any details. The Astwoods were a well-known Bermuda family; nothing more is known of Martha Stokes.[36]

Sexual relations between a black man and a white woman were not unknown in Bermuda; and along with illegal trading, stealing, and running away, they may have been another way in which some blacks asserted their autonomy. That such actions did occur is evidenced by the Assembly's 1704 passage of a bill "to prevent the Insolency of Negros and other Slaves for attempting or Getting White women with Childe, and for furnishing all such White Women."[37] Seventeenth-century records show that at least two white women gave birth to mulatto infants, but it was not until 1723 that a law was passed prescribing the punishment for such women. Under the new law a white woman who gave birth to a child fathered by a black man was to receive a public whipping. The father, if his identity was known, was also subject to a whipping. The instances that may have called forth such a law are not recorded, but its appropriateness was obvious two years later. In 1725 Governor Hope reported that "Mrs [Mistress] Burton," the daughter of Bermuda's former Attorney General Thomas Burton, had given birth to a black child. It is interesting to note that Hope described this child born to a white mother and a black father as a "black" child, not a mulatto. The scandal of such a birth in a high-ranking white Bermudian family can only be imagined. Under the law, Mistress Burton would be subjected to a public whipping, but in this case Governor Hope requested that the justice of the peace remit the legal punishment "until further orders."[38] But Hope's clemency drew the ire of Jonathan Outerbridge, speaker of the Bermuda Assembly, who protested that it was an "inkuragement to sinn." On August 30, 1725, Hope wrote to Outerbridge that he had "suspended punishment of that poor wretch, Mr. Burton's daughter, out of compassion to the afflicted parent."[39] What became

---

Wills, 89, 287. At his death in 1752, Jeremiah Burch's personal property, including his slaves, was worth over £470.

36. Assize records, May 19, 1726, AZ 102/6, 4.

37. *Journals of . . . Assembly,* 2:86–87. In 1705 this act was disallowed by the crown. See *Journal of the Commissioners for Trade and Plantations* (London: H. M. Stationery Office, 1920–1938), vol. 1, April 1704–February 1708/1709, 131–32.

38. Governor Hope to the Duke of Newcastle, in CO 37/28: 34, iv. For the text of the bastardy law, see Smith, *Slavery in Bermuda,* 82 n.

39. Outerbridge to Governor Hope, August 28, 1725, in *CSP,* 1724–1725:445; Hope to Outerbridge, August 30, 1725, ibid., 445.

of Mistress Burton, her child, and her child's father is not recorded. Under the law, the father would also have been subject to a public whipping, but there is no record of his punishment.

Bermudian blacks who were involved in crimes, either as victims or criminals, had no choice but to depend on the mercy of the whites in power. Although some slaveholders, like Will Furblow's master, went to court on a slave's behalf, in at least one instance the mistress of a slave deliberately implicated him in a crime. In July 1691 a black man named Will, belonging to Mrs. Mary Trott, widow of the merchant Perient Trott (and daughter of another merchant, Thomas Richards of Southampton), was indicted for breaking into a storehouse and stealing three bags of "coyned mony" worth £200. The storehouse did not belong to Mary Trott: Perient Trott, who had died on April 2, had left his "new storehouse" and its furnishings in the custody of his two brothers, John and Nicholas, until his son, Perient Jr., reached 22 years of age. Trott's widow received the dwelling house, outbuildings, and two shares of land for use during her lifetime. In the months following the wealthy merchant's death, his brother Nicholas Sr. and his widow evidently had a disagreement over the money in the storehouse.

On Sunday, July 5, "late att night," according to the slave Will's testimony, he broke into the storehouse, found three bags of "coyned mony" worth about £200, took them to Mrs. Trott's, and buried them on the premises. On Tuesday, July 7, Nicholas Trott and a cousin of his (also named Nicholas Trott) seized Will and locked him in the cellar of the storehouse for an hour and a half. Then, said Will, Nicholas Sr. "presented a pistol at mee" and demanded the whereabouts of the money, saying he would "buy mee and give me my freedom If I would carry him where the mony lay." Will complied, and the bags were recovered. Then, according to Will, Trott said, "Now goe thy waie, honest Will. Now thou art— [word missing, page damaged]." Trott also gave Will "a Dram of Strong water."

The testimony of another witness recorded a slightly different version of Will's story. Nathaniel Dunscomb of Hamilton, where Mrs. Trott resided, testified that on July 7 Nicholas Trott and the widowed Mary Trott had a quarrel with "many angry words." According to Dunscomb, Trott threatened the widow with his sword, entered her house to search for money, and "looked under the bed." Then Will appeared, and Trott "put a pistoll to his Breast and said hee would shoot him through if hee would not show him the mony."[40] Mary Jacobson, an indentured servant who had been in service in the Trott

40. CR, 8:418. The surviving records of the case are on pp. 417–19. Nicholas Trott was governor of the Bahamas in 1688. *Early Bermuda Wills*, 587; Books of Wills, vol. 2, pt. 1, p. 1. Nicholas was Perient's brother. Another brother, Samuel, was also a Bermuda merchant and lived in Hamilton in the 1690s. He and Perient Senior had sons named Perient. Samuel's son

family for an undetermined number of years before Perient Trott's death, also testified in this case. Her version was almost identical to Will's, but she did not mention Trott's offer of freedom to Will. She recalled that Nicholas Trott said, "Now goe thy waie, honest Will, now thou art cleare." Shortly after this, a grand jury agreed. Will, who had broken into a storehouse and stolen three bags of money—most likely at the bidding of his mistress—committed a felony punishable by death, but he received a verdict of "not guilty." Mary Trott died the next year, and what became of Will is not known. Whether Nicholas Trott actually offered to buy Will and free him, or whether Will, hoping that his deposition would somehow be legally binding on Trott, inserted that offer on his own, is an intriguing possibility. It is also possible that the damage to the page obliterating the word *free* from the deposition document was done deliberately. In a similar case a few years later, "a Negro man slave" named Tony, belonging to John Burt of Smith's Tribe, was accused of entering the house of Elias Hobald and stealing money (eight pieces of eight) and other unspecified items. There are no surviving depositions, but the grand jury returned a verdict of *ignoramus* (insufficient evidence to send the case to trial).[41] It seems likely that in this case, as in Will's, Tony may have committed a crime at his master's bidding.

In 1705, in another case in Smith's Tribe, three slaves accused of stealing were tried and convicted. Two mulatto girls, Miriam and Nanny, belonging to Martha Gilbert, a widow in Smith's Tribe, and Frank, a black boy of Samson Potter's, were found guilty of stealing two beehives worth five shillings from John Righton's residence. The three culprits were sentenced to be tied to the gallows as a warning. Theft was ordinarily a capital crime. Perhaps because of their youth, they were not executed but were untied from the gallows, "Stript to their hipp," and given 39 lashes "well laid on." But that was not the end of their punishment. The three were apparently suspected of other thefts in the neighborhood, and they were also sentenced to walk through Smith's Tribe and be whipped by the tribe's constables—three lashes at every 30 paces. This part of the punishment was to occur about a month after the first whipping, presumably when their backs had healed. If they walked along the main road that ran the length of Smith's Tribe, they would have walked about two and a half miles with beatings every 30 paces: a painful and unusual punishment, indeed.[42]

---

was living in Providence (R.I.?) at the time of his father's will. See Books of Wills, vol. 2, pt. 1, pp. 172, 104.

41. Assize records, December 9, 1696, AZ 102/1, 150.

42. Ibid., December 1706, AZ 102/3, 60–65. If they only walked along one of the tribe roads that crossed the width of the tribe, the distance could have been about half that.

Adults who burglarized the houses of others did so at the risk of their lives, and some paid the ultimate penalty. For example, Tony Garrett, a mulatto man belonging to Thomas Appowen, a carpenter in Devonshire, and Joe, a "negro man slave" belonging to Captain John Morris, also of Devonshire, were accused of breaking into Colonel Francis Jones's house in nearby Paget Tribe and stealing goods worth £20. Both slaves were found guilty of stealing tobacco, bread, sugar, and fish and were sentenced to death.[43] Whites as well as blacks received the death penalty for theft. In 1726, for example, Thomas Fritts, a mason in Warwick Tribe, was sentenced to death for stealing a hog from a widow, Dorcas Tatem, and killing and dressing it. In another case of similar nature, William Ward and Thomas Bell received the death penalty for stealing a cow from Mrs. Sarah Whitney of St. David's.[44]

Public executions and whippings served not only to punish the guilty party but to warn the rest of the population of the consequences of wrongdoing. Miriam, Nanny, and Frank's walk through the neighborhood allowed slaves and children, who might not have been taken to a whipping at the gallows or to an execution, to see what could happen to thieves. In 1706, the same year as the whippings of Miriam, Nanny, and Frank, another public whipping took place. An Indian man belonging to Thomas Smith was convicted of committing "the abominable crime of buggery" with a mare belonging to Major Michael Burrows. The guilty party was sentenced to be tied to the gallows at St. George's and given 39 lashes.[45] Some years earlier the crime of an Indian in Smith's Tribe became public knowledge, with a more serious result. When an Indian man, "known by the name of Captive" and belonging to Anthony Peniston, was found guilty of fatally stabbing Will, a slave of Thomas Astwood, he receive the death penalty. Captive was executed at the Flatts, where many of Smith's Tribe's residents kept their boats. There was no doubt a large multiracial audience to witness the death of an Indian who had murdered a black man. After the execution, as a further reminder, Captive's severed head was displayed upon a pole.[46]

Another Indian man, known as Samson, in Smith's Tribe was convicted of burglarizing the house of Thomas Persons in 1707, but he was able to escape the death penalty through his own efforts. Sentenced to death for stealing a jug of brandy, a ticking petticoat, and some silk—goods worth a total of £8—Samson, who may have been a free man, submitted a written,

43. Ibid., 50, 56, 64.

44. Ibid., December 1726, AZ 102/6, 12, 19–20, 34.

45. Ibid., December 1706, AZ 102/3, 62. The 1663 survey lists a Thomas Smith as landowner in Paget, and a Michael Burrows as landowner in Hamilton, who had a son, Michael Junior. Hallett, *Early Bermuda Wills*, 85; on Smith, see Books of Wills, vol. 4, p. 48.

46. Assize records, November 1695, AZ 102/1, n.p.

signed petition to the court: "May it please your hon: I Humbly Request that you will make Such a favorable representation of my Case and Condition to our Mercifull Governor that he may be pleased to allow me the benefitt of Transportation." Governor Benjamin Bennett agreed, and the literate, articulate Samson presumably left Bermuda.[47]

In another case about the same time, an accused man asked to be transported, but was refused. A "Negro man Simon" belonging to Mary Jones, a widow living on St. David's Island, and Tom, a slave of Charles Minor, entered the warehouse of Leonard White, a merchant, and took away "pork, sugar, and other things." Simon confessed to the burglary and asked to be transported. In this case, Governor Bennett was not as lenient as he had been with Samson, and Simon's request to be transported was denied. Simon was sentenced to death, while Tom, his accomplice, received a verdict of *ignoramus* and was presumably let go. Mary Jones petitioned the court for reimbursement for Simon, but the executed slave's value is not recorded.[48] In 1721 one of Governor Bennett's slaves, a man named Cuffey, was accused of stealing seven yards of striped linen worth 20 shillings and a linen sheet, also valued at 20 shillings, from the house of one William Brown. Cuffey insisted he was innocent of the theft but admitted to being drunk at the time. Although William Brown and two other members of his family testified as witnesses to this crime, Cuffey was merely "admonished and discharged."[49]

Incomplete evidence precludes statements about the nature of many crimes involving blacks and the ratio of white to black cases and convictions, but the Assize Court records suggest that Bermuda's nonwhites as well as whites received a measure of justice when they sought it and that whites as well as blacks and Indians were punished as the law demanded. By contrast, in Middlesex County, Virginia, in the late seventeenth century, there were "relatively few" court cases involving blacks, and those generally dealt with acts that threatened society. In other slave societies punishment for stealing and unruly behavior was usually a private matter between master and slave.[50] Bermuda slaveholders, on the other hand, were notably lax in controlling and disciplining their slaves, leaving such matters to outside authorities.

Court records suggest that there was a rise in the number of thefts and burglaries committed by both blacks and whites in the early 1700s. Economic

47. Ibid., December 1707, AZ 102/3, 119, 129. Benjamin Bennett was governor from 1701 to 1713 and from 1718 to 1722.
48. Ibid., April 1707, AZ 102/3, 85, 87, 88.
49. Ibid., June 6, 1721, AZ 102/5, 65–66, 67, 71.
50. Rutman and Rutman, *A Place in Time*, 175–76. Kolchin argues that slaveholders tended to handle infractions privately, without recourse to the judicial system. See *American Slavery*, 127. See also Philip J. Schwarz, *Twice Condemned: Slaves and the Criminal Laws of Virginia, 1705–1865* (Baton Rouge: Louisiana State University Press, 1988).

woes may have been partly to blame. The War of the Spanish Succession, or Queen Anne's War (1702–1713), as it was called in England, engaged French, English, and Spanish forces in North America and the West Indies, thus disrupting trade patterns and interfering with the salt trade. In 1710 the Spanish captured the Turks Islands, cutting off salt-raking for a time. Tobacco prices, for the few Bermudians who still grew that crop, hovered around a penny per pound.[51] Fears of a Spanish invasion of Bermuda were rampant. In 1701 British troops were stationed in Bermuda for the first time: The Independent Company, consisting of 50 privates, four noncommissioned officers, and a drummer, under the command of two lieutenants, took up residence in Bermuda and remained there until 1729, when it was reassigned to the Bahamas. The following year Bermudians themselves raised a troop of horse grenadiers. They wore red uniforms, a first for local militia. Bermuda authorities also armed 600 slaves with lances and conducted drills. Around this time, able-bodied male slaves in South Carolina were required to serve in the militia to defend that colony against attack, but a 1712 slave conspiracy scare forbade them to carry guns without the presence or the written permission of their owners.[52] Despite such military readiness, the anxieties continued. In 1712, as noted in the previous chapter, the Governor's Council ordered that no more than one-fifth of a vessel's crew could be white, since white men were needed ashore in case of an attack.

Wartime dislocations and economic troubles went hand in hand with fears of slave unrest. In 1718 Governor Bennett wrote to the Council of Trade and Plantations that "without employing our navigation we must starve, this country not producing sufficient for a quarter part of the people that lives in it, and as for the negro men they are grown soe very impudent and insulting of late that we have reason to suspect their riseing." Bennett also feared that if Bermuda were attacked by pirates, the colony's blacks might join with them. He asked for more troops to augment the Independent Company already stationed there, but he did not receive any.[53] Bermuda's military defenses were precarious, since at any given time nearly half the men on the muster rolls were at sea. A report in 1723 noted that of the monthly militia reviews of 1,009 men listed, the largest number to appear was 569.[54] In January 1729/1730 Governor John Pitt estimated that as many as 2,000 people had left Bermuda since 1725 because of the "poverty of this place." The governor also noted that

51. On tobacco prices, see Kulikoff, *Tobacco and Slaves*, 38–39.
52. See Wood, *Black Majority*, 125–27.
53. Governor Bennett to the Council of Trade and Plantations, July 1718, in *CSP*, 1717–1718:261–62. On the Independent Company, see Rene Chartrand, "Notes on Bermuda Military Forces, 1687–1815," *BHQ* 28, no. 2 (1971): 40–43.
54. Responses to the Questions of the Lords of Trade, 1723, CO 37/11:50.

"a considerable number of blacks" had been transported. In October 1729, Pitt, fearing attacks from the Spanish, petitioned unsuccessfully to keep the garrison of British troops known as the Independent Company, 50 men who had been stationed there since 1701, but they were removed the following year (1730).[55]

Grand juries in the 1720s commented repeatedly on the disruptive behavior of blacks. At the assize of December 1726 a grand jury noted apprehensively that on Sabbaths and fast days, "Negroes or Slaves have then the opportunity to herd and caball together, which may in time prove of Dangerous Consequence, to the Peace and welfare of these Islands." A similar anxiety about the behavior of slaves appeared about this time in South Carolina, a colony frequented by Bermuda vessels and partially settled by Bermudians. In 1721 armed watchmen patrolled the streets of Charleston, with orders to fire upon any black who refused to stop when ordered. There were also patrols in the country parishes. In the 1730s, despite such rules, there were complaints of "Negros publicly cabaling in the streets" of Charleston. A Carolina law forbade the selling of liquor to slaves without their owners' permission.[56] In Bermuda at the assize of December 1728, the grand jury was still concerned about gatherings of slaves as well as the "Impudence & insolency of Negros Generaly Walking with Sticks."[57] The council enjoined the justices of the peace to stricter enforcement in the tribes and to keep "watches with the utmost strictness." A further order stated that "any Negro or Negroes who is or are found upon the Road or otherwise with any cane switch or stick of any kind (except such Negros as are so infirm that they cannot go without a stick) shall have fifty lashes well laid on his or their naked backs." Between 1726 and 1729, during the time of increasing concerns about the insolent behavior of blacks, 20 Bermuda slaves, including one woman, were taken by various Bermuda ships to sell in the port of New York (see appendix B).

In the late 1720s a number of laws were enacted in an effort to control the behavior of slaveholders who were judged to be too permissive with their slaves. In 1729, for example, the Assembly passed "An Act to prevent any person or person allowing and encouraging any Negroes or other Slaves from rioting and meeting at unseasonable times in his or their Houses and possessions."[58] According to the text of this act, certain white Bermudians

55. Pitt to Board of Trade, October 16, 1729, in *CSP,* 1730:78. Oddly, at a time of increasing concern about the insubordinate behavior of blacks, Pitt made no mention of racial tensions in his letter.
56. Assize records, December 7, 1726, AZ 102/6, 37; Wood, *Black Majority,* 272–74.
57. Assize records, AZ 102/6, 159.
58. "An Act to prevent . . . rioting . . . ," February 6, 1728/1729, Miscellaneous Acts, 1711–1759, n.p.

were guilty of encouraging blacks in their transgressions: "Whereas . . . Several good and wholesome Laws for the Regulating negros and other Slaves, have been Enacted, yet frequent Complaints are made by the Inhabitants of these Islands of their daily insolence in meeting together in Companies, Rioting and Dancing of Nights and absenting themselves from their Master or Mistresses Service which is too frequently Encouraged by Sundry white persons knowing and allowing of the Same." References to dancing, beginning in the 1720s, point to the origins of gombey dancing, a custom of African origins that became common among Bermuda's blacks sometime before the mid-eighteenth century.[59]

One of the results of such behavior was the "loss of Provisions in every Kind Stolen from them by such Negroes consorting together at unseasonable times." The penalty was a fine of 40 shillings to "all and every white person or persons soever" who allowed "any meeting of any Negroes or other Slaves to Dance, Cabal, or feast in his or her house or houses . . . after the setting of the Sun." The offending blacks were to be "whipt at the Discretion of the Justice of the Peace." There was apparently some debate over whether the whipping should be the responsibility of the officer of the tribe where the offence took place or of the tribe where the offender resided. The wording of the act was altered in favor of the latter. There was also a five-pound fine for a justice of the peace who might "in any way Connive at the Prosecution" of such offenders.[60]

The grand jury presentments of 1729 and 1730 dealt mainly with the troublesome behavior of slaves, some of whom were contributors to the "cursing, swearing, whoring, excessive gaming & drunkeness too commonly practiced in these islands." Many slaves frequented "tippling houses" on the Sabbath—their day off from work. A 1729 presentment condemned the "Many Lewd and wicked people on such days selling Rum and strong liquors to Negros and other slaves."[61] The grand jury further observed that civil watches were neglected and that justices of the peace were sometimes derelict in their duties. In 1729 another act, noting that the "great Quantitys of Negros and other Slaves in these Islands are very hurtful & prejudicial to the Inhabitants thereof" laid an imposition of £5 on any slaves imported into Bermuda.[62]

59. Zuill, *Story of Bermuda,* 220. There is little or no documentation of this African custom in Bermuda in the 1700s. See Packwood, *Chained on the Rock,* 95–96.

60. See "An Act to prevent . . . rioting," February 6, 1778/1779.

61. Assize records, AZ 102/6, 205. See also 93, 139.

62. "An Act for Imposition . . . on Negroes . . . ," February 6, 1728/1729, Miscellaneous Acts, 1711–1759.

Early in 1730 a 1674 act for "Extirpating all Free Negroes, Indians, and Mulattoes" was repeated, requiring all such persons to leave the islands within six months after receiving their freedom. In South Carolina a "Negro Act" of 1722 required a freed slave to leave the colony within 12 months.[63] The wording of the Bermuda act echoed earlier fears about the growing number of nonwhites in the colony. The 1730 act, however, was more specific about the problem:

> Whereas it is found by Daily Experience that the So great number of negroes, Indians and mulattoes Inhabiting these Islands are very Prejudicial to the Inhabitants of the same by Impoverishing 'em and causing a Scarcity of Provisions, and there being Sundry free negroes, Indians &c. dispersed in and throughout the Several Parishes in the Same, being some or the most part of them Indolent and live purely by theft and rapine, having hutts or Cabbins, in, by and remote places upon Land allowed them by the Owners thereof to the Encouraging of [damaged page] and prejudice of the Inhabitants as well as in the Loss of their Provisions of all sorts as of Sundry Goods and effects by them Stolen.[64]

Moreover, free blacks, mulattos, and Indians were accused of "harbouring, having meetings, and resorting with other negroes not free to the great and apparent damage, as also danger of the Inhabitants in General of these Islands."

But this law, like the law allowing some slaves to stay at home during church and the law allowing infirm slaves to carry sticks, provided for latitude in certain cases. Mulattos "already born free or that hereafter may be born free" were "not Compromised in this Act" but were to "have and enjoy their full and free Liberty as other [of] his Majesties Subjects." Thus the children of white masters or mistresses were protected. This law also prevented "Ancient negroes or Slaves being Inferiour or Decripped" from being declared free and deported by a master attempting to avoid caring for them. There was a fine of £50, however, for any masters who failed to report free blacks "in their custody or possession." This clearly suggests that a number of white Bermudians had free blacks as tenants or employees. All persons "having keeping or holding any such free negroe or negroes &c." were required to swear before their tribe's justice of the peace that they were not violating "the true intent and meaning of this Act." Given such terms, it is no wonder that this act apparently had little effect.

Resistance to slavery could take many forms, and some of Bermuda's blacks asserted themselves by their dress—flaunting the finery they acquired by illegal trading. A grand jury observed in early 1730 that "the Generality of those

---

63. "An Act for Extirpating all Free Negroes . . . ," March 12, 1729/1730, Miscellaneous Acts, 1711–1759, n.p.; Wood, *Black Majority*, 102.
64. "An Act for Extirpating all Free Negroes," n.p.

Negroes can be on Sundays and holy days, so Gaily drest. . . . More especially those whose masters & Mistresses are hardly able to Cover themselves with much Courser Stuff; Such Cloaths are not Legaly purchas't (as we have reason to believe)." A similar concern about blacks who dressed above their station appeared in South Carolina about the same time, indicated by a series of laws against slaves wearing finery and carrying firearms. In Bermuda in 1738 the Governor's Council ordered John Cox, who ran the ferry between St. George's and the mainland, to search all "Bags, Basketts, or bundles whatsoever" carried by slaves using the ferry."[65] There was also a concern about "Negros stealing in the Night and diging out the palmetto topps to the Entire destruction of the Trees." Stolen palmetto leaves could be woven into hats and baskets that were much in demand in both the Caribbean and mainland colonies. Such items could be easily (and illegally) traded for other goods, including clothing, or currency aboard visiting vessels in Town Harbor or Castle Harbor or ashore in foreign ports. Thus many an enterprising black was able to challenge white authority on two counts: to engage in forbidden trade and to flaunt the ill-gotten gains by going about "gaily drest."

The increased efforts to control Bermuda's blacks coincided with a poisoning scare that began in 1729 and sent waves of fear through the white community. How it all started is not clear from the existing records, but the episode proves that slave women as well as men engaged in acts of resistance. In May 1730 the Governor's Council questioned a widow, Mrs. Thomas Minott of Devonshire, and "her negro woman Affey," who were suspects in a poisoning incident the previous year. The outcome of the examination is unfortunately missing in the records, but the Governor's Council issued a warning against "persons either White or Black suspected to have been concern'd in poison or poisoning within your respective tribes."[66] Race relations were obviously tense, and on June 2, 1730, there began one of Bermuda's most notorious trials: a case involving a slave who attempted to murder a slaveholder and his family. A mulatto woman named Sarah Bassett was accused of poisoning not only her master and his wife but also another of their slaves. Bassett was the property of Francis Dickinson, an affluent Southampton blacksmith. Dickinson had died in 1727, and Sarah Bassett was working (presumably for wages) at the Sandys mansion of mariner Thomas Forster, a grandson of Governor Josias Forster. On December 18, 1729, Bassett allegedly gave two bags of poison made of ratsbane and manchineel root to her granddaughter, Beck, a Forster

---

65. Assize records, AZ 102/6, 252. The same presentment, *verbatim*, appears in the assize records of December 1730 and June 1731. See ibid., 274, 295; see also Council minutes, *BHQ* 17, no. 3 (1957): 93. Wood, *Black Majority*, 232.
66. Council minutes, *BHQ* 11, no. 3 (1954): 11.

slave, with instructions to poison Forster and his wife.[67] A "Negro girl called Nancy," another slave in the Forster household, was also an intended victim. Beck did as she was told, placing one dose of poison in the Forsters' food, "where if her Mistress did but smell on't twould poyson her."[68] The other dose of poison was put in the slats of the kitchen door, where the slave Nancy found it, and "by only looking on it ye sd. Nancy was poyson'd."

At Bassett's trial six months later it was reported that the victims were "now sick and Lye in a very Languishing and dangerous Condition." Mrs. Thomas Forster, however, was apparently well enough to testify before the grand jury, along with nine other deponents. There was a suggestion of witchcraft: "for that she, the Sarah Bassett, not having the fear of God before her Eyes, Butt being moved and seduced by ye Instigation of the Devil" had given the two bags containing the lethal mixture to her granddaughter. Beck was exonerated, but Sarah Bassett was convicted of *petit treason* and sentenced to be burned at the stake. The burning, which took place at Crow Lane, passed into the islands' folklore. A very hot day in Bermuda is sometimes called "a Sally Bassett day," and legend has it that a small purple flower known as the Bermudiana first appeared in the ashes of the fire that killed Bassett.[69]

By June 23, about two weeks after the Bassett trial, the Bermuda Assembly drafted an "Act for the further and better regulating Negroes and other Slaves and for the more effectual and Speedy way of prosecuting them in Criminal Causes." The act is long and detailed. The first parts repeat earlier laws against theft, the wearing of finery, the keeping of livestock and poultry, and the trading of goods abroad, but the heart of this legislation deals with acts of slave resistance:

> And whereas many heinous and grievous Crimes as of that Secret and barbarous way of Murdering by Poison and other Murders Burglary & Robbing on the highways

67. Anger toward Thomas Forster might be due to the fact that he and his mother, Martha Forster, were part-owners of the Bermuda sloop *Sarah*, which in 1729 had carried seven Barbadian slaves to sell in New York. Donnan, *Slave Trade*, 3:487. The manchioneel root that Bassett used for poison was commonly known in the West Indies, and it is possible that Bassett had some connection to Barbados. Thomas Forster survived the poisoning attempt and died in 1765. See Books of Wills, vol. 12, pt. 1, p. 393.

68. The manchineel tree is a tropical tree with a toxic, milky juice and a poisonous apple-like fruit. James Clark White, *Dermatitis Venenata: An Account of the Action of External Irritants upon the Skin* (Boston, 1887), 96–97, notes that West Indian slaves used the juice on their backs to simulate beatings. The juice or sap is extremely toxic and causes lesions similar to second-degree burns. The fruit, if ingested, causes stomach cramps, nausea, vomiting, and diarrhea. Recovery is slow, and severe cases can cause death. Bodeau, "A Propos de Quelques Accidents Dus au Mancinillier," *Archives de Medecine et Pharmacie Navales* 126, no. 122 (1910): 122–33.

69. William Edward Sears Zuill, *Bermuda Journey* (New York: Coward-McCann, 1946), 259. The record of the Bassett case is in Assize records, AZ 102/6. See also Packwood, *Chained on the Rock*, 146–49, and Smith, *Slavery in Bermuda*, 100–101.

Thefts Rapes Burning of Houses &c. may be many times Committed by negroes and other Slaves and many times malitiously attempted by them . . . putting Inhabitants in terror dread and jeopardy of their Lives, which said Offenders for danger or fear of Escape are not long to be in prison and being brutish Slaves deserved not for the baseness of their Condition to be tryed by the Legal Tryal of Twelve men . . . which neither truly can be rightly done as the subjects of England are nor is Execution to be delayed towards them in Case of such horrid Crimes.[70]

Instead of a jury of 12 men, two justices of the peace and "four able freeholders," chosen by the said justices, would try the accused. This act was to be published on the Town Bridge immediately, and applied to "the Negroes now imprisoned and in Custody for poysoning or Suspicion of poisoning." The identities of these individuals are not known. In addition to Sarah Bassett, at least one other person—a man—was executed in the poisoning scare.

Besides passing the legislation enjoining slaveholders to control their slaves, the Bermuda Assembly also approved an act designed to protect slaveholders— to "prevent the Forfeiture of Life and Estate upon killing a Negro or other Slave."[71] The wording of the latter act, repugnant as it is to modern sensibilities, reveals a certain uneasiness over the morality of slavery:

Whereas *Negroes, Indians, Mulattoes,* and other Slaves, are very numerous within these Islands, and that the wilful killing of any such Slave . . . comes within the Penalty of Murder, the Judgment whereof is Forfeiture of Life and Estate; and whereas the Privileges of *England* are so universally extensive as not to admit of the least Thing called *Slavery,* occasioned the making such Laws for the Preservation of every individual Subject . . . but here, in his Majesty's Colonies and Plantations in *America,* the Cases and Things are wonderfully altered; for the very Kindred, nay, sometimes even the Parents of those unfortunate Creatures (upon the Coast of *Africa*) expose their Issue to perpetual Bondage and Slavery, by selling them unto your Majesty's Subjects trading there, and from thence are brought to these and other your Majesty's Settlements in *America,* and consequently purchased by the Inhabitants thereof, they being (for the Brutishness of their Nature) no otherwise valued or esteemed amongst us than as our Goods and Chattels or other personal Estates;.therefore our prudent Neighbors in *America* as *Barbadoes,* &c., have thought fit (in Case of killing any such Negro or Slave) to make Laws to prevent the Penalty and Forfeitures aforesaid . . . that then the aforesaid Owner or Possessor shall not be liable to any Imprisonment, Arraignment, or Prosecution . . . whatsoever.[72]

70. "An Act for . . . regulating . . . Criminal Cases," June 23, 1730, Miscellaneous Acts, 1711–1759. Parts of the passage forbidding a jury trial are undecipherable where several words have been crossed out.

71. Ibid. The act to regulate blacks' behavior would be repeated, with modifications, in 1732 and 1733.

72. "Act for the Security of the Subject to prevent the Forfeiture of Life and Estate upon killing a Negro or other Slave," *Acts of Assembly Made and Enacted in the Bermuda or Summer Islands.* . . . (London, 1737), 98. An earlier version of this law was passed by the Bermuda

Bermuda's lawmakers were obviously aware of conditions in England's other colonies, but even though they referred to blacks' "brutish nature," they were not as severe in their views as were some of their counterparts elsewhere. For example, a 1723 Virginia law allowed "dismemberment" as a punishment for runaway slaves or for those who wandered out without permission, and provided that if such a punishment resulted in the slave's death, the master was not punishable by law.[73] Bermuda laws remained vague about the actual punishment meted out to slaves and generally prescribed whippings without specifying the number of lashes. It is worth noting that not until these two laws of 1730, in the climate of fear bred by the poisoning scare, that the word *brutish* was applied to Bermuda slaves.

Reports of the Bassett case and other cases whose records have not survived spread anxiety throughout the Atlantic community. In January 1730/1731 Governor John Pitt reported to the Board of Trade that the authorities had "condemned one wooman to bee burnt and a man Hang'd," along with "severall transported to ye Spanish West Indies wee are now a little easy, but am afraide not quite secure."[74] A letter to Whitehall in February 1730/1731 observed that "Great numbers of merchants trading to and from Bermuda" had reported that "the negroes who are more numerous than the white people have destroyed many of H.M. subjects by poison and many more are lingering under that misfortune whose lives are despaired and altho' some of the actors of that horrid villany have been discovered, convicted and publickly executed in a severe manner for the same, they continue to meet in numbers in a most mutinous manner, which the said merchants conceive to be with an intent utterly to extirpate the inhabitants of that Colony."[75] These unsubstantiated rumors were echoed by Ralph Noden, a London merchant who petitioned the Lords of Trade to put back the Independent Company, which had left Bermuda in February 1729/1730. Noden voiced his fear of the "negroes on that Island who are much more numerous than the white People."[76] Noden's estimate of the number of blacks in Bermuda, however, is clearly based on hearsay. Blacks outnumbered whites in the sugar islands in the Caribbean, not in Bermuda. In 1729 there were 5,086 whites and 3,688 blacks in the

Assembly in 1711 and repeated in 1723. See *Journals of . . . Assembly,* 1:183–84. See also Council minutes, *BHQ* 5, no. 3 (1948): 111.

73. Hening, *Statutes,* 4:132–33. An earlier Virginia law, of 1705, stated that a slaveholder whose slave died while "under correction" would not be accused of a felony but would be free "of all punishment for the same, as if the accident had never happened." Ibid., 3:459.

74. Governor John Pitt to the Lords of Trade, January 27, 1730/1731, in CO 37/12: 13.

75. Sir W. Strickland to Lord Harrington, Whitehall, February 20, 1730/1731, in *CSP,* 1731:44–45. There were other apparently unrelated poisoning cases in 1739 and 1753. See Packwood, *Chained on the Rock,* 149, and Smith, *Slavery in Bermuda,* 101–2.

76. Ralph Noden to the Lords of Trade, in CO 37/12: 77.

colony, and in 1731 there were 4,353 whites and 3,248 blacks—far from a majority.[77] It was true, however, that many whites and a number of blacks had left the islands in recent years. That same year—the year of the poisoning scare—an undetermined number of families emigrated to the island of New Providence, the new British colony in the Bahamas. As the governor there wrote, the newcomers came "from Bermuda which is so full of people and has so little land that they can't be supported there."[78]

If poor economic conditions and a poisoning scare were not worrisome enough, renewed fears of Spanish attacks and pirates in 1731 prompted Governor Pitt to request the Council of Trade and Plantations to station a small man of war in Bermuda's waters. Pirates, he wrote, were "very numerous, and often come into the latitude." Even more frightening, the governor suspected that some pirate ships might be guided through Bermuda's treacherous reefs by former Bermudians. There were, according to the governor, "several negroes borne in these islands aboard their [the pirates'] ship who are excellent pilots and know every creek and bay."[79] Governor Bennett had expressed similar fears two decades earlier, and fears about Bermuda's black pilots aiding outsiders would surface again after the slave plot of 1761. The fact that Bermuda blacks were serving aboard alien ships—pirate vessels or those of a foreign power, such as France—makes clear the fact that at least some of Bermuda's black seamen had managed to escape bondage and were using their nautical skills to their own advantage. Did these skilled seamen, who knew every shoal and reef around Bermuda, manage to steal a boat and sail away from Bermuda? Did they jump ship in a foreign port? Did they have contacts with other slaves in maroon (runaway) communities in Jamaica, for example? The intriguing and unrecorded histories of these men form part of the hidden history of slavery, not only in Bermuda, but in the Atlantic community.

Meanwhile, individual acts of slave resistance in Bermuda became more numerous in the 1730s. The same assize that condemned Sarah Bassett conducted another poisoning trial: A slave woman named Beck, belonging to Martha Durham of Somerset, was indicted on June 4, 1730, for attempting "to poison people."[80] In this case, however, a jury found Beck not guilty. Two slaves were among the deponents. Nan, a slave belonging to Thomas Lea, and

---

77. Bermuda did not have a majority of blacks until well into the nineteenth century. The 1729 census is in Governor Pitt's Replies to Queries of the Board of Trade, April 21, 1730, CO 37/12: 11, i. The 1731 figures are in a report dated July 17, 1731, CO 37/12: 13.

78. Governor Pitt to Mr. Popple, in CO 37/12: 11; Governor Rogers to the Council of Trade and Plantations, October 11, 1730, in *CSP*, 1730:315.

79. Pitt to the Council of Trade and Plantations, November 4, 1731, in *CSP*, 1731:321.

80. Assize records, AZ 102/6, 232–33. Beck was a common name for slave women. Martha Durham was the unmarried daughter of Thomas Durham, a Sandys resident who died in 1714. See Hallett, *Early Bermuda Wills*, 180; Books of Wills, vol. 5, pp. 35, 41.

Peter, belonging to Thomas Dickinson, appeared before the grand jury.[81] In the early 1730s a number of blacks were apprehended and tried, although the surviving records do not specify their crimes or the results of their trials. The council minutes for November 3, 1731, for example, mention expenses for the trials of "Negro Cockoo" and "Negrs. James and Ruth," and the minutes of November 9, 1732, note the bills for the trials of "Negro Sharp, Negro Lewis, Indian Tom, Mrs. Cox Negro, Negro Thyas, Negro Daniel," as well as "Peter a Negro" and Cutto and Jane, whose races are not specified.[82]

In 1732 the grand jury repeated its complaint concerning unacceptable behavior on the Sabbath: "Negros getting together in Companies going a drinking and rowing about in boats." That same year the Assembly renewed an earlier act forbidding whites to allow blacks to meet in their houses to feast or dance after sunset, but added a telling proviso that reveals the close relationships between many Bermuda slaveholders and their slaves. The Assembly agreed that slaveholders could "allow their own negroes to Dance in their own Houses after sun setting."[83] The next two grand juries for the assizes of 1732 voiced further concerns over the continued laxity of enforcement of such rules, citing the "Allowances given to Negros or at least Wink't at to meet together, wear fine Cloths Riot and Cabal" and to frequent "Tipling houses."[84]

Besides these relatively harmless acts of resistance by Bermuda's slaves, there were others more alarming. In the summer of 1739, Phillip, a slave belonging to the Reverend Joseph Horton, who lived on the glebe in Pembroke, was accused of "practising poison & several other misdemeanors."[85] Phillip's master was the pastor of both Pembroke and Devonshire Tribes from 1728 to 1740. The record is unclear as to the specifics of Phillip's actions, but apparently some of the residents of neighboring Devonshire Tribe made accusations against the minister's slave. Horton seems to have been unpopular with some of his Pembroke parishioners, since they voted against giving him the gift of a surplice in 1731. A few years later, in 1738, when his ward, young Samuel Outerbridge, his wife's son by her first marriage, died, Horton

81. Thomas Lea, a mariner of Paget's Tribe, was a cousin of John Wentworth of Warwick. Peter's master may have been the Thomas Dickinson of Pembroke, a blacksmith who died in 1759. Hallett, *Early Bermuda Wills*, 165, 344; Books of Wills, vol. 8, pp. 14, 237.

82. Council minutes, November 3, 1731, *BHQ* 12, no. 2 (1955): 38–39, and November 9, 1732, *BHQ* 12, no. 4 (1955): 113. Jane Prudden submitted a bill for expenses of entertaining the judges and freeholders at "the tryall of Negros" in 1734. *BHQ* 13, no. 4 (1956): 150.

83. *Journals of . . . Assembly*, May 18, 1732, 1:251.

84. Assize records, December 6, 1732, AZ 102/6, 377. See also 389–90, 409–10.

85. Council minutes, *BHQ* 18, no. 1 (1961): 3–4; on the Horton case, see also William Edward Sears Zuill, "Notes on the Darrell Journal," *BHQ* 2, no. 3 (1945): 144; Hallett, *Colonial Church*, 136–37.

allegedly profited from the boy's estate.[86] A legislative committee led by Major Cornelius Hinson, Esquire, of Pembroke Tribe, investigated the matter, and Phillip was jailed to await trial. Horton and his family left Bermuda early in 1740, but the minister died in March of that year, and Catherine Horton returned to Bermuda as the administrator of Horton's estate. What became of Phillip is not recorded. It is possible that he was sold off the island. Catherine Horton, along with three affluent merchants, Henry Corbusier, Samuel Spofforth, and Jeremiah Peniston Jr., was a part-owner of a sloop called the *Mary,* which arrived in New York on June 9, 1742, with one Bermuda slave to sell. That could have been Phillip, the accused poisoner.[87]

The various poisonings and rumors of poisonings in the 1730s left Bermuda's officials shaken and fearful of more plots. No doubt Bermudians heard of the Stono Rebellion in South Carolina, in which 25 whites were killed and 50 slaves executed.[88] After a slave uprising in New York City in 1741, members of the Bermuda Governor's Council requested that Governor Alured Popple write to New York's Governor George Clark to inquire if any Bermuda blacks were involved in the "late plott for burning of that city." The council's assumptions that Bermuda blacks might have had a role in the New York slave conspiracy, like Governor Bennett's earlier apprehensions that black pilots might be piloting pirate vessels, point to the wider perimeters of slavery in Bermuda, where so many slaves went to sea. Black sailors regularly visited seaports (such as New York City) on the mainland as well as in the Caribbean. When ashore, they undoubtedly spoke with other slaves and free blacks, and fraternized with white sailors as well. This informal network certainly existed, although its very existence demanded circumspection on the part of its members. In 1741 New York's Governor Clark answered the Bermudians' query, saying that the judges in New York "could find nothing particularly against any Bermudas Negroes" and that the official inquiries were at an end.[89]

While white Bermudians were no doubt comforted by the news that no Bermuda blacks were involved in the New York revolt, a few years later they

86. Catherine Horton was the widow of Jonathan Outerbridge, a Devonshire resident who died in 1731. See Hallett, *Colonial Church,* 136–37, 382.

87. Donnan, *Slave Trade,* 3:508. The master of the *Mary* was John Vickers, a mariner from Smith's Tribe. His son, John, would figure prominently in the slave conspiracy of 1761 in Bermuda.

88. See Wood, *Black Majority,* 237. The reported conspiracy took place in August 1730, but Wood finds "limited evidence." Blacks had been a majority of Carolina's population since 1708 (36–37). See also Aptheker, *Slave Revolts,* 187–88.

89. Council minutes, April 6, 1742, *BHQ* 28, no. 2 (1971): 35. The New York slave plot, involving 150 slaves and 25 whites, came during a time of anxieties over war with Spain, a hard winter, and high bread prices. Thirteen slaves were burned alive, 10 hanged, and 70 banished. See Aptheker, *Slave Revolts,* 193–95, and T. J. Davis, *A Rumor of Revolt: The "Great Negro Plot" in Colonial New York* (New York: Free Press, 1985).

had reason for further alarm. In 1753 "a barberous murder" was committed by a slave called Quash, who killed his master, Captain John McNeil, a resident of Hamilton Tribe.[90] Quash struck McNeil in the forehead with a hatchet, inflicting "three several blows and . . . three mortal wounds of the length of two inches and down to his Skull, of which the said Mortal wounds . . . John McNeil immediately dyed." Quash slashed his master's body with a knife and threw it over a cliff into the sea. So brutal was the crime, and so eager were Bermudians for justice, that 300 of them signed a petition to bring "Quash the Criminall to Speedy & Exemplary punishment."[91] Quash was tried, found guilty, and sentenced to death by hanging. The execution took place on the highest point on Gibbets (sometimes also called Gallows) Island at the entrance to the Flatts harbor. Hearsay has it that Quash's body hung there in chains for several days before he expired. The pole from which he was hanged remained standing and was for many years afterward known as "Quashi's Pole."[92]

In the years immediately following Quash's trial, the actions of three other blacks further alarmed Bermuda's whites. In 1754 the black pirate Dick, who had run away from Lewis Middleton in the 1720s, was imprisoned on charges of piracy and a murder committed aboard the schooner *Ruby*.[93] The next year two other slaves were suspected of poisoning attempts: Polibius, a slave belonging to Cornelius Hinson, and Judith, a woman slave belonging to Jane Tatem, a widow in Paget Tribe, were arrested. The question of trying these two speedily, under the act of 1711 that denied a jury trial in certain cases, was discussed by the governor and his council, but they rejected that plan, and the two accused slaves received jury trials at the December 1755 assize.[94] The records of Polibius's case are especially noteworthy because they contain the details of his alleged poisoning methods. According to court testimony Polibius was accused of trying to poison Cornelius Hinson and his wife, Ann, by "willfully and maliciously" hiding a poisonous mixture under a stone in the yard near the Hinsons' Pembroke mansion, and mixing a "certain Poisonous Liquor or Composition of a blue Colour in a certain Glass Phiol" designed to put in the Hinsons' food and drink.

The principal witness was Hinson himself. He testified that a Mrs. Elizabeth Wallis (probably a neighbor) had seen Polibius put "some Poisonous Mixture"

90. Council minutes, December 5, 1753, *BHQ* 36, no. 1 (1979): 21. See also Records of the Minutes of Council in Assembly, Bermuda Archives, 1:138–39.

91. Council minutes, November 21, 1753.

92. Packwood, *Chained on the Rock*, 135.

93. Council minutes, *BHQ* 37, no. 4 (1980): 5.

94. Fragmentary records of the trial are in Assize records, AZ 102/9, 12–17. See also Council minutes, *BHQ* 36, no. 2 (1979): 24.

under a stone. This news, according to Hinson, "so much surprized his wife that she fainted." Upon recovering, she "was advised to put it in the fire, which she did, and the Phiol flew, and stuff dispers'd." Hinson reported that he had questioned Polibius, who "told him several notorious lies." But another witness, a black man in the service of a Captain Canton, reported that Polibius had told him that the mixture under the stone was to prevent Hinson from whipping him. Elizabeth Wallis then testified that the liquid in the phial was "like blue stone water" and the other mixture "appeared like Grindstone mudd, and the pairings of Nails & hair, & smelt of rum." The jury, weighing this evidence, returned a verdict of not guilty. Polibius paid his prison and legal fees, then disappeared from the records.

At the same assize, Judith, Mrs. Tatem's slave, was tried, but the records of her trial have not survived. She was sentenced to receive a public whipping at the gallows on Gallows Island at St. George's.[95]

The paucity of documentation in cases such as those of Quash, Dick, Polibius, and Judith is frustrating and leaves a host of questions unanswered: Where had Quash come from, and how long had he been John McNeil's slave? The name Quash, unusual among Bermuda blacks, suggests that he had come from Africa, perhaps by way of the West Indies. His master was a sea captain who may have purchased him in the Caribbean islands. And what of Dick, who ran away and became a pirate? What sort of relationships did he have with other seamen, both white and black? Whom did he murder, and why? What finally became of him? Polibius, like Quash, may have come from Africa or one of the Caribbean islands. It is possible that his use of a conjuring potion to ward off punishment—a practice that may have been unfamiliar to Bermuda slaveholders—frightened his master and mistress and led to his trial. Judith's case remains a mystery, except that she paid for her offense with a whipping.

Sources that reveal something of the everyday lives of Bermuda's blacks—the ordinary folk as well as the notorious—are extremely limited. Besides wills, inventories, and court records, there are almost no firsthand accounts, such as letters, diaries, and narratives. And what few there are come from white observers. Clergymen who ministered to blacks as well as whites sometimes kept journals or diaries that provide unexpected glimpses of black life. For example, there is a fragment of a diary kept by the Reverend James Holiday, pastor of Bermuda's Eastern Parish from 1745 until his death in 1754. Since 1693 the colony had been divided into three "livings," or areas to be served by a clergyman: St. George's, or the public lands; the Eastern, comprising Hamilton, Smith's, Devonshire, and Pembroke Tribes; and the Western, made

95. AZ 102/9, 17.

up of Paget, Warwick, Southampton, and Sandys. St. George's covered an area of approximately two square miles; the two other parishes, eight and one-half square miles each.[96] Holiday resided in Pembroke Parish, and his daily entries afford some views of Bermuda's blacks unrecorded elsewhere. Regrettably, all that has survived of the diary are some entries for 1746 and 1747, but they, along with the journals of two other clergymen, reveal much about life for both blacks and whites in eighteenth-century Bermuda. Besides Holiday's diary, there is the journal of the famous evangelist George Whitefield, who visited Bermuda in the spring and summer of 1748, and the journals of Alexander Richardson of St. George's, where he was pastor from 1755 to 1772 and again from 1778 until his death in 1805.

In the 1740s James Holiday, who lived on the glebe in the center of Pembroke, served a flock of approximately 3,500 souls in the Eastern Parish. A census of 1740 lists 1,996 whites and 1,402 blacks in this area. St. George's had 900 whites and 457 blacks; the Western Parish, the most populous, had 2,573 whites and 1,926 blacks.[97] The totals for the entire colony according to this census were 5,469 whites and 3,785 nonwhites. Bermuda's "blacks, mulattoes, and Indians" in the 1740s made up 40.9 percent of the colony's population. The colony's ministers could hardly ignore them. Holiday's diary reveals that at least some of them went to school. After a list of eight "dame schools" at Spanish Point (an old name for Pembroke Tribe) with a total of 90 "scholars" on November 19, 1746, the sole item for the next diary entry, on November 27, is "At Mrs. Adam's school her negro girl the best scholar by far." On January 18 Holiday noted that he had been "At breakfast with Col. Corbusier to see after setting up a negro school. £1000 may be subscribed for." The idea for a school for blacks may have come from South Carolina, where a school for slaves had been established in Charleston in 1742.[98] Holiday's diary also notes several baptisms of blacks. On February 18, 1746/1747, he wrote, "Negroes to be baptised on St. David's Island. 1 of Mrs. Foxes. 3 of Mrs. Bull's. 1 of Mrs. Picart's. 1 of Wm. Burchall's." Holiday kept careful records of other baptisms, and a surviving register for Hamilton Tribe for 1748 and 1749 has a page listing 23 baptisms—13 males and 10 females—"of Coloured Persons," whose names are recorded along with their owners' names. Six of these may have been free blacks, since the "owner" column opposite their names is blank. None has a surname. Among the owners, the surnames of Somersall, Peniston,

96. Hallett, *Colonial Church*, 116–17.
97. Ibid., 118.
98. See entries in "Diary of the Rev. James Holiday," 84–89. On the Carolina school, see Frey, *Water from the Rock*, 20.

Trott, and Outerbridge indicate the continued prominence of some Bermuda families.[99]

When George Whitefield visited Bermuda around the middle of March 1747/1748, he stayed at James Holiday's home in Pembroke, noting that Holiday received him "in a most affectionate Christian manner." The famous evangelist, weary from his latest triumphant tour of the mainland colonies from New England to Georgia, was to stay in Bermuda until May 22. He gave himself little time to rest, however, and preached to appreciative audiences from St. George's to Somerset. On Sunday, March 27, for example, he preached at Christ Church, Warwick, to a crowd of "about four hundred." Whitefield wrote that an "Abundance of Negroes and many others were in the Vestry, porch and about the house."[100]

On another Sunday later in his stay, Whitefield preached outdoors, "about four miles distant in the fields" from the Warwick church, to "a large company of negroes and a number of white people . . . in all near fifteen hundred people." Since Whitefield had announced his intent to preach a sermon especially for the blacks, it is safe to assume that his audience was predominantly black— perhaps nearly one-fourth of the colony's black population. His description of this service for Bermuda's blacks is worth quoting at length:

> The negroes seemed very sensible and attentive. When I asked, if they all did not desire to go to heaven? one of them, with a very audible voice, said "Yes, sir." This caused a little smiling; but, in general, every thing was carried on with great decency; and I believe the Lord enabled me to so discourse, as to touch the negroes, and yet not to give them the least umbrage to slight or behave imperiously to their masters. . . . Upon inquiry, I found that some of the negroes did not like my preaching, because I told them of their cursing, swearing, thieving and lying. One of two of the worst of them, I was informed, went away. Some said, they would not go any more. They liked Mr. M. . . . .r [Moore] better, for he never told them of these things; and I said, their hearts were as black as their faces. They expected, they said, to hear me speak against their masters. Blessed be God, that I was directed not to say any thing, this first time, to the masters at all, though my text led me to it. It might have been of bad consequences, to tell them their duty, or charge them too roundly with the neglect of it, before their slaves. They would mind all I said

---

99. Rev. James Holiday, "Baptisms of Coloured Persons in Hamilton in the Islands of Bermuda in the Year 1749," Holiday Parish Register transcript, Bermuda Archives. The original is not extant.

100. Whitefield's journal is excerpted in William Edward Sears Zuill, "George Whitefield and His Bermuda Friends," *BHQ* 4, no. 1 (1947): 25–34. Because Whitefield could not produce an official license from the Church of England, Governor William Popple, though hospitable, could not allow him the use of Bermuda's churches. Warwick's Christ Church was the one Independent church in the colony in the eighteenth century, having as its first minister in 1718 one James Paul, who was recommended to that post by Boston's Cotton Mather and who served there until his death in 1751. See Hallett, *Colonial Church,* 221–22. See also Esther K. Law, "Christ Church, Warwick, 1719–1969," *BHQ* 6, no. 2 (1969).

to their masters, and, perhaps, nothing that I said to them. . . . However, others of the poor creatures, I hear, were very thankful, and came home to their masters' houses, saying that they would strive to sin no more. . . .

The old man, who spoke out loud last Sunday, and said "yes" when I asked whether all the negroes would not go to heaven? being questioned by somebody, why he spoke out so? answered, "That the gentleman put the question once or twice to them and the other fools had not the manners to make me any answer; till, at last, I seemed to point at him, and he was ashamed that nobody should answer me, and therefore he did." Another, wondering why I said negroes had black hearts; was answered by his black brother thus, "Ah, thou fool! Dost thou not understand it? He means black with sin." Two more girls were overheard by their mistress talking about religion: and they said, "They knew, if they did not repent, they must be damned." From all which I infer, that these Bermudian negroes are more knowing than I supposed.[101]

The following Sunday Whitefield preached again in the morning at Warwick Church, but in the evening he traveled to Pembroke, near Holiday's house, to preach to an audience of blacks and whites "almost as large" as the crowd that had gathered the previous Sunday. He noted with some satisfaction that "they heard very attentively, and some of them now began to weep. May God grant them a godly sorrow, that worketh repentance not to be repented of!"[102]

As Whitefield's visit makes clear, Bermuda's blacks in the eighteenth century, as in the seventeenth, shared in the religious life of the islands. In this, Bermuda stands in marked contrast to the colonies on the mainland. In the southern colonies with large numbers of slaves, no more than half the whites and a very small percentage of blacks were "churched" in the mid-eighteenth century.[103] A large number of baptisms in one clergyman's records testify to the piety of Bermuda's blacks. The Reverend Alexander Richardson, rector of St. Peter's Church at St. George's, kept meticulous records of baptisms, both black and white. In November 1755 when he arrived, he noted that there had been 54 children baptized in "the four neighboring parishes" (Hamilton, Smith's, Devonshire, and Pembroke) along with "230 Negroes." In 1756, after recording the baptisms of nine children at St. George's he wrote that "142 Children baptized this year in the other parishes and 147 Negroes." In 1759 Richardson wrote that he himself had baptized 41 white children and 63

---

101. Zuill, "George Whitefield," 32–33.

102. Ibid., 33.

103. Frey, *Water from the Rock*, 18. In the Danish West Indies slaves were baptized at birth but attended church only as attendants to their white masters. See Hall, *Slave Society in the Danish West Indies*, 60. For a comparative view of slave religion on the North American mainland, see Frey, *Water from the Rock*, Frey and Betty Wood, *Come Shouting to Zion: African American Protestantism in the American South and British Caribbean to 1830* (Chapel Hill: University of North Carolina Press, 1998), and John Boles, ed., *Masters and Slaves in the House of the Lord: Race and Religion in the American South, 1740–1870* (Lexington, Ky.: University of Kentucky Press, 1988).

blacks.[104] From 1755 to the end of his first ministry in 1772 he calculated that there had been 1,118 whites and 1,535 blacks baptized—more blacks, in fact, than whites. When Richardson returned to this parish in 1778 he continued his record-keeping, noting in 1785 that ministers in other parishes refused to baptize blacks.[105] Of about 2,500 baptisms listed in the parish registers from 1618 to 1826, there are records of the baptisms of 607 blacks by name, not to mention those baptized by Richardson and others who did not record names. The religious experiences of Bermuda's blacks, as recorded by these white clergymen, testify to an active and, as George Whitefield put it, "knowing" participation in church and community life. By the middle of the eighteenth century at least some black children were attending school, and plans were underway for a "negro school." Since Bermuda never had laws forbidding the teaching of slaves to read and write, it is likely that a good portion of adult blacks, both slave and free, were literate.

In Bermuda, perhaps more than in other English colonies, literacy and some knowledge of the wider transatlantic world were part of many blacks' experience, and in 1761 their knowledge of the struggle between England and France for control of North America may have helped to set off the colony's last recorded slave conspiracy. To some degree both black and white Bermudians were drawn into the French and Indian War, which began in 1754. Even before that, French privateers had posed a threat to Bermuda's ships as well as England's, and Bermudians were understandably nervous. Rumors of black Bermuda seamen's collaboration with the French circulated. In October 1752, for example, Captain Joseph Darrell of Devonshire Tribe reported to the Governor's Council that on the evening of October 2 he had overheard a man named John Dobson speaking to "Sam a Negro of Mrs. Stalburrys," who was in Darrell's kitchen garden with three other black men. Dobson reportedly said, "Sam you are a good fellow, it may be easy done, they may then take the country." The council agreed to request the justices of the peace to make inquiry, but there is no further record of the incident.[106] In May of 1761 Bermudians experienced another near panic as French privateers came close to the islands and were repelled by two armed Bermuda vessels.[107]

The unsettled conditions in the islands during this war, which lasted until

---

104. These figures may be somewhat exaggerated, but there is no way to check them.

105. Arthur Tudor Tucker, "Parson Richardson, 1755–1805: Rector of the Parish of St. George, Bermuda," *BHQ* 12, no. 2 (1955): 64–74. A compilation, by alphabetical listing, of the names of Bermuda's whites who were baptized, married, or buried by Alexander Richardson is in Hallett, *Early Bermuda Records*, 147–93, with the note that "many Negroes were baptized and buried by Richardson, but he did not record their names."

106. Council minutes, October 1752, *BHQ* 35, no. 4 (1978): 55.

107. Williams, *Historical & Statistical Account*, 76–77.

1763, may have encouraged some of Bermuda's slaves to plot rebellion. The number of blacks in the islands was growing, and a census of 1764 shows that for the first time in the colony's history there could have been more able-bodied black men than white. As table 9 shows, the total number of black men was 1,225; the total number of white men, 1,520—a difference of 295. That number, however, does not specify the able-bodied men. The number of able-bodied white men listed on the muster roll was 1,070; 450 others were infirm or elderly. The number of able-bodied blacks is not recorded, but it could have been larger than 1,070, the corresponding number of whites. These numbers, combined with the tensions of wartime, may have invited the most serious and widespread slave conspiracy in Bermuda's history.

It began in October 1761, when one white man's overhearing a plot for a general uprising resulted in an embargo on all shipping in December and the imposition of martial law from December 2, 1761, to March 9, 1762.[108] When it ended in April 1762, at least six slaves—five men and one woman—had been executed and an unknown number of other slaves reportedly banished. Records of this event are sketchy, but the surviving documents, especially the governor's speeches and dispatches, suggest a near panic among Bermuda's government officials and fears of a widespread rebellion involving lower-class whites as well as blacks. Moreover, a bloody slave uprising in Jamaica the year before was all too fresh in memory.[109]

On the night of October 12, John Vickers, a mariner who lived in Smith's Tribe, accompanied by one of his mother's slaves, a woman named Frank, was on his way to the house of his father-in-law, Gilbert Bedlow, about eight o'clock. Nearing the house of another resident of Smith's Tribe, Richard Taylor, Vickers came upon a group of "six or eight" black men and overheard what he believed to be a conspiracy plot involving over half the blacks in Bermuda. On October 15, he gave a deposition that apparently set off a mass hysteria among the whites. Vickers declared that he

> heard one of the said Negro Men, and as he believes was a Negro Man late the property of Mr. Thomas Cox, and commonly calld Natt, declare to the other Negro Men, that he (meaning the said Natt) had a Cow, and that no white Body should have any of it, for he would see them all Damned: and hoped to have a Frolick with it; and that would be his part and his Wifes, or Words to that Effect—whereupon another of the said Negroes answered to the following Effect; That the first white Body that should take any thing from him should kill him, or he would kill them—Whereupon another of the said Negroes answered to the following Effect, That

---

108. For the deposition that began the fright, see Records of the Minutes of Council in Assembly, 2:347–48. Other records are in CO 37/19: 20, and *Journals of . . . Assembly,* 2:967–68.

109. For a detailed account of the Jamaica rebellion, see Bryan Edwards, *The History, Civil and Commercial, of the British Colonies in the West Indies,* 2d ed. (London, 1801), 2:75–85.

there would be a very great Victory gained hear soon, or if not, one half, or two-thirds of the Negroes will be hanged in Bermuda.[110]

Besides the slave identified as Natt, Vickers claimed to recognize George, a slave belonging to John Spencer, among the alleged conspirators he saw in the dark on Monday evening. Vickers then recalled that on the morning of that same day he had heard Peter, "late the property of Captain Nicholas Spencer," say that if any white person should take any clothes from him "he would know the reason of it, and be Revenged."[111]

Most of what Vickers overheard could be interpreted as idle boasting: Possessing a cow and planning to feast on it, owning clothes that perhaps violated the law regulating slave wearing apparel, even threatening violence against whites who might challenge a slave's possession of certain goods, were hardly evidence of a murderous plot. Peter, the slave who spoke these words, may have felt freer than most to speak his mind, since his master, Nicholas Spencer, a mariner, had died in 1757 and Peter was in the charge of Spencer's widow, Margaret. But there was the ominous boast of a scheme that involved over half—perhaps two-thirds—of the blacks in Bermuda. And John Vickers was presumably a reliable witness. He came from a long-established Bermuda family, descended from Severin Vickers who had come on the *Truelove* in 1635. His father, the elder John Vickers, was a mariner of substantial means; his father-in-law, Gilbert Bedlow, was a shipwright.[112]

The fears unleashed by young Vickers's accusations resulted in the Assembly's passage, on October 21, of "An Act for the Speedy Trial of divers Slaves, Negroes and others now charged with a Conspiracy and Rebellion as well as other atrocious Crimes with an Intent to take away the Lives of the White Inhabitants of these Islands, and to over turn and totally subvert the Government thereof."[113] Under the provisions of this act, blacks could be tried without a jury, on the testimony of a justice of the peace and six others. The testimony of "one credible white person to the fact or the evidence of one Slave and the circumstance of one credible white person upon oath" was sufficient to convict. On December 2, 1761, Governor Popple proposed to place Bermuda under martial law "till these fatal and threatning dangers lessen or remove." His speech to the Assembly reflects the "Alarms and Fears

110. Records of the Minutes of Council in Assembly, 2:346–48.
111. Nicholas Spencer, a mariner, and John Spencer, a cordwainer, were brothers. Both lived in Smith's Tribe and were related to the Vickers family by marriage. George, John Spencer's slave, was not among the six slaves executed as conspirators in April 1762; nor was Nicholas Spencer's slave, Peter. See Hallett, *Early Bermuda Wills*, 541–42.
112. Ibid., 130. On the Vickers family, see Books of Wills, vol. 12, pt. 2, p. 320.
113. *Journals of . . . Assembly*, 2:931–35, 939. See also Manuscript Acts, 1762–1779, Bermuda Archives.

occasioned by the intended Insurrection of the Negroes, and the Massacre of the white Inhabitants proposed in consequence thereof." The governor voiced his fears that "the small number against whom the sentence of Death . . . may be awarded, will be too few to strike a terror into the Bulk of the Negro's, and will render them rather more cunning, more daring and more desperate than they are."

The governor's next remarks bespeak his further unease, not only over Bermuda's large number of slaves, but over the resulting class tensions as well: "As to the Number of Negroes in these Islands I need not observe to you, that it is much too great for the safety and the Uses for which such Slaves in other places where they have large Plantations, Works and other Calls for them, are required." For the past hundred years, Bermuda's slaves had been encouraged to take up skilled trades, but now the governor perceived that practice as a threat to the colony's social order and class structure. "To breed Negroes to common Trades and Mechanics, if it was only for this single reason, that it prevents the poorer White Inhabitants from following such Vocations and breeding their Children thereto, is the most pernicious practice that can be fallen upon and mustered in impoverishing the poorer sort."[114] Although there is no direct evidence of the involvement of Bermuda's poor whites in the 1761 rebellion plot, this statement, along with the wording of the above act, the proposal for martial law, and subsequent legislation governing whites as well as blacks, suggests that the governor, at least, feared a widespread social upheaval.

On December 3, the day after Governor Popple's speech, the Assembly voted to institute martial law. It would be in effect until March 9, 1762. Other stringent measures were also taken to control the activities of slaves: A watch was ordered to be kept in each tribe, with all owners of one or more slaves to provide one watchman in their turn. Smith's, Paget, and Devonshire were to supply four watchmen per night; Hamilton, Pembroke, Warwick, Southampton, and Sandys, three each; and St. George's, the seat of government, was to have six watchmen. The logic of this distribution may have to do with the fact that the conspirators were discovered in Smith's Tribe, perhaps the designated center of the rebellion. Paget and Devonshire lie immediately to the west of Smith's, and adjacent to Crow Lane, a spot associated with other abortive rebellion attempts. North of Smith's is Hamilton Tribe, more thinly populated and perhaps more easily patrolled because of its separation from

---

114. *Journals of . . . Assembly*, 2:945–46. Blacks in skilled trades continued to be a problem, but a law imposing duties on blacks who took up "mechanic trades" and awarding bounties to whites who did likewise was disallowed by the crown. See James Christie Esten, *A Plan for the Instructions &c., of the Emancipated People of Colour* (London, 1837), 11; Williams, *Historical & Statistical Account*, 184.

Smith's by the narrow neck of land at the Flatts. East of Smith's Tribe lies the island of St. George's, containing the seat of government, and, coincidentally, the colony's store of gunpowder.

The additional number of watchmen for the capital lends credence to the fears of a revolution that could overthrow the government. Watchmen were empowered to search "all Negros Cabbins," and slaves out at night must have a "Ticket in writing" from the owner. This part of the law was not new; tickets had been legally required for the last hundred years. But part of this regulation was different, and it reflects the lawmakers' fears of violence at the hands of rebellious blacks. According to the new provision any black meeting a white and "challenged" must immediately fall to his or her knees. Individuals who did not do so were subject to 100 lashes—a punishment unheard of until then in Bermuda.[115]

Governor Popple's letters during the tense period of martial law reveal his fears, but they are oddly lacking in the details of the conspiracy. Taking Vickers's testimony at face value, he reported that "several others" besides those Vickers named had been examined. These "had informed against many more" who were then apprehended, imprisoned, and examined. The exact number of suspects is never stated. Popple was evidently eager to appoint a special court for the trials, and although the Assembly shared his sense of urgency, they opposed the creation of a special court. According to Popple, they said "the Country (as the Negroes belonged to the Inhabitants) wou'd think their Negroes unjustly try'd by Courts not appointed by Law."[116]

In the end, Popple reported that "several Negroes were try'd, some capitally convicted and executed, others against whom Suspicion only lay, by appreciation of their Owners, transported." The country, said Popple, "was in a general Alarm." Oddly, the parish records for this period do not mention any disturbance.[117]

The Assembly took immediate action to quell fears by drafting "An Act for the better regulating and laying down a Method for the freeing of Slaves, and for the better regulating of them in the future." The Assembly's views of free blacks suggest that such individuals were responsible for much of Bermuda's racial tension. In early March the Assembly noted that free blacks and mulattos "do daily corrupt and debauch" the slaves. They "keep Tipling Houses for the entertainment and reception of our Slaves, they secrete the Inhabitants Goods, encourage our Slaves in Theft, and not only give their Advice and Assistance therein, but by their Example prompt them to Vice and

115. For the full text of the act and its accompanying provisions, see *Journals of . . . Assembly,* 2:967–68.
116. Popple to Board of Trade and Plantations, February 28, 1762, in CO 37/19: 54–55.
117. See Hallett, *Colonial Church,* 367.

Luxury."[118] In a letter to Governor Popple regarding the abovementioned act, the council and Assembly argued that many blacks and mulattos were living in Bermuda "under a pretence of being Free-Born" and that such individuals often corrupted and debauched "those that are Slaves." Moreover, these supposedly free blacks were concerned "in the late intended Conspiracy . . . and are a growing Evil." There was danger that such individuals could "in combination with the slaves subvert the gov't."[119]

The text of the act to control such individuals justified its regulations, on the grounds that "whereas it has been thought fit in His Majesty's Colonys in America to allow of Slaves And whereas where Slavery is allowed the giving Freedom to Slaves unless conducted with great Care may be attended with ill Consequences both as to the general Good of these Islands and private Property."[120] Under this act, an intended manumission would first be declared "by some creditable white Person in the Parish Church . . . at the Time of divine Service and whilst the Congregation is generally present." The slaveholder would then apply to the governor and council, "who upon due Inquiry made of such Slave or Slaves so to be freed hath done any thing meritorious and worthy of Freedom shall and may give leave . . . and grant a license." The duly manumitted slave was required to leave Bermuda within six months. No free blacks would be allowed to reside in the colony except "such Negro Molatto or Indian who having been born free from Father to son and who can produce a Certificate from the Justice of the Peace and two sufficient freeholders of their having lived irreproachably and in strict Conformity to the Laws of these Islands." This act, however, was disallowed by the crown on the grounds that it was "unjust" and "unconstitutional."[121]

At the end of March 1762, after martial law had ended, the governor, council, and Assembly still harbored fears of a French invasion abetted by Bermudian blacks. Popple wrote to England of his government's unease over such an invasion, with the French "joining our disaffected Negroes, who have lately been detected in a dangerous Conspiracy & intended Massacre of the White Inhabitants."[122] If Bermuda should fall into the hands of the French, said Popple, trade between the West Indies and America would be harmed, since ships must pass Bermuda—some within sight of land. In April 1762 Popple lamented Bermuda's scattered population, and the "want of a large body of Inhabitants living together in some part or other of these Islands."

118. *Journals of . . . Assembly,* 2:976.
119. Letter to Governor Popple, March 25, 1762, in CO 37/19: 64.
120. Manuscript Acts, 1762–1779.
121. Ibid.
122. Popple to the Earl of Egremont, March 31, 1762, in CO 37/19: 58.

There ought to be, he thought, a place "where a Body of Men, collected together, might become a means of defence for the whole Community."[123]

The written record for the 1761 plot is fragmentary, and the account of the trial of six slaves on April 30, 1762, has not survived. The only record of the trial is a bill submitted to the council in January 1762/1763 for expenses related to the trial and execution of the six conspirators. They were listed by name, owner, and monetary value. First on the list was Natt (belonging to the late Thomas Cox, a Devonshire shipwright), valued at £70. The others were Juan (whose owner was Joseph Prudden, a Southampton ship's carpenter), £33.06.08; Peter (the property of Edward Parker of Warwick), £91; Ben (belonging to Elisha Prudden, probably of Southampton), £42.13.08; Nancy (the property of Jonathan Tucker, a Sandys merchant), £22; and Mingo (a slave of Richard Jennings of Smith's or Southampton), £40.[124] The ringleader of the plot was said to be Peter, the slave belonging to Edward Parker.[125] As for the great number of other slaves said to be involved, one rumor put the total at between "6 and 700 negro men and women." In the aftermath of the trial an unknown number of slaves were transported, some to Maryland, others to the West Indies. Among the accused were three men named as Cuff, Tom, and Peter (the one whose boast had set off the conspiracy), sentenced to be sent "to some remote part of Maryland never to return here again under pain of Death." Upon further consideration, Governor Popple revoked their banishment, persuaded that their knowledge of Bermuda's waters and skills as ships' pilots would make them too useful to enemies of the colony. Instead, the three were to remain in Bermuda but could "never henceforth Pilot or Conduct any Deckt Vessel coming into or going out" of Bermuda's harbors.[126]

The government's fears eventually gave rise to "An Act for the better Government of Negroes, Mulattoes and Indians, Bond or Free, and for the more effectual punishing Conspiracies and Insurrections of them," passed in 1764.[127] This act added the crimes of plotting insurrection, attempting to poison, and administering medicines to an already-long list of felonies

123. *Journals of . . . Assembly*, 2:989.

124. Joseph Prudden's will is in Book of Wills, vol. 9, pp. 281, 299. Edward Parker, who died intestate in 1783, may have been Governor Popple's secretary. Jonathan Tucker's 1765 inventory is in Books of Wills, vol. 8, pp. 357, 362. See also Hallett, *Early Bermuda Wills*, 427, 466, 316.

125. Williams, *Historical & Statistical Account*, 76–77. The author does not provide any documentation for this reference.

126. Book of Bills, Deeds, and Protests, 1739–1766, 107–9, Bermuda Archives. See also *Annual Register*, 1762, 76, quoted in Smith, *Slavery in Bermuda*, 106–7.

127. *Journals of . . . Assembly*, 2:1076. This act is reprinted in Michael Craton, James Walvin, and David Wright, eds., *Slavery, Abolition, and Emancipation: Black Slaves and the British Empire* (New York: Longman, 1975), 175–78.

punishable by death "without benefit of Clergy." But this law was to remain largely unenforced: The conspiracy of 1761 was Bermuda's last recorded slave plot.

In some ways Bermuda's recorded slave conspiracies reinforce models put forth by scholars of slave resistance in other slaveholding societies.[128] The various explanations for outbreaks of slave unrest elsewhere, such as economic hardships, wars, oppressive treatment, unassimilable elements in the population, weakened forces of control, and frustrated slave expectations fall neatly into place in Bermuda's history. In fact, every one of Bermuda's recorded incidents of organized slave conspiracies can be at least partially explained by one of the aforementioned causes: The 1656 plot followed a witchcraft scare and a time of political and religious turmoil during the English Civil War; the unassimilable Irish caused the trouble in 1661; economic hardships and frustrated slave expectations after the petition of 1669 may have inspired the 1673 conspiracy; in 1682 a Jamaican slave was the ringleader, and political tensions over Bermuda's becoming a royal colony may have weakened the forces of control; in 1761 fears of a French invasion during the French and Indian War unsettled the islands' whites. What must be explained is the remarkable absence of slave conspiracies in Bermuda from the 1760s to the end of slavery in 1834. Besides its atypical chronology of slave rebellion, Bermuda was unique among England's slaveholding colonies in another respect: None of its organized efforts at slave rebellion resulted in the deaths of whites. Moreover, in five conspiracies and one poisoning scare, relatively few slaves lost their lives. There were two executions in 1656, two in 1730, and six in 1761, but in 1661, 1673, and 1682 none of the alleged conspirators was given the death penalty.

When the 1761 crisis had ended, Governor Popple was certain that prompt action had averted a catastrophe: "Is there any one among us," he asked, "that is not convinced but that the Negroes might have butcher'd half the Inhabitants before the other half had known anything of it?" But no whites had been "butcher'd" in the conspiracy of 1761, and that was Bermuda's last recorded slave conspiracy. In the Caribbean, however, the period of slave

---

128. See, for example, Craton's model for the British Caribbean in *Testing the Chains,* 13–14. See also Craton, *Empire, Enslavement, and Freedom in the Caribbean* (Princeton: Marcus Wiener, 1997), and David Barry Gaspar, *Bondmen and Rebels: A Study of Master-Slave Relations in Antigua* (Baltimore: Johns Hopkins University Press, 1985); Mullin, *Africa in America;* Aptheker, *Slave Revolts;* Gerald Mullin, *Flight and Rebellion: Slave Resistance in Eighteenth Century Virginia* (New York: Oxford University Press, 1972); Davis, *Rumor of Revolt.* The political ideology of the American Revolution and the early Republic may have inspired slave revolts. See Frey, *Water from the Rock,* and Douglas R. Egerton, *Gabriel's Rebellion: The Virginia Slave Conspiracies of 1800 and 1802* (Chapel Hill: University of North Carolina Press, 1993); Aptheker, *Slave Revolts,* 209.

rebellions was just beginning. Sixteen of Jamaica's 22 revolts, four of Antigua's five, and all four of the uprisings in the Bahamas took place after 1700, with the majority of revolts in the other British island possessions occurring after the mid-eighteenth century. On the mainland as well, as the Stono Rebellion of 1739, the New York uprising of 1741, Gabriel Prosser's plot in 1800 in Virginia, Denmark Vesey's in South Carolina in 1822, and Nat Turner's rebellion in Virginia in 1831 form a chronology of slave unrest much later than Bermuda's.[129]

Although slave uprisings in Bermuda were comparatively mild in their consequences, the number of attempted rebellions, taken with the frequency of individual acts of resistance, is evidence that Bermuda's slaves craved freedom no less than their counterparts in the Caribbean or on the American mainland. Why, then, did they cease to plot rebellions after 1761? One reason is that by the latter part of the eighteenth century blacks in Bermuda were part of a slave society whose patterns of slaveholding and ways of making a living were unlike those of any other English colony.

129. For the Caribbean, see Higman, *Slave Populations*, 335–39. See also Wood, *Black Majority;* Davis, *Rumor of Revolt;* Edgerton, *Gabriel's Rebellion;* John Lofton, *Insurrection in South Carolina: The Turbulent World of Denmark Vesey* (Yellow Springs, Ohio: Antioch Press, 1964); Stephen B. Oates, *The Fires of Jubilee: Nat Turner's Fierce Rebellion* (New York: Harper and Row, 1975).

6 Families, White and Black

During a time when tensions between England and the 13 colonies on the North American mainland were growing, during a war for independence that disrupted the entire Atlantic community, and during the aftermath of that war that sparked rebellions in Haiti and elsewhere, Bermuda society remained remarkably stable. From the 1770s to the 1830s, while acts of slave resistance and organized uprisings were becoming more frequent on the mainland of North America and in the Caribbean, slaveholders and slaves in Bermuda went about business as usual, with little or no discernible change in their attitudes toward each other. To judge from the extant records, Bermuda's blacks continued to disregard white authority and assert themselves as they had done since 1623, when the first law regulating their behavior was passed. And white slaveholders continued to be lax about enforcing rules, as they had been from the start. But Bermuda had changed in other ways, and some of those changes may help explain why slavery in this island colony took a different turn. Part of that story lies in the patterns of slaveholding and making a living in Bermuda's tribes, or parishes, as they came to be called by the latter part of the eighteenth century.

From the beginning of Bermuda's tribes, slaveholding families and slave families had lived in closer proximity than most slaveholders and slaves in the Caribbean or on the North American mainland, and that intimacy continued to shape the institution of slavery in this island colony. As the decades passed, the size of individual landholdings, most under 50 acres to begin with, grew even smaller, and blacks and whites lived ever closer together as the population grew.[1] One colonial governor remarked that Bermuda was "very well Inhabited; the Houses lying so near, that the whole Country looks like one continu'd Village, or rather like the Neighborhood of some large City."[2] Living so close together, often under the same roof, encouraged a certain familiarity between blacks and whites and broadened the perimeters of acceptable conduct.

1. Greene, in *Pursuits of Happiness*, 153, notes that by 1774, with a population of 11,155, there was a ratio of 1.09 acres of land per person.
2. Hope, "Description of the Bermudas," 214.

George James Bruere, who followed William Popple as governor of Bermuda in 1764, was shocked at the leniency many masters exhibited toward their slaves. In a speech before the Assembly in 1766 he pleaded for the establishment of "a proper order and decency of manners" and reminded his audience of the need to "bring your Negroes to a better regularity and due obedience." The governor exhorted slaveholders to control their slaves, to "prevent their unlawfull Assembly's, Thefts, and pernicious practices of leaving their Masters Houses and going to meetings . . . by night." Bruere proposed a solution completely foreign to the tenor of life in Bermuda: An end to slaves' wandering about without permission, he told the Assembly, could "easily effect by haveing their names called over Evenings and Mornings, or having the Doors lock'd where they are, under the inspection of a white Person, which the British law always intended you should have, I mean in the capacity of an overseer."[3] Governor Bruere's perception of slavery was obviously based on his knowledge of that institution in other British colonies, where large numbers of plantation slaves were controlled by overseers. But Bermuda's slaveholders, with comparatively few slaves, had no overseers in 1764. They had never had any.

Bermuda's 1,250-acre parishes were themselves as large as some plantations in other colonies. But instead of being controlled by a vigilant plantation overseer, a Bermuda slave usually was watched by a nonchalant parish constable. As a result, despite the severity of the laws against a slave's being abroad without a master's permission, slaves continued (as they always had) to visit each other and to move about freely. Members of the parish vestry were supposed to be a force for social order, but until the late eighteenth century they seldom functioned as such. Although an act of 1627 had provided for a vestry of 13 men in each tribe, early records suggest that vestries were elected sporadically and met infrequently, if at all. Governor John Bruce Hope had ordered each tribe to choose a vestry in 1724, but the individual parish records indicate that most did not meet regularly until the 1770s. Pembroke Parish, for example, began annual elections of vestrymen in 1771.[4]

Besides constables, churchwardens, and vestrymen, two other parish officers, a jumper and a poundkeeper, were supposed to help keep order. Not long after the slave conspiracy of 1761, the office of "jumper" was created especially for punishing disobedient slaves. Many masters were evidently reluctant to administer whippings as punishment for their slaves, but by the 1760s a master wishing to discipline an errant slave could hire the parish jumper (so called

3. *Journals of . . . Assembly,* 2:1187.
4. On parish government, including vestries, churchwardens, and assessors, see Hallett, *Colonial Church,* 358–66.

because his whipping made the slave jump) to perform that task. Southampton had a jumper by 1765, and in Pembroke, Daniel Yates, a carpenter, was appointed that parish's first jumper in 1771.[5] The office of parish poundkeeper was established in 1762 to protect individuals' gardens and crops from stray livestock. Under the terms of this act each parish was to build a pound and appoint a poundkeeper to round up wandering livestock and hold them until their owners paid a fine. Pembroke Parish had had a poundkeeper since 1740.

Law enforcement where slavery was concerned was a perennial problem in all the parishes, partly because of lax local officials and also because of the lack of a well-defined and politically powerful slaveholding class. Here Bermuda stands in contrast to the Chesapeake, where the emergence of a patriarchal planter elite and well-defined class system strengthened the institution of slavery.[6] In Bermuda, people from all levels of society owned slaves, and no one group emerged as an advocate for enforcing slavery laws. A slave could as easily have a master of humble means as one of great wealth. Moreover, each class had its own reasons for disregarding the rules. Members of Bermuda's merchant elite, for example, were often at odds with the colony's governors and engaged in smuggling. It was not to their advantage to bring charges for vagrancy or theft upon the loyal slaves who built and sailed their vessels and loaded and unloaded their goods, or on the slaves of their close neighbors who conveniently ignored clandestine trading activities. A valuable slave accused of a crime could spend unprofitable time in jail or, worse yet, be executed for a serious crime. The same argument could be made for the slaveholder of modest or humble means, who could not afford to lose the labor of a slave hired out for wages. Thus none of Bermuda's slaveholders stood to gain by actively prosecuting slaves for petty crimes and misdemeanors.

As for the slaves themselves, they continued to flout the laws in a subtle assertion of autonomy and to flourish in small family groups within their masters' households. A Bermuda slave might belong to a household with one, two, ten, or 15 slaves—never as many as the 50 to 100 or more on a large plantation. Slaveholding in this island colony had always been in small numbers, with the 38 slaves owned in 1773 by Horace Wood, a merchant in Pembroke Parish, the largest number recorded by a single Bermuda slaveholder in the eighteenth century. Although Bermuda's slaves lacked the communal life of

5. On the office of jumper, see ibid., 366–68.
6. See Kulikoff, *Tobacco and Slaves,* 12–13. See also Philip D. Morgan, *Slave Counterpoint: Black Culture in the Eighteenth Century Chesapeake and Lowcountry* (Chapel Hill: University of North Carolina Press for the Omohundro Institute of Early American History, 1998), and the entire collection of essays on slave life in Larry E. Hudson Jr., *Working toward Freedom: Slave Society and Domestic Economy in the American South* (Rochester, N.Y.: University of Rochester Press, 1994).

their fellows on large plantations, they had another kind of community: their parish neighbors—the slaves of households adjacent to their masters' houses. The Bermuda parish was itself a community of many households, black and white, and in the bonds of that parish community may lie some of the reasons for the Bermuda's notable lack of slave rebellions after 1761.[7]

Early census records unfortunately do not give many details of neighborhoods and households, but from time to time in the eighteenth century each parish took its own more detailed census of households and their occupants. Records for one of those parishes, Pembroke, are more complete than the others for the 1770s and may serve as a window through which to view parish life. In 1773 all eight of Bermuda's parishes were surveyed by order of the governor, but only the Pembroke Parish survey, taken in November 1773, has survived.[8] A 1774 summary of its data, along with that of the seven other parishes and St. George's, is in table 6. The Pembroke survey offers a unique portrait of a neighborhood and its residents, black and white. It gives the number of men and women, boys and girls; the number of sailors and "men at sea"; the number of sailing vessels; and the acreage owned by each householder. By comparing it with data from Richard Norwood's survey of 1663 it is possible to see both the continuity of some families and the striking changes in the size of individual landholdings and population over a hundred years.

In 1663, Pembroke had, on its 1,250 acres, 41 households on small plots of land, 28 of them on property of only 12 to 24 acres. In fact, as noted in chapter 3, Pembroke was one of the more crowded neighborhoods in Bermuda. Pembroke slaves and slaveholders knew each other well: They fished together, sailed together, and met often on the "common paths," as they were called, that crisscrossed the parish. Wills sometimes defined bequests of land in terms of their relation to such paths. For example, Pembroke resident John Johnston, who lived near the western end of the parish, defined the land he bequeathed in 1773 to one of his sons by its bordering "the common path down to the sea."[9] In 1773 Pembroke Parish had 147 white households— more than three times as many as in 1663—on the same 1,250 acres. All but 28 of the 147 householders were also slaveholders, most of them heads of

7. The importance of interracial contacts in Bermuda's neighborhoods was borne out by Cyril Outerbridge Packwood, a native Bermudian and longtime librarian of the Bermuda Library, in 1990. Packwood, who grew up near Bailey's Bay in Hamilton Parish, recalled "the white Outerbridges and the black Outerbridges" in that neighborhood. Cyril Outerbridge Packwood, interview by the author, Hamilton, Bermuda, August 1990.

8. "Number of Inhabitants of Pembroke Parish, November 2, 1773," St. John's Church records, microfilm reel 37, Bermuda Archives.

9. Books of Wills, vol. 12, pt. 1, p. 33.

Table 6   Whites and Blacks in Bermuda, 1774

Whites

Parish	Muster Roll	Men Otherwise	Men at Sea	Women	Boys	Girls
St. George's	136	13	68	282	129	131
Hamilton	98	13	21	181	136	111
Smith's	83	14	37	153	77	63
Devonshire	115	16	50	172	129	100
Pembroke	163	8	72	267	155	136
Paget	97	18	25	175	115	89
Warwick	216	12	72	228	123	120
Southampton	152	29	73	293	172	139
Sandys	133	40	80	252	163	185
Totals	1193	163	498	2003	1199	1074

Blacks

Parish	Men	Women	Boys	Girls
St. George's	123	163	150	130
Hamilton	120	148	131	115
Smith's	66	94	80	55
Devonshire	114	112	94	95
Pembroke	178	175	168	143
Paget	152	167	133	110
Warwick	162	187	165	139
Southampton	184	223	164	142
Sandys	176	162	141	164
Totals	1275	1431	1226	1093

"General List of the Number of Inhabitants, Number of Vessels, Number of Sailors . . . 1774 by Order of His Excellency George James Bruere Esquire Governor &c.," in "Reports on Bermuda by Two 18th Century Governors," *BHQ* 25, no. 2 (1968): 60–61.

families, with slave families in their care. With over 80 percent of its residents as slaveholders, Pembroke stands in striking contrast to comparable rural areas in other British colonies with slaves, such as counties in eighteenth-century Virginia or South Carolina, where no more than 60 percent of the residents held slaves, or Georgia, where that figure was around 25 percent. In Middlesex County, Virginia, for example, about half the households held slaves by 1740.[10] In Bermuda, on the other hand, slaveholding was widespread, and only a small number of households were without slaves.

Another marked difference between Bermuda and slave societies elsewhere is that individual properties were small, and they had grown progressively smaller as the population grew larger. In Pembroke, for example, an average of 30 acres per household in 1663 had declined to fewer than nine acres, with many holdings as small as one or two acres. Additionally, in 1663 more than 21 percent of the residents of Pembroke owned the land they lived on; in 1773 more than 42 percent were landowners—but the average size of the properties they owned had shrunk by two-thirds. Pembroke did not then have a town (Pembroke's modern city of Hamilton, which would become Bermuda's capital, was not founded until 1790),[11] but in population density the parish was more like a sprawling modern suburb than a rural area with farms or plantations in the hundreds of acres. In 1773 Pembroke's population was 1,393: 729 were white; 664 were black. They went to church together; their children attended school together, although the documentation of their attendance is not extensive. Pembroke's educated slaves may have played a part in the petition for freedom in 1669, and four slaves from Pembroke were ringleaders in the conspiracy plot of 1673.

Pembroke's people were scattered over a peninsula bordered by the Atlantic Ocean on the north, the Great Sound on the west, and the sheltered harbor of Crow Lane (now called Hamilton Harbor) on the south. On its eastern, or landward, side, Pembroke shares a one-mile-long boundary with its immediate neighbor, Devonshire Parish. In the early days of settlement the land itself was not highly regarded, being heavily wooded with cedar and containing many windswept areas not well situated for growing tobacco or other crops. Consequently, Pembroke's residents had long looked to fishing and seafaring

10. Rutman and Rutman, *A Place in Time,* 184. By the 1770s two-thirds of Virginia colonists in the tidewater regions and about 40 percent of those in the piedmont were slaveholders. Frey, *Water from the Rock,* 9. The Georgia estimate is from Wood, *Slavery in Colonial Georgia,* 107. On other English colonies' slaveholding ratios, see Walvin, *Black Ivory,* 71, 88.

11. On the early history of Hamilton, see Jean de Chantal Kennedy, *Biography of a Colonial Town: Hamilton, Bermuda* (Glasgow: Robert MacLehose and Co., 1961), and Henry Wilkinson, *Bermuda from Sail to Steam: The History of the Island from 1784 to 1901* (London: Oxford University Press, 1973), 50–56.

or to occupations other than farming to make their livings. Timber in the form of Bermuda cedar trees was abundant, and fish from the waters that washed three sides of Pembroke's land provided food if not income. But for most of the seventeenth century Pembroke remained one of Bermuda's less prosperous tribes. Lying toward the center of the main island of Bermuda, Pembroke was not as advantageously situated for local "wrecking" as Sandys and Southampton on the west end, or St. George's on the east end, but Pembroke's residents could still look to trade for their living and perhaps to some "wrecking" in the Caribbean.[12] Since the middle of the seventeenth century Pembroke men like John Stowe, Thomas Wood, John Squire, and others had traded far and wide, both legally and illegally, sailing their sloops to Barbados, Jamaica, Antigua, and other ports in the West Indies, making the run northward to mainland ports from Charleston to Boston. And Pembroke slaves helped to build these vessels, to sail them, to handle the goods that freighted them.

From the great sloops with their tall masts to the tiny Bermuda dinghies, sailing vessels provided a living for many Pembroke residents, and seamanship became a skill of infinite worth to whites and blacks alike. In the latter part of the eighteenth century as many as 50 to 75 Bermuda vessels still made the thousand-mile voyage to the Turks Islands in the salt trade every year, and Pembroke sloops and sailors were a part of those trips, as well as other trading voyages to the mainland and the Caribbean. The crowded conditions of shipboard life, the shared dangers and triumphs over adversities, fostered a camaraderie that must be taken into account in the history of race relations in Bermuda, even though documentation of it is scarce. Pembroke's slaves and slaveholders had ample opportunities for such close relationships. Almost everyone lived close to the water; almost everyone traveled by water. As the map shows, Pembroke has an extensive coastline: more than five miles of inlets and coves and bays both large and small, with virtually no beaches. The coastal waters are deep enough for small craft to dock only a stone's throw from residences or storehouses. Even on the windy north shore, where the Atlantic Ocean washes the rocky coast, steps carved into the limestone here and there lead down to the water, providing lasting evidence of Pembroke residents' connection to the sea. Pembroke people—black and white—traveled by water, engaged in whaling at Whale Bay on the north coast near Spanish Point, and built ships at Daniel's Bay at the western end of Pembroke. Shipbuilding was

12. In 1785 Bermuda's Governor Henry Hamilton (for whom the town of Hamilton was named) remarked that most Bermudians made their livings "mostly from wrecking and smuggling" (quoted in Wilkinson, *Sail and Steam*, 30).

a major part of Bermuda's economic life, and the parish produced 40 to 50 vessels a year, ranging in size from 40 to 100 tons.[13]

As the decades passed, the sea took on an increasing importance in the lives of Pembroke's people, but they were also bound together by other means. For example, whites and blacks, slaveholders and slaves, attended services in St. John's, the parish church. Like other Bermuda churches, Pembroke's church had a "place for the Negroes," usually in a rear gallery.[14] St. John's was located almost in the center of Pembroke, north of Pembroke Marsh. There had been a church in Pembroke since at least since 1618, quite early in Bermuda's history.[15] Like other early buildings this house of worship was built of cedar framing with wattle-and-daub walls and a palmetto-thatched roof. Parishioners had added a 10-by-12-foot vestry in 1663, and in 1677 they had put in 10 casement windows in the main building. St. John's was seriously damaged by hurricanes in 1712 and 1716, and the parish records show the preparation to build a new church in the fall of 1716. That year Pembroke's landowners were required to supply 4,000 twelve-inch-square limestone building-stones, "besides the slate," for a structure 46 feet by 20 feet wide, with a porch and vestry each 16 feet square. By October 1717 a "double row of cedar trees was planted round the church in Pembroke Tribe, all within the bounds of the churchyard." For all that, the church was not large enough. If all of Pembroke's householders, their families, and their slaves attended services, there would have been more than 1,000 people crowded into the church. Although Pembroke's church was larger than some of the other churches, it obviously could not accommodate all its parishioners for a service. In fact, an estimate of church space for all of Bermuda in the early 1800s found seating for 2,383 whites and 610 blacks—or about 50 percent of the white population and 12 percent of the black.[16]

The level of Pembroke families' involvement in church life is suggested by a list of the occupants of the women's pews in the 1770s. Men and women still sat apart, as they had done in the seventeenth century. From Pembroke's

13. Wilkinson (ibid., 37) notes that two-thirds of these vessels were sold off the islands. Shipbuilding took place on the north shore of Devonshire, at the Crawl and Bailey's Bay in Hamilton, and "in every parish." On the salt trade in the late eighteenth century, see ibid., 35.
14. This quotation is from a description of the rebuilding of Smith's parish church in 1717, in Hallett, *Colonial Church*, 272. Bermuda's slaveholders were regularly reminded to see that their slaves attended church.
15. An assize record of 1618 notes that Judith Bayley engaged in "raylings miscallings and all other uncivil speeches in Pembroke tribe church." Assize of October 1618, CR, 1:11A; Lefroy, *Memorials,* 1:132.
16. Hallett, *Colonial Church*, 273, 294, 198. The later estimates are based on the census reports of 1806 and 1832.

147 households there were 122 women who had assigned seats in a total of 16 women's pews, ranging from the two "dubble seats" in the front of the church, where seating was according to age and social rank, to the two pews in the rear called "Maid Seats," where the young unmarried women sat. Among the surnames of the women in the two front pews are names of Pembroke's wealthier men: Hinson, Dunscomb, Stowe, Wood, Joel, Witter.[17] There were also 24 men's pews, owned by the leading mariners and merchants of the parish. A surviving record of the pews for 1781 lists the following names, which include the parish's most prominent men: Cornelius Hinson, Samuel Saltus, Joseph Wood, John Blackbourn, Nicholas Albuoy, Nathaniel Numan, William Leaycraft, William Dunscomb, Edward Dunscomb, Peter Godfrey, Horace Wood, George Darrell, Benjamin Pitt, David Eve, Joseph Stowe, Henry Butterfield, John Beek, Benjamin Dunscomb, William Morris, John Wainwright, and Thomas Whitney.[18] From 1767 to 1775 the pastor of the Pembroke church was the Reverend Thomas Lyttleton. He served as rector of the four "Eastern Parishes"—Hamilton, Smith's, Devonshire, and Pembroke. Pembroke was without a rector from 1775 to 1783, when the Reverend James Barker arrived. In the interim the vestry oversaw the glebe, including land, buildings, and timber.[19] In these years, during the American Revolution, there were only two clergymen—Alexander Richardson and John Moore—in all of Bermuda. Richardson served St. George's, and Moore was obliged to travel to the other parishes, apparently rotating his services. Hamilton, for example, had him "one Sunday in four."[20] Richardson's zeal in baptizing blacks and whites alike is noted in the preceding chapter.

The church provided one focus for parish life; schools provided another, for blacks as well as whites. Bermudians had never opposed blacks' learning to read and write, although the attendance of blacks at schools is not documented until the eighteenth century. Before that time, some slaveholders had favored educating their slaves, but neither whites nor blacks could depend upon public education. Schools came and went, as did their pupils. As early as 1638 the Somers Islands Company had established a free school, appointing Pembroke resident Richard Norwood as master of a school in nearby Devonshire Tribe. But many parents were "not able for to send their children five or six miles to

---

17. St. John's Church records, microfilm reel 37. For a study of sex ratios and the status of women in eighteenth-century Bermuda, see Elaine Forman Crane, "The Socioeconomics of a Female Majority in Eighteenth-Century Bermuda," *Signs: Journal of Women in Culture and Society* 15, no. 2 (winter 1990): 231–58.

18. Three names are unreadable. St. John's Church records, August 8, 1781, microfilm reel 37.

19. Ibid.

20. Hallett, *Colonial Church*, 157.

school." In 1652 a grand jury noted, "The desire of our people is to have their children read English, to write, and cypher" and requested that the land and monetary allocations for a free school be divided among the eight tribes so that "every poor man may have good thereby. And then some honest able men will be encouraged to undertake to teach their children in every parish . . . which now they cannot have it as they desire, which is a very sad thing."[21] Religious disagreements soon forced Norwood to resign from the Devonshire school, and he then opened a private school near his home in Pembroke for selected pupils.[22]

Plans for public schools in other tribes were drafted in 1662, when the Somers Islands Company ordered the Assembly to establish three locations for free schools in addition to the one in Devonshire. There was to be a school at the Overplus in Southampton, one in Warwick, and one at Bailey's Bay in Smith's Tribe. Hugh Wentworth Jr., the tenant on the Warwick school lands, was ordered to build a schoolhouse "of two rooms, one of them with a chimney, each room containing fourteen feet in breadth and sixteen feet in length, with tables, benches and other necessaries."[23] These specifications were very likely the same for the other schools. The Governor's Council was to appoint schoolmasters; the colony sheriff would collect the rents to pay them. Schoolmasters, however, were scarce, and schooling apparently sporadic. A letter from the governor and council to the Somers Islands Company asked "on behalf of the people as to the health of them and their children, that you would be pleased to send us some able physician and a good grammarian schoolmaster, and that the school lands might be united again for his encouragement." The aging Richard Norwood, no longer keeping his school in Pembroke, evidently encouraged this request, but this plan, like the earlier one, was not acted upon. By 1674 Pembroke residents, no doubt at Norwood's urging, began using St. John's Church as a school—with schoolmasters responsible for any damages caused by the students.

Plans for higher education in Bermuda were considered in the next century in a plan proposed by the English cleric George Berkeley. In 1724 he published *A Proposal for the better supplying of Churches in our Foreign Plantations and for converting the savage Americans to Christianity, by a College to be erected in the Summer Islands, otherwise called the Isles of Bermudas.* In this remote place, Berkeley thought, "the students may be safe from the contagion of vice and luxury" in a group of islands that "by their situation, temperament of the air,

21. Lefroy, *Memorials,* 2:37.
22. At one time Norwood had a school on Cox's Hill at Spanish Point. See Joyce Hall, "Norwood," *Bermudian* (December 1958): 48.
23. Lefroy, *Memorials,* 2:188, 206.

plenty of provisions, intercourse with the British plantations and other parts of America, as well by the plainness and frugality of manners observable in the inhabitants, appear a proper place for a college." Berkeley abandoned the plan for a college after he settled in Rhode Island.[24]

Throughout the eighteenth century, schooling in Pembroke, like schooling in the other parishes, was conducted mostly by independent schoolmasters, some brought in by families concerned for their children's education.[25] By 1746 there were at least eight schools in Pembroke, with from four to 20 pupils apiece, for a total of 90 children. These were truly neighborhood schools, held in private homes, much like the "dame schools" in the English colonies on the mainland. Reverend James Holiday, rector of the Eastern Parish, recorded his visits to eight schools in Pembroke in his diary of 1746. The teachers were all women: Mrs. Pitt, Mrs. Robinson, Mrs. Rollins, Mrs. Coverley, Mrs. Salter (Saltus), Mrs. Morris, and two unmarried women, Betty Stovell and Rebecca Dunscomb. The presence of a household's slave children in these schools is suggested by a notation in Holiday's diary in 1746, in which he observed that in one of them, a "negro girl" was the best scholar.[26] In 1748 a parish school for Pembroke was located in the kitchen of the parish rectory. With stone walls 20 inches thick, that structure was 50 feet long and 17 feet wide. It was used as a school until the 1820s.[27]

Schools were not part of the Pembroke census of 1773, but the families of all the women Reverend Holiday mentioned in his diary are listed in the census among the residents of Pembroke 27 years later. For example, among the 10 heads of households bearing the name Pitt were four widows—Mary, Martha, Elizabeth, and Sarah—some of them elderly, and perhaps one who was the young matron-schoolteacher of 1746. The six other Pitt households were married couples, so that one of those wives might also have been the "Mrs. Pitt" in Holiday's list. The number of widows in the Pitt family is silent testimony to the hazards of seafaring: Many of the Pitts, like other Pembroke residents, were mariners. Of the six men bearing the Pitt surname in 1773, four—Benjamin, Richard Jr., and two Williams—are listed as mariners.[28] Families of the other schoolteachers listed were also involved in that trade.

---

24. Hallett, *Colonial Church*, 307. It was some 50 years after Berkeley's proposal that Thomas Lyttleton, Pembroke's pastor, conceived his own plan for a college in Bermuda. See CO 37/11: 109.

25. Hallett, *Colonial Church*, 314–15.

26. "Diary of the Rev. James Holiday," 86.

27. "Journal of John Harvey Darrell," *BHQ* 2, no. 3 (1945): 129–42. The school is described on p. 142. Darrell was a pupil there under the Reverend Alexander Ewing, who was rector from 1791 to 1820.

28. All of the Pitt households contained slaves, ranging in number from the ten each owned by Samuel and one of the Williams, to the one owned by Richard Pitt Junior. See "Number of Inhabitants of Pembroke Parish."

There were four Robinson households in 1773. One was headed by Captain Francis Robinson, the owner of the 40-ton sloop *Fanny* and the master of 11 slaves. He and the other three Robinson men were mariners. Like the Pitts, all the Robinsons were slaveholders. There were three Rollins households in 1773, two headed by married men who were mariners, and neither owned any slaves. The other Rollins household was headed by Mary Rollins, perhaps a widow, who owned three slaves. There were two Stovells in 1773, Samuel and Joseph, both mariners; there were four Dunscombs, including Edward, the owner of the 60-ton sloop *Peggy*, and William, who owned the 50-ton *Jean*. The schoolteacher of 1746 named Saltus was related to Captain Samuel Saltus of 1773, the owner of the 50-ton *Mary*. Thus, of the eight Pembroke families whose women kept schools in their homes in the 1740s, all but one made their livings from the sea, and all but one owned slaves (ranging in number from one to 11) in 1773. Seafaring and slaveholding were an integral part of life in Pembroke Parish.

The importance of seafaring in Pembroke can be measured in the official census of the colony in 1774 (taken from the survey of 1773), which contains headings for both "Men at Sea" and "Sailors." Each white household has a listing, with a wealth of information. The survey lists the names of each householder, followed by columns headed "Whites" and "Blacks" to record the individuals living in a given household. The columns themselves are much more specific. Under "Whites" are the following categories:

Men on the Muster Roll [able-bodied men ages 16 to 65]	163
Men Otherwise [old or infirm]	8
Men at Sea [aboard a vessel or in a foreign port]	72
Women	267
Boys	155
Girls	136
Total white population	729

Under "Blacks" are listed:

Men	178
Women	175
Boys	168
Girls	143
Total black population	664

In addition there is a column headed "Vessels," and under it are spaces for the name and tonnage of the vessel, then "Sailors," and under that, "W" for white, and "B" for black. Last is a column titled "Acres of Land," with amounts ranging from one to 50 acres. All but a few items of the report are legible, and it affords a wealth of detail.

At the time of the 1773 survey there were 163 able-bodied white men in Pembroke, of whom nearly half, or a total of 72, were "at sea." There was also a separate census category for white men who were sailors by occupation as opposed to being "at sea." A man at sea was aboard a vessel under sail or in some foreign port; a sailor, black or white, was a crew member who worked for wages and took orders from the master of a vessel. The household of John Beek, for example, listed no sailors but had one man at sea, who would have been Beek himself. In 1773 he had a wife, three children, and two slaves, a woman and a boy. He did not own any land but made his living from the sea. The household of John Blackbourn listed no men at sea but had one white and one black sailor. Blackbourn was a landholder with 25 acres and a slaveholder with 16 slaves in 1773, but he also had interests at sea, with sailors (one of them probably his slave) working for wages aboard someone else's vessel.

Of the 178 black men in Pembroke, almost one-third, or a total of 59, were sailors. Most, if not all of them, were slaves. The official survey did not consider "at sea" as a census category for slaves, although that term was occasionally used to define a specific slave's status in an inventory. A slave listed as "at sea" in such instances was usually a runaway whose whereabouts were unknown. In 1773 blacks made up the majority of Pembroke's sailors: The survey lists 59 black and 46 white sailors, for a total of 105. Most of them sailed aboard the 11 sloops owned by Pembroke residents.[29] The men listed as white sailors were usually members of the white family, although a few may have been servants. Pembroke and Paget were the only Bermuda parishes in 1773 with more black sailors than white. As table 7 shows, three other tribes—Paget, Southampton, and Sandys—had more vessels and sailors than did Pembroke, but Pembroke is the only one of the eight tribes for which the detailed household census of 1773 has survived.

There were in Bermuda, according to a 1773 report by Governor Bruere, about 200 white "Seafaring Men" (72 of whom were Pembroke residents) and 400 "Negroe sailors [59 of whom were Pembroke residents] . . . besides the Rakers of Salt at Turks' Islands." In all Bermuda there were "between Eighty and One hundred Vessels [11 of which were owned by Pembroke shipowners] generally at Sea."[30] Thus Pembroke could lay claim to an important role in the colony's maritime economy. The 1773 Pembroke survey shows that this parish's sloops ranged in size from 25 to 60 tons, and manned by largely

29. The 10 Pembroke vessels listed in the 1773 survey (table 7) represent owners, not vessels, and hence do not include the Horatio Wood's two: the 50-ton *Ranger* and the 45-ton *Adventure*. In addition to these 11 sloops, Pembroke shipwright William Smith owned a half-interest in another vessel.

30. The text of Governor Bruere's report, along with the extant census data for the colony, is in "Reports on Bermuda by Two 18th Century Governors," *BHQ* 25, no. 2 (1968): 50–61.

Table 7	**Maritime Bermuda, 1774**		
1774: Ships and Sailors			
Area	Vessels	White Sailors	Black Sailors
St. George's	6	87	82
Hamilton	5		33
Smith's			
Devonshire	4	68	33
Pembroke	10	46	59
Paget	16	64	81
Warwick	6	168	70
Southampton	19	59	57
Sandys	20	80	66
Totals	86	572	481

"General List of the Number of Inhabitants, Number of Vessels, Number of Sailors . . . 1774 by Order of His Excellency George James Bruere Esquire Governor &c.," in "Reports on Bermuda by Two 18th Century Governors," *BHQ* 25, no. 2 (1968): 60–61.

black crews, they traded far and wide. "Our chief Trade," Bruere wrote, "is going to Turks' Islands for Salt. . . . And with the Produce from the Salt We buy and fetch all our Corn, Flour, Salt, Pork, Beef and Lumber for all Masts and Yards, Soap and Candles from North and South America, Philadelphia or New York. Our Sloops do frequently go to St. Eustatia, Santa Cruz, and Curacoa, with Ducks, Cabbage and Onions and likewise to our own West India Islands, and they may frequently on their return run Rum, Tea, or Calico's &c. from the above mentioned places, into the different Creeks and Harbours of Bermuda."[31] Mill Creek, Bosses Cove, and Daniel's Bay at the west end of Pembroke had long been places of such trade.

Besides his worries over the amount of illegal trade, Governor Bruere had concerns about the number of blacks aboard Bermuda vessels. In the 1770s black sailors made up the entire crews of most sloops, except for two whites as master and mate, yet there are no recorded instances of mutinies. Ironically, the governor was not so much fearful of the number of black sailors as he was concerned that not enough white Englishmen were acquiring necessary nautical skills: "This matter wants to be better Regulated in some Measure to have more White People, than two in each vessel, for the Benefit of the Nursery

31. Ibid., 52.

for British Sailors." He also thought that there were too many blacks living on the colony's public lands. "Several Widdows and *others*, having too many by far, which occasions very frequent Thefts, and makes the Inhabitants neglect to plant, because they are not certain, to reap the Fruits of their Labour, the Matter calls loudly for Redress, allowed on by most Persons."[32] Official concern notwithstanding, nothing was done. To Governor Bruere, the problem was rooted in the nature of Bermuda society: "The inhabitants are dispersed so much all over the Country that the Thefts are not to be easily prevented or detected, and Idleness and Indolence prevails, and the Cultivation of Corn and Tobacco, totally neglected, and they account their personal Estates from the Number of Negroes that they have, who are distroying their Substance every day, and plundering their Neighbours."[33] Land had always been scarce in Bermuda; slaves, on the other hand, had become plentiful. It is no wonder that an individual's wealth was often measured in the number of slaves rather than acres, but feeding so many mouths could be difficult.

All of the colony's cash, said Bruere, was "carried off to purchase Corn for our Negroes. . . . We buy only from Hand to mouth."[34] Like most colonial governors he feared that the result might be a famine or a slave rebellion and requested a company of British troops be stationed again in the islands, which had had no troops since 1730. Other island colonies, however, had had garrisons of British regulars since the early 1700s, and after 1763 five of the 20 regiments in British America were stationed in the Caribbean islands.[35] In 1771, in the wake of the Boston Massacre and fears of a war with Spain, colonial governors petitioned for more troops, and Bruere added his voice to theirs. Otherwise, he wrote, "how are we to Subdue or correct, the Numerous Negroes in case of any Insurrection." Troops would also provide a defense from privateers in wartime and, last but not least, protect shipwrecked "*Foreigners*" from Bermudians eager to loot shipwrecks. Bruere described the latter as "a rude uncouth sett of People Accustomed to benefit thereby."[36] Bruere's request for troops, however, was not granted.

Part of the reason for Governor Bruere's anxiety about the state of the

32. "The Humble Representation of the Wants and Defects and Improvements Necessary for the better Regulation of the Bermuda or Somers Islands," Bruere to the Earl of Hillsborough, August 18, 1770, in CO 37/20: 164–67.
33. Ibid., 165.
34. Ibid.
35. See Andrew O'Shaughnessy, "Redcoats and Slaves in the British Caribbean," in *Lesser Antilles,* ed. Paquette and Engerman, 105–28. Barbados was the only island colony that did not request troops during this period, perhaps because its ratio of four blacks to one white "was the lowest in the British island colonies." But Bermuda, where the number of blacks and whites was almost equal, is not taken into account here.
36. Ibid.

colony was the increase of Bermuda's black population. By 1773 nearly half (47 percent) of the colony's people were blacks. Bermuda's slaveholders, unlike the owners of slaves in the Caribbean or on the mainland, had little reason to rejoice over the increase in their slave property. Although having a number of slaves conferred a certain social status upon the owner, it also carried an economic burden. It is reasonable to assume that in a place with a mild climate and a fertile soil, one or two adult slaves could plant corn and other food crops for a household's subsistence—but they did not. Male slaves who risked their lives at sea disdained fieldwork and considered tilling the soil as a pastime for children and old people.[37] By the eighteenth century Bermuda did not produce enough food to feed its growing population.

The rate of population growth for whites and blacks in Pembroke may be seen by a comparison of the November 1773 census with two earlier surveys, one taken in September 1764 and one in October 1723 (see table 8). Pembroke's black population was growing more rapidly than the white, and by 1773 there were more black men living in the parish than there were white men.

Of the 147 households in Pembroke in 1773, 118 had slaves. These 118 slave households contained 664 men, women, and children, or 13 percent of Bermuda's black population. Pembroke's 1773 census figures add some detail to that 13 percent, allowing a view of the structure of these slave households and inviting speculation about the quality of slave life in the colony as a whole. The first thing to note is that nearly all of the Pembroke slaves lived in households containing other slaves, usually family members. Of Pembroke's 353 adult slaves—178 men and 175 women—only 14 (seven men and seven women), or less than 4 percent of all the slaves in the parish, lived alone, as the single slave belonging to a white household. This stands in marked contrast to the situations of slaves in other colonies, in which an estimated 18 percent of the slaves lived alone, as the sole black in a white household.[38] Two of the single slaves in Pembroke were members of one-person white households. For example, Sarah Burgess, who lived alone and owned no land, had one slave woman in her household. Burgess's age is not recorded, but she was very likely an elderly widow who was cared for by a family slave. The other single woman with one female slave was Mary Burch, who, like Sarah Burgess, owned no land and was probably a widow. Both women were members of large and long-established Bermuda families: There were Burches and Burgesses living in Sandys Tribe in the 1663 survey. The rest of Pembroke's single female slaves lived in households with families. One was that of the parish minister

37. Wilkinson, *Sail and Steam*, 26.
38. Kolchin, *American Slavery*, 139.

Table 8

White Population of Pembroke Parish

	Men	Women	Boys	Girls	Total
1723	127	202	106	101	536
1764	142	236	154	116	648
1773	171	267	155	136	729

Black Population of Pembroke Parish

	Men	Women	Boys	Girls	Total
1723	75	103	85	96	359
1764	131	157	128	92	508
1773	178	175	168	143	664

"Number of Inhabitants whites and Blacks," in "Responses to the Questions of the Lords of Trade, 1723," CO 37/11: 49; "A General List of all the Inhabitants in His Majesty's Bermuda or Somers Islands . . . 1764," CO 37/19: 257; "General List of the Number of Inhabitants, Number of Vessels, Number of Sailors . . . 1774 by Order of His Excellency George James Bruere Esquire Governor &c.," in "Reports on Bermuda by Two 18th Century Governors," *BHQ* 25, no. 2 (1968): 60–61.

Thomas Lyttleton, who in 1773 lived on the glebe in a house with his two sons. Another single slave woman helped to care for the household of Samuel Stovell, a mariner with a wife and six children. The single slave women in these households generally had housekeeping chores and perhaps some child care and gardening to do, but no heavy fieldwork. Only two households with single female slaves—those of Daniel Beek and his wife, and Richard Stamers and his wife and another woman (most likely a relative)—owned land, and these families had only two acres apiece.

Some of the seven single slave men did some fieldwork or livestock tending as well as other chores, since four belonged to masters who owned from five to 25 acres. Five of the seven belonged to families of mariners or men listed as "at sea," and thus these slaves were the only male presence in households where the heads were often absent. There were obviously close and trusting relationships between these male slaves and the white women and children whom they protected. One of Pembroke's single male slaves was a black sailor whose wages helped support a household consisting of his master and three white women. The one remaining single male slave in the 1773 survey lived in the household of Daniel Yates, a carpenter, who served for several years as the Pembroke

Parish "jumper" responsible for whipping errant slaves. Yates was both jumper and constable in 1774 and 1775, and again in 1782.[39] One wonders if he used his slave to help him in performing his duties, perhaps carrying messages, running errands. Yates's slave would have had plenty of other work to do, both in the house and out of it. In 1773 the Yates household contained two women (one was his wife, Frances), two boys, and three girls. Yates also owned eight acres. Daniel Yates died intestate in 1785, leaving his widow, Frances, a modest estate worth only £87.6.8. Its entire contents are listed below:

a bed bedstead and 1 pr of sheets	£ 3.00.00
a half dozen of low Chairs	1.
1 pine chest 2 Iron Potts & 2 Trivets	.13.04
1 Pot 1 Tea Kettle 1 pine tubb 2 Earthen	.05.04
1 small Tub 1 pine Cupboard 1 Earthen Dish	.06.08
1 spinning wheal 1 Mortar 1 Wood Ax	1.06.08
1 pine Cart 2 planes 1 hand saw 2 stone Jugs	.09.04
1 Water pale 1 Chamber Pot	.01.04
2 Wine Glasses 1 box of knives & forks	02.08
1 tin Jug 1 Coff[ee] mill 1 lamp	.01.04[40]

Besides the household items, the Yates estate included a "Negro Man called James in possession of Mr. Solomon Joell" (a merchant, one of the wealthiest in Pembroke), valued at £80. Why Solomon Joell had taken possession of James, or what became of James afterward, is not known. The Joell family had a large number of slaves, and presumably James became a part of that household in his later years.

Besides the 14 adult slaves who lived alone as the sole servants in white Pembroke households, there were six slave boys who also served by themselves, but life for all of these boys, like that of the single adult slaves, was far from solitary. Two of the boys were in the households of widows with children, and two belonged to the families of men who did not go to sea. The other two were connected to households with maritime occupations. One of these boys served in the household of a sailor, Nathaniel Mitchell, who also owned 20 acres, and the other boy belonged to William White, a sailmaker. All of these households that had a single young black boy as a slave also had one or more white women. Gender roles cannot be documented, but it is likely that traditional women's work such as cooking, laundering, and mending was done by female hands—slave or free—and that young male slaves in a household

39. See entries for April 5, 1774, 1775 (n.d.), and April 1, 1782, St. John's Church records, microfilm reel 37.
40. Books of Administrations, 1782–1835, 2:47, Bermuda Archives.

performed men's tasks such as fence-building, gardening, tending livestock, fishing, and running errands. In a household with white children, the slave boy would also have been a companion and playmate.

Most Pembroke households contained children of both races, and that provided another area of shared experience between slaveowner and slave. Of the 118 slave households, 96 contained children; only 22 households had adult slaves with no slave children. In contrast, on the small farms in slaveholding colonies on the North American mainland, a majority of the slave men and a "substantial" number of the slave women lived with no spouse or children.[41] Of the 664 slaves in Pembroke in 1773, 353, or over half, were adults. In a study of St. George's parish in South Carolina in the 1720s almost two-thirds (62 percent) of the slaves were adults. In that parish of 106 white households, 90 had fewer than 20 slaves, and the rural households were not close together. In Maryland, also, slave family life was "stunted" by isolation and few social contacts. Before 1710 most adult slaves were immigrants, and nearly half of them lived in units of fewer than 10 slaves; one-third were in units of five or fewer. In Virginia in the 1720s slaveholding households generally contained fewer than 10 slaves, but by the 1770s two-thirds of Virginia's slaves lived in households with 20 or more slaves, which facilitated the growth of slave families. In Georgia in the 1760s about one-fourth of the households had slaves, with the average number of slaves per household at 23. In the tidewater areas, half of the slaves lived in groups of 20 or more and another one-fourth in groups of 11 to 20. There as in Virginia the average size of a farm was 200 acres.[42] In Pembroke Parish in 1773 only 22 slave households contained no children, but there were 52 white households with no white children. But most adults lived with children of one race or another: Of the 147 households in Pemboke, only 11 contained no children, black or white. Of the 96 slave households with slave children, 40 contained two or more adult women with a number of children, suggesting two or more family groups.

It is impossible to match parents with children, but the total number of slave children per household yields some interesting facts. The typical slave household in Pembroke was a single-family one with one or two parents and one to four children. Of the 96 slave households with slave children, 84, or 87 percent, had from one to four children. Eleven slave households had from five to 10 children, and two households, which contained several adults and

41. Frey, *Water from the Rock,* 34, states that less than one-fifth of slaves on small farms lived in two-parent slave households.

42. On slave family life on the mainland, see Wood, *Black Majority,* 156–61; Menard, "The Maryland Slave Population, 1658–1730," 29–54, esp. 35–39; Philip Morgan and Michael Nicholls, "Slaves in Piedmont Virginia, 1720–1790," *WMQ,* 3d ser., 46, no. 2 (April 1989): 211–51, esp. 238; and Kulikoff, *Tobacco and Slaves,* 336–37; Frey, *Water from the Rock,* 10–11.

obviously more than one slave family, had 14 children each. Pembroke's slave families with children numbered at least 96, and 95 white families had children. Of the white families, 76 (80 percent) had from one to four children—a figure only slightly less than the slave families' 87 percent. The other 19 white families had from five to eight children apiece; 12 had five children, four had six children, one had seven children, and two families had eight children each. Pembroke's black families had a few more children—311 to 291—than did the white families, but all shared living space, and all shared the experience of family life: the joys and pains of childbirth, the nursing and nurturing of infants, the disciplining of children, and the common bonds between parent and child.

Many slave families, like many white families, shared another experience: the anxieties of having loved ones at sea. Of Pembroke's 118 slave households, 26 had from one to 10 black sailors, and another 46 slave households were attached to slaveholding families with one or more white men at sea. Those left behind, whether white or black, knew the worry of waiting many days, sometimes weeks or months, for loved ones to come home safely from long voyages. Often the head of the household in the master's absence was his wife, who had to take charge of not only her children, but the men, women, and children of her slave household. Of Pembroke's 72 households with men at sea, 34 contained adult male slaves who were under the supervision or control of a woman in the master's absence. Of the other households with men at sea, some contained other white men; others, no women; and some did not have any adult male slaves. While wives often took over for husbands at sea, single women who headed households bore that responsibility all the time.

Most of the Pembroke women listed as the heads of households in 1773 were widows who lived on their late husbands' properties. For example, Mary Whitney, who had 16 slaves in 1773, was the widow of David Whitney, who died in 1761. Her household is listed in the survey as containing one white woman (herself) and a black household with eight men, four women, and four boys. Of the men, at least two were sailors. Mary Whitney also owned 16 acres. In the spring of 1776 the mistress of this establishment, being "weak in Body but of Sound and perfect Mind and Memory," made a will. She died that June. Her will, probated June 18, 1776, offers a glimpse of familial relationships, white and black, in a Bermuda slaveholding household.[43] The childless Mary Whitney made careful division of her land and slaves among various nieces and nephews, and she also provided for her slaves. Bequeathing a "dwelling house" and land with "two Negro Cabbins" to a grand-niece, she specified that some of her slaves were to continue to live on that property: "my now Negroes

43. Books of Wills, vol. 12b, pt. 2, p. 383. For Whitney's inventory, see vol. 9, p. 200.

called Matt, Auber and Tim to live in the said Cabbins during their respective Lives." Mary Whitney also freed her slaves—with some strings attached: "I give to my Several Slaves, namely Old Jemmy, Tim the son of Old Jane, Matt and Auber each their respective freedom from the time of my Death, and my other Negroes namely Joe, Robin, Peter, Ben, Dick, Sam, Martha and Kitt, I give to each of them their respective Freedoms immediately from and after the Deaths of their Mother Matt and their Sister and Mother Auba, and that in the mean while they be under the Controul of my Executors to oblige them to work as well to maintain and support themselves, as to maintain and support their said Mother and Sister during their and each of their Lives."[44]

Besides providing for her slaves, Mary Whitney remembered a friend in her will, another Pembroke widow who had an even larger household and fewer resources than herself. She made a bequest to Mary Eve, who was left with five children at the time of her husband's death in 1773. Her husband, Francis, was evidently ill when he made his will in May of 1773, and he died a few months later. His will was probated October 7, 1773.[45] Francis Eve, like many other Pembroke men, was a mariner, and he owned the *Mary,* a sloop named after his wife. He may have ventured more than he could afford in trade, for in his will he ordered his executors to sell the *Mary,* along with "three Negro Wenches." The money from the sale was to be added to the appraisal value of his estate. This is one of the rare documentations of a Bermuda slaveholder's sale of slaves. It indicates the seriousness of Francis Eve's illness and his desire to provide as much as he could for his wife and children. He had good reason to be concerned: After his death Mary Eve's household would consist of 26 people: herself and her five children, her adult slaves (two men, four women), and their children (eight boys, six girls). In 1773 they all lived on a half acre, which contained a dwelling house, storehouse, and wharf. For income they depended on one white "man at sea," who may have been one of Mary's sons, and one black sailor, who was one of her slaves.

Another slaveowning widow was Martha Joell, in 1773 the owner of 12 slaves. But unlike Mary Eve, Martha Joell was well off. She had been married to Solomon Joell, a mariner, one of the richest men in Bermuda. His personal property at his death in 1767 came to £2,980.11.6, including £545 in slaves.[46] Joell was a part owner of two trading vessels, the *Savanna* (of which he had eleven-twelfths share), and the *Industry* (of which he owned two-thirds). His interest in these two vessels was valued at £951; his ships' stores and other merchandise came to £403. Joell's inventory also contained £379 in "ready

44. Ibid., vol. 12b, pt. 2, p. 383.
45. Ibid., vol. 12, pt. 1, p. 375.
46. Ibid., vol. 8, pp. 417–19.

Money with stores" and 1,200 gallons of rum valued at £160. There were 12 slaves in the inventory of Joell's estate: six sailors, a carpenter, four men listed as "Plantation Negroes," and one woman, Rosilla. One of the "Plantation Negroes" had no recorded value and was described as "Peter at Sea."

Runaway slaves seldom appear in Bermuda records, but Peter had apparently managed to get himself aboard a vessel and make a bid for freedom. Most Bermuda slaves were familiar with the ways of ships and the sea, and many besides Peter had opportunities to escape. Except for the occasional notation by a disgruntled slaveholder of a missing slave, the record is silent as to the number and frequency of such runaways. Peter, the runaway, was not a sailor by trade, but he, like most Bermudians, probably knew how to sail a boat. His work as a "Plantation Negro" may have included fishing, perhaps from the "large sailboat" listed in Joell's inventory. He may also have helped to load and unload his master's sloops, and no doubt he heard from his fellow slaves who sailed aboard these and other Bermuda vessels the tales of faraway destinations such as Antigua and St. Eustatias, Charleston and Philadelphia.

Solomon Joell's widow, Martha, had no black sailors among her 12 slaves in 1773, but she did have one white man at sea. That would have been the Joells' only son, Solomon. There were three white women, including the widow, in the household, two of whom were probably her unmarried daughters. The Joells had nine children in all. Six of the daughters were unmarried at the time of their father's death in 1767, and some may have been still single in 1773. Two of the daughters had married by 1767: A daughter whose name was also Martha was the wife of Pembroke's George Robinson; Susanna had married Richard Robinson, who may have been a relative of George. The other daughters were Mary, Hannah, Jane, Jehosheba, Frances, and Esther. Mary is listed as the occupant of a pew in St. John's Church, Pembroke, about 1773.[47] Martha Joell had 14 slaves—more than enough to tend her 12 acres. There were seven adult men, two women, two boys, and three girls. It is interesting to note the growth of slave families in this household: Six years earlier there had been only one woman, Rosilla, and no children among the dozen Joell slaves. Now there were five slave children. It is also interesting that where Solomon Joell had had six black sailors, Martha Joell had none. She is the only one among the four Pembroke widows who owned 10 or more slaves who did not have at least one black sailor. Mary Whitney had two black sailors; Mary Eve, one; Elizabeth Eve had 10 slaves, with one black sailor; Sarah Tuzo, with 13 slaves, had two black sailors.

Sarah Tuzo, like Mary Joell, presided over a slave household that multiplied after the death of her husband, Benjamin Tuzo, in 1766. At that time he

47. See Hallett, *Early Bermuda Wills*, 318.

had only four slaves—three men and one woman. But seven years later the survey of 1773 lists his widow as the owner of 13 slaves: three men, five women, three boys, and two girls. Like the slave household of Solomon and Martha Joell, the Tuzos' slaves had formed families within a few years. At least one, and perhaps two, of the Tuzos' slaves had been in the Tuzo family for many years. In 1748 Benjamin Tuzo's father, Luke, a Pembroke sailmaker, bequeathed his "Negro Boy named Rigg" to his son, Benjamin. The elder Tuzo also left a "Yellow Wench named Anne" who is later referred to as Nanny in his will, to his wife and two daughters, "to wait upon them during their Life and hers, and in case of death in my Family said Nanny to belong to the oldest Survivors." In 1766, the inventory of Luke Tuzo's son Benjamin lists a "Negro woman Nancy" at £5, who was almost certainly the same person as the Nanny of 1748. The "Negro Boy," Rigg, was a grown man in 1766.[48] Sarah Tuzo, whose husband left her four slaves named Nancy, Rigg, Pompey, and Sam, had only a modest estate worth £288.18.4, £210 of which was the value of the slaves. Seven years later, however, Sarah Tuzo had a much larger slave household to support: Rigg, Pompey, and Sam had acquired wives and children by 1773. The slaves had multiplied from four to 13, and Sarah Tuzo had two other white adults, a man (perhaps a son) and another woman besides herself to feed, clothe, and shelter—all on one acre. Benjamin Tuzo's inventory mentioned "1/4 sloop at sea" but did not give any monetary value. It may have been lost. And so the widow Tuzo's large household depended for its livelihood on the efforts of one white "man at sea" and two black sailors.

Elizabeth Eve, the other widow with a relatively large number of slaves, was also the wife of a mariner.[49] Her husband was William Eve, whom she married in 1744. The date of her husband's death is not known, but she was a middle-aged widow in 1773. She lived in a household with two other women, who might have been her unmarried daughters. Her slave household consisted of 10 people: three men, two women, three boys, and two girls. All of these individuals lived on two acres. Elizabeth Eve, like most of the other widows in Pembroke, hired out one of her slaves as a sailor.

Hiring out slaves for wages was one way for a woman heading a household to ease economic burdens. Manumission was another. Martha Pitt, who is listed in the 1773 survey as the head of a household with seven slaves, freed three of them in her 1779 will. She may have been the daughter of John Pitt of Pembroke, who died in 1762. Aging and unmarried (her will describes her

---

48. Luke Tuzo's date of death is not known.
49. Elizabeth Eve was the daughter of Pembroke resident Lewis Johnson. See Books of Wills, vol. 8, pp. 40, 398, 399.

as an "ancient woman"), Martha Pitt had one man, two women, two boys, and two girls in her slave household. She wrote in her will:

> I give unto my Negro Woman Ruth at my decease her entire Freedom, for and in consequence of her faithfull services, to be to her own use and behoofe for Ever.
> I give unto my Negro Woman Dinah at my decease her entire freedom for and in consideration of her faithfull services, to be to her own use and behoofe for Ever.
> I give unto my Negro girl Little Ruth her entire Freedom for an in consideration of her being Lame, to be to her own use and behoofe for Ever.[50]

Manumissions were not always motivated by unselfish interests, as the above suggests. Martha Pitt freed two women, probably past their prime, and a little lame girl, but she kept her able-bodied slaves: the man, two boys, and a girl. She left most of her estate, including "all the rest of my Negroes and their Issue," to her widowed sister, Mary Wood. Perhaps she did not wish to impose upon her elderly sister the care of slaves who were old or unable to work.

Of 33 Pembroke households headed by women in the survey, 25 had slaves. Sixteen of the 25, including that of Martha Pitt, had no white men in their households, but 10 of them had slave households containing one or more adult black men. One wonders what relationships existed in these households where the voice of authority was a lone female, perhaps an elderly one at that. Some of these Pembroke women's households may have been the ones Governor Bruere referred to as those with slaves allowed to range freely and to pilfer goods from others. Many of these female-headed households were poor: The women in charge had households of slave men, women, and children ranging from one to 20, not to mention their own families. What did they live on? Most of them did not grow any crops; only 10 of Pembroke's women slaveholders were listed as holding land, and that was in small amounts. The rest were dependent on the labor or the wages of their slaves to feed their households. Often the number of adult, able-bodied slaves to hire out was not large. Ten, or nearly half, of the women slaveholders had only one or two slaves. Five of these women had only a single slave (four had a female slave; one, a slave boy). Among the remaining female slaveholders, the number of slaves they had ranged from one to 20, with five widows—Elizabeth Eve, Sarah Tuzo, Martha Joell, Mary Whitney, and Mary Eve—holding ten, 13, 14, 16, and 20, respectively. But slave children were numerous in all these households, and all their members, both white and black, depended upon the labor of the blacks for their sustenance.

The labor of blacks who worked as sailors is easy to document, but the work of other slaves, both male and female, is less obvious in the extant records. Besides sailing, Pembroke slaves, like the rest of the slaves in Bermuda,

50. *Behoof* is defined in the *Oxford English Dictionary* as utility or application.

contributed to their owners' welfare by their skills at carpentry, masonry, and blacksmithing, spinning, weaving, and candlemaking, as well as ordinary house and field tasks. For example, Francis Dickinson, a blacksmith whose ancestor had followed that occupation in Bermuda in the 1660s, had taught at least one of his slaves the trade. In 1773 the large Dickinson household consisted of Francis Dickinson, his wife, three other women, and a boy (the Dickinsons' son), and their slave household had at least one other family, perhaps two: two men, a woman, two girls, and a boy. At his death in 1785 Dickinson's modest inventory listed just one slave: "1 Negro man (a Smith)."[51]

Some details of other slaves' work, as well as descriptions of slave living quarters, can be pieced together from wills and inventories. For example, the inventory of Cornelius Hinson, Esquire, is one of the few that lists slaves' occupations as well as their names and values. Hinson, a merchant and one of Pembroke's wealthiest residents, was the son of the earlier-mentioned Cornelius Hinson whose slave, Polibius, was tried for poisoning in 1754. Hinson owned a 50-acre tract that stretched the width of Pembroke from the Atlantic Ocean to Crow Lane harbor. He thus had access to the sea on both the north and south ends of his property. He was the largest landowner in Pembroke. To the east of Hinson's land were five small lots occupied in 1788 by William Place, Thomas Place, James Vaughan, and Thomas Nelmes; on the west of Hinson's property were the lots of Samuel Smith, Nathaniel Numan, John Numan, Richard Stiles, and Robert Gantlett. Such small individual holdings are illustrative of the closeness of Pembroke households in the late eighteenth century.[52] Hinson also owned land in Sandys Parish. His household in 1773 consisted of six men, three women, four boys, and one girl. He was also one of the largest slaveholders in the parish. In the survey of 1773 the Hinson slaves numbered 19: four men, seven women, five boys, and three girls, among whom there could have been as many as four family groups consisting of two parents and their children. Some of these individuals were still in Hinson's household when he died in 1789. His estate inventory lists 17 slaves—eight men, four women, one boy, three girls, and a "young child"— and their estimated values:

Joe a Mason	£30
January a Carpenter	25
Enos a Blacksmith	100
Jemmy a "	90

51. Books of Wills, vol. 10, p. 158.
52. Hinson's will is ibid., p. 289. The estate inventory, dated March 9, 1790, is in Books of Administrations, 2:44–48. There were several Hinsons named Cornelius, all related, in the late 1700s. See Hallett, *Early Bermuda Wills,* 285–86.

Nat a Fisherman	40
Charles a "	75
George a Field Negro	65
Harry a "	55
Dick a Boy	33
Pamelia a Cook	20
Amarillas a Washerwoman	45
Tent a House Maid	33
Jane and a Young Child	10
Sue a Girl	25
Nancy a "	15
Marriam a "	19

Cornelius Hinson's inventory is one of a handful of Bermuda slaveholders' inventories that contains items used by slaves. Among the furniture in the "kitchen chamber" (not the kitchen, but a chamber adjacent to it where some of the slaves lived) were a "Bedstead, Bed & Curtains," "One large Cedar Press," a looking glass, an ironing table, and four cedar chairs. Some of his slaves—most likely house servants—lived in the kitchen chamber. The others may have lived in the house as well, in the "wash room," the kitchen, and the cellars on the lower floor. There may also have been slave quarters separate from the Hinson house. These slave families tended the Hinson acreage, some of which was put to growing corn or tobacco, and looked after the large house, which had eight rooms, plus the cellars. It was a handsomely furnished house, with mahogany furniture, silver, framed pictures, and luxury items such as a "Japannd tea pott and stand." Hinson was a wealthy man by Bermuda standards; his total personal estate, including the slaves, came to £1,381.11.8.

The 1786 inventory of John Blackbourn, a prosperous Pembroke mariner who wrote "Gent." after his name, also provides a glimpse of slave living quarters in the "Cellars" of his house.[53] The furnishings there included a large bedstead with curtains and bed, two "field bedsteads" (one of them "old"), a calico coverlet, "Pine Cribb," a small cedar table, a large oval table, an old cedar table, six cedar chairs, a cedar chest, six small cedar chairs, a "Queens Ware Lamp," an "old Copper Tea Kettle," a coffee pot, and various earthen jugs and dishes. In 1773 when the census was made, the Blackbourn slave household consisted of 16 people: two men, four women, four boys, and six girls, among them at least two sets of parents with children. At the time of the inventory 13 years later there were 15 slaves: five adults—three men and

53. Blackbourn died intestate. The inventory, dated November 16, 1786, is in Books of Administrations, 2:41–46.

two women—and 10 children—five boys and five girls.[54] All shared the slave quarters at the Blackbourns' house.

Some of these slaves' activities can be reconstructed from the contents of Blackbourn's cellars and the list of the slaves' occupations. The three men were Jemmy, a carpenter; Tony, a mason; and George, also a mason. Tony and George would have worked outside the house for wages, helping to construct Bermuda's limestone buildings, walls, and fences. Jemmy, the carpenter, would also have been hired out. It was he who used the paint, pine boards, and timber listed among the cellars' contents, and no doubt it was he who built the pine crib. In 1773 Blackburn's household included two sailors, one white, one black, whom he hired out for wages, probably as crew members on one of Pembroke's 11 sloops. He shared in the profitable Turks Islands salt trade; among the contents of his cellars in 1786 was "some Salt about 10 Bushells." Other items in the cellars suggest that Blackbourn's slaves themselves were knowledgeable in matters of trade: A slate for figuring and a scale for weighing goods were part of the furnishings. There was also an "old Spie Glass" for looking out to sea. In 1786 one of the five boys among the Blackbourn slaves was "at sea with Cn [Captain] Godfrey," Blackbourn's father-in-law. The other boys, along with the women and girls in this slave establishment, would have helped to care for the Blackbourn livestock—a cow and her calf, a small heifer, and three sheep—that grazed on Blackbourn's 25 acres. The women and children probably gardened, planting a little corn and perhaps some potatoes and other vegetables. There were two hoes in the kitchen, along with an axe and a hatchet for chopping wood.

Slave women's work is also evident in the contents of the cellars and kitchen. One can imagine candles made from the set of candle molds, clothes washed in cedar tubs and ironed with the two pairs of smoothing irons heated in the fireplace, milk (from the Blackbourns' cow) stored in the earthen jugs, meat roasted on the iron spit, spices ground with the mortar and pestle, and the savory products of baking irons, Dutch oven, and chafing dish served up to the Blackbourns and their guests. On cool nights the warming pan full of hot coals was carried upstairs to the Blackbourns' beds. Meanwhile there was mending and scrubbing and polishing, and tending young children. There were two women, Mary and Dinna, in John Blackbourn's slave household at the time of his death. Dinna was the mother of a girl eight months old. She and Mary had four other girl children—Sue, Phillis, Patience, and Jean—

54. Blackbourn had 16 slaves—two men, four women, four boys, and six girls—in the 1773 survey. Their names and occupations are not given, but in the inventory of his property at his death 13 years later, in 1786, some of the same individuals were no doubt those in the 1773 listing.

and five boys—Sam, Will, Tom, Daniel, and Joe. At the time of the 1773 survey Blackbourn and his wife, Susanna, whom he had married in 1768, had two young children, a son and a daughter both under the age of five. The Blackbourn children would have played with the slave children as the slave women watched over them all. The relationships between the black family or families in the cellar quarters and the white family who lived upstairs can only be imagined, but it was very likely an intimate one.

John Blackbourn's wife was the daughter of the Pembroke shipwright Peter Godfrey. One measure of the close relationship between slaveholders and slaves in this family is that Tom, one of the Blackbourn slave children, went to sea with Captain Godfrey, no doubt learning to sail and perhaps to become an apprentice shipwright. John Blackbourn also had ventures at sea, but in the 1773 census the "men at sea" column is blank. Blackbourn himself was not at sea at the time, but his pursuits seemed to require him to be well armed: His 1786 inventory lists a pair of brass-mounted pistols, a silver and brass-mounted cutlass, a silver-hilted sword, and one "Small Arm." Privateering may have been part of his occupation, as it was for a number of Bermuda's men.

Blackbourn was also active in the affairs of Pembroke Parish. He owned one of the 24 pews in St. John's Church (his inventory included a "Large Family Bible"), served as a churchwarden and poundkeeper in the 1770s, and was selected several years as a juror along with his father-in-law.[55] Susanna and John Blackburn were obviously active in Pembroke society. Their household furnishings suggest a fondness for entertaining, and they lived as well as many of their counterparts in other colonies or in England. The inventory includes six cedar chairs and six caned chairs, all with blue cushions, eight Windsor chairs, six mahogany chairs, and three small cedar chairs; three tables—a square mahogany table, a round cedar table, and a round tea table; a brass tea kettle with stand, a silver teapot, one "set of China compleat, red & white," a brass chafing dish, three decanters, a tureen, and an assortment of silver and china compotes and serving dishes. Elegant dinners took place in that household, with slaves in attendance. The Blackbourns visited other Pembroke residents, sometimes riding horseback together: The inventory lists both a saddle and a sidesaddle.[56]

Some of Pembroke's more modest slaveholding households left inventories that offer other glimpses of slave life in this seafaring parish. William Leaycraft,

55. St. John's Church records, microfilm reel 37. On Blackbourn, see entries dated May 24, 1770, April 13, 1773, November and December 1773, May 15, 1775, and November 6, 1776.
56. Susanna, widowed in 1786, was living in a house on eight acres in Pembroke in the 1790s, owned by the representatives of Captain John Blackbourn. "Survey of Bermuda," *BHQ* 3, no. 2 (1946): 107–18, and no. 3 (1946), 171–84, 223–45. See esp. 178. She was buried on January 26, 1810, in Pembroke Parish.

a mariner, had two acres and seven slaves in 1773: three women, a boy, and three girls. They lived in the "old Cabbin" referred to in Leaycraft's 1778 will. In good health, but "being forthwith to depart on a voyage to Turks Islands," he made a will for the benefit of his wife, Deborah, and their three sons, Benjamin, William, and John. He bequeathed to Deborah "one Negro Boy called, or known by the name of Peter, together with one Negro Girl called by the name of Dinah"; but in an act unusual in Bermuda wills, he ordered the rest of his slaves (perhaps the three women and the other two girls he had in 1773 were among them) sold at his death, the money from the sale to be equally divided among his wife and sons. William Leaycraft returned safely from Turks' Islands and lived another 11 years.[57] When he died in 1789 his wife received the two slaves her husband had left to her in his will. The boy and girl named Peter and Dinah were then a grown man and woman and had known each other for more than 20 years. They remained in the family until Deborah's death in 1795. It is likely that they had become man and wife and that they had children: The inventory of Deborah Leaycraft's slave property also lists two girls, Ruth and Auber, and a boy named Brown.[58]

Many of the same families who lived in Pembroke in 1663 had descendants living there in 1773. From the 1773 parish census and surviving wills and inventories it is possible to describe some of these parish households and their occupants, both white and black, and also to trace some of the changes in these families and their property since the survey of 1663. The first thing to note is the continuity: Of 40 families listed in Pembroke in Richard Norwood's survey of 1663, 14 had descendants living there more than a century later.[59] Among the families who continued to live in Pembroke Parish were the Johnsons, the Lingars, the Moores, the Sanderses, the Swans, and the Watermans. For the most part, these families had held onto their positions on the economic ladder, and some had advanced. For example, Thomas Johnson was a tenant on one share of land in 1663; in 1773 a Lewis Johnson was a landowner with six acres. Lewis, listed as a mariner, had five slaves—a woman, three boys, and a girl. He also had one white sailor in his employ. Lewis Johnson was a Pembroke juryman in 1773 and 1776. His brother, Anthony, also lived in Pembroke in 1773 with his wife and two children, but owned no slaves. Lewis and Anthony's father, John Johnson, died in September 1773, leaving Lewis his "mansion house" and all of his land except two acres, which he bequeathed

57. Leaycraft's will is in Books of Wills, vol. 10, p. 299. The will was probated May 6, 1789. An inventory of the goods of William Leaycraft dated 1798 was probably that of his son. It lists three slaves: an "old Negro Woman Sary," another woman named Doll, and a boy, Ned. See Books of Administrations, 3:85, 110.
58. Deborah Leaycraft's inventory is in Books of Administrations, 3:43.
59. For the 1663 survey, see Lefroy, *Memorials,* 2:645–731.

to Anthony.[60] In some instances the economic advancement was not in real estate but in chattels. In 1663 one Richard Lingar had been a tenant on land near Mill Creek and the common land at the west end of Pembroke; in 1773 one Thomas Lingar occupied the same land, but not as an owner. Thomas Lingar did, however, own 11 slaves: five men, three women, two boys, and a girl. In 1663 Henry Moore had owned 50 acres near Mill Creek; in 1773 a David Moore, who may have been a descendant, owned only four acres but had seven slaves—three men, a woman, and four boys.

Some families had kept the status and property they had in 1663. Richard Sanders had been a tenant on the free school land in 1663, occupying 12 acres there, where he lived to be 103 years old. In 1773 Joseph Sanders, his grandson, was one of Pembroke's landowning residents, with a half-share (very likely the same 12 acres his grandfather held as a tenant) but no slaves. Thomas Swan lived as a tenant on another 12 acres in 1663; a William Swan lived in Pembroke in 1773. That Swan did not own land, but he did own one slave. Nathaniel Waterman owned 25 acres in Pembroke in 1663; a descendant, William Waterman, who was either a bachelor or a widower with no children, owned and lived on five acres in 1773, with one male slave.

The size of an individual's acreage was much diminished in Pembroke by the latter part of the eighteenth century; but as we have seen, a considerable number of Pembroke's residents had prospered, with incomes derived from seafaring and trading ventures, and owned relatively little land. Most, in fact, according to the 1773 survey, owned no land at all. Many nonlandowners owned a number of slaves—often more than they needed—while a few owned land and no slaves. Joseph Sanders, who had a wife and five children, had 12 acres but no slaves. Besides Joseph Sanders, three other men headed households and owned land but no slaves. One of these, Jonathan Rollins, owned only one acre and lived on it with his wife and five children. He was either ill or disabled, since he was not on the muster roll and was listed as "otherwise." One of his sons may have been the mariner named John Rollins, who also lived in Pembroke in 1773 but owned no land and no slaves.[61] The other two nonslaveholders with land, Luke Tilley and Daniel Gibbs, do not appear in any other extant records. They were heads of households with wives and children, and they owned land—eight and 12 acres, respectively—but had no slaves listed in the 1773 survey.[62]

60. John Johnson's will is in Books of Wills, vol. 12, pt. 2, p. 33; an inventory of his estate is ibid., vol. 9, pp. 126, 129.
61. A John Rawlings was a juror in 1775 and 1776, and at his death in 1792 owned four slaves, worth £174 of his £230 estate. For his inventory, see Books of Administrations, 2:30. See also Hallett, *Early Bermuda Wills*, 472.
62. Luke Tilley is listed as head of a household with four women, two boys, and four girls; Daniel Gibbs had a wife, two sons, and four daughters.

Of the 147 Pembroke householders in the 1773 survey, only 28—among them, 19 men and eight women—had no slaves.[63] Pembroke slaveholders made up a remarkable 80 percent of the population. If Pembroke is typical, these figures suggest that slaveholding in Bermuda was far more widespread than in any of the Caribbean or mainland colonies. Little is known about the Pembroke residents who had no slaves. These, some of whom were among the poorer sort, nonetheless deserve a place in this portrait of a slaveholding society. Of the eight nonslaveholding households headed by women, only one, that of Ann Dill, had a man on the muster roll in 1773. That was probably her son, David.[64] Of the other seven women's households, four belonged to widows young enough to have children under the age of 15, and three may have been headed by elderly widows living with adult daughters or other female relatives. Only one household contained a single woman with no other residents.[65] None of these women owned land. All have surnames belonging to other Pembroke families, although the exact relationships cannot be established from the existing records. These women with no land and no slaves had relatives—children, siblings, aunts or uncles, cousins, or in-laws— who could help them if the need arose.

Of the more affluent Pembroke households, a substantial number belonged to families who were living there in 1663; but in 1773 the source of their wealth was, not the land, but the sea. The Stowes, for example, were one of three of families who had established themselves as landowners in Pembroke in the 1660s and made their fortunes from the sea in the 1770s. The Stowes, the Woods, and the Dunscombs had all been large landowners in 1663. The Stowes, who were the largest landowners in the 1663 survey, maintained that distinction in 1773, with 75 acres at Point Shares and Mill Shares. Captain Joseph Stowe Sr. (the great-great-grandson of Captain John Stowe who purchased the land in the early 1660s) occupied the family property and owned a 40-ton sloop, the *Jane*. At the time of the 1773 census six of Stowe's 12 children were still living at home with him and his wife, Susanna. Captain Stowe had 16 slaves listed: four men, four women, four boys, and four girls, possibly as many as four family groups. Some or perhaps all of the men were sailors, since the *Jane* was manned by a crew of two white and three black sailors.

---

63. Of the 28 householders without slaves, the gender of one—J. Holly—cannot be determined.

64. A David Dill is listed as the executor of the will of Pembroke resident William Leaycraft in 1778, which suggests he was living in the parish at the time. See Hallett, *Early Bermuda Wills*, 385.

65. This is one of three spaces in which the name is left blank on the last page of the survey and the household with only one woman resident has been inserted between the lines.

Captain Joseph Stowe, who styled himself "Gent.," lived on 50 acres at Mill Shares. He was the grandson of the Joseph Stowe mentioned in an earlier chapter and the son of Joseph Stowe Jr., who died in 1746. His widowed mother, Christian Nature Stowe, occupied the remaining share of the family property. She lived there with a female companion, perhaps one of her two daughters, and four slaves—two women and two boys. Christian and Joseph Stowe had three sons and two daughters. It is possible that one of these daughters was also a widow by 1773 and lived with her mother. Christian Stowe, who was probably in her early forties at the time of her husband's death, had a long widowhood and was in her eighties when she died in 1784.[66] Her household inventory offers a view of an elderly, wealthy widow's lifestyle: three feather beds and one bedstead, a round walnut table and seven chairs with cane bottoms, a large armchair, two cedar joint stools, and a large looking glass with a frame were among her household furnishings, along with curtains and bed covers of white calico and dimity, and "1 bed Quilt worn." Of the Stowe family silver, she had only a porringer and basin, three table spoons, a pepper box, a pair of tea tongs, and 11 teaspoons. She had only one tablecloth and one set of eight napkins, and one china plate and one wine glass. There were, however, assorted other plates, both "deep" and "flat," and a pair of brass candlesticks and a snuffer. She had a tea kettle and a china teapot, a vinegar cruet, a "salt glass," a mortar and pestle, an "old trivet," and an iron pot. Her two slave women would have done the cooking and cleaning, also the washing and ironing: There were two washing tubs of oak and cedar and two smoothing irons. No slaves are listed in the inventory, but it is likely that Mrs. Stowe's slaves were placed in the households of other family members at the time of her death. The Stowes, like most other Bermudians, kept their slaves within the family. The widow Stowe's slaves might have gone to a nephew who lived on property adjacent to hers. Joseph (designated Joseph Jr. to distinguish him from his cousin, the captain) also lived on the Stowe family land, occupying six acres with his wife and five children. At the time of the 1773 survey the slaves in his household consisted of two men, a boy, and a girl.[67]

Like the family of Captain John Stowe, the family of Thomas Wood had been in Pembroke since the 1660s, and by the 1770s the Woods were one of the parish's shipowning families. They, like the Stowes, had enhanced their social status over the years. By the 1770s Horatio Wood, a great-grandson of Thomas Wood, like Captain John Stowe's great-great-grandson Joseph Stowe, wrote "Gent." after his name. Wood owned two vessels, the 50-ton *Ranger*

66. Hallett, *Early Bermuda Wills*, 562.
67. On the Stowe family, see Hallett, *Early Bermuda Wills*, 561–64. See also Darrell, Genealogical Note Book, 56–67.

and the 45-ton *Adventure*. At the time of the 1773 survey Horatio Wood's household contained a wife and seven children—six girls and a boy. His slave household, however, was even larger. There were 12 men, 12 women, eight boys, and six girls, by far the largest number of slaves owned by one Pembroke resident, making Horatio Wood also one of Bermuda's largest slaveholders. There may have been as many as a dozen families among Wood's slaves. Like Captain Stowe, Wood used his slaves as crews for his sailing vessels. The census lists 10 black and four white sailors in Wood's employ.

When Wood died intestate in 1789 the inventory of his goods and chattels listed only 11 slaves in what were probably three family groups: three adult men (Jim, David, and Tom), three adult women (Sary, Martiter (Martita?), and Sary), three boys (Addam, Sam, and Dick), and two girls (Rose and Sara).[68] What had become of the other 27 slaves listed in Wood's 1773 household, as well as his two sloops, is not known. He was by Bermuda standards a rich man, with slaves and household goods valued at £744.14.0. Like most affluent Bermudians he kept some livestock—three cows, two sheep, and a hog—for the use of his family and his slaves. His household furnishings included a mahogany chest of drawers, "11 Frame Pictures," china plates and wine glasses for 20, and a dining room with three tables.

Over the decades the original Wood family property of 50 acres had become divided among a succession of other Horatio Woods as well as their siblings, and this Horatio lived on 10 acres of the original property surrounding a small cove called Bosses Hole (now called Bosses Cove) bordered by the Stowes' land near Mill Creek. The number of people under Wood's care was unusually large by Bermuda standards, but no doubt he found plenty of work for his slaves to do, tending the gardens and caring for the livestock necessary to feed his own family plus the several other slave families who lived and worked on the premises. If 10 of Wood's male slaves were at sea, that left only two adult males to work in the fields, fish, care for livestock, and do the heavy labor. They would of course have been helped by some of the 12 female slaves, but the women would have had housework and child care as well. Counting the white and black households, even with most of the men at sea, there were at least 40 mouths to feed in Horatio Wood's establishment.

Another member of the Wood family, perhaps a brother of Horatio, was Stowe Wood, whose name demonstrates the closeness of the Stowe and Wood families over the decades. He is listed in the 1773 census as head of a household with a wife, three sons, a daughter, and 10 slaves. By the time he made his will in 1785 he and his wife, Frances, had had two more daughters. To each of his

68. The inventory of Wood's estate, administered by Samuel Wood (perhaps a son) is in Books of Administrations, 2:148.

six children, Stowe Wood bequeathed a young female slave, as well as land at Bodkin Bay and Ireland Island, across the Great Sound from Pembroke.[69] He, like several other men in his family, was a seafaring man, although the records do not show that he owned a vessel. However, as an owner of property on Ireland Island he no doubt profited from wrecks off its coasts. The 1773 record shows that Wood had one man at sea at the time of the survey, and one white and one black listed under "Sailors." Including Wood himself, there were three adult white men in the household, two of whom may have been his older sons. Like many Bermuda slaveholders, Stowe Wood had more slaves than he needed. He held only four acres, but he had three men, three women, a boy, and three girls to tend it and to work as house servants.

The Dunscomb family, whose matriarch, Hannah Dunscomb, had owned 50 acres in 1663, by 1773 had only two acres—but they owned two ships: Edward Dunscomb had the 60-ton *Peggy*, the largest of Pembroke's 11 vessels; his brother William owned one of the next-largest, the 50-ton *Francis*. The Dunscomb brothers both married into the family of Pembroke shipwright Peter Godfrey, who lived near the Dunscombs at Spanish Point. Edward married Christiana Godfrey in 1768; William married Love Godfrey in 1773. Christiana and Love Godfrey were sisters of John Blackbourn's wife, Susanna.[70] Edward and William were the sons of Thomas Dunscomb and Prudence Waterman, whose 1717 marriage had united two longtime Pembroke landowning families. Both Dunscomb brothers made their livings from the sea, and both kept what was, by Bermuda standards, a substantial number of slaves. Edward was listed in 1773 as having 10 slaves: three men, three women, two girls, and two boys—presumably three family groups. The three men, plus one white sailor, were crew members of the *Peggy*. William Dunscomb had eight slaves—three men, two women, a boy, and two girls. No doubt William, as the owner of the *Francis*, also had sailors, but that part of his listing in the survey is damaged and unreadable.

Besides the Dunscombs, Stowes, and Woods, all of whom lived within a half-mile radius of each other at the west end of the parish, Pembroke's other shipowning families were those of Thomas Burch, Francis Eve, Joseph Gibson, James Prudden, Francis Robinson, and Samuel Saltus. In 1773 Thomas Burch, Esquire, was listed as the owner of the 48-ton sloop *St. George*. He also owned 25 acres in Pembroke. Burch died intestate in 1777. Unfortunately there are no surviving wills or inventories for the rest of these Pembroke shipowners, but the inventory of the household goods of Thomas Burch's widow, Elizabeth, who died in 1787, suggests that Pembroke's elites lived

---

69. Stowe Wood's 1785 will is in Books of Wills, vol. 10, p. 416. He died in 1791.
70. The Dunscombes' marriages are recorded in Hallett, *Early Bermuda Records*, 105, 163.

as luxuriously as their counterparts in England or on the mainland of North America. Elizabeth Burch's inventory, taken in 1787, describes a household of considerable affluence.[71] The house, like those of most wealthy Bermudians, was not large, but its seven rooms contained such items as damask table linens, china (including soup plates, tureens, and sauce boats), wine glasses and decanters, silver (including a silver coffee pot, tobacco box, and silver spoons of "wash't gold"), mahogany tables and chairs, and a satin quilt. The total value of Elizabeth Burch's possessions was £484.5.4. In 1773 her husband had owned 12 slaves—two men, three women, six boys, and one girl—but Elizabeth Burch's inventory, taken nearly two years after her death, does not list any slaves.

There were other affluent residents of Pembroke, including families who had been there since 1663. Not all of them had kept their property intact. The Woods and the Stowes, as we have seen, had maintained their property on the west end of Pembroke, dividing smaller portions among their descendants. The family of Richard Norwood, the surveyor of 1663, did the same thing. His daughter, Elizabeth Witter, who lived on his property after his death in 1674, bequeathed the "mansion house" and a single house at the water's edge, which was the slave quarters, to her daughter, Elizabeth Vincent, in 1691. Vincent sold the property to Samuel Saltus, a Pembroke merchant, in 1707. Then, in 1722, Vincent's daughter, Esther, married Samuel Saltus, and thus the house was again lived in by a descendant of Richard Norwood. Esther Saltus was his great-great-granddaughter.

In 1773 the old Norwood house was the residence of Saltus's son, also named Samuel, and his wife, Mary. He and his wife had two sons, Witter and Hinson, at the time of the census. (These names, like Stowe Wood's name and others, suggest the closeness of certain Pembroke families.) The Saltuses were also connected to the Hinsons: Mary Saltus was the daughter of Cornelius Hinson. At the time of the 1773 census Saltus owned 16 acres and a 50-ton sloop called the *Mary*. This vessel carried a crew of three white sailors and one black, the black sailor being one of the nine slaves (three men, two women, two boys, and two girls) in the Saltus household.[72]

In 1773 Richard Witter, Richard Norwood's great-great-grandson, was a mariner who owned no land. He had a wife, two sons, two daughters, and six slaves: two men, a woman, two boys, and a girl. At the time he made his will in 1780 he lived in a mansion house in Pembroke (not the old Norwood

71. Elizabeth Burch's will, dated April 13, 1786, is in Books of Wills, vol. 10, p. 212. The administration of her estate was turned over to Henry Butterfield on October 22, 1787. See Books of Administrations, 2:122.

72. On the Saltus family, see Hallett, *Early Bermuda Wills*, 496–98. There is also a Samuel Saltus in Southampton, with a wife named Esther.

house), which he left to his son, John. By 1780 Richard Witter was a widower, but in the meantime his family had been enlarged by another son, Norwood. In his will Witter ordered that one of his slaves, Peter, be "Set Free" at his death and provided for another slave, Bess, to have "her choice of living with whom she pleases" among his five children. When Witter died in 1791 his estate inventory listed only two slaves: "one Negro Woman Old Bess" and "One Negro Man"—presumably Peter.[73] Richard Witter's estate, including his slaves, came to only £142.17. He had little china or silver, but he had two large round cedar tables and 12 chairs, which suggests a fondness for entertaining, even if his guests supped from 12 pewter soup plates instead of china ones.

George Darrell, a descendant of the merchant John Darrell, who resided in Warwick Tribe in 1663 and also owned 25 acres in Pembroke, was a wealthy merchant in Pembroke in 1773. He was one of 10 children born to John Darrell's son, also named John.[74] George Darrell also had a large family: five children by his first wife, who died in 1758, and at least four by his second wife, whom he married sometime before 1762. At the time of the 1773 survey the household of George Darrell, "Gent.," comprised three sons old enough to be in the Pembroke muster, three still listed as boys, three older daughters, and two girls. Darrell had 10 slaves: three men, three women, a boy, and three girls. A merchant, he owned only one acre. Darrell took an active part in Pembroke life and served as a juror every year from 1770 to 1776. He also owned a pew in the parish church.[75]

Families like the Darrells, the Stowes, and the Woods had prospered, trading widely and profitably, sometimes engaged in privateering. Their counterparts (and their relatives, since many of Bermuda's leading families had intermarried over the years) could be found all over Bermuda, and all were equally willing to ignore established authority. When Governor Bruere had arrived in 1764 he found the capital, St. George's, "almost deserted by the greatest number of Inhabitants," who were "dispersed over the whole country with their Sloops and little store Houses, so extended and scattered, not withstanding they scarce grow a bushel of corn, or raise any other staple commodity."[76] Although a census of 1764 (table 9) belies Bruere's estimate of St. George's desolate condition, his first impression was probably correct.

73. Books of Wills, vol. 10, p. 406 (for the will), vol. 9, p. 495 (inventory).
74. George, born in 1721, married Jane Albouy, the daughter of Captain Thomas Albuoy, and a relative of Pembroke resident Nicholas Albuoy. See Darrell, Genealogical Note Book, for more on the Darrell family genealogy.
75. See entries for May 24, 1770, November 7, 1771, May 1773, May 21, 1774, and April 1776, in St. John's Church records, microfilm reel 37.
76. Bruere to John Pownell, Secretary, Lords of Trade and Plantations, in CO 37/19: 20, 282.

Table 9 **Census of St. George's and the Tribes, 1764**

Tribe	White Men	White Women	White Boys	White Girls	Black Men	Black Women	Black Boys	Black Girls
St. George's	154	244	128	150	125	176	138	134
Hamilton	131	191	132	90	135	148	139	125
Smith's	106	163	85	87	94	116	104	82
Devonshire	114	149	115	81	82	117	100	90
Pembroke	142	236	154	116	131	157	128	92
Paget	115	180	102	77	145	152	117	109
Warwick	206	294	234	199	160	191	172	152
Southampton	350	419	0	0	186	213	198	149
Sandys	202	302	166	166	167	243	232	202
Totals	1,520	2,188	1,120	966	1,255	1,513	1,328	1,135

"A General List of all the Inhabitants in His Majesty's Bermuda or Somers Islands . . . 1764," CO 37/19: 257.

A few years before Bruere's arrival, his predecessor, Governor Popple, had bowed to the wishes of residents who claimed that St. George's two harbors were inconvenient and had authorized another harbor. Popple at last had allowed what many Bermudians had sought for years: that "vessels might load and unload at the west End, provided it was under the inspection, and in the preserve of a searcher." The "west end" referred to was Crow Lane harbor on Pemroke's south shore. This port could serve the four western parishes of Pembroke, Warwick, Southampton, and Sandys. But Crow Lane was remote from the capital at St. George's, and enforcement of customs regulations at the newly authorized port was notoriously lax, when it existed at all. Upon his initial survey of the arrangements at Crow Lane in 1765, an exasperated Governor Bruere reported that the customs inspector there had been "dead some years, and no Person appointed in his Room."[77]

In 1773 Governor Bruere's report to the Lords of Trade describes what all Pembroke and other Bermuda mariners knew well: "In the middle part of the Country is the great Sound [Pembroke's south shore bordered on

77. Bruere to Lords of Trade, May 24, 1765, in CO 37/19: 273.

it, from Daniel's Bay and Mill Shares to Crow Lane]; but very difficult of Access from Sea, by the Entrance called Hog Fish Cut, nigh the West part of the Mainland and Chub Cut North West, lies far out and by the Rocky Windings very difficult for any but Bermudian Navigators [many of whom were Pembroke seamen] to get to the Harbours through those rocky and narrow channels, yet most of the Inhabitants choose to go there away from the Seat of Government or Customs House."[78] To curtail this illegal trade would take customs officers who were "not Natives of the Place" and who should be "exchanged by Rotation as the Inhabitants are somewhat intermarried." The governor was right: In 1773, the year of this report, the comptroller of customs was Copeland Stiles, Esquire, and the "Searcher [customs officer] at the West End" was John Stiles. These two were "kin" (John Stiles referred to Copeland's son, Samuel, as such in his will). John Stiles was the son of a Pembroke mariner, Captain Richard Stiles.[79] The Stileses were also related to the Saltuses, Burches, the Hinsons, and the Butterfields—four of Bermuda's leading merchant families—of whom all but the Butterfields lived in Pembroke.[80]

These families and others like them were Bermuda's elites, making their living from the sea as the generations before them had done. With their slaves, they lived and traded as they pleased, largely free of government control. In times of war, they profited from privateering and shipbuilding. As Governor Bruere observed, Bermuda's sloops and brigs, "being the very best and the Swiftest Sailing vessels, get freighted readily, at a better price than the vessels of any other Country."[81] In the 1770s as the American Revolution began, Bermuda's families were not eager to join the 13 mainland colonies in a revolution against the mother country. As one of the Stowes' twentieth-century descendants remarked, Bermuda's trading families already had their "independence" from Great Britain.[82] The rhetoric of revolution permeated the transatlantic community, but Bermuda's slaves, living in families within their masters' households, building and sailing their masters' ships, sharing with them the pleasures and dangers of a seafaring life, saw no point in

78. For the text of the report, see "Reports on Bermuda by Two 18th Century Governors," 50–61.
79. On the relationships of these families, see Hallett, *Early Bermuda Wills*, 550–52. Captain Richard Stiles died intestate in 1805. His son, John Edmund, was the administrator of his estate. Books of Wills, vol. 10, p. 212.
80. John Stiles's will is in Books of Wills, vol. 15, p. 414.
81. "Wants and Defects . . . . of Bermuda," Governor George James Bruere to the Earl of Hillsborough, August 18, 1770, in CO 37/20: 164.
82. John Stow, "Three and a Half Centuries of Bermuda History," *Bermuda* 30, no. 5 (July 1959): 30–31.

plotting rebellion. In the lives of Bermuda's families, both white and black, lie multiple answers to the social and political stability of England's smallest colony. Bermuda was a slave society, but unlike others in which a deep-rooted racism bred long-lasting and bitter conflicts, that society was bound by ties of economic, geographic, and personal reality.

Conclusion

Slavery and racism, racism and slavery: This chicken-and-egg relationship has confounded scholars for decades. What does Bermuda's history add to the search for answers? The fragments of many lives—white, black, mulatto, Indian, mustee—uncovered in this book, like shards of pottery unearthed, leave much to the imagination. Wills and inventories, laws and court cases, governors' reports and council minutes, are public documents. They can furnish only a part of what the thousands of private voices in Bermuda's early history would tell us if we could hear them: Slavery happened to people. Slavery was personal. It was individual. And it bound slaveholders as well as slaves. Once it took root, neither group was free.

The English colonists who came to live in Bermuda, like those who came to England's other colonies, did not arrive with the intent to enslave other human beings for life. But the larger world had already adopted slavery, and as Bermudian vessels plied the Atlantic and the Caribbean in search of trade (and sometimes plunder), they could not avoid contact with a highly profitable labor system. It was a system based on the enslavement of Africans, a people exotic and mysterious to the English, as unlike white Anglo-Saxons as it was possible for them to imagine. Bermudians knew about "Negroes," and in the first years of settlement they eagerly sought them for their special skills: to dive for pearls, to cultivate cassava and melons and tobacco, to turn palmetto leaves into baskets and hats—to teach the English settlers things that they did not know. What these first whites and blacks in Bermuda thought of each other, what they said to each other every day, what patterns of dominance and deference grew between them, remain matters of conjecture. Much of the history of the first contacts between the two races is hidden in the interstices of the public record. That history is not documented; it must be inferred. In the extant documents of early Bermuda's history there are no black voices, and relatively few white ones, to suggest how each race perceived the other.

From their actions, if not their words, these first-generation Bermudians, black and white, reveal something of their attitudes toward each other. For example, Roger Wood and other whites thought blacks should learn to read, study the Bible, live together as man and wife, and refrain from insulting their betters. Francisco and other blacks no doubt thought themselves superior in some ways to whites who did not know how to grow and cure tobacco, cook cassava, or swim, much less dive for pearls. Scraps of evidence suggest that blacks and whites worshipped together, worked together, and in their leisure time undoubtedly sailed and fished together. By the second generation some of them had even closer relationships, as the number of mulattos proves. Bermuda's first blacks married and had children, just as the whites did, and as the population grew, so did concerns about social order and servitude. Some blacks were free, and their assertive ways led whites to call them "insolent." Other blacks were bondservants who might become free. For them, white Bermudians found a solution: the 99-year indenture. That did not make an individual a slave—legally—but it conveniently kept him or her in the service of a master or mistress for life. The status of children born to a person with a 99-year indenture remained uncertain and was often spelled out in wills and presentments. But as the years passed, as servants with 99-year indentures died, and as English settlers on Providence, Barbados, and other island colonies eagerly adopted slavery, Bermudians accepted it, too. But they did not need it. And they did not enforce its laws with the same rigor as the other colonists did.

Here is the central paradox of Bermuda's racial history: A tiny island colony with little need for a large labor force soon had more slaves than it could put to work. Unlike the mainland colonies, where slavery grew slowly in the seventeenth century and where the slave population did not reproduce itself for several decades, and unlike the Caribbean colonies, where harsh conditions and grueling labor in the sugarcane fields wore out slaves faster than they could be brought in, Bermuda, almost from the beginning, had a healthy and prolific slave labor force. Efforts to limit a slaveowner's number of slaves, like the efforts to rid Bermuda of its free blacks, were largely unsuccessful. Instead, slaves and slaveholders lived in ever closer quarters, sharing family life, often sharing given names. Naming practices in Bermuda, like the 99-year indentures, are telling evidence of Bermudians' reluctance to conform to the racial attitudes that reinforced slavery. While slaves in other colonies often kept African names, or derivatives of African names such as Juba, Sambo, or Mingo, or bore fanciful, classical, or humorous names given them by whites, such as Jumper, Cicero, or Pokey, Bermuda slaves usually had the same ordinary, serviceable English names that slaveholders had: John, Peter, Kate, Mary. Regardless of who chose the names, the similarity and even the sharing of given names among slaves and slaveholders indicate a certain level of acculturation and illustrate the close bonds that often existed between master and slave. While other colonies were using blatantly racist words such as *barbarous, wild,* and *heathenish* to describe blacks, the worst that Bermudians could say about them was that they were "insolent" and "not free."

As the generations passed, Bermuda's slaves and slaveholders, crowded together on land that no longer produced enough to feed them, had to find other ways to make a living. The transformation from an agricultural to a maritime economy also transformed race relations. Whites and blacks— working, eating, and sleeping side by side in the cramped space aboard a sloop, each man standing his watch, all sharing the dangers and uncertainties of a thousand-mile voyage in a small sloop—formed relationships quite unlike those of master and slave or white and black in other societies. The bonds that existed among crew members, and between crew members and the master of a vessel, are largely undocumented. There are no diaries or letters describing them. But that such bonds existed, there can be no doubt. Black sailors, of course, were not unique to Bermuda, but Bermuda was unique in the large proportion of its men—black and white—at sea.

Bermuda's maritime economy gave its slaves two things that few of their counterparts in slave societies on the mainland or in the islands had: a large measure of autonomy and a sense of identity. A sailor working for wages, sharing in the booty from "wrecking" or privateering, bartering goods in faraway ports, was far more his own master than a plantation slave could ever be. A sailor with specialized knowledge of ships and the sea, or a boatwright with finely honed skills in building vessels known for their excellence through- out the Atlantic community, had a certain pride, a sense of self-worth, that came to few field hands. For Bermuda's slave women, the maritime economy meant that many of them shared with their white mistresses the hardships and anxieties of having men at sea. In Bermuda's small households the bonds of womanhood, of female companionship, like the bonds between men aboard a ship, undoubtedly transcended race. White and black families in Bermuda lived in much closer proximity than those in England's other colonies, and the harshness of slavery was constantly mitigated by the personal nature of contacts between slaveholder and slave.

Besides the irony of too many slaves in a society that did not need them, there is another incongruity in Bermuda's racial history, one that clearly reflects the degree of racial tolerance in the colony: Laws to control and to punish blacks were passed repeatedly, but both whites and blacks found ways to ignore or circumvent such laws. Violent confrontations between blacks and whites were few, and punishments were relatively mild compared to other slave societies. There were rebellion plots, yes, but no whites were ever killed in them, and whites were often reluctant to inflict the death penalty on accused rebels. Although slave plots elsewhere resulted in the deaths of whites, and scores of rebel slaves were tortured, mutilated, and cruelly executed, Bermuda had only one episode of brandings and nose-slittings, a handful of hangings, and one documented burning at the stake. Bermuda was an anomaly, putting weapons in the hands of its adult male slaves soon after conspiracy plots and sending vessels out to sea with a white master and an all-black crew. There is nothing in Bermuda's history to compare with the white response to black uprisings elsewhere. In Providence Island's first slave rebellion, for example, fearful whites retaliated by executing 50 blacks.

This not to say that Bermuda was free of racial violence, or that Bermuda's slaves were more docile or more content than those of other slave societies. On the contrary: Bermuda's slaves, like the colony's first blacks, found ways to assert themselves, to procure food, clothing, and enjoyment, to intimidate whites who stood in their way, and, most remarkably, on two occasions, to present formal petitions for their freedom. Ironically, the enslaved turned the tables on their white masters by adopting the very method Englishmen had traditionally approved: the written petition. Bermuda's officials preserved the governor's proclamation and the council's minutes referring to these petitions—but, regrettably, not the petitions themselves. Like slaves elsewhere, Bermuda's slaves sought their freedom by plotting rebellion; but unlike slaves elsewhere, they offered no organized resistance to slavery after the 1761 conspiracy.

At a time when rebellions on the mainland and in the Caribbean occurred with increasing severity and frequency, through the tumultuous years of the American, French, and Haitian revolutions, Bermuda remained largely untouched by the rhetoric of revolution.[1] In fact, in 1782 one chance of freedom offered by liberty-loving Americans to the slave crew of a Bermuda privateer was rejected. The episode provides some telling insights into both the history of slavery in Bermuda and the racial interpretations of that history.

The story begins with the *Regulator,* a 160-ton vessel built of Bermuda cedar in 1782. Armed with 20 guns, she was one of many Bermudian privateers that preyed on American shipping during the American Revolution.[2] In May 1782 the *Regulator* captured an American ship, loaded with rice, off the

1. Bermuda did play a brief role in the American colonies' struggle: On the night of August 14, 1775, as two American vessels hovered off shore in Bermuda's waters, eager hands, both white and black, took 100 barrels—1,182 pounds—of gunpowder out of the magazine at St. George's and stealthily moved them across the island to Tobacco Bay on the north shore, where a small fleet of whaleboats was waiting. Piloted through the treacherous reefs by skilled blacks, these vessels sailed from St. George's to Somerset under cover of darkness and delivered their cargo to the American ships. George Washington's army desperately needed gunpowder, and Bermuda's shipowners desperately wanted to continue their lucrative salt trade with the North American colonies. On the "Gunpowder Plot," see Wilfred Brenton Kerr, *Bermuda and the American Revolution, 1760–1783* (Princeton: Princeton University Press, 1936), 49–52. See also Isaac J. Greenwood, *Bermuda during the American Revolution* (Boston, 1896), 4; "Some Repercussions of the Gunpowder Plot," *BHQ* 12, no. 2 (1955): 45–56; A. E. Verrill, *Relations between Bermuda and the Colonies in the Revolutionary War* (New Haven: A. E. Verrill, 1907).

2. On Bermuda privateering, see Packwood, *Chained on the Rock*, 38–46.

coast of South Carolina. She was then herself captured by a larger American vessel, the 32-gun frigate *Deane,* and taken to Boston. The *Regulator* carried a crew of about 75, 70 of whom were blacks. The American authorities offered their black captives two choices: They could remain in Boston as free men, or they could return as slaves to Bermuda. All 70 men chose to return to the islands. Their reasons, like their personal histories, went unrecorded. Did they talk to other blacks in Boston? The irony of the American Revolution, with its rhetoric of liberty, was not lost upon American slaves. Did the Bermuda slaves hear, perhaps, that freedom for blacks was a mockery in the mainland colonies? Or was it simply the ties of home and family that moved them? At any rate, Massachusetts' governor, John Hancock, arranged for the Bermudians to sail from Boston to Bermuda via New York. Sixty of them embarked on the American ship *Duxbury* out of Boston, but not trusting the Americans, the Bermudian seamen seized command of the vessel as she neared Cape Cod. They set their course for home, where they arrived on June 24, 1782. Nine of the other black seamen returned to Bermuda later from New York. Thus all 70 black crew members of the captured *Regulator,* except one who died in America or at sea, returned to their various homes and families, to take up their lives again as part of Bermuda's slave society.

In later years the story of the *Regulator* was often used by white Bermudians to illustrate the mildness of slavery in the colony. In 1824, for example, Bermuda's chief justice, James Esten, made a speech before the Bible Societies in England, in which he cited the willingness of the *Regulator* slaves to return to Bermuda as "proof of their kind treatment."[3] In the twentieth century, historians who recounted the story of the *Regulator* echoed Esten's sentiments, marveling that "the slaves might have taken their liberty, but they preferred returning to their owners in Bermuda." Why? A nineteenth-century clergyman, pondering that question, had a simple answer: "Blacks were more attached to their homes and masters, than would readily be imagined."[4] Twentieth-century Bermuda historian Cyril Outerbridge Packwood put the matter clearly: It was not to their masters that these Bermuda slaves were attached, but to their homes—"their families, mothers, wives, and children."[5] It was this attachment, not contentment under slavery, or lack of a love of liberty, that drew the *Regulator*'s crewmen back to Bermuda. They were, as white Bermudians had long ago described them, "not free."

3. Cited ibid., 45.
4. The first quotation is from Henry Wilkinson, *Bermuda in the Old Empire* (London, Oxford University Press, 1950), 257; the second, from Williams, *Historical & Statistical Account,* 137 n; the third is the Methodist clergyman Joshua Marsden, quoted in Packwood, *Chained on the Rock,* 45.
5. Packwood, *Chained on the Rock,* 45.

It is nonetheless clear that in this small island colony slavery had wider perimeters that in other slave societies. In 1782, the same year as the *Regulator* incident, Hector St. Jean de Crèvecoeur, a French émigré to America, recorded his impressions of slavery in Bermuda, which he visited after seeing Jamaica:

> What a contrast! What an immense difference! What a happy comparison did I draw between the rich and splendid Jamaica and this simple home of poverty, of simplicity, and of health! . . .
>
> All land not cultivated is covered by red cedars, with which they build sloops of 200 tons, well known in every sea for durability and speed. The great number of these vessels are manned by negroes, a race of men long since refined not only by their stay on this island but by education that they have received from their Masters. They aid in building ships and afterwards sail them to the Islands where they are preferred above other boats for navigation and smuggling. Their ability as sailors and shipbuilders, their faithfulness as supercargoes, the punctuality with which they direct the business of their masters, and bring home their vessels is indeed a truly edifying sight. I have seen several of these black managers at the tables of rich Jamaican planters, treated with all the consideration which their intelligence and faithfulness merit.[6]

Between Crèvecoeur's lines is a portrait of masters as well as slaves: Bermuda's slaveholders allowed their slaves a degree of independence but were at the same time dependent on them. Masters, like their slaves, were "not free." When emancipation came at last in 1834, as a descendant of the Bermuda slaveholder Perient Trott wrote, "Bermuda grasped its freedom with both hands, master and slave alike, one glad to be relieved of the responsibility, the other eager to assume it."[7]

6. *Lettres d'un Cultivateur Americain* (Paris, 1784), 1:235 ff., excerpted in "A Description of Bermuda: Extract from 'Lettres d'un Cultivateur Americain' by Jean Crevecoeur, 1784," trans. Louis S. Friedland, *BHQ* 3, no. 4 (1946): 201–3. Crèvecoeur also visited South Carolina, and his other description of slavery, a horrific image of a black man starving to death in a cage, stands in stark contrast to his portrait of slavery in Bermuda.

7. Helen M. Fessenden, "Childhood Memories of Bermuda in the '70s," *BHQ* 5, no. 1 (1948): 20–38 (quotation, p. 22).

Bermuda-Registered Vessels Bringing Blacks into the Port of New York, 1716–1742

Date	Vessel	Owner(s)	Slaves & Origins
1716	*Wall*	John Trott, Tobias Wall of Nevis	6 (Bermuda)
1718	*Seaflower*	S. Hawkes, Wm. Stone	2 (Bermuda)
1719	*Rubie*	P. Paynter, J. Burch	4 (Antigua)
1721	*Success*	S. and P. Spofforth	1 (Bermuda)
1721	*Overplus*	S., W., and H. Tucker	1 (St. Eustatias)
1722	*Eliza*	J. Peniston, J. Williams, Eliz. Walker, E. Woolrich	1 (Jamaica)
1723	*Prudence*	F. and J. Burrows, Rachel Seymour, J. Conyers	8 (Jamaica, Bermuda)
1723	*Elizabeth and Anne*	P. Mallory, J. Jennings, J. Foster, J. Gibbs	1 (Turks I., Bermuda)
1723	*Benjamin*	B. Hinson	5 (Jamaica)
1724	*Henry*	E. Clark, J. Trimingham, N. Butterfield Sr. & Jr., J. Butterfield	1 (Bermuda)
1724	*St. Andrew*	R. Dinwiddie	2 (Bermuda)
1724	*Eliza and Martha*	J. Gibbs Jr., C. Hinson, C. Conyers, P. Mallory	1 (Barbados)
1725	*Rubie*	R. Leacraft, J. Burch, P. Paynter, P. Burrows	11 (Jamaica)
1725	*Thomas and Mary*	T. Gilbert Sr. & Jr.	1 (Bermuda)
1725	*Glassco*	W. Orem	2 (Bermuda)
1726	*Sincerity*	G. and T. Smith	1 (Barbados)
1726	*Mary and Ellinor*	S. Spofforth, T. Withers, T. Harrison	2 (Bermuda)

Date	Vessel	Owner(s)	Slaves & Origins
1726	*Speedwell*	E. Styles, W. Mallory, R. and Angelina Hunt	1 (Barbados)
1726	*Sarah and Elizabeth*	M. and E. Burrows, J. Wells	1 (Bermuda)
1726	*Bruce Hope*	T. Handy, R. Dinwiddie	1 (Bermuda, a woman)
1727	*Dolphin*	J. Jones, H. Corbusier, J. Maydman	2 (Bermuda)
1727	*Bruce Hope*	J. Jennings, T. Handy	1 (Bermuda)
1727	*Blessing*	E. Gilbert, J. Janny	3 (Bermuda)
1728	*Old Soldier*	W. Mitchell, H. Corbusier, Wm. Mitchell	3 (Bermuda)
1728	*Susanah*	P. Burrows, P. Paynter, S. Burrows	1 (Bermuda)
1729	*Susanah*	P. Burrows, P. Paynter, S. Burrows	4 (Bermuda)
1729	*Little Marys*	J. Jennings, D. Stiles	1 (Bermuda)
1729	*Unity*	S. Paynter, P. Paynter Sr. & Jr., J. Evans	3 (Bermuda)
1729	*Friendship*	T. and J. Hunt, W. Burrows	2 (Barbados)
1729	*Content*	J. Harvey, R. White, J. Catling, N. Bascomb	4 (Barbados)
1729	*Sarah*	F. Seymour, T. Forster, J. Appleby, Martha Forster	7 (Barbados)
1730	*Exchange*	J. Gibbs Jr. & Sr., E. Gilbert, P. Mallory	3 (Antigua)
1730	*Lancashire*	Wm. Mitchell, S. and R. Spofforth	5 (Bermuda)
1730	*Rose*	N. Butterfield, B. Butterfield, F. Jones	1 (Jamaica)
1731	*Mary*	S. Spofforth, J. Woodley of Nevis	3 (Nevis)
1731	*Unity*	S. Paynter, P. Paynter Jr. & Sr., J. Evans	1 (Curacao and Bermuda)

Date	Vessel	Owner(s)	Slaves & Origins
1732	*Charming Joanna*	W. Seymour Sr., F. Seymour	8 (Barbados)
1732	*Neptune*	H. Corbusier, W. Mitchell, J. Jones	2 (Bermuda)
1733	*Heron and Dolphin*	A. Heron, W. Mitchell, S. Judkins, B. Wright	1 (Antigua and Bermuda)
1733	*Riddle*	G. Seacraft, W. Riddle, W. Albuoy	1 (Bonaire and Curacao)
1733	*St. Andrews*	W. Riddle, W. Keel	2 (Bermuda)
1733	*Happy*	J., T., and K. Hunt, E. Burrows, D. Hinson	1 (Antigua)
1734	*Warwick*	J. Darrell Jr., M. Darrell, Wm. Riddle	1 (St. Lucia)
1736	*Olive Branch*	R. Durham, J., T., and K. Hunt, W. Burrows	3 (Curacao)
1737	*Unity*	S. Paynter, W. Leacraft, P. Payner	1 (Jamaica)
1738	*Industry*	H. and S. Outerbridge	4 (Antigua)
1738	*Unity*	P. Paynter Jr. & Sr., Ruth Evans	2 (Barbados)
1738	*Delight*	S. Burrows, J. Henry, T. Gilbert, T. Jenoux, P. Trimingham	1 (Jamaica)
1738	*Blessing*	J. Wells, R. Mathelin, Mary Bassett	3 (Jamaica)
1738	*Unity*	P. Paynter Jr. & Sr., Ruth Evans	1 (Madeira)
1738	*Frances*	B. Stiles, Mary Stiles, G. Gibbs	1 (Bermuda)
1739	*Hopewell*	E. Young, J. Tucker, P. Mallory	1 (Turks I.)
1739	*Mary and Margaret*	W. Burrows, J. Hunt, D. Hinson, T. Fowle	1 (St. Thomas)
1739	*Retrieve*	T. Seymour, C. Williams, C. Willis, R. Burr	5 (Bermuda)

Date	Vessel	Owner(s)	Slaves & Origins
1739	*Black Jake*	H. Tucker, Wm. Riddle, S. Lightbourn	4 (Bermuda)
1740	*Dove*	Wm. Riddle, J. Gibbs	1 (Jamaica)
1740	*Frances*	W. Mallory Sr. & Jr., Wm. Riddle	1 (Bermuda)
1740	*Elisabeth*	R. Mathelin	9 (St. Christopher)
1740	*Charming Jane*	W. Seymour	2 (Antigua)
1740	*Olive Branch*	T. Hunt, R. Durham, N. Marston of New York	3 (Jamaica)
1740	*Mary*	F. Jones, J. Sears	1 (Jamaica)
1741	*Anne*	D. Whitney, G. Jones, J. Butterfield, J. Taylor	3 (Jamaica)
1741	*Anne*	F. Jones, R. Voden of London, J. Dickinson, S. Burrows	1 (Bermuda)
1742	*Mary*	H. Corbusier, S. Spofforth, J. Peniston Jr., Catherine Horton	1 (Bermuda)

Source: Donnan, *Slave Trade*, 3:462–512.

Bermuda-Registered Vessels Bringing Blacks to Virginia, 1710–1766

Date	Vessel	Master	Slaves & Origins
1710–1718	*Industry*	Jno. Smith (m)	2 (Providence)
	Love	Samuel Saltus	1 (Bermuda)
	Elizabeth	Thos. Bell	2 (Barbados)
	Dragon	Thoms. Eve	1 (Bermuda)
	May Flower	John Dorrell	3 (Barbados) 1 drawn back[1]
	Content	Jno. Argent	2 (Bermuda) 1 drawn back
1727	*Resolution*	Daniel Gibbs	1 (Turks Islands)
1734	*Warwick*	John Darrell	18 (Barbados)
1734	*Mary*	Peter Pruden	1 (Barbados)
1735	*Ann*	Francis Jones & Co.	10 (Bermuda)
1735	*Henry*	Edw. Todd	23 (Bermuda)
1735	*Sarah and Ann*	Thos. Joell	3 (Antigua)
1736	*Ann*	Francis Jones & Co.	3 (Bermuda)
1736	*Neptune*	John Harvey	1 (Bermuda)
1736	*Saunders*	John Sears	4 (Bermuda)
1736	*Reb'a and Batchelor*	Jno. Robinson	1 (Bermuda)
1736	*Bermuda Merchant*	Giles Corbusier	6 (St. Christopher)
1736	*Increase*	Will. Riddell & Co.	1 (Barbados)

1. Not sold; returned.

Date	Vessel	Master	Slaves & Origins
1737	*Mary and Elizabeth*	Nathaniel Bascomb	4 (Bermuda)
1737	*Elizabeth*	Francis Jones	2 (Bermuda)
1737	*Ann*	Jas. Dickinson & Co.	4 (Bermuda)
1737	*Pembrooke*	Joseph Stowe	1 (Bermuda)
1738	*Frances*	Nathaniel Butterfield	1 (Bermuda)
1738	*Ann*	Sam. Barrons	3 (Bermuda)
1738	*Ruby*	Richd. Leycraft	5 (Bermuda)
1739	*Martha and Mary*	Nich. Hinson	11 (Barbados)
1739	*Eagle*	Will. Riddle	15 (Antigua)
1739	*Mary*	Francis Jones	7 (Bermuda)
1739	*Mary*	Isr. Brownlow	8 (Bermuda)
1740	*Bredah*	Jeremiah Burch	4 (South Carolina)
1740	*Breda*	Jeremiah Burch	4 (Lower James)
1740	*Charity*	George Gibbs	1 (Bermuda)
1740	*Mary*	Isr. Brownlow	1 (Bermuda)
1741	*Roy'l Ranger*	Nathaniel Bascome	3 (Barbados)
1741	*Friendly*	Thom. Tucker	26 (Barbados)
1741	*Joseph*	John Butterfield	1 (Bermuda)
1741	*Martha and Susanna*	Hubbard Outerbridge	15 (Antigua)
1741	*Endeavour*	John Pitt	18 (Barbados)
1741	*Fanny*	Henry Darrell	1 (Bermuda)
1741	*Mary*	Israel Brownlow	3 (Bermuda)
1741	*Joseph*	John Butterfield	1 (Bermuda)
1741	*Sarah and Elizabeth*	Joseph Stowe	1 (Bermuda)
1741	*Elizabeth*	Will. Higgs	2 (Bermuda)
1741	*Diamont*	Fra's Jones	1 (Bermuda)
1741	*Elizabeth*	Fra's Jones	4 (Bermuda)
1741	*Delight*	Thom. Gilbert & Co.	1 (Bermuda)
1741	*Endeavour*	Soloman Joell	1 (Barbados)

Date	Vessel	Master	Slaves & Origins
1741	*Molly*	Joseph Darrel	1 (Bermuda)
1741	*Industry*	Solom. Joell	1 (Bermuda)
1742	*Industry*	William Morris	1 (Hampton, Va.)
	Nonpareil	Henr. Tucker	1 (Bermuda)
	Breda	Jerem. Birch of Birmingham	1 (Bermuda)
	Nonpareil	Henry Tucker & Co.	1 (Bermuda)
1742	*Friendship*	Henry Jennings & Co.	1 (Bermuda)
	Charming Molly	Nath. Butterfield & Co.	1 (Bermuda)
	Elizabeth	Robt. Robertson	1 (Bermuda)
	Molly	John Harvey & Co.	1 (Bermuda)
	Esther	Thos. Parsons & Co.	2 (Lower District)
	Robert	James Congers & Co. of Virg.	5 (Bermuda)
1743	*Royall Rangers*	Wm. and Mary Burrass	2 (Bermuda)
	Windsor Castle	John Pigot	2 (Bermuda)
	Diamond	Henr. Corbusier	3 (St. Christopher)
	Joseph	John Butterfield	1 (Bermuda)
	Industry	John Argent & Co.	2 (Barbados)
1744	*Joseph*	John Butterfield	8 (Antigua)
	Sea Flower	Thom. Hunt & Co.	1 (Montserrat)
	Deborah	Nath. Bascombe & Co. of V.	1 (Bermuda)
	Esther	Thom. Parsons & Co.	1 (Bermuda)
	Endeavour	Fra's Jones & Co.	50 (St. Christopher)
	Elizabeth	Robt. Brown & Co.	2 (Bermuda)
1746	*Jolly Batchellor*	Henr. Corbusier	3 (Barbados)
1747	*Delights Change*	Solo'n Joell	2 (Angola)
	Elizabeth and Mary	Fran. Guichard & Co., St. Kitts	1 (St. Christopher)
1751	*St. George*	Ric. Baker	6 (St. Christopher)
1754	*Luckey*	Richard Pitts & Co.	3 (Providence)
1754	*Charming Ann*	George Tucker	4 (Bermuda)

Appendix B

Date	Vessel	Master	Slaves & Origins
1754	*Lucky*	Rich'd Pitts & Co.	2 (Turks I.)
1755	*Charming Ann*	Edward Godfrey & Co.	4 (Bermuda)
1756	*Charm'g Ann*	Richard Cocks & Co.	2 (York River, Va.)
1762	*Molly*	Sam. Peniston, Jno. and Saml. Paynters	1 Man 4 Women (Bermuda)
1763	*John*	Wm. Seymour & Co.	4 (Barbados)
1765	*Mary*	Wm. Riddle & Co.	2 (Barbados)
	Esther	Thos. Joell & Co.	11 (Nevis)
	Sally	Thos. Hutchins	3 (Barbados)
1766	*Dolphin*	John Outerbrize	4 (Montserrat)

Source: Donnan, *Slave Trade,* 3:462–512.

A Note on Bermuda Sources

Since Bermuda lies outside the mainstream of either American or Caribbean colonial history, a brief description of its rich and largely unused seventeenth- and eighteenth-century materials is in order. Thanks to the compilations of two Bermudians, Helen Rowe and A. C. Hollis Hallett, the sources for Bermuda history have been listed in two works useful to scholars. I am indebted to Rowe's *A Guide to the Records of Bermuda* (Hamilton, Bermuda: Government Stationery Office, 1980) for a compilation of public documents and private papers in the Bermuda Archives, and to Hallett's *Bermuda in Print: A Guide to the Printed Literature on Bermuda,* 2d ed. (Hamilton, Bermuda: Juniperhill Press, 1995).

Bermuda's earliest public records date from the founding of the colony in 1612. The collection known as the Colonial Records in the Bermuda Archives contains documents such as the commission of the first governor, Richard Moore, letters and instructions of the Somers Islands Company, governors' correspondence and proclamations, minutes of the Governor's Council, acts of the Bermuda Assembly, assize court records, and various other public documents through the 1680s. Among them are the remarkable map and real estate survey of the colony in 1663 by Richard Norwood— the "Domesday Book" of Bermuda—that describes every property and lists the owner or tenant of every acre in Bermuda in 1663. The seventeenth-century court records and grand jury presentments date from the first assize in 1616 and run through 1677, with gaps totaling twenty years. Assize records from the 1680s, the decade of Bermuda's transition from the control of the Somers Island Company to the status of a royal colony, are not extant. From 1693 to 1797 the assize court records continue, with some years missing. They are an invaluable source for Bermuda's early social history and racial history, for they include trials of Indians, blacks, and mulattos as well as whites. Equally valuable for this study were the Books of Wills and Inventories, 15 bound manuscript volumes that contain documents from 1629 to 1835. The Colonial Records and Books of Wills are now on microfilm. The Colonial Records are excerpted in J. Henry Lefroy, *Memorials of the Discovery and Early Settlement of the Bermudas or Somers Islands, 1515–1685,* 2 vols. (London,

1877, 1879; reprint, Toronto: University of Toronto Press, 1981). Wills and related documents for hundreds of Bermuda families are listed alphabetically in C. F. E. Hollis Hallett, comp., *Early Bermuda Wills, 1629–1835* (Pembroke, Bermuda: Juniperhill Press, printed by University of Toronto Press, 1993).

Church records for the seventeenth and eighteenth centuries are fragmentary and have been microfilmed. There are parish registers of baptisms, marriages, and burials at St. Anne's Church in Southampton dating from 1619 to 1700, with some later additions in the 1750s and 1760s; St. John's Church in Pembroke from 1645 to 1720; and Devonshire from 1668 to 1706. There are a few pages from a register kept by the Reverend James Holiday of Hamilton Parish from 1745 to 1748, a register for Smith's Parish, 1758–1761, and some partial records kept by two other clergymen, Reverend John Moore from 1743 to 1776, and the Reverend Alexander Ewing, 1755 to 1802. Parish records of baptisms, marriages, and burials, along with miscellaneous other records, have been compiled by A. C. Hollis Hallett in *Early Bermuda Records, 1619–1826: A Guide to the Parish and Clergy Registers with Some Assessment Lists and Petitions* (Pembroke, Bermuda: Juniperhill Press, printed by University of Toronto Press, 1991).

Government and court records in the Bermuda Archives include the minutes of the Governor's Council meetings starting in 1645. The minutes from 1684 to 1756 were printed in sequence in the 38 volumes of the *Bermuda Historical Quarterly,* a publication that existed from 1944 to 1981. A listing of the council minutes in these volumes can be found in Hallett, *Bermuda in Print.* Complete sets of the periodical are in the Bermuda National Library and in the Bermuda Archives, both in Hamilton, Bermuda. Legislative records are in *Ancient Journals of the House of Assembly of Bermuda from 1691 to 1785,* 2 vols. (Hamilton, Bermuda, 1890), and in Miscellaneous Acts, 1711–1759, and Manuscript Acts, 1762–1779, manuscript collections in the Bermuda Archives. The correspondence of Bermuda's royal governors with the Board of Trade, including reports and census records, is in the Colonial Office papers (CO 37) in the Public Record Office in Kew, England. There are microfilm copies in the Bermuda Archives.

Bermuda did not have a newspaper until 1784, when the *Bermuda Gazette and Weekly Advertiser* began publication on January 17. The Bermuda National Library has a complete file of this newspaper through 1827, continuing to the present as the daily *Royal Gazette.*

Archival collections of private letters and papers for seventeenth- and eighteenth-century Bermuda are rare. For the seventeenth century, the correspondence of Robert Rich, Earl of Warwick, one of the principal shareholders of the Bermuda colony, his cousin, Nathaniel Rich, also a shareholder, and Nathaniel's brother, young Robert Rich, manager of the family's holdings in

Bermuda, have been preserved. The Rich family's letters to each other and to their various Bermuda connections—factors, government officials, clergymen, tenants, and servants—provide an extraordinary record of the colony's first three decades. Once part of the Manchester Papers in the collection of the Duke of Manchester in England, these letters were purchased in 1970 by the Bermuda National Trust. They were edited by Vernon A. Ives in *The Rich Papers: Letters from Bermuda, 1616–1646* (Hamilton, Bermuda: Bermuda National Trust, printed by University of Toronto Press, 1984). Other private papers relating to the seventeenth and eighteenth centuries in the Bermuda Archives include the Jennings "family book," a manuscript journal containing a history of that family, 1697–1746, and some letters of the Reverend Alexander Ewing in the 1780s. The Bermuda National Trust has a collection of Tucker family papers from the mid- to late-eighteenth century.

Bermuda's rich architectural history, with many seventeenth- and eighteenth-century buildings still in use, is being preserved in the Historic Buildings Book Project, a series published by the Bermuda National Trust. These are histories of each of Bermuda's parishes, plus the colonial capital, St. George's. Drawing on private collections of family papers, drawings, and photographs as well as wills, inventories, and land records, these volumes offer a unique chronicle of Bermuda's development, beginning in the seventeenth century. The first volume in the series, *Bermuda's Architectural Heritage: Devonshire,* a collaborative research effort by the trust, with a text by Andrew Trimingham, was published in 1995. The second, *Bermuda's Architectural Heritage: St. George's* (1998), was the work of Michael Jarvis and a trust research team. Other volumes are in the making.

Works Cited

Archival Materials

Bermuda Archives

PRINTED WORKS

Acts of Assembly Made and Enacted in the Bermuda or Summer Islands . . . . London, 1737.

Ancient Journals of the House of Assembly of Bermuda from 1691 to 1785. 4 vols. Hamilton, Bermuda, 1890.

Bermuda Acts, 1690–1883. Compiled by Reginald Gray. 2 vols. London, 1884.

Bermuda Statutes, Laws, and Acts of Assembly, 1690–1714. London, 1719.

MANUSCRIPT SOURCES

Action Book. 1739–1766. Folder AZ 101/6.

Assize Court Records.

   1693–1697. Folder AZ 102/1.

   1704–1709. Folder AZ 102/3.

   1710–1719. Folder AZ 102/4.

   1720–1725. Folder AZ 102/5.

   1726–1735. Folder AZ 102/6.

   1755–1764. Folder AZ 102/9.

Books of Administrations. 1782–1835. 4 MS vols.

Book of Bills, Deeds, and Protests. 1739–1766.

Books of Wills and Inventories. 1629–1835. 15 bound MS vols. Also on microfilm.

Colonial Records of Bermuda. 1616–1713. 9 MS vols. Also on microfilm.

   Volume 1 (1616–1640), reel no. 495: Assize records, Council minutes, Acts of Assembly.

   Volume 2 (1636–1661), reel no. 496: Indentures, deeds, bills of sale.

   Volume 3 (1647–1661), reel no. 497: Assize records, Council minutes.

   Volume 4 (1647–1683), reel no. 502: Letters to and from the Bermuda Company, Whale Fishery.

   Volume 5A (1622–1676), reel no. 503: Deeds.

Volume 5B (1661–1676), reel no. 507: Council, Assizes, etc.

Volume 6 (1663), Richard Norwood's Survey of Bermuda.

Volume 7 (1676–1689), reel 510: Council, Assizes, etc.

Volume 8 (1677–1692), reel 511: Warrants, Indentures, Bonds.

Volume 9 (1677–1713), reel 512: Bonds, Bills, Grants, etc.

Fragmentary Books A–E (miscellaneous letters and documents, 1622–1635), reel 508.

Fragmentary Books G–H (Shipping Register, 1656–1671; General Assembly, 1663; Oaths of Public Office, 1693), reel 509.

Darrell, William Hall. Genealogical Note Book. 1872.

Holiday, Rev. James. "Baptisms of Coloured Persons in Hamilton in the Islands of Bermuda in the Year 1749." Holiday Parish Register transcript.

Manuscript Acts. 1762–1779.

Miscellaneous Acts. 1711–1759.

Norwood, Richard. "A Mapp of the Sommer Ilands." 1626.

Records of the Minutes of Council in Assembly. 1746–1765. 2 MS vols.

St. Anne's Church Records. 1619–1751. Microfilm reel 19.

St. John's Church Records.

Baptisms, Marriages, and Deaths. 1645–1722. Microfilm reel 25.

Registers. 1663–1791. Microfilm reel 37.

Wood, Roger. Letter Book of Roger Wood. 1631–1634. Colonial Records. Fragmentary Book F. Microfilm reel 720.

Public Record Office, Kew, England.

Colonial Office Papers. CO 37. CO 700.

Other Sources

Abrahams, Roger D., and John F. Szwed, eds. *After Africa: Extracts from British Travel Accounts and Journals of the Seventeenth, Eighteenth, and Nineteenth Centuries Concerning the Slaves, Their Manners, and Customs in the British West Indies.* New Haven: Yale University Press, 1983.

Andrews, Charles M. *The Colonial Period of American History.* 4 vols. New Haven: Yale University Press, 1938.

Andrews, Kenneth R. *The Spanish Caribbean: Trade and Plunder, 1530–1630.* New Haven: Yale University Press, 1978.

Aptheker, Herbert. *American Negro Slave Revolts.* New York: Columbia University Press, 1943.

Arton, Mary Alicia Juliette. *Trade and Commerce of Bermuda, 1515 to 1839.* Hamilton, Bermuda: Island Press, 1965.

Axtell, James, "The White Indians of Colonial America." *William and Mary Quarterly,* 3d ser., 32, no. 1 (January 1975): 55–88.

Bailyn, Bernard, and Philip Morgan, eds. *Strangers within the Realm: Cultural Margins of the First British Empire*. Chapel Hill: University of North Carolina Press, 1991.

Barbour, Philip L., ed. *The Complete Works of Captain John Smith*. 3 vols. Chapel Hill: University of North Carolina Press, 1986.

Beckles, Hilary. *White Servitude and Black Slavery in Barbados, 1627–1715*. Knoxville: University of Tennessee Press, 1989.

Benbow, Colin. "Norwood's First Survey." *Bermuda Historical Quarterly* 32, no. 3 (1975): 48–52.

Berlin, Ira. "From Creole to African: Atlantic Creoles and the Origins of African-American Society in Mainland North America." *William and Mary Quarterly,* 3d ser., 33, no. 2 (April 1996): 251–88.

———. "Time, Space, and the Evolution of Afro-American Society on British Mainland North America." *American Historical Review* 85 (1980): 44–78.

Berlin, Ira, and Philip D. Morgan, eds. *Cultivation and Culture: Labor and the Shaping of Slave Life in America*. Charlottesville, Va.: University Press of Virginia, 1993.

Bernhard, Virginia. " 'Men, Women, and Children' at Jamestown: Population and Gender in Early Virginia, 1607–1610." *Journal of Southern History* 58, no. 4 (November 1992): 599–618.

Bluck, Laura A. "The Evolution of the Town of Hamilton." *Bermuda Historical Quarterly* 13, no. 3 (1956): 111–35.

Bodeau. "A Propos de Quelques Accidents Dus au Mancinillier." *Archives de Medecine et Pharmacie Navales* 126, no. 122 (1910): 122–33.

Boissevain, Ethel. "Whatever Became of the New England Indians Shipped to Bermuda and Sold as Slaves?" *Man in the Northeast* 21 (1981): 103–14.

Boles, John. *Black Southerners, 1619–1869*. Lexington, Ky.: University of Kentucky Press, 1983.

———, ed. *Masters and Slaves in the House of the Lord: Race and Religion in the American South, 1740–1870*. Lexington, Ky.: University of Kentucky Press, 1988.

Bolster, Jeffrey. *Black Jacks: African American Seamen in the Age of Sail*. Cambridge: Harvard University Press, 1997.

Breen, T. H., and Stephen Innes. *'Myne Owne Ground': Race and Freedom on Virginia's Eastern Shore, 1640–1676*. New York: Oxford University Press, 1980.

Breslaw, Elaine G. "The Salem Witch from Barbados: In Search of Tituba's Roots." *Essex Institute Historical Collections* 128, no. 4 (October 1992): 230–33.

———. *Tituba, Reluctant Witch of Salem: Devilish Indians and Puritan Fantasies*. New York: New York University Press, 1996.

Bridenbaugh, Carl. *No Peace beyond the Line: The English in the Caribbean, 1624–1690*. New York: Oxford University Press, 1972.

Brown, Kathleen M. *Good Wives, Nasty Wenches, and Anxious Patriarchs: Gender, Race, and Power in Colonial Virginia*. Chapel Hill: University of North Carolina Press, 1996.

Bruce, Philip Alexander. *An Economic History of Virginia in the Seventeenth Century*. 2 vols. 1895. Reprint, New York: P. Smith, 1935.

Burns, Alan Cuthbert. *History of the British West Indies*. London: Allen and Unwin, 1965.

Butler, Nathaniel. *Historye of the Bermudaes or Summer Ilands*. Edited by J. Henry Lefroy. London: Hakluyt Society, 1892.

Calendar of State Papers, Colonial Series, America and West Indies. 41 vols. Edited by Noel Sainsbury et al. London, 1860–1953.

Carr, Lois Green, Russell R. Menard, and Lorena S. Walsh. *Robert Cole's World: Agriculture and Society in Early Maryland*. Chapel Hill: University of North Carolina Press, 1991.

Carr, Lois Green, Lorena S. Walsh, Gloria L. Main, and Jackson Turner Main. "Toward a History of the Standard of Living in British North America." *William and Mary Quarterly*, 3d ser., 45, no. 1 (January 1988): 116–70.

Carson, Cary, Ronald Hoffman, and Peter J. Albert, eds. *Of Consuming Interests: The Style of Life in the Eighteenth Century*. Charlottesville, Va.: University Press of Virginia, 1994.

Chamberlain, John. *The Letters of John Chamberlain*. Edited by N. E. McClure. 2 vols. Philadelphia: American Philosophical Society, 1939.

Chartrand, Rene. "Notes on Bermuda Military Forces, 1687–1815." *Bermuda Historical Quarterly* 28, no. 2 (1971): 40–49.

Cody, Cheryl Ann. "There was No 'Absalom' on the Ball Plantation: Slave-Naming Practices in the South Carolina Low Country, 1720–1865." *American Historical Review* 92 (June 1987): 563–96.

Conniff, Michael L., and Thomas J. Davis. *Africans in the Americas: A History of the Black Diaspora*. New York: St. Martin's Press, 1992.

Considerations touching the New Contract for Tobacco. London, 1625.

"Constructing Race: Differentiating Peoples in the Early Modern World." *William and Mary Quarterly*, 3d ser., 54, no. 1 (January 1997).

Council minutes, 1684–1756. *Bermuda Historical Quarterly* 1, no. 2 (1944): 56; 2, no. 1 (1945): 14–19, and no. 4 (1945): 160; 3, no. 1 (1946): 15–24, and no. 2 (1946): 63–73; 4, no. 2 (1947): 46; 5, no. 3 (1948): 111, and no. 4 (1948): 157, 161; 8, no. 1 (1951): 3; 11, no. 3 (1954): 11; 12, no. 2 (1955): 38–39, and no. 4 (1955): 113; 13, no. 4 (1956): 150; 17, no. 3 (1957): 93; 18, no. 1 (1961): 3–4; 28, no. 2 (1971): 35; 35, no. 4 (1978): 55; 36, no. 1 (1979): 21, and no. 2 (1979): 24; 37, no. 4 (1980): 5.

Crane, Elaine Forman. "The Socioeconomics of a Female Majority in Eighteenth-Century Bermuda." *Signs: Journal of Women in Culture and Society* 15, no. 2 (winter 1990): 231–58.

Craton, Michael. "Reluctant Creoles: The Planters' World in the British West Indies." In *Strangers within the Realm,* edited by Bernard Bailyn and Philip D. Morgan. Chapel Hill: University of North Carolina Press, 1991.

———. *Testing the Chains: Resistance to Slavery in the British West Indies.* Ithaca, N.Y.: Cornell University Press, 1982.

———. *Empire, Enslavement, and Freedom in the Caribbean.* Princeton: Marcus Wiener, 1997.

Craton, Michael, and Gail Saunders. *Islanders in the Stream: A History of the Bahamian People.* 2 vols. Athens, Ga.: University of Georgia Press, 1992.

Craton, Michael, James Walvin, and David Wright, eds. *Slavery, Abolition, and Emancipation: Black Slaves and the British Empire: A Thematic Documentary.* London: Longman, 1976.

Craven, W. F. "The Earl of Warwick, A Speculator in Piracy." *Hispanic American Historical Review* 10 (1930): 457–79.

———. *An Introduction to the History of Bermuda.* Williamsburg, Va., 1938. Originally published in *William and Mary Quarterly,* 2d ser., 17, nos. 2, 3, 4 (April, July, October 1937), and 18, no. 1 (January 1938).

Crèvecoeur, Jean Hector St. Jean de. "A Description of Bermuda: Extract from 'Lettres d'un Cultivateur Americain' by Jean Crevecoeur, 1784." Translated by Louis S. Friedland. *Bermuda Historical Quarterly* 3, no. 4 (1946): 201–3.

Curtin, Philip D. *The Atlantic Slave Trade: A Census.* Madison, Wisc.: University of Wisconsin Press, 1969.

Darrell, John Harvey. "Journal of John Harvey Darrell." *Bermuda Historical Quarterly* 2, no. 3 (1945): 129–42.

Davis, Thomas J. *A Rumor of Revolt: The "Great Negro Plot" in Colonial New York.* New York: Free Press, 1985.

Deal, Douglas. *Race and Class in Colonial Virginia: Indians, Englishmen, and Africans on the Eastern Shore during the Seventeenth Century.* New York: Garland Press, 1993.

Demos, John. *Entertaining Satan: Witchcraft and the Culture of Early New England.* New York: Oxford University Press, 1982.

Donnan, Elizabeth, ed. *Documents Illustrative of the History of the Slave Trade to America.* 4 vols. Washington, D.C.: Carnegie Institution of Washington, 1932.

Dunn, Richard S. "The Downfall of the Bermuda Company: A Restoration Farce." *William and Mary Quarterly,* 3d ser., 20, no. 4 (October 1963): 487–512.

————. *Sugar and Slaves: The Rise of the Planter Class in the English West Indies, 1624–1713.* Chapel Hill: University of North Carolina Press, 1972.

Dunn, Richard S., James Savage, and Letitia Yeandle, eds. *The Journal of John Winthrop, 1630–1649.* Cambridge: Belknap Press, 1996.

Earle, Carville V. "Environment, Disease, and Mortality in Early Virginia." In *The Chesapeake in the Seventeenth Century: Essays on Anglo-American Society,* edited by Thad Tate and David Ammerman. Chapel Hill: University of North Carolina Press, 1979.

————. *The Evolution of a Tidewater Settlement System: All Hallow's Parish, Maryland, 1650–1783.* University of Chicago Department of Geography Research Paper 170. Chicago, 1975.

Edwards, Bryan. *The History, Civil and Commercial, of the British Colonies in the West Indies.* 2d ed. 2 vols. London, 1801.

Egerton, Douglas R. *Gabriel's Rebellion: The Virginia Slave Conspiracies of 1800 and 1802.* Chapel Hill: University of North Carolina Press, 1993.

Engerman, Stanley L. "Europe, the Lesser Antilles, and Economic Expansion, 1600–1800." In *The Lesser Antilles in the Age of European Expansion,* edited by Robert Paquette and Stanley L. Engerman. Gainesville, Fla.: University Press of Florida, 1996.

Esten, James Christie. *A Plan for the Instructions &c., of the Emancipated People of Colour.* London, 1837.

Fessenden, Helen M. "Childhood Memories of Bermuda in the '70s." *Bermuda Historical Quarterly* 5, no. 1 (1948): 20–38.

Forbes, Jack. *Africans and Native Peoples: The Language of Race and the Evolution of Red-Black Peoples.* Urbana: University of Illinois Press, 1993.

Frey, Sylvia. "In Search of Roots: The Colonial Antecedents of Slavery in the Plantation Colonies." *Georgia Historical Quarterly* 68, no. 2 (summer 1984): 244–59.

————. *Water from the Rock: Black Resistance in a Revolutionary Age.* Princeton: Princeton University Press, 1991.

Frey, Sylvia, and Betty Wood. *Come Shouting to Zion: African American Protestantism in the American South and British Caribbean to 1830.* Chapel Hill: University of North Carolina Press, 1998.

Games, Allison F. "Opportunity and Mobility in Early Barbados." In *The Lesser Antilles in the Age of European Expansion,* edited by Robert Paquette and Stanley L. Engerman. Gainesville, Fla.: University Press of Florida, 1996.

Gaspar, David Barry. "Ameliorating Slavery: The Leeward Islands Slave Act of 1798." In *The Lesser Antilles in the Age of European Expansion,* edited by Robert Paquette and Stanley L. Engerman. Gainesville, Fla.: University Press of Florida, 1996.

————. *Bondmen and Rebels: A Study of Master-Slave Relations in Antigua.* Baltimore: Johns Hopkins University Press, 1985.

Genovese, Eugene D. *From Rebellion to Revolution: Afro-American Slave Revolts in the Making of the Modern World.* Baton Rouge: Louisiana State University Press, 1979.

Golding, William. *Servants on Horseback, or . . . A Representation of the dejected state of the Inhabitants of Summer Islands.* London, 1648. Reprinted in *Bermuda Historical Quarterly* 9, no. 1 (1952): 183–213.

"The Governors of Bermuda." *Bermuda Historical Quarterly* 22, no. 4 (1965): 111–15.

Gragg, Larry D. *The Salem Witch Crisis.* New York: Praeger, 1992.

————. " 'To Procure Negroes': The English Slave Trade to Barbados, 1627–60." *Slavery and Abolition* 16, no. 1 (April 1995): 65–84.

Greene, Jack P. *Pursuits of Happiness: The Social Development of Early Modern British Colonies and the Formation of American Culture.* Chapel Hill: University of North Carolina Press, 1988.

Greenwood, Isaac J. *Bermuda during the American Revolution.* Boston, 1896.

Hall, Joyce. "Norwood," *Bermudian* (December 1958): 19–27, 47–49.

Hall, Kim F. *Things of Darkness: Economies of Race and Gender in Early Modern England.* Ithaca, N.Y.: Cornell University Press, 1995.

Hall, Neville A. T. *Slave Society in the Danish West Indies: St. Thomas, St. John, and St. Croix.* Edited by B. W. Higman. Baltimore: Johns Hopkins University Press, 1992.

Hallett, A. C. Hollis. *Bermuda in Print: A Guide to the Printed Literature on Bermuda.* 2d ed. Hamilton, Bermuda: Juniperhill Press, 1995.

————. *Chronicle of a Colonial Church: Bermuda, 1612–1826.* Pembroke, Bermuda: Juniperhill Press, 1993. Printed by University of Toronto Press.

————, comp. *Early Bermuda Records, 1619–1826: A Guide to the Parish and Clergy Registers with Some Assessment Lists and Petitions.* Pembroke, Bermuda: Juniperhill Press, 1991. Printed by University of Toronto Press.

Hallett, C. F. E. Hollis, comp. *Early Bermuda Wills, 1629–1825.* Pembroke, Bermuda: Juniperhill Press, 1993. Printed by University of Toronto Press.

Harlow, Vincent T., ed. *Colonising Expeditions to the West Indies and Guiana, 1623–1667.* London: Hakluyt Society, s. 2, no. 56, 1925.

Harris, Jane. "History under Siege: A Review of Marine Archaeology in Bermuda." *Bermuda Journal of Archaeology and Maritime History* 45, no. 4 (July 1990): 15–16.

————. "Shipwrecks Reveal a Wealth of Maritime History." *Bermuda* 31, no. 11 (October 1, 1996): 85.

Hayward, W. B. "St. Peter's Churchyard." *Bermuda Historical Quarterly* 11, no. 1 (1954): 41–43.

Hening, William Walter, comp. *The Statutes at Large: Being a Collection of all the Laws of Virginia . . .* 13 vols. Richmond, Va., Philadelphia, and New York, 1819–23.

Higman, B. W. *Slave Populations of the British Caribbean.* Baltimore: Johns Hopkins University Press, 1984.

Holiday, James. "Diary of the Rev. James Holiday, 1746–1747." *Bermuda Historical Quarterly* 2, no. 2 (1945): 84–89.

Hope, John Bruce. "A Description of the Bermudas or Summer Islands in America in the Year 1722." Colonial Office Papers. Public Record Office, London.

Hudson, Larry E., Jr. *Working toward Freedom: Slave Society and Domestic Economy in the American South.* Rochester, N.Y.: University of Rochester Press, 1994.

Hughes-Hallett, Lt. Col. C. M. "Yellow Fever." *Bermuda Historical Quarterly* 11, no. 2 (1954): 101–4.

Hutchinson, Thomas. *History of the Colony and Province of Massachusetts.* Edited by Lawrence Mayo. 3 vols. Cambridge: Harvard University Press, 1986.

Inikori, Joseph E., and Stanley L. Engerman, eds. *The Atlantic Slave Trade: Effects on Economies, Societies, and People in Africa, the Americas, and Europe.* Durham, N.C.: Duke University Press, 1992.

Inscoe, John. "Carolina Slave Names: An Index to Acculturation." *Journal of Southern History* 49, no. 4 (November 1983): 529–30.

———. "Generation and Gender as Reflected in Carolina Slave Naming Practices: A Challenge to the Gutman Thesis." *South Carolina Historical Magazine* 94 (October 1994): 252–63.

Ives, Vernon A., ed. *The Rich Papers: Letters from Bermuda, 1615–1646.* Toronto: University of Toronto Press, 1984.

Jones, Norrece T. *Born a Child of Freedom, Yet a Slave: Mechanisms of Slave Control and Strategies of Resistance in Antebellum South Carolina.* Middleton, Conn.: Wesleyan University Press, 1989.

Jordan, Winthrop. *White over Black: American Attitudes toward the Negro, 1550–1812.* Chapel Hill: University of North Carolina Press, 1968.

Journal of the Commissioners for Trade and Plantations. 14 vols. London: H. M. Stationery Office: 1920–1938.

Karlsen, Carol F. *The Devil in the Shape of a Woman: Witchcraft in Colonial New England.* New York: W. W. Norton, 1987.

Kennedy, Jean de Chantal. *Biography of a Colonial Town: Hamilton, Bermuda.* Glasgow: Robert MacLehose and Co., 1961.

Kerr, Wilfred Brenton. *Bermuda and the American Revolution, 1760–1783.* Princeton: Princeton University Press, 1936.

Kiple, Kenneth F., and Kriemhild C. Ornelas. "After the Encounter: Disease and Demographics." In *The Lesser Antilles in the Age of European Expansion*, edited by Robert Paquette and Stanley L. Engerman. Gainesville, Fla.: University Press of Florida, 1996.

Kolchin, Peter. *American Slavery, 1619–1877*. New York: Hill and Wang, 1993.

Kulikoff, Allan. *Tobacco and Slaves: The Development of Southern Cultures in the Chesapeake, 1680–1800*. Chapel Hill: University of North Carolina Press, 1986.

Kupperman, Karen Ordahl. "Apathy and Death in Early Jamestown." *Journal of American History* 66 (June 1979): 24–40.

———. *Providence Island, 1630–1641: The Other Puritan Colony*. Cambridge, Eng.: Cambridge University Press, 1993.

Law, Esther K. "Christ Church, Warwick, 1719–1969." *Bermuda Historical Quarterly* 6, no. 2 (1969): 43–53.

Lefroy, J. Henry, ed. *Memorials of the Discovery and Early Settlement of the Bermudas or Somers Islands, 1515–1685*. 2 vols. 1877. Reprint, Toronto: University of Toronto for the Bermuda National Trust, 1981.

Levy, Babette. "Early Puritanism in Southern and Island Colonies." *American Antiquarian Society Proceedings* 70, pt. 1 (1960): 69–348.

Ligon, Richard. *A True and Exact Account of the Island of Barbadoes*. London, 1673. In *After Africa: Extracts from British Travel Accounts and Journals of the Seventeenth, Eighteenth, and Nineteenth Centuries Concerning the Slaves, Their Manners, and Customs in the British West Indies*, edited by Roger D. Abrahams and John F. Szwed. New Haven: Yale University Press, 1983.

Littlefield, Daniel C. *Rice and Slaves: Ethnicity and the Slave Trade of Colonial South Carolina*. Baton Rouge: Louisiana State University Press, 1981.

Lofton, John. *Denmark Vesey's Revolt: The Slave Plot that Lit a Fire to Fort Sumter*. Kent, Ohio: Kent State University Press, 1983.

———. *Insurrection in South Carolina: The Turbulent World of Denmark Vesey*. Yellow Springs, Ohio: Antioch Press, 1964.

Lower Norfolk County Virginia Antiquary. Edited by Edward W. James. Vols. 1–5. Baltimore: The Friedenwald Co., 1895–1906.

MacFarlane, Alan. *Witchcraft in Tudor and Stuart England: A Regional and Comparative Study*. New York: Harper and Row, 1970.

McCallan, E. A. *Life on Old St. David's*. Hamilton, Bermuda: Bermuda Historical Monuments Trust, 1948.

McColley, Robert. "Slavery in Virginia, 1619–1660: A Reexamination." In *New Perspectives on Race and Slavery in America: Essays in Honor of Kenneth M. Stampp*, edited by Robert H. Abzug and Stephen Maizlich. Lexington, Ky.: University of Kentucky Press, 1986.

McCusker, John J., and Russell R. Menard. *The Economy of British America, 1607–1789*. Chapel Hill: University of North Carolina Press, 1988.

McIlwaine, H. R., ed. *Minutes of the Council and General Court in Virginia*. Richmond, Va.: Colonial Press, Everett Waddey, 1924.

Martyr, Peter. *Legatio Babylonica*. 1511.

Menard, Russell R. "British Migration to the Chesapeake Colonies in the Seventeenth Century." In *Colonial Chesapeake Society*, edited by Lois Green Carr, Philip D. Morgan, and Jean B. Russo. Chapel Hill: University of North Carolina Press, 1988.

―――. "From Servants to Slaves: The Transformation of the Chesapeake Labor System." *Southern Studies* 16 (December 1977): 355–90.

―――. "The Maryland Slave Population, 1658–1730: A Demographic Profile of Blacks in Four Counties." *William and Mary Quarterly*, 3d ser., 32, no. 1 (January 1975): 29–54.

Mintz, Sidney W., and Richard Price. *The Birth of African-American Culture: An Anthropological Perspective*. Boston: Beacon Press, 1992. Originally published as *An Anthropological Approach to the Afro-American Past* (Philadelphia: Institute for the Study of Human Issues, 1976).

Morgan, Edmund S. *American Slavery/American Freedom: The Ordeal of Colonial Virginia*. New York: W. W. Norton and Company, 1975.

―――. "The First American Boom: Virginia, 1618 to 1630." *William and Mary Quarterly*, 3d ser., 28, no. 2 (April 1971): 169–98.

Morgan, Philip D. "British Encounters with Africans and African-Americans, circa 1600–1780." In *Strangers within the Realm: Cultural Margins of the First British Empire*, edited by Bernard Bailyn and Philip D. Morgan. Chapel Hill: University of North Carolina Press, 1991.

―――. *Slave Counterpoint: Black Culture in the Eighteenth Century Chesapeake and Lowcountry*. Chapel Hill: University of North Carolina Press for the Omohundro Institute of Early American History, 1998.

―――. "Slave Life in Piedmont Virginia, 1720–1800." In *Colonial Chesapeake Society*, edited by Lois Green Carr, Philip D. Morgan, and Jean B. Russo. Chapel Hill: University of North Carolina Press, 1988.

Morgan, Philip, and Michael Nicholls. "Slaves in Piedmont Virginia, 1720–1790." *William and Mary Quarterly*, 3d ser., 46, no. 2 (April 1989): 211–51.

Mullin, Gerald. *Flight and Rebellion: Slave Resistance in Eighteenth Century Virginia*. New York: Oxford University Press, 1972.

Mullin, Michael. *Africa in America: Slave Acculturation and Resistance in the American South and the British Caribbean, 1736–1831*. Urbana: University of Illinois Press, 1992.

Newton, Arthur P. *Colonising Activities of the English Puritans: The Last Phase of the Elizabethan Struggle with Spain*. 1914. Reprint, Port Washington, N.Y.: Kennikat Press, 1966.

———. *The European Nations in the West Indies, 1493–1688*. 1933. Reprint, New York: Barnes and Nobles, 1967.

North Atlantic Ocean: Bermuda Islands. Navigational chart. Hamilton, Bermuda, 1996.

Norwood, Richard. *The Journal of Richard Norwood*. Edited, and with an introduction, by W. F. Craven and Walter B. Hayward. New York: Bermuda Historical Monuments Trust, 1945.

———. "Relations of Summer Islands . . ." In *Hakluytus Posthumus or Purchas His Pilgrimes*, edited by Samuel Purchas. 20 vols. Glasgow: J. MacLehose and Sons, 1905–1907.

Oates, Stephen B. *The Fires of Jubilee: Nat Turner's Fierce Rebellion*. New York: Harper and Row, 1975.

O'Shaughnessy, Andrew. "Redcoats and Slaves in the British Caribbean." In *The Lesser Antilles in the Age of European Expansion*, edited by Robert Paquette and Stanley L. Engerman. Gainesville, Fla.: University Press of Florida, 1996.

Packwood, Cyril Outerbridge. *Chained on the Rock: Slavery in Bermuda*. New York: Eliseo Torres and Sons, 1975.

Packwood, Cyril Outerbridge. Interview by the author. Hamilton, Bermuda, August 1990.

Palmer, Margaret. *The Mapping of Bermuda: A Bibliography of Printed Maps and Charts, 1548–1970*. Edited by R. V. Tooley. London: Holland Press, 1983.

Palmié, Stephan, ed. *Slave Cultures and the Cultures of Slavery*. Knoxville: University of Tennessee Press, 1995.

Patterson, Orlando. *Slavery and Social Death: A Comparative Study*. Cambridge: Harvard University Press, 1982.

Percy, George. "A Trewe Relacyon of the Procedeinges . . . in Virginia." *Tyler's Quarterly Historical and Genealogical Magazine* 3 (April 1922): 259–82.

Pope, F. J. "Sir George Somers and His Family." *Bermuda Historical Quarterly* 4, no. 2 (1947): 57–61.

Rawley, James A. *The Transatlantic Slave Trade: A History*. New York: W. W. Norton Company, 1981.

The Records of the Virginia Company. Edited by Susan M. Kingsbury. 4 vols. Washington, D.C.: Government Reprint Office, 1906–1935.

"Report of Governor Robert Robinson to the Lords of Trade, 1687." *Bermuda Historical Quarterly* 2, no. 1 (1945): 14–19.

"Reports on Bermuda by Two 18th Century Governors." *Bermuda Historical Quarterly* 25, no. 2 (1968): 35–61.

Rivera y Saabedra, Juan de. "Shipwrecked Spaniards, 1639: Grievances against Bermudians." Translated by L. D. Gurrin. *Bermuda Historical Quarterly* 18, no. 1 (1961): 14–28.

Robinson, W. Stitt. "The Legal Status of the Indian in Colonial Virginia." *Virginia Magazine of History and Biography* 56 (July 1953): 247–59.

Rose, Willie Lee, ed. *A Documentary History of Slavery in North America.* New York: Oxford University Press, 1976.

Rutman, Darrett B., and Anita H. Rutman. *A Place in Time: Middlesex County, Virginia, 1650–1750.* New York: W. W. Norton, 1984.

Schwarz, Philip J. *Twice Condemned: Slaves and the Criminal Laws of Virginia, 1705–1865.* Baton Rouge: Louisiana State University Press, 1988.

Scott, Julius S.. "Crisscrossing Empires: Ships, Sailors, and Resistance in the Lesser Antilles in the Eighteenth Century." In *The Lesser Antilles in the Age of European Expansion,* edited by Robert Paquette and Stanley L. Engerman. Gainesville, Fla.: University Press of Florida, 1996.

Seed, Patricia. *Ceremonies of Possession in Europe's Conquest of the New World, 1492–1640.* Cambridge, Eng.: Cambridge University Press, 1995.

Sheehan, Bernard. *Savagism and Civility: Indians and Englishmen in Colonial Virginia.* Cambridge, Eng.: Cambridge University Press, 1980.

"Shipwrecks Reveal a Wealth of Maritime History." *Bermuda* 31, no. 11 (October 1, 1996).

Sluiter, Engel. "New Light on the '20 and Odd Negroes' Arriving in Virginia, August 1619." *William and Mary Quarterly,* 3d ser., 54, no. 2 (April 1997): 395–98.

Smith, James E. *Slavery in Bermuda.* New York: Vantage Press, 1976.

Smith, Peter J. C. "Presbyterianism in Bermuda." *Bermuda Historical Quarterly* 6, no. 2 (1969): 36–53.

"Some Repercussions of the Gunpowder Plot." *Bermuda Historical Quarterly* 12, no. 2 (1955): 45–56.

Stow, John. "Three and a Half Centuries of Bermuda History." *Bermuda* 30, no. 5 (July 1959).

Strachey, William. *For the Colony in Virginia Brittania: Lawes Divine, Morall and Martiall.* Edited by David Flaherty. Charlottesville, Va.: University Press of Virginia, 1969.

———. "A True Reportory of the Wracke, and Redemption of Sir Thomas Gates Knight; upon, and from the Ilands of the Bermudas. . . ." In *Hakluytus Posthumus or Purchas His Pilgrimes,* edited by Samuel Purchas. 20 vols. Glasgow: J. MacLehose and Sons, 1905–1907.

"Survey of Bermuda." *Bermuda Historical Quarterly* 3, nos. 2, 3, 4 (1946): 104–18, 171–84, 223–45.

Thorndale, William. "The Virginia Census of 1619." *Magazine of Virginia Genealogy* 3 (1995): 155–70.

Thornton, John. *Africa and Africans in the Making of the Atlantic World.* Cambridge, Eng.: Cambridge University Press, 1992.

Tucker, Arthur Tudor. "Parson Richardson, 1755–1805: Rector of the Parish of St. George, Bermuda." *Bermuda Historical Quarterly* 12, no. 2 (1955): 64–74.

Tucker, Terry. *Bermuda's Story.* Hamilton, Bermuda: Island Press, 1970.

———. "Bermuda Tribes or Parishes as Placed on Norwood's Maps." *Bermuda Historical Quarterly* 32, no. 4 (1975): 75–77.

———. *The Islands of Bermuda.* Hamilton, Bermuda: Island Press, 1970.

Twombly, Robert C., and Robert H. Moore. "Black Puritan: The Negro in Seventeenth Century Massachusetts." *William and Mary Quarterly,* 3d ser., 24, no. 2 (April 1967): 225–28.

Usner, Daniel H., Jr. "Indian-Black Relations in Colonial and Antebellum Louisiana." In *Slave Cultures and the Culture of Slavery,* edited by Stephan Palmié. Knoxville: University of Tennessee Press, 1995.

Vaughan, Alden T. "Blacks in Virginia: A Note on the First Decade." *William and Mary Quarterly,* 3d ser., 29, no. 3 (July 1972): 469–78.

———. *Roots of American Racism: Essays on the Colonial Experience.* New York: Oxford University Press, 1995.

Verrill, A. E. *Relations between Bermuda and the Colonies in the Revolutionary War.* New Haven: A. E. Verrill, 1907.

The Voyages of Captain William Jackson (1642–1645). Edited by Vincent T. Harlow. Camden Miscellany, vol. 13, no. 4. London: Royal Historical Society, 1923.

Wallenstein, Peter. "Indian Foremothers: Race, Sex, Slavery, and Freedom in Early Virginia." In *The Devil's Lane: Sex and Race in the Early South,* edited by Catherine Clinton and Michelle Gillespie. New York: Oxford University Press, 1997.

Walvin, James. *Black Ivory: A History of British Slavery.* New York: Harper Collins, 1992.

———. *Questioning Slavery.* New York: Routledge, 1996.

Watlington, Hereward T. "The Bridge House, St. George's, Bermuda." *Bermuda Historical Quarterly* 28, no. 1 (1971): 9–18.

Watson, Alan. *Slave Law in the Americas.* Athens, Ga.: University of Georgia Press, 1989.

Watts, David. *The West Indies: Patterns of Development, Culture, and Environmental Change since 1492.* Cambridge, Eng.: Cambridge University Press, 1987.

Wells, Robert V. *The Population of the British Colonies in North America before 1776: A Survey of Census Data.* Princeton: Princeton University Press, 1975.

White, James Clark. *Dermatitis Venenata: An Account of the Action of External Irritants upon the Skin.* Boston, 1887.

Wiecek, William. "The Statutory Law of Slavery and Race in the Thirteen Mainland Colonies of British America." *William and Mary Quarterly,* 3d ser., 34, no. 2 (April 1977): 258–80.

Wilkinson, Henry. *Adventurers of Bermuda: A History of the Island from Its Discovery until the Dissolution of the Somers Island Company in 1684.* London: Oxford University Press, 1933.

——. *Bermuda from Sail to Steam: The History of the Island from 1784 to 1901.* London: Oxford University Press, 1973.

——. *Bermuda in the Old Empire.* London: Oxford University Press, 1950.

Williams, William Frith. *Historical & Statistical Account of Bermuda.* London, 1848.

Wood, Betty. *The Origins of American Slavery: Freedom and Bondage in the English Colonies.* New York: Hill and Wang, 1997.

——. *Slavery in Colonial Georgia, 1730–1775.* Athens, Ga.: University of Georgia Press, 1984.

——. *Women's Work, Men's Work: The Informal Slave Economies of Low Country Georgia.* Athens, Ga.: University of Georgia Press, 1995.

Wood, Peter H. *Black Majority: Negroes in Colonial South Carolina from 1670 through the Stono Rebellions.* New York: Knopf, 1975.

Zuckerman, Michael. "Identity in British America: Unease in Eden." In *Colonial Identity in the Atlantic World, 1500–1800,* edited by Nicholas Canny and Anthony Pagden. Princeton: Princeton University Press, 1988.

Zuill, William Sears. "Norwood's Second Survey." *Bermuda Historical Quarterly* 32, no. 3 (1975): 53–56.

——. "Bermuda, Salt, and the Turks Islands." *Bermuda Historical Quarterly* 8, no. 4 (1951): 162–68.

——. *The Story of Bermuda and Her People.* London: Macmillan, 1973.

Zuill, William Edward Sears. *Bermuda Journey.* New York: Coward-McCann, 1946.

——. "George Whitefield and His Bermuda Friends." *Bermuda Historical Quarterly* 4, no. 1 (1947): 25–34, 258–80.

——. "John Somersall." *Bermuda Historical Quarterly* 29, no. 2 (1972): 168.

———. "The Maligan Family." *Bermuda Historical Quarterly* 29, no. 4 (1972): 246.

———. "Notes on the Darrell Journal." *Bermuda Historical Quarterly* 2, no. 3 (1945): 144.

———. "The Second Mrs. Somersall." *Bermuda Historical Quarterly* 29, no. 3 (1972): 203–212.

Index

Adderley, Abraham: family of, 173, 203; career of, 175
Africans, 49, 83, 84, 96, 141, 273; in slave trade, 17; acculturation of, 23. *See also* Blacks; Slaves
Agriculture, 111, 131; decline of, 148, 179. *See also* Crops; Land; Tobacco
Albouy, Nicholas, 242
Alcohol: consumption of, 44, 45, 191; aqua vitae, 14; "bibby," 107. *See also* Rum
Alden, John, 161
Aldworth, Elizabeth, 100
Allen, Doll and William, 74
Ambergris, 4, 149
Antigua, 91, 188; slave revolts in, 198, 199
Appowen, Thomas, 207
Apprentices, 10, 29, 31, 49, 58, 53, 99. *See also* Servants
Assembly, 91, 113; formation of, 7; dissolved, 141; and salt trade, 169; and rebellion plot, 228–30. *See also* Government
Assizes, 28, 29, 45, 46–47, 65, 67, 90, 113, 191. *See also* Crime
Astwood: Francis [Frances], 204; Thomas, 207
Atkins, Thomas, 113
Atkinson, Alise, 47
Atwell, Henry, 46
Atwood, Thomas, 157

Bahamas, 80; Bermudian emigration to, 117; slave revolts in, 199–200
Bailey, John, 53
Bailey's Bay, 161
Bailiff, 29
Ball, George, 108
Ballard, Mr., 46
Barbados: slaves in, 41, 51, 66, 137; population, 51, 66, 97, 98, 101, 187, 200; Indians in, 58, 66; slave revolts in, 84, 197, 199; blacks from, 90, 188; trade with, 160, 167
Barker, Rev. James, 242
Basden, William, 73; family of, 140
Bassett: Mary, 188; Sarah, 213–15
Bayley: John, 46; Judith, 46
Bedlow, Gilbert, 226, 227
Bedwell: Grace, 69, 70; John, 69
Beek: Daniel, 250; John, 242, 246
Bell: Philip (governor), 34, 35, 41; Thomas, 207
Bennett, Benjamin (governor), 168, 185, 187, 208, 209
Berkeley: Rev. George, 243–44; William, 44
Bermuda: founding of, 3–6; geography, 13, 115
Bermuda Hundred, 9
Bermudez, Juan de; 2
Blackbourn: John, 242, 246; Susanna, 261, 267
Blackman, Sarah, 120
Blacks: first brought to Bermuda, 17–19, 23, 32; status of, 19, 21, 27–28, 31, 36, 41, 42, 47, 49–52 passim, 108; as skilled labor, 20, 23–24, 50, 58, 72, 107, 170–71, 228, 231, 258, 260; white attitudes toward, 22, 30–31, 40–42, 48, 66, 71, 93, 107, 108–9, 145–46, 189; as wage earners, 28, 36, 54, 56, 74; laws controlling, 30–31, 48, 73, 91–92, 145–46, 202–3, 204, 210–12, 214–15, 227, 231; acculturation of, 40, 107, 274; in militia, 42, 198–99; free, 47, 56, 62, 74, 76, 82, 84–88 passim, 92; surnames of, 74–75, 76; proclamations concerning, 87–88, 91, 135, 139, 142; as seamen, 141, 143, 153–54, 180–81, 183–87, 189–90, 217, 219, 246, 247,

275; free, required to leave Bermuda, 212, 229–30. *See also* Africans; Slaves
Black Will, 83, 135
Blake, Jeames, 68
Bodkin Bay, 267
Bolton, Mary, 124
Bond, Rev. Sampson, 107, 143–44
Bosses Cove [Bosses Hole], 247, 266
Boston, Massachusetts, 172, 277
Bowen, Anne, 60
Bowley, Edward, 46
Brangman, Lt. Edward, 122
Briggs, Zachariah, 63
Brown, William, 208
Browne, John, 52
Bruere, George James (governor), 235, 246, 248, 269–70
Buckley, Thomas, 36
Buller, Katherine, 56
Burch: Elizabeth, 267–68; Jeremiah, 203; Thomas, 267; William, 135, 191
Burgess, Thomas, 109
Burrows: Capt. Christopher, 134; Capt. Thomas, 84, 86, 88; Ellen, 88; Jeremiah, 158; John, 53; Mary, 53; William, 203
Burt, John, 206
Burton, Thomas, 180, 204
Bushell, Capt. Leonard, 193, 194
Butler, Nathaniel (governor), 7, 13, 14, 22, 29, 32, 33, 34, 43, 96, 152–53
Butterfield: Henry, 242; John, 62
Byshop, Robert, 83

Caribbean islands, 1, 19. *See also* Colonies
Carolina, 60, 61, 62, 101, 120, 159, 167
Carpenter, Samuel, 168
Carter: Christopher, 4; Mary, 47
Cassava, 15, 18, 20, 44, 273
Casson, John, 194–95; family of, 124, 196
Casson, Thomas, 194–95
Castle Harbor, 54, 160, 161
Cattle. *See* Livestock
Cedar, 9, 12, 162, 196, 239, 240
Census: of 1622, 26–27; of 1698, 97–98; of 1740, 222; of 1764, 226, 270; of 1774, 238. *See also* Population
Chaddock, Thomas (governor), 83, 154
Chard, Edward, 4
Charleston, South Carolina, 52, 210
Children, 28, 45, 47, 50, 51; illegitimate, 46, 52–55 passim, 85, 122–23, 191–92; disposition of slaves', 63–64, 71

Churches, 16–17, 44, 45, 75, 241–42. *See also* Religion
Churchwardens, 201, 202, 235
Clark: Elizabeth, 100; George, 219
Class structure, 192, 236
Clergy, 8, 16–17
Climate, 2–3, 12, 34, 96. *See also* Hurricanes
Clothing, 13–14, 15, 32, 35, 45, 46, 112, 212–13
Cobler's Island [Gallows Island], 86, 113
Collins, George, 116
Colonies: Portuguese, 18; Spanish Caribbean, 18, 20–21, 23, 49, 51, 55; Dutch, 146, 182, 188
—Chesapeake, 34; blacks in, 23, 33, 38, 39; population, 50–51; demography, 97–98, 102; class structure, 236
—English Caribbean, 49, 51, 90; demography, 97–98, 137, 186; slave revolts in, 199–200, 232–33; troops in, 248
—English North American, 49; demography, 97–98, 149; slave revolts in, 200, 233; slave households in, 252
Coney, Richard (governor), 54, 150, 176–78, 198–99
Coney Island, 17
Constables, 201–2, 235
Copeland, Rev. Patrick, 87, 162
Corbusier, Henry, 219
Courts. *See* Assizes
Coverley, Mrs., 244
Cox, Thomas, 226, 231
Crèvecoeur, Hector St. Jean de, 278
Crime: sexual assault, 28, 47, 204; theft, 30–32, 45, 47, 65, 67, 136, 201, 205–9, 248; fornication and adultery, 43, 46–47, 65, 69, 122–24, 191–92, 207; murder, 193, 207, 220
Crofts, Lt. John, 71, 72
Crops, 15, 16, 20; corn, 4, 8, 9, 16, 44, 180, 196; potatoes, 15, 16, 31, 44, 161. *See also* Agriculture; Tobacco
Crow Lane, 64, 142, 161, 182, 270
Cuba, 18
Curacao: trade with, 168, 184, 247
Custis, Edmund, 158
Customs regulations: evasions of, 177, 182–83, 270–71

Dando, Marmaduke, 11–15, 21, 33,

35, 36; family of, 12, 26, 37, 44, 45, 124–27, death of, 130
Daniel's Bay, 240, 247
Darrell: Capt. Joseph, 225; George, 242, 269; Sir John Harvey, 158
—Capt. John, 101, 133, 140, 143, 161, 166; career of, 117; family of, 118, 269
Dart, Jane, 100
Davis: Hugh, 28; John, 54–55
Dawes, Ann, 132
Day, Samuel (governor), 202
Devale, John, 89
Devitt, John, 56, 79, 84, 86, 89, 163
Devonshire Tribe, 16; described, 132
Dickinson: Francis, 213, 258; Robert, 58, 130, 158; Thomas, 218
Dill, Ann, 264
Disease, 4–6, syphilis, 9, 21; smallpox, 96, 116, 138; yellow fever, 97
Dobson, John, 225
Dorsett, John, 193–95 passim
Downum, Thomas, 25
Dunscomb: Benjamin, 242; Edward, 242, 245, 267; Hannah, 103, 267; Nathaniel, 205; Rebecca, 244; Thomas (family of), 128, 267; William, 242, 245, 267
Durham: Martha, 217; Thomas, 24, 25, 29, 36, 37, 40, 41, 49, 197
Dutton, John, 9, 10, 22, 24, 25, 29, 41

Eaton, James, 120
Education, 43, 178; literacy, 13, 44, 68–69, 77, 124, 146, 225; of blacks, 40–41, 42, 68, 139–40, 222, 225; schools, 44, 56n, 242, 244–45
Eleuthera: emigration to, 80, 87, 88
Elfrith, Capt. Daniel, 22, 24n, 25, 30, 32
Ely's Harbor, 182
England, 23, 31, 89, 90, 148
Esten, James, 277
Evans, Lewis, 47; Ruth, 188
Eve: David, 242; Elizabeth, 256, 257; Francis, 254, 267; Mary, 254, 257; William, 256
Ewer, Jerome, 118, 128, 149
Executions, 47, 66, 68, 69, 83, 113, 193; of blacks, 83, 85–86, 136, 214, 215, 220, 231, 232; black executioners, 85, 136

Families, 12, 24, 26, 27, 37, 94, 99, 261; black, 25, 26, 37–39, 52, 55, 60, 71–72, 76–82; 252–53; Indian, 58–64 passim,

70, 114; white, 175–76, 271; 261, 262–69. See also Children; Marriage
Fforce [Force], William, 46, 84–88 passim, 129
Fish and fishing, 2–3, 5, 13, 35, 45, 107, 171, 178, 202, 239
Fitzhugh, William, 109
Flatts, the, 17, 111, 131, 165, 182
Food, 31, 32; abundance in early Bermuda, 2–3, 35; of ordinary people, 14–15, 44; Bermudians obliged to import, 180, 196, 249. See also Agriculture; Crops
Force, Ann, 129
Ford: Henry, Jr., 120–21; John, 192
Forster: Hanna, 128; Josias (governor), 54, 68, 86, 87, 128, 134, 155–56; Josias, Jr., 119; Martha, 188; Mrs. Thomas, 214; Thomas, 213
Forts, 6, 13
Freedom. See Manumission
French: islands, 182, 184; French and Indian War, 225, 230; Revolution, 276
Frith: George, 185; Henry, 45; Mary, 45
Fritts, Thomas, 207
Furblow, William, 203

Gabriell, Nicholas, 29
Gantlett, Robert, 258
Gardiner: Jeane, 67, 69; Ralph, 67
Garrett: George, 137–38; Tony, 207
Gates, Peter, 36
Georgia: slaves in, 97, 200, 252
Gibbs: Daniel, 263; Thomas, 173, 174; 175
Gibson, Joseph, 267
Gilbert: Martha, 206; Richard (family of), 128
Godfrey, Capt. Peter, 242, 260, 261; family of, 267
Godwin, Edward, 83
Goffe, Marie, 100
Gombey dancing, 211
Goodwin, Mr., 118
Government: formation of, 7–8; of tribes, 201–2
Governor's Council: and slave revolts, 141–42, 196; rules on looting of shipwrecks, 155; on illicit trade, 176; on slave petition, 193; and poisoning scare, 213
Great Sound, 12
Greene, William, 173, 175; family of, 174
Griffin, Thomas, 89, 138

Haiti, revolution in, 276
Hall: John, 163; William, 191
Hamilton (town), 239
Hamilton Tribe, 16, 62, 111; described, 131
Hamman, John, 193–94
Hancock, John, 277
Hanmore, John, 24
Harding, Symon, 62, 65
Hariot, John, 116
Harper, John, 89
Harris, Marie, 192
Harrison, John (governor), 30, 34, 153
Harvie, Henry, 118
Havard, Goodwife, 37
Hernandries [Hernandes]: Amie, Antony, Ellon, 73
Herne [Heron] Bay, 86, 182
Heydon, John (governor), 137, 141–42, 159, 164, 191
Heyling, John and Margaret, 45
Hill, Gilbert, 84, 86, 109
Hingson, William, 31
Hinson: Daniel, 2–3; Edward (family of), 128
—Cornelius, 219, 242; household of, 220, 258–59
Hispaniola, 18
Hobald, Elias, 206
Hogs. See Livestock
Holiday, Rev. James, 221–23 passim, 244
Holloway, Hannah, 11, 136
Hooper, John, 54
Hope, John Bruce (governor), 97, 150, 183, 184, 185, 189, 199, 204, 235
Hopkins: Jane, 69; John, 83
Horton: Catherine, 188, 219; Rev. Joseph, 218–19
Houses: earliest structures, 6, 12, 16, 44; numbers of in 1663, 102; described, 108; numbers of in 1687, 178
Hubbard, Capt. John, 70–71, 142
Hughes, Rev. Lewis, 5, 10, 32, 43
Hunt: Angelina, 188; Frances, 88, 125
—Richard, 84–85, 130, 157; family of, 125
Hurricanes, 179, 180, 196, 241
Hutchinson, Thomas, 56, 62

Independent Company: stationed in Bermuda, 209–10, 216
Indians, 1, 6, 49, 56–63, 103, 114; Powhatan, 11; Carib, 19; first brought to Bermuda, 19; Pequot, 56, 114; attitudes

toward, 60–61, 63, 64, 65, 66; free, required to leave Bermuda, 62, 212; Wampanoag, 63, 114; Mohican, 114; Narragansett, 114
Ingham, John, 127
Interracial sex, 46, 52–55, 59, 65, 69, 92, 123–24, 192, 204
Inventories: household goods, 129, 251, 261, 265; estate values, 149, 169, 172, 173–75, 254–55, 259, 266, 268
Ireland, Thomas, 116
Ireland Island, 134, 151, 267
Irish: in Bermuda, 88, 90, 91, 117

Jackson, Capt. William, 52, 55–56, 63
Jacobson, Mary, 205–6
Jamaica, 55, 58, 91, 100, 161; Bermuda emigrants to, 173; slave markets in, 184; population, 187; slave revolts in, 197–98, 199–200
James, 60, 61, 62, 63–64, 75, 126, 218, 251. See also Sarnando, James
James Bay, 12
Jamestown, Virginia, 2, 5, 10, 33
Jeames: Capt. W., 161; Frank, 84–89 passim
Jennings: Capt. Thomas, 32
—Capt. Richard, 61, 76; property of, 126, 131; career of, 150, 158, 165; family of, 164
—John, 164; will of, 171
—Richard, Jr., 61–62, 175, 199, 231; will of, 121, 171–72
Jennyns, Francis, 54
Jenour, Anthony, 142, 149
Joell: Martha, 254–57 passim; Solomon, 251, 254–55
Johns, Richard, 71
Johnson: Anthony, 262; Daniel, 147, 184, 189; Daniel, Sr., 189; John, 262; Lewis, 262; Nathaniel, 183–84; Thomas, 262
Johnston: John, 237; William, 52–53
Jones: Arthur, 194; Col. Francis, 207; Mary, 208; Richard, 63, 121
Jumper, office of, 235–36, 250
Juries, 8, 215; grand, 45, 90, 122, 155, 164, 191; efforts to control slaves, 210–12, 218
Justices of the peace, 8, 201–2, 211; in trials of blacks, 215

Keele: Daniel, 128, 185; William, 128
Keith, Rev. George, 17

Kendall, Miles (governor), 22, 30
Kennish, Ann, 135–36
Kersey, Thomas: household of, 128, 129
King Philip's War, 62, 63, 66
Kirby, Capt., 22, 30, 32
Knowles, Damon, 45, 76; family of, 126–27
Kupperman, Karen O., 40

Labor, skilled trades: cooper, 8, 63, 69; blacksmith, 8, 130, 158, 193, 195, 258; carpenter, 8, 207, 258, 260; stonemason, 8, 207, 258, 260; weaver, 53, 58; tailor, 58; boatwright/shipwright, 58, 72, 231, 261; midwife, 64; cordwainer, 65; sailmaker, 256
Land, 9; size of holdings, 7, 102, 104, 131, 239; shortage of, 34, 100, 179
Larkin, George, 159
Lea: Capt. Christopher, 84, 86; Capt. Philip, 63, 64, 71, 117, 133, 161–62, 169; Copeland, 162; Thomas, 217
Leacraft: Thomas, 142
—Richard, 75, 129; family of, 130
Leaycraft [Loucraft], William, 242, 261–62; family of, 262
Leaycraft, Deborah, 262
Lee, Edward, 122
Leeward Islands: trade with, 161, 167
Lesser Antilles, 18, 19
Lewis, Roger, 72
Lightbourn, Joseph, 168
Lingar: Richard, 185, 263; Thomas, 263
Little Sound, 17, 111
Livestock, 12, 20, 31, 32, 78, 107; hogs, 2, 3, 15, 30, 31, 32, 35, 44, 171, 174, 266; poultry, 8, 14, 15, 30, 31, 35, 44, 45; cattle, 12, 44, 171, 174, 260, 266; horses, 17, 142, 171; sheep, 129, 171, 174, 260, 266; bees, 171, 174
London, 6, 12
Longbird Island, 54, 58, 113
Longbottome, Dorothy and Thomas, 46
Lyttleton, Rev. Thomas, 242, 250

MacKenny, John, 203
Makeraton, John, 68–69
Mangrove Bay, 182
Manumission: of individuals, 52, 53, 60, 65, 72, 88, 112, 119–22, 128, 254, 256–57, 269; slave petitions for, 74, 137–39, 141, 193–96; rules for, 230

Marriage, 25, 42, 43, 46, 73; of Indians, 11, 63; of blacks, 25, 39, 42–43, 60, 72–73, 118. See also Families; Women
Marteene, Christopher, 56, 86
Maryland: blacks in, 23, 50, 252
Massachusetts, 56, 66
McNeil, Capt. John, 220
Merchants, 110, 115; rise of, 169–76, 189; as slaveholders, 236
Mestizo, 59. See also Mustee
Mexico, 19
Middleton: Anne, 53; Capt. Lewis, 186, 220; Elizabeth, 68; John, 68, 69; Solomon, 81
Militia, 50, 93, 209
Mill Creek, 247, 266
Millson, Thomas, 192
Minor, Charles, 208
Minott, Mrs. Thomas, 213
Miriam, 206, 207
Miscegenation. See Interracial sex
Mitchell, Nathaniel, 251
Montague, Edward, Lord Mandeville, 49–50
Montserrat, 91
Moore: David, 262; Henry, 142, 263; Rev. John, 242; Richard (governor), 3–6, 18
Morgan, Henry, 127
Morris: Capt. John, 207; Mrs., 244; William, 242
Mortality, 5, 96, 98. See also Disease
Motton, Thomas, 176
Mulattos, 1, 52–55, 66, 69, 91–92, 96, 99, 103; free, required to leave Bermuda, 212
Murrell, Thomas: family of, 128
Mustee, 59, 91–92, 96

Nailor, Walter, 56
Nash, Thomas, 194–95
Negroes. See Blacks
Nelmes, Thomas, 258
Nevis, 91, 188
New England, 56, 58, 62, 75, 100; population, 66–67
New Jersey, 97
New Netherland, 23
New Orleans, 200
New York, 85, 100; trade with, 161; Bermuda vessels to, 187–88, 279–82; slave uprisings, 200, 219
Noden, Ralph, 216
Nonconformists, 17. See also Religion

North, John, 62
North America, 1, 49, 90. *See also* Colonies, English North American
North Carolina, 82, 187
Norwood, Richard, 130, 143, 150; survey of 1617, 6–7, 16; family and servants of, 59–61, 268; survey of 1663, 101–8 passim, 134; schoolmaster, 144, 242–43; "wrecking," 158, 165
Numan: John, 258; Nathaniel, 242, 258

Oranges, 15, 16, 44, 161, 179, 180, 196
Outerbridge: Jonathan, 204; Samuel, 218
—Thomas, 164, 174; family of, 175
Overseers, 29, 31, 235
Owen, Lazarus, 64
Owen's Island, 64

Packwood, Cyril Outerbridge, 277
Page, Elizabeth, 69
Paget Tribe, 16, 133
Palmettos, 12, 101, 107, 166, 213, 273
Parishes: law enforcement in, 221–22, 235–36; census of, 237, 238. *See also* Tribes
Parker: Christopher, 42; Edward, 231
Paulson, Mr., 42–43
Paynter, Stephen, 79; family of, 81, 157; house of, 110, 152; career of, 162–63, 188
Pearls, 6, 18, 19, 23, 24, 55
Peasley, William, 123, 168
Pecke, Damian, 51
Peirce, Mr., 56
Pembroke Tribe, 16, 46, 75; described, 132; 138; census records of, 237–39, 245–46, 249–57 passim
Peniston: Anthony, 89, 156, 196, 198, 207; Jeremiah, Jr., 219; Samuel, 189; William, 142
Persons, Thomas, 207
Peru, 19
Philip, King of Wampanoags, 63
Pirates, 165, 168, 184, 185; fear of, 209, 217
Pitt: Benjamin, 242, 244; Elizabeth, 244; John, 256; John (governor), 209–10, 216; Martha, 244, 256–57; Mary, 244; Richard, Jr., 244; Sarah, 244; William, 244
Place, Thomas and William, 258
Pocahontas, 11, 59

Popple, William (governor), 219, 227–32 passim, 270
Population (of Bermuda), 1; in 1615, 5; in 1622, 16, 26–27; in 1630s, 35; 1670s, 66, 97; in 1676, 165; in 1687, 178; in 1690s, 98, 179–80; in 1700, 180; in 1720s, 187, 216–17; 1770s, 99. *See also* Census
Porter, Judith, 123
Port Royal, 11
Potter, Samson, 206
Poundkeeper, 235–36
Powell: Capt. Henry, 41; Capt. John, 20–21, 22, 28; Daniel, 70; Joane, 69, 70, 122; Robert, 69, 70, 112–13
Pratt, Lewis, 53
Preston, Capt. Bartholomew, 56, 61, 63
Priestley, Robert, 69
Privateers, 22, 23, 148, 167, 185–86, 276; French, 225
Prosser, Symon, 32
Providence Island: Bermuda emigrants to, 35, 84, 94; slaves on, 40–41, 50, 56, 61, 75–76, 84
Prudden: Elisha, 231; James, 267; Joseph, 231
Puerto Rico, 18; trade with, 160; runaways to, 186
Puritans, 40–41, 43, 51n, 55, 75, 79–80, 87. *See also* Religion

Queen Anne's War, 209

Racism. *See* Blacks, attitudes toward
Ramsbotome, Frances, 47
Randolph, Edward, 167, 180
Rayner, Samuel, 193
Rebellion plots, 83–89, 90, 91, 140–45, 196–99, 226–33, 275; fears of, 135, 146, 198–99, 209, 213, 216, 219–20, 228–32; poisonings, 213–15, 217–19, 220–21
Religion, 43, 45, 55, 75; baptism of blacks, Indians, mulattos, 25, 37, 50, 73, 75, 137, 138–39, 222, 224–25; religious life of blacks, 223–24. *See also* Churches; Clergy; Puritans; Sabbath
Rich: Nathaniel, 7, 11, 12, 15, 21, 26, 125; Robert, the younger, 11, 12, 14, 15, 16, 19–25 passim, 41
—Sir Robert, second Earl of Warwick, 7, 11, 26, 49, 79, 81; privateering, 20, 22, 55

Richards: Ann, 129, 156
—Capt. Thomas, 129, 150; career of, 155–57; 178
Richardson: John, 127; Rev. Alexander, 222, 242
Richier, Isaac (governor), 98, 179
Ridlie, Daniel, 192
Righton: John, 206; Stephen (inventory of), 174, 175
Rivera, Juan de, 44–45, 47, 48, 100, 153–55, 179
Robinson: Capt. Francis, 245, 267; Mrs., 244; Robert (governor), 96–97, 178, 179
Rolfe, John, 11, 18, 59
Rollins: Jonathan, 262–63; Mary, 244, 245
Rookes, William, 47
Round Hill Island, 70
Rum, 117, 120, 163, 168, 183, 211, 247, 255
Runaways, 76, 82–83, 88–89, 135–36, 185–86, 255

Sabbath: observance of, 37, 45, 46, 75; breaking of, 191, 202–3, 211, 218
Sailing vessels, 13, 16, 153, 178, 182, 188, 240, 271; Dutch, 1; Spanish, 2, 19; Brazilian, 20; French, 20; numbers of in Bermuda, 137, 138, 178, 181; 246–47; numbers of sailors, 180–81; 202. *See also* Seafaring
—by name: *Adventure,* 266; *Anne,* 155; *Bruce Hope,* 184; *Charles,* 56; *Christopher,* 189; *Deane,* 277; *Deliverance,* 3; *Dorset,* 99–100, 164; *Duxbury,* 277; *Dymond,* 79; *Eagle,* 157; *Edwin,* 19; *Elizabeth and Anne,* 90, 163, 164; *El Salvador,* 155; *Endeavour,* 185–86; *Fanny,* 245; *Fortune,* 161, 177; *Francis,* 267; *Friendship,* 157; *Hope,* 161; *Hopeful James,* 161–62; *Hopeful Luck,* 155–56; *Hopewell,* 20; *Jane,* 264; *Jeames,* 161; *Jean,* 245; *La Viga,* 153–54; *Mary,* 219, 245, 254, 268; *Matthew and Francis,* 161; *Molly,* 189; *Patience,* 3; *Peggy,* 245, 267; *Plough,* 3; *Ranger,* 265; *Recovery,* 117; *Regulator,* 276–77; *Resolution,* 193; *Ruby,* 220; *Samuells Adventure,* 164; *San Antonio,* 152–53; *Savanna,* 254; *Seaflower,* 153; *Sea Venture,* 2, 3; *Speedwell,* 163; *Truelove,* 99–100, 156, 157, 227; *Virginia Merchant,* 157; *William,* 87

Salt Kettle, 167, 182
Saltus: Mary, 244, 268
—Capt. Samuel, 242, 245, 268; family of, 267
Sanders: Joseph, 262; Nathaniel, 120–21; Richard, 121, 263
Sandys, Sir Edwin, 3, 34
Sandys Tribe, 16, 26, 133–34
Sarnando, Hanna, 26, 77–80, 82
Sarnando, James, 21, 22, 24, 25, 26, 32, 36, 41, 76–78, 80–82
Sayle: Capt. William (governor), 52, 55, 87, 91, 117, 121, 131, 137, 161; James, 164; Nathaniel, 138
Schools. *See* Education
Scots: in Bermuda, 65, 68, 88, 90
Scrogham, Samuel, 62
Seafaring, 148, 239, 246, 247. *See also* Blacks; Sailing vessels; Trade
Seamer, William, 42–43
Servants, 99, 123; indentured, 21, 22, 36, 49, 51–52, 57, 58, 99, 100, 107, 274; care of, 31–32; Irish, 90. *See also* Apprentices; Slaves
Seymour: Capt. William, 47; Florentius (governor), 134, 135, 136, 150, 194, 196; Rachel, 188
Sharp: Capt. Boaz, 63, 114; Henry, 164
Shaw, Thomas, 55
Sheriff, 8
Sherlock: Edward, 65, 108; Samuel, 171
Shipbuilding, 170–71, 177, 182, 240–41. *See also* Labor, skilled trades
Shipwrecks: salvaging ("wrecking") of, 151–59, 177, 179, 184–85, 240, 275
Simon: Daniel, 75; Josias, 81
Simonson family: Ann, Elizabeth, Rebecca, Simon, 75
Slaveholding: patterns of, 36, 99, 115, 237–38, 264
Slavery: origins of, 18, 49, 76–82; use of *slave,* 29–30, 41–42, 48, 50
Slaves, 1, 115; prices of, 20, 57, 58, 59, 79, 109, 123, 170, 258–59; in inventories, wills, and lists, 38–39, 57, 59, 62, 103, 109, 112, 114, 116–23 passim, 170, 258–59; naming of, 39–40, 60–61, 127–28; care of, 54, 115–22 passim, 134–35; housing of, 108, 110, 116, 229, 253, 259, 262; sale of, 116, 174, 187–88, 210, 254, 262; importation banned, 146–47; households of, 170,

252–53, 258–61, 262–63, 266. *See also* Blacks; Indians; Mulattos
—by name: Addam, 266; Affey, 213; Allen, 87; Amarillas, 259; Andrew, 63, 70, 114; Ann, 75, 112; Anna, 38, 72; Anne, 46, 60, 62, 65–66, 256; Anthonia, 36, 41; Anthonie, 89; Anthonio, 39, 40; Anthony, 46, 75, 126; Antonio, 37, 75; Antonye [Antony], 21, 22, 24, 32, 36, 76, 121; Argee, 59, 143–44; Auber, 254, 262; Barbarye, 57; Beck, 121, 213–14, 217; Ben, 204, 231, 254; Besse [Bess], 57, 59, 60, 71, 121, 123, 128, 191; Betty, 203; Black Anthony, 84–88 passim, 125; Black Bess, 135, 163; Black George, 118; Black Hanna, 119, 128; Black Harry, 84; Black Hester, 118; Black Jack, 84–85; Black Laddie, 118; Black Mathew, 136–37; Black Moll, 118, 191; Black Nan, 118, 135; Black Robin, 84–86; Black Tom, 84–86, 88, 191; Black Will, 83, 135; Bridget, 38, 41; Brown, 262; Cabilecto, 84, 85; Captive, 207; Catalena, 38, 41; Charles, 259; Christopher, 118; Ciscilly, 57; Clemento, 88–89; Cockoo, 218; Cuff, 231; Cuffe, 196–98; Cuffey, 208; Daniel, 46, 128, 218, 261; David, 120, 266; Deborah, 192; Diana, 120; Dicke [Dick], 59, 60, 63, 88–89, 175, 220, 254, 259, 266; Dickey, 121; Diego, 124, 140, 195; Dinah, 63, 65, 114, 119, 257, 262; Dinna, 260; Dorothy, 38; Edward, 72; Elizabeth, 53, 57, 58, 59, 60; Ellicke, 76; Enos, 258; Fortune, 173; Francis [Frances], 63–64, 122, 128; Francis, 88, 119; Francisco, 20–21, 24, 25, 32, 36, 41, 273; Frank, 118, 143, 145, 206, 207; Frank (female), 226; George, 57, 60, 61, 65, 74, 129, 194–95, 227, 259–60; Grace, 89, 163; Gregorie, 116; Guindolin, 38; Hanna, 118, 121; Hannah, 121; Harry, 120, 259; Hercules, 143–44; Huba, 118; Isabella, 39, 41; Jack, 71, 116; James, 60, 61, 62, 63–64, 75, 126, 218, 251; Jane, 57, 63, 75, 126, 128, 254; January, 258; Jeames, 128; Jean, 260; Jefferie, 118; Jemmy, 254, 259, 260; Jenny, 63; Jim, 266; Joan, 121, 128; Joane, 57, 58, 70, 109, 113, 122; Joanna, 54–55; Job, 118; Joe, 207, 254, 261; John, 38, 53, 65, 73, 81–82, 89, 120, 121, 126, 135–36,

193; Judah, 135, 191; Jude, 114; Judith, 71, 220–21; Justina, 38; Kate, 69, 122; Katherine, 73, 75, 121; Kitt, 143–45, 254; Lewis, 119, 218; Libby, 120; Louis, 71, 72; Lucea, 121; Lucretia, 38; Luke, 128; Maneno, 38, 40; Maneno mayor, 38, 40; Margret, 81; Margret (daughter of Margret), 81; Maria, 38, 39, 41, 46, 65, 71, 72, 85, 118, 164; Marie, 121, 191; Marrea, 59; Marriam, 259; Martha, 254; Martiter [Martita], 266; Mary, 57, 58, 59, 60, 61, 75, 128, 260; Marye, 57; Matt, 254; Matthew, 126; Megge, 57; Michaell, 123; Mingo, 39, 40, 231; Mingo (female), 46; Mingo Grando, 38, 40; Miriam, 206, 207; Mischall, 57; Moll, 118, 121; Nall, 57, 58, 61; Nan, 59, 60, 61, 63, 217; Nancy, 214, 231, 256, 259; Nanny, 63, 206–7, 256; Nat, 59; Nathaniell, 80; Natt, 226, 231; Pamelia, 259; Paraketa, 46–47; Patience, 260; Pedro, 57; Penelope, 38, 75; Penny, 75; Peter, 73, 75, 89, 121, 122, 126, 135–37, 218, 231, 254, 255, 262, 269; Philip (female), 63; Phillass [Phyllis], 37, 75; Phillip, 114, 218–19; Phillis, 260; Pimpro, 197–98; Plenthento, 89; Polassa, 38; Polibius, 220–21, 25; Pompey, 256; Populo, 70, 113, 122; Priscilla, 38; Quash, 220; Queen, 118; Quicke, 163; Rabb, 121; Rachell, 118, 135; Ralph, 120; Richard, 38, 75, 80; Rigg, 256; Robin, 141, 143, 144–45, 254; Rose, 114, 266; Rosilla, 255; Ruth, 114, 120, 218, 257, 262; Salvadoro, 89; Sam, 121, 122, 123, 128, 225, 254, 261, 266; Sambo, 42, 121, 140; Samson, 207–8; Samuel, 80, 82; Samuel (son of Salvadoro), 89; Sand., 38; Sander, 49, 76, 83, 120, 126; Sara, 266; Sarah, 54, 57, 65, 73, 80, 118, 128, 129, 140; Saray, 38; Sary, 266; Sharp, 218; Simon, 75, 208; Sissie, 121; Stephen, 121; Susan, 37, 38, 53, 75; Symon (boy), 66, 68–69; Symon, 28–29, 32; Symon, Martha, 74; Tabitha, 70, 113; Tent (female), 259; Thomas, 53, 75, 126, 128; Thyas, 218; Tim, 254; Tituba, 66; Tom, 59, 60, 123, 143, 145, 195–98, 208, 218, 231, 261, 266; Tomackin [Tomakin], 57, 88–89; Tomasin, 67, 69, 112; Tony, 63, 80, 84–85, 121, 206, 260; Venturilla, 19;

Whan, 119–20; Will, 59, 144, 186, 205–8, 207, 261; William, 38, 39, 128; Wylliam [William] 38–39

Slave trade, 17, 146–47, 187–88, 189; Royal African Company, 184

Smith: Capt. John, 5, 6, 33, 94, 96; Christopher, 122; Henry, 53; John, 85; Rev. Samuel, 137; Samuel, 258; Sir Thomas, 3; Thomas, 198, 207; William, 11, 12–13, 15, 21, 35–36

Smith's Island, 4

Smith's Tribe, 16, 131–32

Smuggling, 165, 183. *See also* Trade, illicit

Smythe, Alexander, 47

Somers, Sir George, Admiral, 2, 3

Somersall, John, 121, 131

Somerset, 17

Somers Islands Company, 18, 35, 94, 101, 137, 141, 150, 151; settlement of Bermuda, 3, 6, 10; servants and slaves of, 19, 22, 36, 42, 54, 55, 61, 71, 74; trade regulations of, 33, 160; factions in, 34; ends control of Bermuda colony, 176, 243

Southampton Tribe, 16, 33, 74, 111, 151; as multiracial community, 25–26, 75, 94, 124–30

South Carolina, 97, 145, 172, 187, 202, 209, 212, 239; Stono Rebellion, 219, 233. *See also* Carolina

Spanish Point, 196, 222, 240

Sparkes: Elizabeth, 122; Thomas, 112

Spencer: John, Margaret, and Nicholas, 227

Spofforth, Samuel, 219

Squire, John, 143, 145, 191

St. Anne's Church, 73, 76

St. David's Island, 4, 26, 56; Indians on, 62, 114–15

St. Eustatius, 184, 188, 247

St. George's (island), 2, 7, 9, 26

St. George's (town), 4, 16, 62, 86, 154; social structure, 111, 113

St. John's Church, 241, 261

St. Kitt's [St. Christopher], 84, 91, 188

St. Lucia, 94

St. Peter's Church, 75, 113

St. Thomas, Virgin Islands, 184, 188

Stafford: Richard, 96, 119–20, 170, 191; William, 39

Stalburry, Mrs., 225

Stalvers: Ann and Capt. George, 111–12

Stamers, Richard, 250

Stiles: Capt. Richard, 271; Copeland, 271; Mary, 188; Richard, 258

Stirk: Agnes, 157; Rev. George, 43, 157

Stirrup, James, 58, 61; family of, 113

Stokes: Jonathan, 65; Martha, 204

Stone: Capt. Edward, 161; Elizabeth, 116, 117; Samuel, 116, 149, 168

Stovell: Betty, 244; Joseph, 245; Samuel, 245, 250

Stowe: Christian Nature, 265; Elizabeth, 164; Joseph, 242

—Capt. John, 90, 117, 150; slaves and servants of, 58, 72, 76, 143, 163–64; career of, 163–64; family of, 163–64, 171, 265

—Capt. Joseph, Sr., 264; family of, 265

—Joseph, 164; household of, 169–71

Strachey, William, 1, 2

Strange, Penelope, 54–55

Sugarcane, 15, 16, 18

Swan, Thomas and William, 262

Swimming, 23–24, 107, 178–79

Symon: George, Martha, and Susannah, 74

Tatem: Jane, 220; Nathaniel, 193

Taylor, Richard, 226

Tempest, The, 1

Tenants, 9, 11, 36–37; as heads of households, 103, 106. *See also* Apprentices; Servants

Thornton: Benjamin, 118; Nicholas, 118–19

Tickner, Mr., 9

Tilley, Luke, 263

Tobacco: as staple crop, 6, 13, 44, 148, 183; cultivation of, 9–10, 24, 101; prices, 11, 33, 34, 36–37; smoking of, 14; contraband, 161, 177

Todd: Edw., 188; John, 128, 188

Tortoises, 2, 3, 7, 9

Town Harbor, 113, 152, 160

Trade: blacks and, 30, 31, 92, 93, 176, 183, 213; transatlantic, 148–49, 159–61; illicit, 161, 165, 176–77, 183–84; salt trade, 166–69, 182, 185, 209, 240, 247. *See also* Customs regulations; Smuggling

Tribes, 7. *See also* Parishes

Trimingham: John, 89; Mrs. Anne, 88–89; Paul, 89, 161

Trott: John, 187, 205; Mary, 155, 205–6; Nicholas, 205; Nicholas, Sr., 205; Perient, 120, 126, 155, 192, 278;

Perient, Jr., 205; Samuel, 164, 177, 193, 194
Tucker's Town, 26
Tucker: Capt. George, 74, 117, 161, 184; Daniel (governor), 6, 18, 19, 29; Henry, 142, 162; Jonathan, 231; St. George, 194, 195
Turks Islands, 166–67, 168, 188
Turner: Capt. Thomas (governor), 53, 68, 134; Jonathan, 84; John, 53; Moll, 192
Tuzo: Benjamin, 255; Luke, 256; Sarah, 255, 257
Tynes, David, 185

Vaughan: Ann, 112, 128; Anne, 192; James, 258; John, 68, 112, 128
Vestries, 201, 235
Vickers, John, 226–29 passim; family of, 227
Vincent: Edward, 83; Elizabeth, 268
Virginia: early settlement of, 5–6; blacks in, 18, 27–28, 31, 67, 141, 147, 186, 208, 252; tobacco in, 24; population, 32–33, 50; laws concerning blacks, 32–33, 50, 52, 54, 216; estate values, 172; Bermuda vessels to, 187–89, 283–86
Virginia Company, 2, 3, 9, 10
Virgin Islands, 185, 186

Wages: of English laborers, 4; of Bermuda tradesmen, 8; of Bermuda laborers, 99. *See also* Blacks, as wage earners
Wainwright: George, 65, 119; John, 242; John, 65, 80, 119, 133, 142, 150; John, Jr., 82
Walker, Elizabeth, 188
Wallis, Elizabeth, 220–21
Walmesley, Thomas, 203
Ward: Aron, 194, 195; Elizabeth, 70; Henry, 70; William, 207
Waterman, Nathaniel, 51, 263; family of, 263, 267
Waters, Robert, 4
Watlington, Francis, 122, 149
Waylett, Capt. William, 134, 135, 191
Weaverley, Thomas, 203
Welch, John, 136
Wellman: Francis, 191; Martin, 109; Sarah, 191
Wells, Thomas, 37, 75; family of, 125–27
Welsh, John, Sr., 63

Wentworth: Hugh, Jr., 78, 101, 117, 133, 143, 145, 243; John, 78, 133, 146
—Hugh, 21, 26, 36, 49, 118; family of, 77–79
West Indies, 56; blacks from, 20, 22, 23, 96; Danish W.I., 186; geography, 186; slave punishments, 200–201
Wethersby, Henry, 24
Whale Bay, 152, 240
Whaling, 117, 150, 240
Whalley, Samuel, 149
Whan [Juan]: Elon, 73; John, 73, 74, 89
Whipping, 31, 45, 46–47, 140, 191–92, 204, 206, 211
White: Anthony, 196, 198; Cornelius, 142; Katherine, 100; Leonard, 71; Rev. Nathaniel, 79, 80, 87; William, 251
Whitefield, Rev. George, 222, 223–25
Whitney: David, 191, 253; Mary, 253, 257; Sarah, 207; Thomas, 242
Whitteares: Dorothy and Jeremy, 45
Williams: Capt. William, 63, 64, 119; George, 192; Phillip, 119
Willis, Ruth, 119
Wilson, John, 124
Winthrop: Henry, 41; John, 56, 100
Wiseman, Joseph, 84; family of, 128
Witchcraft: trials, 66–71
Witter, Elizabeth Norwood, 60, 133, 144, 268; James, 60, 133; Richard, 268–69
Women, 14, 27, 100, 178, 241–42; Indian, 11, 57–61, 65–66; black, 25, 38–41, 46–47, 52–53, 54, 275; mulatto, 54–55, 66, 67; as heads of households, 103, 105, 253–57, 264; as part-owners of vessels, 188; as slaveholders, 253–57. *See also* Families; Marriage
Wood: Dorothy, 121; Horace, 236, 242; Horatio (family and household of), 266; Joseph, 242; Mary, 257; Roger (governor), 14, 15, 16, 34, 35, 38–42 passim, 71–72, 273; Stowe (family of), 266
—Roger, 71–72; family of, 72
—Thomas, 119, 141; family of, 121, 265
Wormeley, Ralph, 172
Wright, James, 58

Yates, Daniel, 236, 250–51
Young, John, 85